MECHANICS-
MERCANTILE
LIBRARY.

My Years as Prime Minister

MY YEARS AS PRIME MINISTER

JEAN CHRÉTIEN

A RON GRAHAM BOOK

ALFRED A. KNOPF CANADA

PUBLISHED BY ALFRED A. KNOPF CANADA

Copyright © 2007 Jean Chrétien Consultants Inc.

www.randomhouse.ca

Library and Archives Canada Cataloguing in Publication
Chrétien, Jean, 1934–
My Years as Prime Minister / Jean Chrétien.
ISBN 978-0-676-97900-8
1. Chrétien, Jean, 1934-. 2. Canada—Politics and government—
1993–2006.
3. Prime ministers—Canada—Biography. I. Title.
FC636.C47A3 2007   971.064'8092   C2007-902468-8

Text design: CS Richardson

First Edition

Printed and bound in the United States of America

2 4 6 8 9 7 5 3 1

CONTENTS

To

France and André, Hubert, and Michel,

Olivier, Maximilien, Philippe, and Jacqueline,

and above all Aline.

Without you, nothing

ENTRE NOUS

Not long ago, in April 2007, I was in Moscow to attend the funeral of Boris Yeltsin, the former president of Russia and a person whom I greatly admired. He was a good man who spoke the truth, and his convictions changed the course of history, not only in his own country but around the world. The ceremony, full of dignity and beauty, took place in the cathedral that had been rebuilt to mark the return of freedom of religion in what had been the Soviet Union. Even a heathen would have bowed before the priests dressed in their majestic robes, and everyone present was moved to hear the old hymns of Mother Russia that so pierce the soul.

Looking around, I saw many former world leaders, now plain citizens, come to bid farewell to the one-time enemy who had later become their brother in arms. There was the elder

George Bush, whose son I had gotten to know so well, and at his side foreign kings and presidents who seemed, in this holy place, mere mortals, as were we all. I said hello to John Major, the ex–prime minister of Great Britain, and we were joined by another famous retiree, though younger than either of us, Bill Clinton. When Bill and I shook hands on the steps of the church, I felt as though we were two parishioners meeting after Mass on a Sunday morning back home. With us was Lech Walesa, the former president of Poland, who had captured the imagination of the world when he was nothing but a courageous electrician from Gdańsk daring to defy the might of the Soviet Union. We talked of the good old days and of the present, which didn't seem so bad either, and swapping stories about our friend Boris reminded us of our own impermanence. The friendships and the memories warmed us in the cold spring air of Moscow, just as they continue to warm me in my advancing years. They are what propelled me to write this book, not to puff up my reputation but to record a moment in the all too brief span of time we human beings are given on earth.

Whether foreign or domestic, I've always had a passion for politics. The other day I heard a young man say on television that he was standing for election because he wanted to serve. I said to myself, "My friend, you seem nice, you have some charm, but you're not telling the whole truth. Going into politics is both simpler and more complicated than that." To be frank, politics is about wanting power, getting it, exercising it, and keeping it. Helping people comes with it naturally, because you'll never be elected if you treat people badly. But no one will ever convince me, with all the experience I've had, that the motivations are strictly altruistic. No—we throw ourselves into politics because we love it.

Politics is a sport in which the desire for victory is everything, because the ultimate reward is the power that lets you do some good for your constituents as a member of Parliament, for the stakeholders as a minister, and for the entire country and maybe even the rest of the world as prime minister. The more you succeed and the higher you climb, the more the wish to win becomes an obsession that consumes you day and night—but also gives you satisfactions too numerous to count, from helping the unemployed in your riding find a job to sending Canadian peacekeepers to the rescue of besieged Bosnians. It's in that sense, I suppose, that you can say that you're in the game to serve, since politics gives you the opportunity to help others.

I was fortunate to have been given that opportunity. The joy of serving, to pick up on the young man's idea, allows you to forget all the miseries that come too—when you freeze your feet campaigning from door to door; when the doors slam in your face; when the hand you extend is refused; when the neighbour you've known all your life pretends not to see you across the street; when old friends betray you or laugh at you when you meet or, worse, behind your back. A dirty business, you say to yourself in those moments. I've known many of their kind, but I've also known how quickly the next victory erases them from memory.

This book picks up the political story of Canada, as I lived and breathed it, from where the updated edition of my earlier memoir, *Straight from the Heart,* left off, following my return to politics in January 1990 after a four-year absence, my election as leader of the Liberal Party the next June, and my time as leader of the Opposition until the autumn of 1993.

It is hard for most Canadians to remember how bleak our days looked at that point in our history. To be frank, Canada was in terrible shape—exhausted, demoralized, and fractured. The federal, provincial, and municipal governments were virtually bankrupt, and their combined debt was greater than the country's total GDP, its gross domestic product. Unemployment was stuck at 11.4 per cent. Our interest rates seemed permanently fixed higher than U.S. rates, despite our lower inflation rate, and many of our best scientists, researchers, and scholars were leaving for greener pastures. Though none of that was solely the fault of nine years of Progressive Conservative rule, Ottawa had to bear the blame for creating a "made in Canada" recession—one of the worst since the 1930s—through its ideological monetary policy and its failure to help Canadian industry adapt to the new realities of free trade, financial globalization, and rapidly changing technology.

Moreover, because Prime Minister Brian Mulroney had defeated the Liberals in 1984 by promising to restore prosperity, reduce the debt and deficit, and create "jobs, jobs, jobs," his government's record of broken promises, coupled with a string of corruption charges, ministerial resignations, and patronage appointments, produced a feeling of cynicism and betrayal that plunged public respect for Canada's politicians and democratic institutions to a historic low.

Even so, in my opinion, Mulroney might have survived to fight and win a third term if he hadn't also put the country in a constitutional pressure cooker, as though reopening the *Constitution Act* of 1982 was somehow going to solve the real problems we were facing as a people. He and I used to joke with each other in the House of Commons about the great fight it would be, him against me, and he had a twinkle in his eye whenever he spoke about winning the triple crown of a third majority. Instead, by using exaggerated rhetoric and divisive tactics to try to sell two successive constitutional packages to Canadians—and then failing to deliver either one—he reignited separatist sentiments in Quebec and rekindled a sense of alienation in Western Canada. As a result, his close friend and key lieutenant Lucien Bouchard quit the Tories and launched the Bloc Québécois, which was dedicated to advancing the cause of

Quebec independence within the federal House; Preston Manning funnelled Western discontent into his populist movement, the Reform Party; and Mulroney himself, with his personal popularity level lower than the percentage of people who believed that Elvis Presley was still alive, decided to retreat from the field in February 1993.

Ten years later, at my retirement from public life on December 12, 2003, Canada was enjoying the longest period of economic expansion since the 1960s, Ottawa was on the verge of announcing its seventh surplus budget in a row, unemployment had fallen to around 7 per cent and was still dropping, the Parti Québécois had been defeated in Quebec, Western Canada had never been more prosperous, Canada's international reputation as an economic miracle and independent force for peace in the world had never been higher, and the Liberal Party of Canada was guaranteed by every poll and pundit to be ready to win its fourth consecutive majority. So how did this remarkable turnaround happen? What critical decisions or mistakes did we make along the way? Why did we choose one solution rather than another?

My intention is not to produce a weighty, comprehensive account of the "Chrétien years." I'll leave that task to scholars and historians. Instead, I want to write an informative and highly personal recollection of my decade as prime minister—to tell it as I saw it, to share a few entertaining stories as I do with my friends, to correct the record where necessary, to brag a bit, and to be as candid as possible. That said, I hope readers will understand and forgive me if I refrain from going into my family's private matters or commenting unnecessarily on the foibles and failures of individual personalities. No human being is perfect, and there are always more than enough people ready and eager to remind politicians of that fact every day of the week. I couldn't bring myself to write a warts-and-all description of the members of my staff and Cabinet or even of my political opponents. If that proves a weakness in the book, so be it, but it's a strength in life—and especially in politics—to learn to take people as they are and accept what they are not.

Another caveat: I have also limited myself to writing about events that occurred during my period in office. Except in a few places where I felt it necessary to mention what happened after December 2003 (and even there without much comment or detailed analysis), I don't believe that these memoirs are the proper forum in which to air my thoughts about subsequent political issues. In earlier drafts, however, I was prepared to jump ahead in time and write at some length about my successor's decision to launch the Commission of Inquiry into the Sponsorship Program under Mr. Justice John Gomery, partly because I understood the public's curiosity about my views, but mostly because I wanted to make use of the opportunity to express my grave concerns about the commission, its findings, and its ramifications. Unfortunately, by the time the book was ready to go to press, the matter was still before the courts—and might remain there for months, even years, to come. Under these circumstances, and out of respect for judicial protocol and the judicial process, it would be at least inappropriate and probably impermissible for me to comment on the work on the Gomery Commission.

Though I haven't always been able to avoid the habit all politicians share of repeating the same arguments and anecdotes over and over again, I have tried to spare the hundreds of thousands of Canadians who made *Straight from the Heart* a national bestseller the irritation of reading about my childhood and early career a second time (which allows me, of course, to encourage everyone else to demand an immediate reprint of the first volume). As well, a few of my former associates—both Cabinet ministers and public officials—have already delved into certain areas in depth or from their own perspective. Two books in particular, because they were written by key advisers in my office, might be read as interesting complements to mine: *Rollercoaster,* by James Bartleman, on foreign affairs between 1994 and 1998, and *The Way It Works,* by Eddie Goldenberg, on domestic issues.

Prime ministers cannot—must not—get bogged down in the details of government or try to micromanage the business of the nation. Rather, it is their job to establish priorities, develop strategies, supervise crises, handle the toughest problems, communicate the complicated issues in simple ways, and delegate as much as possible to their ministers. My recollections, not surprisingly, reflect those preoccupations.

My purpose was perhaps best described by a man whose songs and books I have long admired: Félix Leclerc. Even though he and I didn't always share the same political ideas, we came from the same region of Quebec, La Mauricie, and neither of us ever forgot that special corner of the globe. Once, when accounting for the inspiration behind his own work, he said, "I had a happy childhood. I want to share it." In my case, I had a happy life as prime minister, and I would like to share some of my memories with you.

ONE

AT LAURIER'S DESK

I n victory or in defeat, I wanted to be with my family and supporters in Shawinigan, Quebec, on election night, Monday, October 25, 1993. Shawinigan is where I was born in 1934, the eighteenth of nineteen children, to Wellie Chrétien and Marie Boisvert. Shawinigan is where I was first elected to the House of Commons as a Liberal member of Parliament in April 1963. And Shawinigan, an industrial town located on the St. Maurice River halfway between Montreal and Quebec City, is where I always returned to renew my strength for the next political battle or to reconnect with the wisdom of Main Street. Now, with the seven-and-a-half-week campaign drawing to an end, I had come home to cast my vote and await my fate alongside my wife, Aline, our daughter, France, her husband, André Desmarais, their four young children, and our son Hubert. Our youngest child, Michel, was living in the North at the time, but he was on the phone regularly, full of anticipation and encouragement.

We were quite a crowd, huddled around the stack of seven TV sets (each on a different French- or English-language channel) in the living room of the compact A-frame chalet I owned on Lac des Piles, a beautiful lake fifteen kilometres from downtown Shawinigan with water so pure that it serves as the reservoir for the municipality of Grand'Mère. As a kid I used to go there for picnics with my parents or swimming with my friends—sometimes at the popular beach, other times at the various places my sisters rented after they became nurses. As a teenager I passed several glorious summers at the cottage of my eldest brother, Maurice, already a doctor with a wife and six children of his own. I really loved that lake, bordered by steep cliffs and northern woods, and I could think of nowhere else I'd rather be if and when I was elected to become Canada's twentieth prime minister.

I was hopeful, even though the Liberals had gone into the campaign running neck and neck with the Progressive Conservatives. Brian Mulroney's successor, Kim Campbell, had come out of her victory at the leadership convention in June riding high as the young, intelligent, glamorous politician from the West—and as Canada's first woman prime minister—and her love-in with the public and the press had lasted all summer long. As soon as the writ was dropped, however, Campbell discovered that Canadians weren't quite so ready to forgive and forget the legacy of the government in which she had been a senior minister. At the same time, her relative inexperience resulted in some stumbles and gaffes that caused the same media that had lifted her up as a star to turn and bring her crashing down to earth.

The unstable coalition of Quebec nationalists and Western conservatives that Mulroney had skilfully held together with carrots and sticks quickly dispersed to the Bloc Québécois and the Reform Party, while many moderate Conservatives in Ontario and Atlantic Canada started looking to the Liberal Party as their alternative. In the final ten days of the campaign, when the Tories went into freefall, the governing party gave up on policy issues altogether and launched a series of nasty, extremely personal attack advertisements, dismissing me as Yesterday's Man because of my thirty years in politics, insulting me as some kind of hick who would embarrass Canada on the world stage, and even ridiculing my facial paralysis, the result of a birth defect that also left me deaf in my right ear. But the fundamental decency and common sense of Canadians prevailed, and the Progressive Conservatives sank even lower in the eyes of the voters.

At 8:45 p.m., local time, all the networks had proclaimed a Liberal majority. There was then a long wait until the polls closed in British Columbia and Prime Minister Campbell conceded defeat. Not that the result was anything like a cliffhanger, given that the Tories had been reduced to just two seats. The biggest surprise that evening was the size of our win in Ontario, with 98 of its 99 seats. The only uncertainty was whether the Bloc Québécois or Reform, hovering at 52 seats each, would emerge as the official Opposition, though I knew I would be in a strong position to take on either party. It was well after midnight before Aline and I went to greet the hundreds of happy partisans who had gathered at our campaign headquarters to cheer the return of the Liberals after nine years out of office. From there we joined a more intimate gathering in a local motel and partied until three in the morning with my brothers and sisters (who could scarcely believe what had become of their Ti-Jean), my cousins and in-laws, and the key organizers and supporters who had helped deliver my tenth electoral victory by more than 6,000 votes.

I was proud, of course, but I didn't have time to stop and think much about it amid the pace and the excitement of the celebrations. The reality didn't sink in until the next morning, when Aline woke me up with the words, "Do you want a coffee,

Prime Minister?" Shortly afterwards President Bill Clinton telephoned to offer his congratulations, and I let my three grandsons lie on the bed and listen to my first conversation with an important head of state. Clinton and I had a friendly, informal chat that lasted about ten minutes—and that, oddly enough, was interrupted when the line went dead for a moment. "I hear there were a remarkable number of similarities between your campaign and my campaign last year," the president joked.

"Well," I countered, "I've been in politics a lot longer than you've been around, so maybe it was you who copied me." It was the first of the many laughs Clinton and I were to share.

Later that morning, en route to the airport, I asked the RCMP driver to stop in La Baie so I could visit the small brick house in which I had grown up. The occupant, the daughter of a friend of mine, asked for a souvenir, and I gave her the first of the thousands of autographs I was to sign as prime minister. Then Aline and I were driven up the hill to the nearby cemetery where my parents are buried, and we offered a prayer at their graves. It was emotional for me—still is, remembering it now—to think that they were not alive to see one of their children, the most mischievous and worrisome of the bunch, take up the mantle of their hero, Wilfrid Laurier.

The Chrétiens had been active Liberals since the nineteenth century, and Laurier was like a saint to the family. When I was a high school student, I identified with him and even made a pilgrimage to his birthplace. Laurier, a rural Quebecer who became Canada's first French-speaking prime minister, was a flesh-and-blood symbol to French Canadians that they had a place of respect in Canada, and his election was the realization of their hope for a founding partnership between the French and English cultures. He rejected the extreme views on both sides because he understood that a nation as diverse and far-flung as Canada could not survive that kind of polarization.

He welcomed immigrants, supported free trade with the United States, and opened up the West to settlers, including French Quebecers such as my maternal grandfather, who went out to a farm north of Edmonton in 1907. Laurier's essential optimism struck a chord in me as well. He truly believed in the promise of Canada, and he inspired Canadians to make that promise a reality by calling on them to look beyond their particular region, language, or religion. People often forget that Laurier had opposed Confederation at first, but he was a man with an open mind, and once he was convinced of the merits of the new arrangement, he became the most ardent Canadian of his era. He wanted us to be a strong, independent country whose voice would be heard on the international stage, and the first modern nation to celebrate diversity, tolerance, and generosity.

One day I was thrown out of class for daring to challenge a history teacher's nationalistic claim that because Laurier had studied law at McGill University, he had been an anglophone. Never a shy person or easily intimidated by authority, I rose to the defence of my hero. "That's not true, sir," I said. "Laurier was born in St-Lin, he went to school in L'Assomption, and after McGill he practised law in Arthabaska." (Years later, when I became minister of finance, that same teacher wrote me a touching letter in which he said that he never thought he would see the day when a French Canadian was appointed to that position, let alone a former student of his.)

Among all the mementos I have gathered in my life, I especially cherish four items that once belonged to Laurier: his walking stick, his horseshoe-shaped cravat pin, a sterling-silver epergne that had been presented to him in 1905 by the mayor of Manchester in England, and a heavy silver drinking cup that had been a gift from Lord Aberdeen at a farewell dinner at the end of Aberdeen's term as governor general. The cup is inscribed to his friends Sir Wilfrid and Lady Laurier, "*Oublier nous ne le pouvons.*" And now I was to sit at Laurier's own desk in the office of the prime minister of Canada on Parliament Hill.

—

I flew to Ottawa on the campaign plane and was met by the media, most of our national "war room," and the cheering local Liberal candidates and campaign workers. For a moment, after all the long hours and emotional roller coaster of a hard-fought election, it was pleasant to bask in their warm wishes and to savour the sweetness of victory together, but I was eager to get to work right away. Though I knew there would be some rough days ahead, I have always enjoyed big challenges and rarely spend a lot of time fretting about what terrible things might happen down the road. There was a job to be done, and all I could give it was my best. The mantra of my life has been, "When I look in the mirror, I despair, but when I compare myself to others, I am consoled." However great my imperfections, I probably wasn't worse than anyone else—and I certainly had much more experience than most.

"Suppose you're going into the hospital for surgery," I asked Canadians during the election, "and have the choice between two doctors—one a recent graduate from a top-notch university, the other with a track record of thousands of successful operations. Which one would you choose?"

Both to their credit and to their disadvantage, before reaching the age of forty, Lester Pearson had been a diplomat and civil servant, Pierre Trudeau a professor and essayist, and Brian Mulroney a lawyer and businessman. My path had been a long, patient climb up through the political system, propelled by hard work, relentless optimism, and a lifelong ambition to keep striving ever higher. My father, a paper-mill machinist, had inherited a love of politics from his own father, who had been the mayor of a nearby village for thirty years, and might have been a federal or provincial candidate himself if he hadn't had such a large family to support. Politics was Dad's sport, his hobby, his fun. He served as a Liberal Party organizer in our parish for forty years and never failed to win his polls. His dream was for one of his children to become a politician, and when he didn't have any success with my brothers and sisters, he decided to train me from an early age—much like those hockey dads who drive their four-year-olds to practices before dawn.

When I was still a kid, he had me distributing pamphlets door to door or setting up chairs for the candidates' meetings. By the time I was fifteen, I was already arguing on behalf of the Liberals in the pool hall next door during the 1949 federal election. While in university in the late 1950s I campaigned for St. Laurent, was elected president of the Laval University Liberal Club, organized student protests against Quebec premier Maurice Duplessis, and debated policy resolutions at party conventions as vice-president of the Canadian University Liberal Federation. Though I had flirted for a while with the idea of becoming an architect, my dad said, "No, you'll never get elected as an architect." He pushed me into law, not so much to make a career of it but as a route to public office.

Not that I felt I was born with an entitlement to be prime minister or ever told my confessor that God had ordained it. Given where I began, I knew I had to work harder than those who had arrived in this world destined for greatness. I had to become tougher and more competitive than those who had grown up with privileges and contacts, and I had to earn the encouragement of Lester Pearson and Pierre Trudeau every step of the way. In quick order, I rose from the backbenches to Pearson's parliamentary secretary; from minister without portfolio attached to the Department of Finance to the minister of national revenue; from the minister of Indian affairs and northern development to the president of the Treasury Board; from the minister of industry, trade and commerce to the first French-Canadian minister of finance. I served as the minister of justice in Trudeau's last government as well as the minister of state for social development and the minister responsible for the negotiations that led to the patriation of the Constitution and the Charter of Rights. I was the minister of energy, mines and resources when I first ran for the leadership of the Liberal Party in 1984, and I took on the responsibilities of deputy prime minister and secretary of state for external affairs under John Turner. I was never timid about accepting a promotion. My attitude was, when you don't speak much English and the prime minister of the day asks you to become the youngest Canadian Cabinet minister in a century, you do it.

A great deal of my success was due to the fact that I deliberately chose to undersell and outperform rather than oversell and underperform. Whenever Trudeau gave me a job of some importance, such as Finance or the Constitution, there were always a few people who openly expressed surprise that I had been moved ahead of the big stars in the party. The press never saw me as a star either, but that was fine with me because I didn't want to be seen as a star. Trudeau valued performance above image. He knew he could give me a shovel if there was a mess to clean up, and he kept moving me from one mess to another. And that was going to remain my basic approach now I was my own boss. Crises and confrontations were to be avoided or downplayed rather than manufactured or blown out of proportion. I had no interest in creating any more problems than we already faced simply to set myself up as the messiah who was going to solve them. But if there were problems that had to be tackled, I was ready to roll up my sleeves and get at them.

The changeover of government was one of the shortest and smoothest ever, despite the fact that I had resisted the pressure to put a huge transition team in place beforehand. Most of that heat came from some party members who wanted to be on any transition team for only one reason: to appear powerful, well connected, and influential. But if the public looks at your list and sees the same old insiders, they jump to the conclusion that nothing is going to change once you are elected. It won't matter whether those insiders are good, bad, or indifferent as advisers— it's the perception that usually counts in politics. And the media, because they need an angle, pick over the list to see who's in and who's out, who's up and who's down, all of which breeds rivalry and discontent. Instead, a year earlier, I had asked David Zussman, dean of the School of Management at the University of Ottawa and a former assistant of mine, to compile a set of briefing notes on the structure and management of the federal government, to add to the nine fat volumes of background material I knew I would receive from the civil servants in the Privy Council Office (PCO).

Drawing on the advice of a very small, discreet, and professional team of non-partisan outsiders, Zussman produced a superb document that became a model of its kind in public policy circles. It contained over four hundred pages of information and some three dozen priorities—everything from the structure of the Cabinet committee system to an analysis of the most urgent policy matters, from the logistics of moving into 24 Sussex Drive to a data bank containing more than three thousand applications for staff jobs. However, after three decades and nine departments inside Ottawa, I already felt I had a good grasp of what I wanted to do, and I had found time during the election campaign— between meetings and speeches, during flights and car rides—to make notes, exchange ideas with Zussman and others, and reflect on the kind of government I wanted.

I was helped, too, by being able to build from the core team I had as leader of the Opposition. Jean Pelletier, a distinguished former mayor of Quebec City, agreed to stay on as my chief of staff to run the Prime Minister's Office (PMO). He and I had been good friends since our last year at a Catholic boarding school in Trois-Rivières, where we had special beds side by side in the dormitory because we were tall for our age. Beneath his patrician manner and warm smile, Pelletier was extremely disciplined, well organized, and as hard as nails. He ran a very tight—and tight-lipped—ship. He neither wanted nor needed to be in the news, and he told all the staff to stay out of the spotlight too unless a matter had to do directly with their jobs. As a result, we didn't suffer from the public feuding, backbiting gossip, and anonymous leaks that had plagued other PMOs. Even those columnists and academics who were no fans of the Liberal Party had to concede that Pelletier's operation was among the most efficient and harmonious in memory, despite having been reduced from 120 to 80 employees as a cost-saving measure.

While Pelletier managed the office and served as my chief political adviser, Eddie Goldenberg and Chaviva Hošek worked on the policy side, though they were as astute about nitty-gritty politics as about program ideas. Goldenberg, a law graduate from Montreal who had first started working for me as a summer student in 1972, focused on economic issues, federal-provincial matters, and Canada-U.S. relations in his capacity as senior policy adviser. Hošek, a Harvard-educated professor, ex-president of the National Action Committee on the Status of Women, and former Cabinet minister in David Peterson's Ontario government, concentrated on social issues and directed policy development in the PMO. In practice, however, Goldenberg's and Hošek's files constantly overlapped, and they worked in close collaboration, thinking, reaching out, researching, writing reports and speeches, and troubleshooting on my behalf.

On the communications side were Peter Donolo, a bright, funny young Montrealer of Italian descent who had been

Toronto mayor Art Eggleton's press secretary, and Patrick Parisot, an eloquent and personable Radio-Canada journalist. On paper, Donolo was the director in charge of a staff that looked after the overall public relations strategy for the government and the prime minister, while Parisot, as my press secretary, was concerned with more day-to-day issues. But, for me, they worked as equal partners on how to get our message out to the people, with Donolo focusing on the English-language media, Parisot on the French-language media, and both on speeches and policy ideas.

Among the other key players were Jean Carle, director of operations; Penny Collenette, director of appointments; Maurice Foster, the caucus liaison; Michael MacAdoo and, later, Bruce Hartley, as executive assistant in charge of my schedule; and Monique Bondar, my long-time secretary. I was gratified by the number of these trusted associates who stayed close by me for all or most of the decade I was prime minister. As far as I was concerned, they made a hell of a good team—smart, self-effacing, professional, and keen.

Though they all had their own duties and expertise, it was obviously impossible to separate politics from research from communications in an action-oriented office, so every morning at 8:45 the senior staff met with Jean Pelletier to coordinate the matters of the day. I also tried to make sure that everyone had fair and regular access to me. The common perception was that I was closer to Jean Pelletier and Eddie Goldenberg, because I had known them so long and because they, in turn, thoroughly understood my thinking. For sure, Pelletier and I met formally at least once a day, and Goldenberg was always in and out of my office, but they weren't necessarily involved in every decision or meeting. I probably talked with Peter Donolo and Patrick Parisot more often during the course of a week; I had frequent one-on-one discussions with Chaviva Hošek and Jean Carle; I relied heavily on Maurice Foster when Parliament was in session; and Bruce Hartley was as close as my own shadow. The fact was, because the role of a prime minister is so diverse, I got advice from everybody. Sometimes I accepted it, sometimes I didn't. Everyone was influential because everyone was good—anyone who wasn't good didn't stay long. I certainly wasn't aware of much juggling for position around me. They all knew their area of responsibility; they all had a job to do; and I deliberately chose not to release my daily agenda widely to avoid any rivalry about who was seeing me more often.

For the same reason, though there was a remarkable amount of laughter and camaraderie in the office, I rarely mixed business with pleasure. All members of the staff worked long hours. They rested with their families or travelled on weekends. And, except for farewell dinners at 24 Sussex or the occasional quiet moment, I didn't usually socialize with them or get involved in their personal lives. They were friends, yes, but they were also constantly aware that I was both their boss and a head of government. That created an inevitable distance between us, despite all the years in which we worked side by side. As I had seen with Pearson and Trudeau, and as I was to discover through my own share of disillusionment, a prime minister has little room for friendship. Even people who hardly knew me claimed to be my buddy, especially in Ottawa, where politicians, bureaucrats, lobbyists, and party activists were always trying to get their way by dropping the boss's name without my knowing or being able to do anything about it. Name-dropping may not be the most admirable trait, but it exists in all walks of life, and if others choose to be impressed, it's not against the law. That, however, doesn't mean that it can't cause plenty of trouble in the hands of the opposition or the press, so it requires constant alertness and caution. This unnatural distancing is why family becomes so important to a prime minister. It's also part of the shared understanding that quickly binds political leaders as human beings whenever they get together, no matter what their affiliations or ideologies.

One very influential member of the staff was my mentor Mitchell Sharp, then in his early eighties, who had retired after a long and distinguished career as a public servant in Finance and Trade, an elected politician, a senior Cabinet minister under Pearson and Trudeau, and a policy thinker. Sharp had taken me under his wing soon after I arrived in Ottawa as a unilingual know-nothing from rural Quebec. He had been my first choice to succeed Pearson in the 1968 Liberal leadership race, and I always looked up to him as a man of great wisdom, experience, and integrity. He was the person I went to when I had problems or was feeling under siege. I would walk over to his house after dinner for a half-hour chat when I was a minister, and he would play some Schubert or Mozart on the piano while I turned the pages.

One day, soon after the 1993 election victory, he and I were discussing the importance of ethics in government, which was one of his many areas of expertise. Suddenly I got a bright idea. "Hey, Mitchell," I said, "why don't you come and be a personal adviser to me in the PMO? It would reassure me to have you nearby when I need help, and it would send a signal to people that ours is going to be a serious government. You can work as hard as you want and set your own hours."

His first reaction was to say no. "People will think that I've asked for a job from my friend," he said.

"In that case," I replied, "I'll pay you the grand sum of a dollar a year, and nobody will be able to complain."

Though I later regretted not forcing him to accept a salary commensurate with the tremendous value of his contribution to the government, I thought his selfless commitment to the service of his country for a token amount would be a fitting symbol in the frugal times we faced, just as it had been during the Second World War, when powerful CEOs from the private sector had volunteered to work in Ottawa. Happily, he agreed. (I confess I forgot to pay him for the first few years and eventually handed him a five-dollar bill.) He stayed on to the very last day of my term, dying just three months later at the age of ninety-two, after a decade of providing good counsel not only to me and my staff but also to all the journalists and opposition members who came to consult with him.

One of the first tasks I asked Sharp to perform for me was to interview likely Cabinet members regarding any potentially embarrassing problems and to report back to me with his recommendations. The candidates all had to answer fourteen questions to test their suitability. As far as I remember, there were only a couple of people he had to disqualify, because of conflicts of interest. As for their marriages, sexual orientation, or other private matters that had no bearing on their ability to serve the public well, I didn't think these were any of my business.

In my judgment, Canadian Cabinets had been getting too big, with Mulroney having set the all-time Canadian record at forty ministers. Prime ministers are always pushed to ensure a fair representation from all the various regions, ethnicities, and interests across the country. At the same time, because every minister also has a full-time job serving constituents as a member of Parliament, there's a practical advantage in spreading the workload among more people. And, human nature being what it is, the larger the Cabinet, the greater the number of happy MPs in the caucus and the easier the prime minister's job. In my experience, however, large Cabinets aren't efficient decision-making bodies. They suffer from having too many voices, too many subcommittees, too many officials. I also wanted to send a signal that this was to be a downscaled government, appropriate to a time of fiscal restraint and broader bureaucratic cutbacks. My solution was to restrict the first Cabinet to twenty-three ministers—including myself—and appoint eight secretaries of state. These were, in effect, junior ministers, who would be kept informed through the confidential Cabinet documents and invited to join the weekly meetings two or three at a time, on a rotating basis, or whenever there was a matter relevant to their particular responsibilities. I decided not to tamper much with the departmental changes that Prime Minister Campbell had introduced a few months earlier— I didn't want the ministers and bureaucrats wasting their precious hours writing memos about who was now running what or dealing with questions of structure rather than substance.

Building a Cabinet is perhaps the most private and personal duty a prime minister has to perform. The sad fact is that you cannot make every caucus member a minister. You read their CVs; you watch them in action in the Commons and the committees; you observe their personalities; you look at how they're perceived by the bureaucrats and the press; you factor in gender, language, region, and background; and you make a decision. It's complex, and it's not always fair. You spot one good person here and an equally good person in the riding next door, but because you don't have room for two people from the same region of the same province, one gets into the Cabinet and the other does not. I usually began my planning with a clean sheet of paper, though I sometimes used to jot down names and positions on little yellow Post-it notes in spare moments, and once, in January 1996, I scribbled a few ideas for a major shuffle on two cocktail coasters in the Regent Hotel in Kuala Lumpur, Malaysia, during a trade mission.

Many of the decisions for my first ministry were easy to make because I knew I would have enough places in Cabinet for only the most obvious choices. First I listed all the provinces, and then I put down the names of the leading contenders from each, based on their experience, reputation, personal attributes, or support for me over the years (which I liked to joke was an indication of their superb political judgment). Newfoundland was Brian Tobin; Nova Scotia, David Dingwall; New Brunswick, Doug Young; Prince Edward Island, Lawrence MacAulay; Manitoba, Lloyd Axworthy; Saskatchewan, Ralph Goodale. Quebec, too, was relatively simple, for the unhappy reason that there were only nineteen Liberal MPs to choose from out of seventy-five seats. André Ouellet was a Cabinet veteran; Marcel Massé and Michel Dupuy were star recruits; and Paul Martin Jr.—the son of a famous Liberal minister, a successful business-man in Montreal, a member of Parliament since 1988, and my principal opponent for the leadership in 1990—clearly deserved a major portfolio.

Alberta, with four possibilities, all from Edmonton, was more complicated. David Kilgour and John Loney were experi-enced MPs, but both were regarded with suspicion by some Liberals because they had switched from the Tories. Judy Bethel, an educator and investment broker, would have been a good choice, though I leaned towards another woman, Anne McLellan, dean of law at the University of Alberta. However, the race in her riding had been so tight that a recount was under way and her victory was far from assured. When McLellan was finally declared the winner by a mere eleven votes late on the night before the swearing-in, I rushed her into the Cabinet and named Kilgour Deputy Speaker. British Columbia, with only six Liberal MPs out of thirty-two seats, also had a complication. Besides David Anderson, a former leader of the BC Liberal Party in the provincial legislature, I wanted to make Herb Dhaliwal, a Sikh immigrant and successful businessman, the first South Asian minister in any national government in the Western world. At the time, however, his company was doing business with the federal government, and he couldn't simply tear up the contract without hurting his partner's financial interests. So, at the very last minute, Jean Pelletier phoned Raymond Chan in Vancouver and told him to grab a dark suit and jump on the overnight red-eye to Ottawa. Chan arrived mere hours before the ceremony and became the first Chinese Canadian ever appointed to a federal Cabinet.

Ontario was the toughest, because it was such an embarrassment of riches. Herb Gray, Sheila Copps, and John Manley were senior in the caucus and represented Windsor, Hamilton, and Ottawa, respectively. David Collenette had been an MP since 1974 and a minister under Trudeau and Turner. Roy MacLaren brought his experience as one of Turner's ministers as well as his connections to the Toronto business community. Art Eggleton had been a long-time mayor of Toronto. Ron Irwin, a good friend of mine, was from northern Ontario, though he almost didn't make it into the Cabinet because he had gone into the woods to recover from the election and no one had been able to find him for a week. Diane Marleau, elected in 1988, represented Sudbury. Allan Rock, though he had no political experience, was a very distinguished lawyer and had been a star candidate. Things got trickier when I wanted to have at least one representative of the Italian-Canadian community from among the many loyal and competent Liberal MPs elected in the Greater Toronto Area. Ultimately I went with Sergio Marchi. Some of the older caucus members resented the fact that he was so young, but Marchi had worked hard for me and turned out to be an excellent minister. All leaders need what's termed (most appropriately, in this case) a "Roman guard" around them—people who have been there from the start, who believe in them, and who can therefore create a zone of comfort and security.

If I had picked someone other than Marchi, all the rest would still have been just as disappointed and resentful. In politics, as in life, it's normal to have ambition, but very few MPs like to admit that they may not be as good as the person sitting beside them. They've managed to get themselves elected by the people, after all, and they're respected and influential in their ridings, so it's natural for them to assume they deserve a place in Cabinet. This expectation adds an undercurrent of jealousy and grievance to governing in Canada that doesn't exist in the American system, where the president selects his Cabinet members from outside Congress. The Australian Labor Party tries to get around the problem by having its caucus select the Cabinet, but as a result there's a lot of ugly backroom politicking, the prime minister isn't always able to make use of his best MPs, and he loses a great deal of authority over the ministers simply because they don't owe him their jobs. Although a few of our MPs used to complain bitterly that they hadn't been chosen for this political reason or that, the main reason they hadn't been chosen was that I had found someone I thought was better.

I didn't give much consideration to trying to balance the left and right wings of the Liberal Party. We had all rallied around the election platform, and I saw us as partners in a collective effort to implement it. Nevertheless, the various emphases and interests of different caucus members were a factor when it came to allocating their responsibilities. It made sense to give the economic portfolios to people with whom the business community would feel comfortable, and the social portfolios to those on the progressive side. I knew, for example, that we would be facing a number of difficult reforms in the human resources field, some because of outdated programs and others because of money issues, so I gave the job to Lloyd Axworthy, figuring that he would have the credibility as a well-known, respected social activist to do what had to be done, as well as the skill to be able to explain why and, as a former minister of employment and immigration, the experience required for the task. Axworthy had his heart set on Foreign Affairs, but so did André Ouellet, and at that stage I preferred to have a francophone in that prestigious position if we had to fight the separatists in another referendum in Quebec. I also knew that Ouellet wasn't intending to remain in public life much longer, so I could dangle the hope of Foreign Affairs like a carrot to get Axworthy to take on Human Resources Development in the meantime.

The reality is, when you're the prime minister, you don't have to engage in a lot of bargaining. Of course, if someone wants something and that person is also the best for the job, you'd be crazy to ignore it. But most MPs are grateful to be given any seat at the Cabinet table, and they know there's a line of hopefuls waiting at the door if they don't accept what's offered. I often kept the fire under the feet of my A team by lightly reminding them how many good people I had in reserve on the B team.

Nevertheless, I didn't have an easy time getting Paul Martin to accept Finance. I thought he would be the most suitable choice, because of his knowledge of the field and his popularity among the business community, but Martin was keen to have both Industry and International Trade, as Michael Wilson had had under Mulroney, or the Environment portfolio, which had been Martin's area of responsibility in opposition. Maybe, too, he was afraid that, during a period of deficit reduction and program cuts, Finance would be the graveyard of his political ambitions. "Look," I told him, "I know you want to take over from me someday. But if we don't solve the deficit, there will be nothing left to take over. It's the biggest problem we have." I also reminded him that both John Turner and I had survived Finance to become prime minister. Still he refused. So I got ready to offer the job to Roy MacLaren or John Manley, both of whom had experience in business and Parliament, though MacLaren really wanted International Trade and Manley certainly wasn't as well known in financial circles as Martin.

In the meantime, I heard that others were pressuring Martin to change his mind, and I know he was disappointed to learn that I had decided to appoint a full-time minister to handle all the important and complicated trade issues Canada was facing. By our third meeting—to Martin's own good fortune, as it turned out—he agreed to accept Finance after all. When I told Manley that he was going to Industry instead, he never uttered a word of complaint and went on to do an excellent job there. In retrospect, history might have been very different if Paul Martin had gone to some other department. I find it ironic that I practically had to force him to take the job that would launch his reputation and help make him party leader and then prime minister.

—

The swearing-in ceremony, presided over by Governor General Ray Hnatyshyn in the ballroom at Rideau Hall on Thursday, November 4, 1993, was a solemn occasion for my family and me, though I mostly remember having some trouble reading the oath of office because I hadn't wanted to wear my glasses. Aline sat in the front row, of course, and she was particularly chic that day.

"Do I look like a prime minister's wife?" she asked David Zussman going in.

"Madame Chrétien," he replied, "you look like a prime minister!"

After the official reception, Aline and I walked hand in hand down the long drive, through the gates, and across the street to our new home at 24 Sussex Drive, where we had a less formal reception with our relatives and closest friends. The two of us had come a long way together from our humble beginnings and the basement apartment that had been our first home as newlyweds in 1957, when I was still a law student at Laval University in Quebec City.

Considering where we had started in life and how hard we had worked to get here, neither Aline nor I had anything to complain about, and it wasn't in our nature to care about a grand style of living, but I think that Canadians would have been as surprised as we were by the structural condition of the prime minister's official residence in 1993. The reality, let me put it, didn't always match the glamorous image. In fact, Stornoway, the home of the leader of the Opposition in Rockcliffe Park, is a much better house—better built, better maintained, better laid out—except for the fact that nobody wants to stay there for long and nobody wants to be sent back to it.

For all its prestige, its fabulous views, its indoor pool, and its lovely garden, 24 Sussex is more like an old hotel than a modern home. When the wind blew from the north in winter, the second-floor sitting room was too cold to allow me to sign documents or read late at night in my favourite chair overlooking the river. In summer we had to turn off the three noisy fans in the dining room during lunch to allow a visiting dignitary's remarks to be audible. And when U.S. vice-president Al Gore came for lunch in July 1994, he sweated under his bulletproof vest all through the meal. Even so, when the National Capital Commission immediately requested $150,000 to repair the fifty-year-old cedar-shingle roof and $200,000 to install an emergency power generator, I said no, it's not right to spend money here when we're asking Canadians to tighten their belts everywhere else. But in 1998 the Great Ice Storm tore so many tiles from the roof that doing nothing was no longer a practical option, and a generator became necessary for the operation of the government.

Aline, too, hesitated to spend anything on the interior decoration, no matter how bad the wear and tear from thousands of people coming through the house every year. The worst was in the dining room, where the linen on the walls was so warped with age that it would soon have to be replaced. A solution presented itself in 1995 when Canada hosted the Group of Seven (G7) meeting in Halifax. Though the meeting was dubbed the Chevrolet Summit because of our efforts to streamline the agenda and minimize costs, we still had to jazz up the meeting room we had rented on the fourth floor of an office tower. The cheapest and most attractive option was to cover the walls with a beautiful green cloth, frame the windows with matching drapes, and warm the floor with a new carpet. It all looked so nice, in fact, that Aline decided to ship everything back to Ottawa in boxes after the summit was over and recycle it in the dining room at 24 Sussex. When the time for a renovation was past due, the material was used to cover the walls and two dozen chairs, with still more left over for tablecloths, at virtually no extra expense.

I added a personal touch of my own a few weeks after settling into the residence when I noticed a painting in the living room at 7 Rideau Gate, the government's official guest house, where I had gone to do a series of year-end television interviews. It was a pastoral scene by the famous nineteenth-century artist Cornelius Krieghoff, of a river with a high waterfall. "I know that place," I said. Sure enough, according to the label, it was the Little Shawinigan, which runs into the St. Maurice not far from where I grew up. I recognized the rocks on which Aline and I used to sit and kiss when we were young.

"Gee," I said to the woman in charge of the house, "my brothers and sisters are coming for Christmas and they'll get some fun out of seeing this. I'm going to take it with me."

"No, no, Mr. Chrétien," she said. "You can't take it until I ask my boss."

"*He's* your boss now," one of my bodyguards piped up.

"Yes," I said, "I'm your boss now, so I guess I'll only be stealing this from myself. Seriously, Madame, inform the curators that I have taken it, and I will bring it back at once if they have any problem." Then I lifted the painting off the wall, carried it under my arm across the street, and hung it in the living room, where it stayed until I left office.

The move into 24 Sussex was made faster and easier than usual because Kim Campbell had chosen not to occupy the house after her election as Tory leader the previous June. When I spoke to her on the phone to discuss the transfer of power, which I wanted to happen as quickly as possible, I discovered that she was in a bind, with no seat in the Commons, no income, no pension, no office, no secretary, and no plans. So we gave her an office, a budget, and a staff of two to help her organize her papers for the national archives, and in 1996 I appointed her consul general in Los Angeles, where she continued to serve her country with great spirit and dedication.

"The PM's courtesy was widely discussed," Campbell wrote in her own memoirs, "as evidence that the Liberals were treating me better than my own party."

I have always thought it a matter of civility to be generous in victory and important not to be narrowly partisan. It rarely pays to be vengeful in life or to try to undo everything that has gone before. For example, even though Glen Shortliffe, whose position as clerk of the Privy Council made him the federal government's highest-ranking public servant, was known to have been close to Brian Mulroney and had quickly offered me his resignation, I asked him to stay on for a few more months, much to his surprise, because he was doing a good job and I needed his help during the transition. I left Benoît Bouchard as Canada's ambassador to France and appointed Perrin Beatty as president of the Canadian Broadcasting Corporation, though both had been Mulroney Cabinet ministers; and I named Tory MPs and Tory political assistants to boards and senior bureaucratic positions if I thought they were capable people who needed a job. Above all, I made sure that my two opponents in the 1990 Liberal leadership race, Paul Martin and Sheila Copps, were given important Cabinet posts.

From the first meeting with the new ministers on the afternoon of our swearing-in, I wanted to establish my own style of government. There weren't to be any more of Trudeau's six-hour marathons, which used to waste everyone's valuable time and leave us totally exhausted. My Cabinet meetings weren't graduate seminars or discussion groups; they were a place to make decisions. I started them at precisely ten o'clock on Tuesday mornings in the Cabinet Room down the hall from the prime minister's Centre Block suite, gave a half-hour overview of the country's current issues, went down the agenda item by item for approval or further consideration, and wrapped up precisely at noon. If ministers agreed with one of their colleagues, they didn't have to repeat the same arguments ad nauseam, and if someone talked too often or too long, I became visibly edgy. When they saw me packing up my binders, they knew I was about to read a list of the latest government appointments, which everyone was always eager to hear, and that was both a signal and an incentive to bring the session to a close. I believe the ministers were happy to be able to plan the rest of their day around a firm schedule and to get out of there promptly. In addition, we had two or three Cabinet retreats a year—less formal meetings that took place in a conference room in the Pearson Building on Sussex Drive over the course of a couple of days—during which we freely discussed our priorities as both a government and a party.

For the same reasons, I reduced the number of permanent Cabinet committees from more than a dozen to two—Economic Policy and Social Policy—though the Treasury Board and the Special Committee of Council that administers government orders and regulations were technically Cabinet committees as well. Occasionally, if the government needed to examine a particular issue in more depth, such as health care or the airlines industry, I set up an ad hoc committee, but only on a temporary basis. When you have too many committees and too many documents, everyone gets dragged down in the details and fewer decisions get made. Moreover, there's little to be gained from having the minister of fisheries, for example, perpetually involved in the business of the Department of Veterans Affairs, or vice versa. I wanted the ministers to be spending most of their time in their own offices, looking after what needed to be done and making decisions, rather than behaving like quasi–prime ministers trying to tell the whole government what to do.

Contrary to the myth of the prime minister as dictator— friendly or otherwise—I saw myself as the head of a team of ministers charged with the management of their own departments. I had no intention of breathing down their necks, looking over their shoulders, or interfering with their officials as long as everything was functioning smoothly, nor did I expect them to come running to me with every little problem. I also gave strict instructions to my PMO staff that it was their role to coordinate the work of the departments, not to tell the ministers what to do. My job was to act like the orchestra conductor, not the pianist or the drummer, and because I insisted on being given time between meetings for reflection and strategy, I found most days surprisingly less strenuous than when I had been responsible to someone else for the day-to-day operations of a large ministry—until, of course, a crisis hit or the really tough decisions landed on my desk.

During the first Cabinet session, as a way of illustrating to the ministers what I expected of them, I repeated a favourite story of mine. One day when I was minister of Indian affairs, Trudeau phoned and asked if I was angry with him.

"No," I answered. "Why do you ask?"

"Well, I've noticed that you have not asked to see me for a year," he said, "and I thought there might be something wrong. Are you mad at me?"

"Nothing's wrong. It's just that, knowing how busy you are, I didn't want to call you for no reason. And I'm happy that you never called me, because I assume that means you're satisfied with the way I'm doing my job."

"Believe me, Jean," he said, "if all my ministers had the same idea, being prime minister would be much, much easier."

The effect was gratifying. Some ministers even took pride in testing how long they could go without saying a word to me. Lyle Vanclief, for example, who was an old friend and an excellent minister of agriculture from 1997 to 2003, once boasted that he had come to see me only four or five times despite all the serious issues he faced.

The process worked quite efficiently. If ministers were looking for a new program or policy change, they sent a report to the Cabinet's Social Policy or Economic Policy Committee for discussion and a decision. Someone from the PMO, usually Chaviva Hošek or Eddie Goldenberg, attended all those meetings on my behalf, and they knew my mind well enough to be able to predict my reaction to any particular initiative and warn ministers away from wasting a lot of effort on something they assumed I would reject. Eddie was accurate about 90 per cent of the time, because of all the years he had spent working at my side. I liked to tease him that the other 10 per cent occurred only when he was pursuing some agenda of his own. Once the committee reached an agreement, it was brought to me for analysis and approval before being taken to the full Cabinet for a collective decision, subject only to the budget considerations of the Treasury Board and the Department of Finance, and then back to me for a final signoff.

In the Canadian system, prime ministers can change a decision of the Cabinet simply because they have the power to switch any or all of the ministers at any time. There's no formal vote because everybody knows exactly who has the last word. During my term, any objections or concerns within the bureaucracy were communicated from a deputy minister to the clerk of the Privy Council and, at the political level, from a minister to my chief of staff, senior policy adviser, or director of research. I would listen to the arguments, review the material, and make any amendments I thought were necessary. In practice, however, a prime minister who continually goes against the views of the majority of the Cabinet or his most powerful ministers might be able to impose his will for a short while but probably won't last long as leader.

—

Because building a Cabinet is so complicated, your instinct is to stay with the same team so long as it's a good one. It's usually wise to keep ministers in their department long enough to let them learn the ropes and master the issues. But too little change can create frustration and agitation among those backbenchers who see no movement and, therefore, no possibility of advancement in their own careers. Though no one can demand to be made a minister, a prime minister is under constant pressure to make room for new people, even if there's no real need for a shuffle, because there's an unfortunate misconception in Ottawa that if you're not a minister, you're not a success. But that's simply not true. Some people can be extremely effective MPs without ever being in Cabinet, and some can have more influence in the caucus or the party than many ministers.

Charles Caccia, for example, had been in Trudeau's Cabinet, and though I never named him to one of mine, he was a great promoter of environmental causes and an articulate defender of social liberalism. Whenever he rose in caucus, he was well prepared, passionate, and interesting, so members listened closely to whatever he had to say. Caccia had his own way of being effective. He used to enter every caucus meeting by the aisle in front of where I normally sat and slip me an envelope containing a note full of advice about the current debates. Most weeks I would talk to him on the way out if an answer was needed or simply to thank him for his ideas. Clifford Lincoln and Ted McWhinney were another two of the many worthy backbenchers who come to mind. Like Caccia, they were older men of broad experience and deep expertise. Unfairly, perhaps, their age may have hurt their chances of becoming ministers because I wanted my Cabinet to project a youthful image to counter the impression that I had been around the political scene forever. Nevertheless, Lincoln and McWhinney made a valuable contribution to the government without having chauffeur-driven cars and fancy titles.

As I saw it, I was prime minister because enough Liberal MPs had run for public office and succeeded in getting elected, so it was both just and useful that those MPs should feel respected. I always tried to attend the weekly Wednesday-morning caucus meetings, and I instructed every member of the Cabinet to go as well. Often arriving early, I used to survey the room and write down the name of each minister I saw. Sometimes, just for fun, I pretended to skip over one of them, and the ignored individual would immediately wave frantically to catch my attention. The MPs felt good knowing they could make their pitch directly to the prime minister and maybe boast back home that they had changed the course of Canadian history. After the various regional and special caucuses presented their reports, a couple of dozen members a week were able to stand up and express their views without any of the PMO or ministerial staffs present. If they had problems with a certain department or if a particular minister was refusing to meet with them, they got a chance to air their grievances in front of their colleagues. And, if necessary, I didn't hesitate to order a minister to be more helpful. At other times I had to remind caucus members that they couldn't always get what they wanted or that a certain minister had acted in accordance with government policy.

Though I didn't chair the caucus meetings myself, I made certain they were kept orderly and on schedule: thirty or forty minutes of reports; an hour of questions or comments, with each speaker limited to three minutes; then ten or fifteen minutes for me to reply to the points I had noted. If I didn't have the proper information at hand or wanted to speak privately with an MP, I invited individual members to come and see me in my office at three o'clock, following Question Period in the House of Commons. As well, two or three times a month, I used to lunch with a dozen members of the caucus at 24 Sussex.

Because issues are never completely black or white, I often changed my views in the evolution of a file after listening to the caucus. You may decide to do something, but if you encounter an obstacle, you have to change direction or figure out a way around it. That is the art of politics. But these tactics help you implement the policies that your government thinks the country needs. In my mind, if you make a mistake in administration, it will hurt you politically; and if you make a mistake politically, it will hurt your ability to govern with the support of the people. The two have to mesh if you want to do what is right as well as what is possible.

—

My first piece of advice to the members of the Cabinet at our first meeting was that they become allies with their deputy ministers—the senior bureaucrats in charge of each department. From my own experience, I know there is a strong community of interest between the political masters and their public servants, even though they have completely different responsibilities. I was bothered by the trend that had developed under

Prime Minister Mulroney in which ministers built up large political offices headed by a chief of staff who often competed with the deputy minister for power and the final word. I got rid of the ministerial chief of staff as a title, reined in the empire-building habits of a few old-style ministers who wanted to have more assistants than everyone else, and tried to set an example by keeping the PMO small.

Part of that was to demonstrate fiscal restraint by saving as much as $13 million a year, but I also preferred to have a smaller staff. It meant fewer turf wars and avoided the overly complex lines of authority that plague so many large teams. I didn't feel the need to have a lot of yes-men standing around me. As Mitchell Sharp once put it, the bigger the staff, the smaller the minister. Even when I was simultaneously minister of justice, attorney general, and minister of social development, as well as Trudeau's minister in charge of the referendum and the Constitution, I had no more than a handful of assistants working for me in my office.

One of them, I remember, was a particularly eager young man who loved all the responsibilities and decisions I kept delegating to him. "I'm having a ball," he told his grandmother, an elderly, conservative-minded lady from rural Nova Scotia. "I'm attending important meetings, I'm dealing with deputy ministers, I'm writing speeches, I'm preparing for Question Period, I'm travelling the country. Mr. Chrétien is giving me more authority than I ever expected at my age."

"I always knew," she said, "that those French Canadians are lazy."

The battles between the chiefs of staff and the deputy ministers not only created tension and confusion around the minister but promoted the false notion that there is a separation between good politics and good administration. Some academics and theorists have even recommended that a kind of wall be established between politicians and public servants, as though it were desirable or even possible for the two not to talk to each other. They don't think that the clerk of the Privy Council should be both the prime minister's chief bureaucratic adviser and the head of the civil service, for instance, nor do they want the deputy ministers to be responsible to the ministers for the administration of their departments. In reality, the result would be that the elected government would not be in charge of running anything.

The role of the politician in a democracy is to set policies based on a party platform and to receive representations from constituents. The Americans even hire and fire almost ten thousand government officials, right down to the middle ranks, with every change of administration. When Canadians have a problem, they can go to their MP, who then takes it, within a set of rules and procedures, to a bureaucrat for a solution. That's not exercising undue influence—that's doing the job. But what would happen if the bureaucrat wasn't accountable to the minister? Who would be responsible for any action or inaction? Conversely, it's part of the job of a civil servant in charge of implementing a policy to take note of the political environment, to caution whether the policy will be unpopular, unworkable, or unfair, and to help the elected government do the best job possible. That may not be exactly the same as helping it to win re-election, but it's political advice nonetheless.

"If you look good, so will the other," I told the ministers, and I delivered the same message to all the deputy ministers when I met with them the next day. "If you look incompetent, so will the other. So it is a partnership that you will have to develop. The political staff should deal with political matters; the deputy ministers should deal with legislative and administrative matters; and all of them should remain on their own turf. If they do that, the ministers will be well advised by both and will make good decisions." To the deputy ministers I added, "If any of you think you'll feel uncomfortable serving this government for any reason, let me know now." No one spoke. And the pattern was set for the next ten years.

The second thing I emphasized to the Cabinet was the high ethical standard I expected all of us to uphold. I was determined to restore the tarnished reputation of parliamentarians in the minds of the Canadian people. That meant keeping our election promises as best we could and staying beyond reproach, whether as ministers, MPs, or ordinary citizens. At the very start of my political life, when I was still a student at Laval University, I was invited to give a speech at a riding association meeting at the time of the 1958 federal election. It was a pretty good speech, I thought, but what I remembered for the rest of my life was the advice a woman gave me afterwards. "Young man," she said, "don't become a politician if you're not honest, because you're extremely convincing."

"Don't even try to make money when you're here," I now told the ministers, "because there is no money to be made in politics. But if you work hard and build a solid reputation, you'll earn your chance to find a good job afterwards." In my own case, I said, I had started in politics when I was twenty-nine and retired with almost nothing in 1986. Within four years I wrote a successful book, helped open a branch of a law firm in Ottawa, worked for an investment company in Montreal, and saved enough money to give myself the freedom to return to public life without any obligations to anybody. "But if you get tempted in office and do something wrong, that's it," I cautioned. "You will have a black eye for the rest of your life."

To reinforce my resolve, I wanted to move quickly to fulfill our election promise to appoint an independent ethics counsellor to advise both public officials and lobbyists about the rules by which ministers, MPs, senators, political staff, and public servants were to deal with lobbyists. But Mitchell Sharp, in particular, warned me that the idea could lead to runaway costs and political chaos. Making the ethics counsellor independent, he explained, would require establishing a large, expensive, and complicated new office at a time when the government was trying to downsize, tighten its belt, and simplify its operations. Even more significant, an independent ethics counsellor would be able, in effect, to decide—rather than simply advise—on the fitness of a particular minister to hold his or her portfolio. In other words, Canadian prime ministers would be delegating part of the responsibility to choose the members of their Cabinet to a public servant, because they would be surrendering the right, as it currently exists in our system, to forgive a minister's mistake and risk the political fallout in the House of Commons, the press, or the next election.

Since the position would be new and nobody could be sure how it was going to work out in practice, I decided that the responsible action was to back away from our full election commitment, at least for the time being, and make Canada's first ethics counsellor only an adviser to the prime minister. In June 1994 I appointed a highly regarded public servant, Howard Wilson, to the post. I had never met him, but he was already overseeing the *Lobbyists Registration Act* as assistant deputy registrar general, and we increased his authority by strengthening the act and introducing a more comprehensive conflict of interest code as his guideline. Though the government had to take a hit for reneging on a promise we had made during the campaign, Wilson did a very professional job. His reports were objective, judicious, and available for intense public scrutiny. I certainly never tried to influence them in any way, and he had enough clout with the opposition parties and the media to have withstood any pressure from me. Imagine the political damage if I had ever tried to fire him. However, his credibility was hurt—especially on those occasions when he found no fault with the government—by the technical fact that he had been hired by the prime minister, could be fired by the prime minister, and reported to the prime minister.

Rather than getting the credit for having created the position in the first place, we were criticized for not making it completely independent. Even some of our own caucus members used to wonder if we hadn't made a mistake in setting it up at all. In October 2002, therefore, the government agreed to reform the position as part of an updated ethics package that was eventually put into effect by my successor. By that time, experience had convinced me that the advantages of an independent ethics counsellor reporting directly to the House of Commons now outweighed Sharp's initial fears. We had had almost a decade to test the system and to establish clearly that the last word on who was, or was not, fit to serve in the Cabinet remained the prime minister's prerogative and duty.

—

With my office and Cabinet all in place, I got to work on cleaning up the mess the Tories had left behind and checking off the Liberals' election promises item by item. There were, as I saw it, three fundamental priorities facing the government as a result of the Mulroney legacy: to reduce our horrendous deficit and prevent the International Monetary Fund from coming into Canada to fix our finances; to reassert our independence and protect Canada from being seen as the fifty-first state of the United States; and, in the face of the separatist threat in Quebec and the sense of alienation in other parts of the country, to keep Canada united.

To manage those issues, we basically had to change the mood of the country from cynicism to optimism, from despair to hope. Political leadership always has as much to do with creating a positive mood as solving any particular problems. Why? Because a country's economy and quality of life are made up of the millions of decisions its citizens make every day. If people are worried or depressed, they won't build for the future, and no government program on earth can pick up the slack. If they are content and confident, they'll spend, they'll invest, and they'll build. In fact, though I was no fan of Ronald Reagan's policies as president of the United States, I think he did an exemplary job of making Americans proud and confident again. Similarly, at the risk of being accused of wearing rose-coloured glasses, I felt it was essential to put our problems in perspective and give Canadians back their sense of confidence. My underlying message was always positive and practical. I talked about creating jobs, not changing the Constitution, and I never ceased reminding Canadians of all the people around the world who would willingly sacrifice everything they owned to be able to share our so-called miseries.

Once, near the beginning of my term, an American reporter asked me how I would like to be remembered. "As a competent prime minister," I replied. Perhaps it seemed a modest ambition, but I didn't feel I had to be great. Canada was great, and my task was to make it even greater by dealing with our problems as they arose and letting Canadians get on with their own business and pleasures.

If you read Plato or Montesquieu, as I did at school, you see that the basic problems of government haven't changed over the centuries, because human nature hasn't changed. Of course, the mechanics of life will change, so there must always be different solutions for dealing with different situations, but there are no miracles that will solve everything and there are few good ideas that are new. Furthermore, the basic problems of government almost always come down to questions of money. You can have all the dazzling visions and bright ideas you want, but they are nothing next to finding enough money to do what you want, establishing the proper priorities, and exercising sound judgment in pursuit of a better society. As a result, every leader ends up confronting the same complex problems and unpredictable crises that make visions virtually impossible to realize or sustain.

For me, "vision" is perhaps the emptiest and most ill-used word in politics. It's easy for someone to wake up in the middle of the night and say he or she has a "vision." But what does that mean? Nothing. It's just a word that's used by speechwriters and reporters to build up some politicians as wise and omnipotent saviours—until the inevitable day comes when they're brought down as disappointments, failures, or mere humans. John Diefenbaker said he had a vision of the Great North; Pierre Trudeau, of a Just Society; Brian Mulroney, of a National Reconciliation. Was Diefenbaker's vision of Canada bigger than Louis St. Laurent's? Was Trudeau's more compassionate than Lester Pearson's? Was Mulroney's better than Joe Clark's?

Instead of visions, I preferred to talk about values—Canadian values, Liberal values, personal values. Values shape the principles and perspectives that are brought to bear on the priorities and problems of governing. In my own case, though I had originally been drawn to politics as a competitive sport, I quickly learned how parties and governments can be a force for tolerance, justice, and prosperity. I grew up fighting the reactionary policies and corrupt practices of Premier Maurice Duplessis's Union Nationale government in the 1950s. I picked up the anti-clerical, democratic, and reformist agenda of the Liberal Party in Quebec and the progressive record of the federal Liberals under Laurier, King, and St. Laurent. Before becoming a candidate, I took on loads of small cases as a defence lawyer—often pro bono, for people without any money or influence who were trying to prove their innocence when the entire system of police, prosecutors, and judges seemed to be against them—and I represented the unions in their battles against the big companies. Defending the underdog was part of my values as a Liberal. I certainly didn't need to make a lot of money to be happy. Even after I began to do quite well, I preferred to build a house near my blue-collar friends in an area that became known as La Place Rouge, rather than in a bourgeois part of Shawinigan.

My reputation as a defender of the little guy helped get me elected at the age of twenty-nine, no doubt about it, as did my down-to-earth, fun-loving, optimistic personality. In the 1960s, as we tend to forget, the major opposition to the Liberals in rural Quebec was not the Tories but the Créditistes—folksy types who had picked up the "funny money" monetary theories of the Social Credit movement in Alberta and launched a conservative protest party in Ottawa with great success. Their leader, Réal Caouette, was a dynamic orator with a terrific sense of humour, and both he and his ally, Camil Samson, were from the Shawinigan region. Indeed, Samson and my wife, Aline, had been neighbours and classmates. So, while my style may have caused the intellectuals and snobs in Quebec City and Montreal to look down on me, it made me a winner with the people of my riding—as, in due course, it did with the people of Canada—and it suited my position on the centre-left of the Liberal Party when I arrived in Ottawa as a young MP.

In the United States, a Liberal is almost a communist; in Europe, a Liberal is a kind of conservative; but in Canada, as I would tell foreigners whenever they asked about the difference, you're a good Liberal when the left says you're on the right and the right says you're on the left. I've always been both amazed and proud at how close the values of the Liberal Party are to the values of the nation. This country is fundamentally liberal. In fact, Canada's values of moderation, sharing, tolerance, and compassion are very much the product of all the progressive policies that have been introduced by Liberals since Laurier's time.

Some people like to say that we stole them from the CCF/NDP. That's not exactly true, but even if it were, so what? Anyone from any part of the political spectrum can have a good idea, but the courage and capacity to implement that good idea are more important. By definition, a Liberal is not an ideologue. Liberals don't reject any good idea just because it isn't one of our own, nor do we keep implementing bad ideas after they've been shown not to work.

"No vision?" I used to ask rhetorically. "I want Canada to be the best nation in the world, that's all. Imagine if I had a vision!"

TWO

THE VIRTUOUS CIRCLE

———

I f I had proclaimed any grand visions before being elected prime minister of Canada, they would have been smashed to pieces by the cold, hard facts the government faced on its first day at work. Even though the country was slowly emerging from a recession, the Progressive Conservatives left us with a $42 billion deficit, representing 6 per cent of Canada's gross domestic product and $10 billion over the Tories' last budget prediction. The federal debt was soaring above $500 billion, and we were spending about $40 billion a year, or 37 cents of every tax dollar, just to service the interest on the debt. That was more than we were spending on Unemployment Insurance and Old Age Security combined.

I can't say I was taken by surprise. Every outgoing government tries to paint a rosier picture of reality than is generally the case, and I had been watching the fiscal projections very closely in opposition. But even the Finance Department was alarmed by how quickly the numbers had worsened over the summer. It was a dreadful legacy to have inherited. I saw myself as a Liberal who had always been preoccupied with fixing social problems, but Ottawa couldn't spend money it didn't have. So our first task had to be to restore the integrity of the nation's finances, not for their own sake but to stimulate the jobs and growth we had promised during the election campaign.

Soon after being elected, I visited a classroom in Vancouver full of kids from different races and religions, and there was one little guy, maybe twelve years old, who was already worried about his pension. "Hey, wait a minute," I told him. "Get an education, get a job, work hard, and then you can worry about your pension." But his concern struck me as an indication of how many ordinary citizens were uncertain about Canada's prospects, as were the international investors and currency speculators whose decisions had so much power over the value of our dollar and the cost of our interest payments.

The fact was that governments everywhere and of all stripes had been caught for way too long in a vicious circle in which high spending led to high deficits that led to high interest rates that led to high unemployment and low growth. At the same time, governments had to adjust to fundamental changes in the global economy and in the role of the state, to the expansion of international trade, to the revolution in technology, and to the consequent pressure on social programs. In Canada, meanwhile, the Liberal Party got itself trapped between a nostalgia for Trudeau's interventionist policies and a fiscal conservatism that wasn't all that different from where Mulroney's Progressive Conservatives had been. By the 1990s we were divided, confused, and uncertain about where we wanted to go. We had been in opposition too long and had become accustomed to being negative, quarrelsome, and unaccountable. Left fought against right, protectionists against free traders, isolationists against those who wanted to engage with the bigger world. We needed to establish a unified middle course between social justice and fiscal responsibility—not just to win an election, but to have a reason to win an election, at a point in history when no one could predict with any certainty what the future held in store.

While still leader of the Opposition, inspired by the Liberal Party's historic conferences in Port Hope in 1933 and in Kingston in 1960, I had invited 125 economists, political scientists, academics, and politicians from across Canada and around the world, representing the left, the right, and the centre, to come together to explore the issues Canada faced. The conference, which took place in November 1991 at a hotel in Aylmer, Quebec, across the river from Ottawa, never received enough credit for uniting Liberals and setting us on the road to our 1993 victory. If nothing else, it allowed us to state what we stood for clearly and unequivocally when we launched our election platform a week into the campaign. *Creating Opportunity: The Liberal Plan for Canada,* commonly known as the Red Book, was produced under the direction of Paul Martin and Chaviva Hošek after widespread consultations across the land. Though every party lays out its policies and commitments for the voters, the Red Book had a particular impact because it was remarkably detailed, unusually prudent, fully costed, and presented as a complete, integrated package. It was especially welcomed by those Canadians who felt duped by the unfulfilled and unrealistic promises of the Mulroney Conservatives.

I didn't go to the Aylmer Conference with the idea of telling everybody what to do; rather, I went to listen and learn. I read all the background papers, attended every session, and was pleased when the non-partisan discussions led to many of the same conclusions I had already reached myself—not because I was brilliant, but because they were obviously necessary. We had to create the conditions for more jobs and more growth. We had to balance the budget and reduce the federal debt. We had to open Canada's borders to trade and prepare for the new knowledge-based economy through investment in education and research. We had to be pragmatic centrists, feeling the pressure from left and right equally, coping with problems realistically, and ready to bring in the best ideas without giving a damn where they had originated. After all, that's how we behave in our own lives. If we're bankrupt, we have to face the fact that we have no money to pay our bills. If we're rich, we have to decide whether to indulge ourselves with luxuries or help feed the poor. Why should good government be any different?

"At this conference," I said at its conclusion, "we have learned that the old concepts of right and left do not apply to the world of today and tomorrow. What is important are policies that contribute to the well-being of all our citizens. Protectionism is not left-wing or right-wing. It is simply passé. Globalization is not right-wing or left-wing. It is simply a fact of life."

The thorniest problem we faced in the two years between the Aylmer Conference and the Red Book was how far and how fast we should promise to bring down the deficit. The Tories and the Reform Party were talking about getting to zero within three years. Some Liberals wanted us to do the same, but most thought it unnecessarily severe. For me, it was a nice idea in theory but probably impossible to achieve in practice, and I was concerned that pulling tens of billions out of the economy so quickly would plunge the country back into a recession. Instead, picking up on the target set by the Maastricht Treaty for membership in the European Community's monetary union, I decided that our goal would be to reduce the deficit to 3 per cent of GDP by the end of our third year. Cutting government spending by some $20 billion in three years was enough of a challenge and, to be frank, as optimistic as I am by nature, there were days when I didn't really believe we could make it in one term.

"If 3 per cent is good enough for the Europeans, it should be good enough for Canadians," I told Paul Martin, who was feeling the heat from his former colleagues in the business community and wanted us to adopt the tougher, more macho stand of the parties on the right. "If we do better, everyone will applaud, but if we promise zero and hit only 2 per cent, then everyone will say that we've failed."

Setting a realistic target and meeting it is always a better course of action than aiming too ambitiously and failing to deliver. Too many politicians think they have to make extravagant promises to attract votes. On the contrary: people are highly suspicious of those who make big promises. Rather than claim to be able to do everything, I preferred to admit that there were things I might not be able to do, if only because the future doesn't always evolve according to our fondest hopes and best predictions. Mulroney took Trudeau's $160 billion federal debt, for example, and "reduced" it after eight years to $450 billion and climbing. That's why it's unreasonable to promise spending programs or tax cuts around how many dimes you're going to have ten years from now, and that's why I insisted we keep our budget projections to two years.

It was very much both my style and my desire to be as honest and straightforward with the voters as possible. Give them the facts, tell them what you hope to do, explain the challenges ahead, and then let them decide. That had been my approach ever since my first days in politics. The economy was tough on Shawinigan during the 1960s. Technologies and customers were changing, the old industries were closing or downsizing, and several thousand jobs were lost in a riding of seventy thousand people. People were desperate and wanted easy answers. But there were no easy answers. Yesterday our great-grandfathers were driving horse carriages; today we are driving cars; tomorrow our great-grandchildren could be driving rockets. In the same way, just as the refrigerator put the men who used to deliver ice out of business, so petrochemicals caused the collapse of the big electrochemistry plants in Shawinigan. That's how humanity evolves, and it really has little to do with whether there's a good or a bad administration in power. All we can do, I would tell my constituents, is stick together and work hard to overcome the difficulties. The people respected the fact that I was telling them the truth and promising nothing more than to do my best.

"Mr. Chrétien says he will do what is possible," one of my opponents said during an election campaign. "I will do what is impossible."

"Yes," I shot back, "but what is impossible for you will be easy for me."

Similarly, when I was minister of finance, I resisted any calls from the Liberal caucus and strategists to produce a free-spending budget to try to buy the 1979 election. The left-leaning members of the party—those who had already branded me as Dr. No when I was president of the Treasury Board—blamed our defeat on my stubbornness, but I had been well trained by Mitchell Sharp not to risk the long-term health of the nation for short-term electoral advantage.

Saying no wasn't something I enjoyed doing. I'm a Liberal, after all, and I have been preoccupied my entire political life with job creation, health and welfare, and social justice. However, coming into office in 1993, we had no choice but to cut the deficit drastically or face an economic crisis in which the proverbial twenty-five-year-old brokers with their red suspenders would drive down our currency, push up our interest rates, and compel the global financiers to step in and take charge of our spending decisions in exchange for a loan—a humiliation I wanted to avoid at all costs. At first it was extremely difficult to convince most of the Liberal caucus that we had to undertake a strict austerity program, but they soon understood I was determined to do it, even if it meant I would be prime minister for only one term. I wanted to run and win a second time, no doubt about it, but this was my last job, and doing it well was more important to me than repeating an honour I had already achieved. I immediately warned the ministers to prepare for some stormy weather, because we were going to do what we had promised.

After our first Cabinet meeting, Lawrence MacAulay, the secretary of state for veterans, called his wife and said, "I listened to the prime minister this morning and I think I'm toast in the next election, so we might as well enjoy this while it lasts."

To set an example, I had insisted on arriving at the swearing-in ceremony in an ordinary Chevrolet rather than in one of the fleet of Cadillacs that had been bought in Mulroney's day. That caused security concerns with the RCMP, and I was subsequently forced to accept an armoured Buick, but I didn't use a Cadillac except for occasional trips to the airport to pick up distinguished visitors for the drive back into town. I also refused to fly in Mulroney's renovated Airbus, which I had branded Air Farce One and the Flying Taj Mahal during the election campaign. For many Canadians, the plane had become a symbol of government extravagance at a time when the Conservatives were asking them to accept cutbacks in social programs. When some reporters began begging me to use the plane, because most of its space—and much of its cost—had been allocated to facilitating their ability to file stories from the air, I said, "I know you guys. If I use it, you'll give me hell. But if you insist, fine, just send me a petition and I'll agree." They were as trapped as I was, of course, by our cheap shots, but it didn't make any difference to me personally.

More significant in terms of savings—but just as important as a symbol—was the Cabinet's decision, taken at its first meeting, to fulfill our campaign promise and cancel the Conservative government's order for forty-three new EH-101 military helicopters, even though it meant having to pay a $500-million contract penalty. Given the size of the deficit the Tories left us, we would have had to borrow $6 billion to pay this additional bill and, as a result, been that much farther from balancing the books. Indeed, when all items were accounted for, we would have had to borrow even more than that: it's a reasonable calculation that those helicopters would have cost the people of Canada at least another $6 billion in interest over ten years. Compared to that bill, the penalty didn't look quite so bad.

Eventually, when we had managed to get from deficits to surpluses by taking hard decisions such as this one, we were again pressed by the military to replace its forty-year-old Sea King helicopters. "Okay," I said. "If they're so dangerous to life and limb, go buy some good used ones from the Americans right away." And do you know what our Defence Department discovered? One, the same model Sea King was still in use by the United States military to ferry the president from the White House to his retreat at Camp David. And, two, the helicopters our generals looked at turned out to be in worse shape than the ones we already had.

Another immediate decision the government had to confront concerned John Crow, governor of the Bank of Canada since 1987, whose seven-year term was about to expire. In my mind, Crow was an impressive, competent, knowledgable fellow I had enjoyed chatting to whenever I met him out for a walk in my old neighbourhood, but he was also a professor by attitude and doctrinaire to a fault. The problem with professors in power—unless they're as agile as Pierre Trudeau or Stéphane Dion—is that they tend to place their abstract ideas ahead of practical consequences in order to prove some theory or other.

I had been dealing with governors of the Bank of Canada ever since Lester Pearson appointed me minister without portfolio attached to the Ministry of Finance in April 1967, and I had learned my way around the complex issues of fiscal management from Crow's eminent predecessors, Louis Rasminsky and Gerald Bouey. One budget day when I was minister of finance, I attended a reception with a few dozen senior officials from the department and the Bank of Canada. I invited them to wager twenty-five cents each on whether the market's reaction would send the Canadian currency up or down the next morning. All but three of us bet it would go up. Eddie Goldenberg and I guessed it would go down, not because we were better analysts but because we're cautious by nature. The third person to guess correctly was an economist in the Finance Department.

"How did you figure that out?" I asked him.

"Well, Minister," he said, "I taught economics at the University of Toronto for years, I worked at the Bank of Canada, and now I'm with Finance, and everything I've learned from the textbooks told me that the dollar should go up. But the market is crazy, so I bet it would go down."

In Crow's case, I didn't agree with what he had done under Mulroney by opting to wrestle inflation to the ground with high interest rates in the middle of a recession and with a high Canadian dollar, just when our economy needed to adjust to the Canada–United States Free Trade Agreement that the Conservatives had negotiated in 1988. Those policies not only made unemployment worse but caused the fight against the deficit and the debt to be all the harder. Nor did I agree with his desire to lower the target for what was an acceptable level of inflation. Still, Crow was highly regarded among economists, international financiers, and the business elites as their champion in the struggle against inflation. Changing the governor at this particular time was risky, especially as the bond salesmen and currency speculators were keeping a close watch on Canada's fiscal policies under a new government. The Liberals had just been elected; we had yet to produce our first budget cuts; the nation's credit rating was in jeopardy because of the size of our debt and the threat of another referendum in Quebec; and, as ever, the financial establishment was suspicious of any kind of change.

"If you want to have John Crow, you can have him," I told Paul Martin when we met in my office on Monday, December 20, "but I bet that, within two years, either you or he will have to go, because he will have stifled the first signs of our coming out of the recession."

We didn't need to have a long debate about it, however, because Martin didn't want to keep him either. We also agreed that Crow's highly experienced deputy, Gordon Thiessen, would make an able successor whose appointment would serve as a signal of continuity and stability; and we kept the inflation band for the next three years to between 1 and 3 per cent, a range that was still competitive with that in the United States. I admit I was nervous about what the reaction would be. I even suffered one of the rare nights in which I didn't sleep soundly—needlessly, as it turned out. Thiessen was well received by the financial community, and the dollar actually went up the next day.

—

As the Crow decision had demonstrated, the finance minister and I tried from our first day in office to set aside the tensions that had arisen between us during the 1990 leadership race and to work in tandem to restore Canada's economic and fiscal health. I can't remember when I first met Paul Martin Jr. It may have been as early as 1958, when I had supported his father for the party leadership, or perhaps during one of my visits to the family home in Windsor. Though Paul Martin Sr. wasn't happy with me for not backing him again in 1968 for the leadership, he made a joke out of it by observing that I had shown better judgment when I was younger.

I had a friendly enough relationship with his son whenever we met during the 1970s and 1980s at Liberal events or in the offices of Power Corporation, the Montreal-based financial and industrial conglomerate where Martin worked alongside my son-in-law, André Desmarais, and my former executive assistant John Rae. Martin and I fished and golfed together a few times, talked about the political scene, and crossed paths during the 1984 leadership race, in which I was a contender and Martin was the neutral moderator of the all-candidates' debates. We weren't buddies, but we weren't rivals either, until he decided to run against me in 1990. "Paul fighting Jean," I remember his mother saying, "that's a big problem for us." But I told her not to worry. "I don't mind," I said. "It's a free country." I could afford to be generous because I didn't really see him as a serious threat. Indeed, after I won the leadership, Paul Martin and his supporters held key positions, and I gave him joint responsibility for the Red Book, to help unite the party and prepare it for the election.

Moreover, because I had myself been minister of national revenue, president of the Treasury Board, and minister of finance, I understood the difficult issues he was facing. Even when out of politics, I enjoyed reading about economics and the budgetary policies of government, and nature had blessed me with a good head for numbers. I can read them; I can remember them; I love playing with them. If I'm on a plane with nothing else to do, I start fooling around with mathematical puzzles. Examining Canada's economic performance in minute detail, checking all the budget calculations with my pen, asking questions about where we were heading never seemed like work to me. It was a pleasure, and I could hardly wait for the beginning of every month when Finance issued its Fiscal Monitor report about the deficit, interest rates, and so forth. Every year I used to bet Paul Martin $100 over whether the deficit or the surplus would be lower or higher than his budget prediction, and each time I won. (He has yet to pay me, though. If he ever does, I won't cash the cheque—just frame it.)

In many ways, by evolution rather than design, the government's annual budget has become a more significant document in terms of the policies and priorities of the year ahead than is the traditional Speech from the Throne. In the old days, when the House of Commons used to meet for only six months, the throne speech was an annual occurrence at the start of each new session, followed by endless days of general debate and a vote of confidence. As the work of Parliament began to stretch from one calendar year to the next, there were longer and longer periods between throne speeches. As well, especially in a majority situation, it was better to spend the time in the House debating specific legislation, though some days were still set aside for general issues. By default, therefore, the budget emerged as a kind of "state of the nation" address. And, while its crafting and presentation remained the most important job of the minister of finance, it increasingly reflected the work of the entire government.

Certainly, no other PMO had ever been as consistently involved in the budget-making process as mine. Martin kept me well briefed on what was happening in his department, usually through Eddie Goldenberg, whose job as my senior policy adviser on economic issues required him to be in constant communication with Martin in person or by phone, especially around budget time. I also met with Martin several times during the year to help establish the government's strategic targets and spending priorities. Just as the combination of government experience and political instinct had led me to insist on the 3 per cent target in the Red Book, for example, so it caused me to ask for a budget reserve of $2.5 billion, rising to $3 billion a year in 1997–98, solely dedicated to funding any increases in the debt that resulted from rising interest rates. Although we had other contingency funds on the books for natural disasters, military interventions, national unity, and so forth, we basically removed this new reserve from the grasp of departmental demands with one quick stroke, and if rates went down instead of up, we would apply it to paying down the federal debt.

Every December, Martin would present me with the specific options he had before him and ask me to make the really tough decisions. Thus, on February 15, 1994, a week before our first budget, he and I got together to consider the last four outstanding issues.

Throughout 1994, unfortunately, inflation fears in the United States and concern about another referendum in Quebec pushed up borrowing costs higher than our first budget's conservative assumptions, and the financial markets kept reacting negatively to the size of our deficit and debt, even after we announced our intention to cut program spending by $17 billion over three years from previously planned levels—by reducing costs in the Department of National Defence, tightening the qualifications for Unemployment Insurance, freezing the transfers to the provinces for health and higher education, and so forth. Since a jump of 2 per cent in interest rates represented almost $3.5 billion in increased expenditures, we were under renewed pressure to cut more and more just to stay on track to our three-year target, even with the contingency reserve.

On May 2, 1994, I met with Paul Martin to review the economic, employment, and fiscal outlook for the remainder of the year and get a sense of his plans for his make-or-break budget. Were we still going to meet the 3 per cent commitment? Did Finance's agenda dovetail with our other objectives of job creation and social security reform? How did he plan to establish his budget goals and attain them? We also discussed the financial impact of a possible victory by the Parti Québécois in the upcoming provincial election and the potential economic consequences of another separatist referendum.

Three weeks later, on May 24, after Martin presented an especially grim picture to the Cabinet if we failed to meet the fiscal targets set out in the 1994 budget and show more progress beyond year three, I again met with him to consider his general direction. What about our jobs strategy, not just in the long term but in the short term as well? Was he right to base his fiscal planning on an extreme interest-rate scenario, or should he prepare a separate backup plan for that unlikely event?

In the meantime, on a second track, I asked Marcel Massé, the minister of intergovernmental affairs and public service renewal, to chair an ad hoc committee of seven ministers to undertake a systematic review of every federal program (except for transfers to individuals and the provinces), department by department, for a total of about $52 billion, with an eye to cutting costs and rationalizing services. To Massé's initial consternation, I made sure that the deficit "doves" were a majority on the committee. Making the big spenders an integral part of the process would help build Cabinet solidarity around the extremely tough decisions ahead, I reasoned. If we weren't able to convince our own colleagues of what had to be done, we would never be able to convince Canadians. The task of the Coordinating Group of Ministers on Program Review, as the committee was called, was to ask six simple but very far-reaching questions of each program. Does this program continue to serve a public interest? Is there a legitimate and necessary role for government in this program? Should this program be transferred in whole or in part to the provinces or the municipalities? Should this program be transferred in whole or in part to the private or the voluntary sector? If this program continues, how can it be made more efficient? Finally, are the remaining programs affordable?

Marcel Massé rarely got the public recognition he deserved, not least because he never sought it. A francophone from Montreal with degrees from the Université de Montréal, McGill, Warsaw, and Oxford, he had been deputy minister of finance and Cabinet secretary in New Brunswick under Richard Hatfield's Conservatives, clerk of the Privy Council in Ottawa during Joe Clark's brief regime, president of the Canadian International Development Agency, and, in 1984, undersecretary of state for external affairs while I was the minister. When he mentioned one day that he was tired of being a civil servant, I invited him to run as a Liberal in the 1993 election. To my surprise and delight, he agreed. Because of his intelligence, his capability, and his excellent judgment, I even made him my Quebec lieutenant despite his lack of experience as a politician. Politics is an art, not a science, and for that you need common sense. Massé had plenty of common sense, and I missed him greatly when he decided to retire for health reasons in 1999.

No one I knew had the practical skills to understand the workings of government better than Massé. He understood, for instance, that in a pyramidal organization such as the federal government, an important element in determining the bureaucrats' pay is the number of people they have working under them. If bureaucrats build bigger departments, they increase their own salary. If they cut staff, they take a hit themselves. As a result, there's not much incentive to scale back, and often a great deal of resistance. I saw it happen at Harrington Lake, the prime minister's retreat, where boss A told his assistant B to cut, B told his assistant C to cut, and so on down to the bottom. By the end, the guys who pushed paper were still on the payroll while those who pushed lawnmowers were gone. When they were cut, the grass was not.

On the whole, however, the federal civil servants understood as well as—or even better than—most Canadians the gravity of the country's fiscal situation, and they made extraordinary efforts and many personal sacrifices to help the government achieve its goals. Even when our decisions weren't in their own interests, they took early retirement, laid off staff, cut costs to the bone, and did what was necessary. In short order, thanks to their incredible cooperation and skill, we managed to reduce the number of people on the federal payroll by about sixty thousand, including military personnel and those employees whose jobs were transferred to the private sector or to other levels of government. It was painful in human terms and discouraging for those of us who believe in government as an instrument for good in society. We lost the talent and potential of many young people, who either couldn't join the federal public service or left to find more lucrative work elsewhere. The morale of those who remained obviously suffered a serious blow. Yet it wasn't a mortal blow, I believe, because everybody could see that we were acting even-handedly and out of absolute necessity. And when we finally won the war against the deficit, we emerged with a more efficient, modern, responsive public service.

By the summer of 1994, faced with the challenge of reducing spending by billions of dollars without simply slashing programs across the board, Paul Martin and I asked Finance officials to come up with rough, reasonable, and relatively arbitrary targets for how much money the departments were to get in the next budget. The decisions about how to allocate it were left to the ministers and their officials. Then, from September through November, Massé's Program Review Committee and civil servants in the PCO assessed each department's recommendations. In December the committee members met twice a week to take a look at the integrated picture, identify further savings, and come up with a package of reforms. By the time I met with

Paul Martin on November 28, 1994, for our next discussion of the 1995 budget, the departments had found about $4.3 billion in savings over the next two years—but we needed $6.8 billion to reach our 3 per cent target. So the Coordinating Group sent the ministers back for even more reductions or came up with its own choices, which Massé presented to the Cabinet on December 20.

Massé's hardest challenge was to resist the demands for more money from ministers who wouldn't take no for an answer. Though the majority respected the program review process and didn't try to circumvent it very often, ministers or their deputy ministers always had the right to bring their complaints to the clerk of the Privy Council, who then wrote a memo for my consideration, or to make an appeal to me through Jean Pelletier and Eddie Goldenberg. I might test a few options on my staff and try to arbitrate a solution, or I might summon those responsible to meet with me to discuss the problem. I seldom brought a large number of people into the room, because that kind of meeting rarely gets anywhere. And I usually ended up backing Massé anyway.

The level of consensus was remarkable, given the disparate views and interests of the members of the committee and the number of extremely sensitive policy issues that pitted department against department, region against region, minister against minister. The minister of public works didn't want the federal government to get out of making new commitments in the area of social housing, on the grounds that Ottawa had a legitimate role in helping to meet the housing needs of low-income Canadians. The minister of industry objected to a 35 per cent reduction in federal assistance to business because it was inconsistent with our efforts to build a more innovative economy. The minister of Canadian heritage argued against cuts to the Canadian Broadcasting Corporation, the National

Film Board, and Telefilm Canada, for the simple reason that the private sector cannot preserve and foster the cultural sector in Canada all by itself. And while the minister of transport offered to save $560 million a year by abolishing the Western Grain Transportation Subsidy, a historic federal policy that in effect paid for much of the cost of shipping wheat by rail, the minister of agriculture wanted the savings to go directly into the pockets of Prairie farmers. Each had a strong case, but nobody could get everything. Deficit reduction was the mandate Canadians had given the government, and we simply couldn't risk failure.

If Paul Martin and I got most of the credit for aiming to balance the books, it was Marcel Massé and the rest of our Cabinet colleagues who really deserved it. "It's easy for you to make decrees," Industry Minister John Manley argued in Cabinet after having his department's budget cut by 50 per cent, "but we're the ones who have to do the dirty work, who have to let good people go, who have to cancel sound programs, who have to increase productivity, who have to tell our clients that there's no money left for fresh ideas or good projects, and who have to deal with all the bitterness and hardships." Ouch. What made his objection even sharper was that he was absolutely right.

Some unhappy ministers used to accuse the Finance Department of deliberately demanding more cuts than were necessary so it could consistently outperform the budget forecasts. I didn't think that was true, but I wouldn't have objected anyway. Prudence was better than the unrealistic and ultimately disappointing predictions that the Mulroney government had made, and underselling was still at the root of my political technique. "As you are undoubtedly aware," went my stock answer to most of those who appealed to me to spare a regional program or pet project, "the minister of finance faces many difficult choices in preparing the budget, and there are no easy solutions." If the ministers persisted, I sometimes hinted that they seemed to be having difficulty doing the job they had been asked to do—and that was usually enough to make them back away.

At the end of the day, the minister of finance is the minister of finance, and even though I kept a close watch on what Paul Martin was doing, it was critical that I be seen to support him. I had never forgotten the humiliation of being let down as finance minister by Trudeau in August 1978, when he announced $2 billion in spending cuts during a televised speech to the nation on the economy without first seeking my final signoff, and I had watched the political fiasco that took place in 1985 when Mulroney failed to back up Michael Wilson in the face of public protests over a budget proposal to partially de-index old age pensions from the rate of inflation. As a result, I made sure that everybody knew how involved I was in Martin's decisions and how high a priority I placed on reducing the deficit according to our schedule. Conversely, if I expressed a strong desire for some item, Martin conceded it to me, and we rarely had any serious policy disagreements.

One of the few exceptions took place in the days leading up to our second budget in February 1995. The recent Mexican peso crisis shook Ottawa and Canada's financial community to the core. By showing how vulnerable we were to the sudden, sometimes irrational reactions of the world market, it strengthened the government's resolve not to move off our set course. Through no fault of our own, the Canadian dollar fell, our interest rates rose, and a credit warning from Moody's threatened to drive interest rates up even higher. The *Wall Street Journal* declared that Canada had become "an honorary member of the Third World," and there was a lot of loose talk on Bay Street that the Canadian economy was going to "hit the wall" if the government failed to meet its targets. As a precautionary measure, Martin wanted to dig into the $20-billion-a-year Old Age

Security (OAS) benefit. Among his proposed reforms was the idea of pooling the pensions of husbands and wives into a single payment and taxing it back from high-income families. In theory this idea made sense. It would certainly save some money, and there seemed no logical reason why married couples shouldn't be happy to share everything, even taxes. However, I didn't think it would fly either socially or politically, because it didn't take into account the real lives of ordinary people.

Isolation is an occupational hazard in Ottawa. Politicians and public servants always have to make deliberate efforts to stay in touch with the needs and desires of Canadians. As a senior minister in Trudeau's government, I had made a point of going back to Shawinigan almost every weekend to meet with my constituents, and I realized I could always attract the prime minister's attention by mentioning the opinions of the workers at Alcan or Consolidated Bathurst, some of whom Trudeau had known and whose judgment he respected from his days as a union lawyer in Quebec. He came to rely on me to report their reactions, especially if they refused to buy a particular policy or thought some of our ideas were nuts.

Now, whenever I had the chance, I still liked to drop into a beer parlour or coffee shop in my riding, without any fuss, to talk politics, and I used to call a number of people on a regular basis—lawyers, entrepreneurs, union leaders, party organizers, artists, teachers, all sorts of ordinary citizens across the nation—because I felt comfortable with them and trusted their discretion. No one else knew who they were, and if they ever bragged about the fact that the prime minister had called them, they wouldn't have been called again. I didn't want them to tell me how great I was—I had enough people around me who thought their jobs depended on doing just that. Rather, I wanted to know what the government should do in regard to this or that, what criticisms they were hearing, or what was happening in their communities.

One evening Aline and I were having dinner with Pierre and Angèle Garceau, old friends of ours from university days, and we began to discuss Martin's idea about old age pensions. "Are you serious?" said Madame Garceau. "For women who have been at home all their lives, that little cheque is the only bit of money they can ever call their own. After thirty or forty years of begging their husbands for every cent, they can buy themselves a new hat or take a friend out for cake and coffee without answering to anybody. So they're not going to be very happy if you take it away from them or put it into a joint account, because some husbands are really cheap and selfish."

I laughed at the colourful way she had expressed it. It reminded me of a story that Rachel Bournival, the able assistant in my Shawinigan office for seventeen years, had told me about a woman who had shown up one day. She was about to turn sixty-five and had a list of questions about the old age pension, how it worked, what forms she needed to fill out, how much she would get, and so on. A few months later Madame Bournival saw her on the street. "Oh, thank you, thank you for all your help," the woman said. "I've never been so happy. The day I received my first cheque, I threw my old man out of the house. 'Go to your mistress and have her wash your dirty socks,' I told him. 'I don't want to have anything more to do with you.' Now, with my pension and the money I picked out of his pocket when he was drunk, I finally have enough to have a nice life of my own." That kind of anecdote, the trouble Mulroney had when his finance minister tried to tamper with the pension, and Aline's own warnings alerted me to the importance of the old age pension to many women, no matter how small the amount of money involved, and it reinforced my instinct to tell Paul Martin to pull back.

Martin did not come himself but sent his adviser Peter Nicholson one Saturday afternoon to 24 Sussex to argue his case.

The budget was about to be printed, and there were rumours that Martin was ready to quit over the issue. "The minister doesn't think he has enough cuts to meet his target," Nicholson told me.

"Really?" I said. "You know, it's been the dream of my life to be my own minister of finance. I'll be happy to read the budget speech myself." Martin did not resign, and though I offered to let him come back with his proposal the following year, he reached the decision on his own that it was no longer necessary.

—

No government in the history of Canada had ever gone through such a thorough and methodical exercise as we did with our program review, the results of which were incorporated into the 1995 and 1996 budgets. Our decision to abolish the Western Grain Transportation Subsidy was an enormous political gamble, with regional and structural implications that would change western agriculture forever. We eliminated or substantially reduced other transportation subsidies, dairy subsidies, and business subsidies. We integrated the Canadian Coast Guard with the Fisheries Department fleet and consolidated the food inspection system of three different ministries. We transferred inland water responsibilities to the provinces and handed over the management of airports to local authorities, because there wasn't any practical reason to have them operated by federal bureaucrats. We sold off the Canadian National Railways, most of Petro-Canada, and the Air Navigation System, because they no longer served any national public-policy objective. We modified or trimmed whatever remained through a new expenditure management system and innovative service deliveries, not just to gain short-term savings but for long-term productivity. In these and other ways, we managed to reduce Ottawa's program spending from $120 billion in our first year to $104 billion in 1996–97.

No department emerged unscathed, with the single exception of Indian Affairs. The dire and deep-rooted problems of Canada's Aboriginal peoples, who had remained so close to my heart ever since my six years as their minister, meant that we as a society could not let up, even for a moment, in our pursuit of social justice and equal opportunity for them. I knew, of course, that there were no quick fixes, that the leadership had to be fiscally responsible, and that progress would be slow and long term. The land claims negotiations were complex; there were administrative difficulties in the bureaucracy and on the reserves; and it's never easy for people—especially people who have been colonized and discriminated against—to make the transition from living off the land to living in towns or cities. It often takes two or three generations to adjust to the dramatic economic and social changes of modernization while staying true to an ancient culture and community. In the meantime, we have to deal with the issues of high unemployment, alcohol and drug abuse, infant mortality, teenage suicides, and chronic poverty.

I firmly believed that we were making progress. I deliberately appointed, as Indian affairs ministers, individuals in whom I had a lot of confidence—Ron Irwin, Jane Stewart, and Bob Nault—and they knew that I would always try to be with them in a crunch. We initiated partnership programs for early childhood development, youth centres, business and economic strategies, education reform, housing, heritage and language preservation, and health services. Our 1998 action plan, "Gathering Strength," acted on many of the recommendations of the Royal Commission on Aboriginal Peoples, which reported in November 1996. We reaffirmed the inherent right to self-government, sped up the land claims process, acknowledged the tragic legacy of the residential school system, and presided over the creation in 1999 of the new territory of Nunavut. Sometimes I look through the Northern magazines that arrive in our house for my son Michel, whom Aline and I adopted as a baby during a trip to Inuvik in 1971, and I am fascinated to read about how the people of the North, in their own words, are striving to balance their respect for the past with their ambitions for the future.

There were some areas, I have to admit, in which we went too far with our cuts. Some, such as our investments in technological innovation and cultural institutions, we were able to correct after we balanced the books; others were irreversible. In retrospect, to take but one example, we should not have closed down the Collège Militaire Royal (CMR) in St-Jean-sur-Richelieu, Quebec, in the 1994 budget. That was a mistake. At the time, however, we desperately needed the savings, and once we had decided to close Royal Roads in Victoria, we couldn't be seen to be playing favourites. It was also our hope that moving CMR to Kingston might turn Ontario's military college into a fully bilingual institution. Unfortunately, the number of francophones at the higher levels in the armed forces decreased as a result, something I especially regret given my commitment to bilingualism and to a strong French-Canadian presence in our national institutions. The only upside was that it provided yet another opportunity to expose the absolute hypocrisy of the separatists: all of a sudden the same MPs who had always complained about Canada's military spending and the presence of the federal government in Quebec began denouncing us for shutting down a national defence institution in a Bloc riding.

As they cut, all the ministers struggled hard to keep their priorities consistent with our national values. Canadians didn't want us to eliminate the deficit on the backs of those in need of help, nor did they want us to slash and burn essential government services. They wanted us to be both compassionate and clever with our cuts. Thus, while we were closing military bases and slicing business subsidies, we put new money into programs for the young, the disadvantaged, and the vulnerable, especially for single-parent families, people with disabilities, and children grow-ing up in poverty. We funded the Prenatal Nutrition Program to provide low-income pregnant women with food supplements and nutrition counselling. We restored the National Literacy Program to deal with the startling statistic that 38 per cent of Canadians were unable to deal consistently with everyday reading require-ments. We started Youth Service Canada and the youth internship program to let thousands of young people get work experience. We put $1.7 billion into the Atlantic Groundfish Strategy (TAGS) to deal with the plight of the East Coast workers whose livelihood had been destroyed by a moratorium on cod fishing on the Grand Banks, and we established a $1.6 billion transition fund to help Western Canadian farmers transport their products.

Similarly, while Lloyd Axworthy had to extract significant savings from the Unemployment Insurance program, which had skyrocketed from $4.4 billion to $20 billion annually in just ten years, he used it as an opportunity to launch a much-needed review of Canada's social security system. Not only was UI no longer meeting its primary purpose to help people get work and keep working, but it had actually created disincentives to full-time employment. The level of long-term unemployment had tripled between 1976 and 1993. Twice as many Canadians were living on social assistance as had been in 1981. Among house-hold heads receiving social assistance, 45 per cent were consid-ered employable; 38 per cent of UI claimants had received payments at least three times in five years; and too many seasonal workers were employed for only the minimum weeks required to collect benefits for the rest of the year. In April 1994, I remember, I got into really hot water for saying that we could no longer afford to keep people sitting at home drinking beer. The response was terrible and I had to apologize, though there were also many letters of support, including one funny note from a woman who told me I was damn right.

Lloyd Axworthy was another of the unsung heroes in our battle against the deficit. He was very much on the left of the Liberal Party, a progressive thinker with a serious mind and earnest manner who obviously hadn't been delighted when I gave him the job of putting order and restraint into Canada's social programs. Still, he handled the challenge well, and though he probably came to me with his concerns and disappointments more than most ministers, he had a bigger, trickier portfolio than almost anyone else. As far as I was concerned, he did an excellent job under very trying circumstances.

Human Resources Development lost a third of its budget over two years, but Axworthy fought hard to retain $800 million with which to launch innovative pilot projects to try to break the cycle of dependency through work experience and retraining programs. He wanted to help people get jobs in a cheaper and more cost-effective manner and, at the same time, to provide the labour force with the upgraded skills needed for Canada to compete in the global economy. Jobs were going begging in Canada because people didn't have the right set of skills, yet more than a million Canadians were still unemployed, three million were stuck on social assistance, and over a million children were living in poverty. I recall meeting a New Brunswick woman who said, "Mr. Chrétien, I have been on welfare all my life, and now I have the dignity of learning something. There's nothing to beat it. When I come home at night to do my own homework while my kids are doing theirs, they see that they'll never have to be on welfare, as I was, if they get the training and the education." I wished we could have afforded to assist more people like her.

We also chose to invest new money in several strategic areas in order to stimulate growth and jobs. First, we kept our campaign promise to spend $6 billion over two years toward rebuilding Canada's infrastructure through an equal partnership with the provinces and the municipalities. Wherever I went in the country, I noticed the neglected condition of so many of our roads, bridges, water plants, and other public facilities, especially in comparison with those in the United States and Europe, and I came to believe that a national infrastructure program would help kick-start the economy, create tens of thousands of jobs within a very short period in every region, and signal the return of hope across the land. Though the Tories had denounced this Red Book promise as a waste of money, it actually cost the federal government much less than our one-third share of the program because of the greater revenues we recouped through various taxes and the lower expenditures required in Unemployment Insurance and welfare payments.

We fulfilled another Red Book promise by investing immediately in Canada's scenic beauty, cultural activities, and recreational opportunities. My personal commitment was whetted in November 1993 after a conversation I had at 24 Sussex with Israeli prime minister Yitzhak Rabin, the first international leader to visit me after my election. Following our discussions about the situation in the Middle East, we got into the practical preoccupations that are the daily concern of every politician: the economy, unemployment, job creation, trade, and the deficit. "You know, Mr. Chrétien," Rabin said, "creating new jobs in high tech and scientific research is very expensive, very capital-intensive, but that's not the case with tourism. Israel is doing well with that sector at almost no cost. All you need is promotion, which should be easy because you have such a beautiful country."

In May 1994 I asked Judd Buchanan, a Trudeau Cabinet minister who had been working successfully in the tourism industry since leaving public life, if he would serve as my special adviser in that area. Knowing the Opposition would be quick to accuse me of patronage for hiring a former Liberal politician, I was grateful when, because he really believed in the integrity of public service and the importance of the mission, he agreed to become my second dollar-a-year man. In fact, Buchanan saved the taxpayers fifty cents by finishing his report in six months.

After visiting every province and territory and consulting with over 350 experts in the field, he reached the conclusion that tourism was a big business that could—and should—get bigger. Tourism activities employed more than half a million Canadians, generated $33 billion in spending, and provided quick and relatively inexpensive work opportunities for young and old, skilled and unskilled, in cities and rural areas in every corner of Canada. But developing the industry would require a coordinated approach. Tourism depends on a variety of disparate elements, from currency fluctuations to road repairs, from visa requirements to golf courses, and I remember thinking how inefficient the lack of coordination was when I saw a two-page ad for the Yukon, paid for by the Yukon government, in the pages of *The Economist* magazine one day. Since it seemed unlikely that the average British tourist would fly the length of Canada just to visit the Yukon, why was no other part of the country mentioned to make an even more attractive package?

Based on Buchanan's recommendations, therefore, we took a cooperative approach in which Ottawa, the provincial and territorial governments, and industry officials sat on the board of the new Canadian Tourism Commission, with Buchanan himself serving as its first chair. Reasoning that people don't go to places they've never heard of, we also agreed to increase advertising in the tourism sector at home and abroad from $15 million to $50 million a year by cutting back in other areas, and we managed to persuade the industry to match us dollar for dollar. After four years of success, we increased our annual commitment to $65 million, and the balance-of-payments deficit in tourism dropped from $6 billion in 1993—more than one-quarter of our current account deficit at the time—to $1.5 billion in 2002 before it began to creep up again with the higher Canadian dollar, the tightening of border security after the terrorist attacks on New York and Washington in 2001, and the SARS epidemic scare in Toronto in 2003. In my riding alone, the industry created more than a thousand jobs in seven years and helped reduce the level of unemployment by half.

On the revenue side, although we benefited greatly from the upswing in economic growth spurred on by the fiscal measures we were undertaking, by the advent of lower interest rates, by the boom in the United States, and by a lower Canadian dollar, there wasn't much we could do in terms of raising taxes. Canadians were already overburdened, and even the social activists in the Liberal Party had come to recognize that the people were in no mood for a tax hike beyond introducing a few user fees, closing an unfair loophole for family trusts, putting a special tax on bank profits, eliminating the $100,000 capital gains exemption, and increasing the federal excise tax on tobacco and gasoline. We also gave some new funds to the Department of National Revenue, for one obvious reason: if you want to collect more delinquent taxes, you need more tax collectors to do it.

Certainly there was no room for significant tax cuts until the happy day when we moved into surpluses. I never bought into the Laffer curve, a theory, named after an American supply-side economist who had been an adviser to the Reagan administration, that essentially argues that a government will increase its revenue by reducing its taxes. If it were that easy, everybody would do it. What politician doesn't want to reduce taxes in order to win votes? Taken to its logical extreme, the Laffer curve makes no sense because, if you lower your taxes to zero, how are you going to get higher revenues? In practice, every government that toyed with this theory ended up with larger deficits, higher interest rates, and greater social inequality.

For most Canadians, the best tax cut they ever received from the Liberal government—more than they ever would have received from the Reform Party or the Tories—was the reduction in interest rates. During a flight from Ottawa to Halifax, for instance, a young Liberal member of Parliament came and thanked me for what we had done for him by striving to balance the books. He was able to renew his $100,000 mortgage at a rate of 6 per cent rather than 11.5 per cent, an annual saving after taxes of $5,500 that went directly into his pocket—money he could spend on his family.

One promise I never made was to abolish the 7 per cent federal Goods and Services Tax. True, in opposition, the Liberal Party had tried everything in its power to stop Mulroney's government from introducing the GST in 1989, but I had been virtually alone during the 1990 leadership race in saying that we should not promise to scrap it until we knew how we were going to replace the lost revenue. True, too, I had been pushed as leader of the Opposition into going along with the caucus's anti-GST stand. But after a committee of three experts reported back that they couldn't see a better solution, I made sure that our election platform stopped short of a commitment to abolish it altogether unless we could find a viable replacement. "A Liberal government will replace the GST," the Red Book read, "with a system that generates equivalent revenues, is fairer to consumers and to small business, minimizes disruption to small business, and promotes federal-provincial fiscal cooperation and harmonization."

What we were promising to do was clear enough in my own mind—*replace*, not abolish, the GST—but I made a mistake by trying to be a bit too clever with the nuanced argument. My party and I certainly paid a political price in terms of our credibility by creating the impression in the minds of many voters that we were promising to get rid of the sales tax even if we couldn't find an alternative system. I myself sowed some confusion during the election campaign by making a slip of the tongue one day when I was tired, and, though I issued a clarification the very next morning, the press had no interest in reporting it. Then Sheila Copps muddied the water by making an imprudent pledge during the heat of a TV "town hall" meeting that she would resign her seat if a Chrétien government didn't scrap the GST altogether. I thought it was gutsy of Copps to follow through on her promise to resign after she failed to convince me to change my mind. As I had told the ministers at the start, if anyone ever hands me a letter of resignation, I figure it must be a serious matter, so I won't argue about it. If Copps thought she had to resign, that was up to her, but I didn't think that I or anyone else in my government, including my minister of finance, needed to apologize to the voters for breaking a promise the party had never made. Even Copps's constituents didn't seem too perturbed—they sent her back to Ottawa in the by-election.

Lord knows it was in the party's interest, the government's interest, and the national interest to find a better way to tax manufactured products or individual consumption. I certainly pushed Paul Martin and the Finance Department to come up with a proposal as quickly as possible. And they tried their hardest. In June 1994, for example, I received a detailed memo that weighed the pros and cons of replacing the GST with a single federal-provincial value-added tax, a business transfer tax, or a manufacturers' sales tax. The reality was, though, that once the GST had become law and been put in place, it proved impossible to find another system that was fairer or more efficient, and we simply couldn't afford to give up the $15 billion the GST brought into the federal coffers every year. However, we were able to make some progress toward harmonizing the collection of the tax in some provinces, reducing its administrative costs, and avoiding duplication in every province but Quebec. That might not have been the replacement that we—or the Canadian public—had hoped for, but it was the best we could do at the time.

—

By the end of our third year in office, instead of reducing the federal deficit to 3 per cent of GDP as we had promised in the Red Book, we had got it down to 1 per cent. A year after that, we were at zero. The vicious circle had become a virtuous circle, in which lower spending produced lower deficits that produced lower interest rates, lower unemployment, and greater growth. But what made me even more pleased was that Canadians had once again faced a formidable challenge and overcome it with patience, discipline, understanding, and a willingness to share the burden fairly. Even after the very tough budget in 1995, the opinion polls showed that 40 per cent of the people thought it was okay and that 40 per cent thought it wasn't tough enough; and, except in Atlantic Canada and parts of rural Quebec, the voters didn't punish us unduly at the next election for doing what they knew was the right thing to do. Though I was hollered at by union workers in Shawinigan and burned in effigy by a crowd in Bathurst, New Brunswick, it didn't hurt too much and, remarkably, we never had to go through a major national strike. The union leaders and the activist organizations ultimately understood that we were trying to treat everybody as justly as possible, given the terrible situation we had inherited, and that we would never back down from a confrontation.

From the start, consistency and resolve were very important, as was maintaining a united front as a government. While most ministers weren't happy about having to downsize their departments and their programs, Cabinet solidarity prevailed. We all bought into the Red Book's target, even if it contradicted our activist ideals and risked our defeat at the polls. I don't doubt that being Liberals gave us credibility. Canadians knew that a Liberal wouldn't fool around with social programs just for the fun of it. They understood that we were not acting out of abstract or ideological sport. Lloyd Axworthy obviously didn't find any delight in cutting social programs; André Ouellet wasn't reducing foreign aid for doctrinaire reasons; Sergio Marchi wasn't introducing a $975 landing fee for new immigrants because he wanted to curtail their numbers; and so each of them was able to do what had to be done without losing his credibility as a progressive.

There were times when I had to be tougher than Brian Mulroney had ever been. But Canadians were willing to give me the benefit of the doubt, I think, because I never got as close to the corporate establishment as he did. If you're perceived as a big shot, you create a suspicion that your government is too pro-business and not really concerned with the plight of ordinary Canadians. Though it was common knowledge that I had been a Cabinet minister since 1967, that I had worked for Gordon Capital and been a director of the Toronto-Dominion Bank while out of politics, and that my daughter, France, had married into the wealthy Desmarais family, in the minds of most people I was still the little guy from Shawinigan.

At the same time, the opposition in the Commons was weak, divided, and inconsistent. The Bloc Québécois was preoccupied with the separation of Quebec. The NDP had virtually vanished into its marginalized, outdated rhetoric. As for the right, split as it was between Reform and the two lone Tories, it was hardly in a position to oppose budget cuts and deficit reduction, and it proved incapable of articulating a clear, middle-of-the-road alternative. If it's a fatal flaw of all politicians to promise the moon and not be able to deliver it, right-wing politicians have a particularly hard time living with the contradictions within their ideology. On the one hand, they're always blaming the state for spending too much. On the other, they're always criticizing cuts to defence contractors, to business subsidies, to the provinces, and to their own ridings, even while they're demanding more cuts in taxes. They are invariably negative, seldom consistent, and blind to the fact that the military establishment, corporate CEOs, and provincial premiers will always believe they need more.

To fiscal conservatives, from whom I never expected many votes even when they told me they were happy with what we were doing, the accomplishments of the Liberal government were simply good luck. The timing was undoubtedly fortunate, but, in politics, if you make a good decision, people think you're lucky, and if you make a bad decision, they think you're incompetent. Good management was a more important factor than good luck, I believe, and so, apparently, did the delegations from France, Germany, Japan, and scores of other countries that came to study our success, and all the heads of government who quizzed me whenever I travelled abroad. They shook their heads in amazement that we had managed to cut both our program spending and the federal bureaucracy by about a fifth without having had a revolution on our hands.

The reality was that, through the debt-inflicted years of the eighties and nineties, every Western country, every Canadian province, every municipality—conservative, liberal, and socialist—was caught between the same rock and the same hard place, and the Canadian people had probably been ahead of their politicians in recognizing the crisis. They were willing to go along with us because we had set a realistic interim target of 3 per cent in three years—and then had more than met it. Without setting that target, we would have had a harder time maintaining our fiscal and political discipline. Without meeting it, we would have raised expectations only to dash them to the ground. Instead, after the years of darkness, Canadians could see some light at the end of the tunnel. It helped, too, that we tried to make the entire process transparent and fair by preparing everybody at the same time for what was coming through committee debates or policy papers.

No government is ever perfect, to be sure, and no society is ever free of problems, but Canadians should be very proud of what we achieved together in so short a time.

THREE

YANKEE TRADERS

———

I hadn't even been sworn into office before I had to make my first crucial decision involving Canada's relationship with the United States of America: whether we should sign into law the North American Free Trade Agreement (NAFTA) that Brian Mulroney's government and the U.S. administration had negotiated with Mexico but which had not yet been ratified in either Ottawa or Washington. In November 1992, despite vigorous opposition from the protectionist elements among both the Republicans and the Democrats, Bill Clinton had been elected president of the United States with a pledge to support NAFTA, subject only to getting side agreements concerning labour and environmental standards. A year later I had won a majority on a similar platform. We would sign, but with some conditions of our own.

During the 1993 campaign, in an attempt to embarrass me with apparent contradictions and flip-flops, the Tories had put

together a little book of statements I had made over the course
of my long career, and one of them was from a speech in 1971
in which I proposed a free trade agreement with Mexico and the
United States. I can't remember what business I had thought it
was of mine, since I was the minister of Indian affairs and northern development at the time, but it did show that I have always
been a free trader. More than most countries, Canada was, is,
and ever shall be dependent on the export of goods and services
for jobs and growth. Exports accounted for about 40 per cent of
the private sector's total output by 1993, and promoting trade
was as essential to our economic recovery as balancing the books
and bringing down interest rates. To strengthen Canada's presence in the world's fastest-growing regions, I created two new
Cabinet positions: secretary of state (Latin America and Africa)
and secretary of state (Asia-Pacific). Within a year of taking
office, the government organized Team Canada, a remarkably
successful initiative in which I led the premiers, the territorial
leaders, and hundreds of business executives on a series of trade
missions to Asia, Latin America, Russia, and Germany.

I had been out of politics when John Turner set the
Liberals in opposition to the initial Canada-U.S. Free Trade
Agreement. When Mulroney decided to fight the 1988 election
on the FTA, I tried to warn the party that it wasn't a good issue
for us to campaign on. With the nation divided almost exactly
in half over the agreement, I was concerned that we would end
up splitting the protectionist vote with the New Democrats. I
also thought we would do better to attack Mulroney's disastrous economic and political record. Liberals have generally
been free traders since the days of Laurier, who courageously
opposed the Conservatives' cry of "No truck or trade with the
Yankees" during the 1911 reciprocity election; and though a
nationalist faction has been active in the party since the 1960s,
I preferred the sounder theory and more pragmatic approach of

my mentor, Mitchell Sharp. I don't know if my message ever got to the top—probably not—but Turner decided to take a position that was very popular among the intellectuals and the *Toronto Star* crowd in Ontario. There just weren't enough of them, however, and we had to share them with the NDP.

When I became leader in 1990, I decided that the party needed to clarify its position on free trade. We had to show Canadians that we were not just better managers than the Tories, we were philosophically different. We also had to demonstrate that our ideas were evolving with the modern realities of globalization and common markets. Without attacking or repudiating Turner's stand in a negative way, I began to talk positively about what I was going to do as prime minister, and I used the Aylmer Conference and the Red Book to help elucidate and communicate the party's new direction. By the time of the 1993 campaign, we were united around the promise to work for an expansion of free and fair trade through the General Agreement on Tariffs and Trade (GATT), the creation of the World Trade Organization (WTO), and NAFTA—as long as we could get a few improvements, just as Clinton had proven able to get with labour and the environment in August 1993.

"A Liberal government will review the side agreements to ensure that they are in Canada's best interest," the Red Book stated. "A Liberal government will renegotiate both the FTA and NAFTA to obtain a subsidies code; an anti-dumping code; a more effective dispute resolution mechanism; and the same energy protection as Mexico." We later added water to the list, so that Canadians could never be forced to export water to the United States against our own interests.

Washington was concerned that any sign from me that I might renege on the deal as prime minister would probably kill Clinton's chances of getting congressional approval for his NAFTA deal. Almost immediately after our election victory, in fact, I received a phone call from Ross Perot, the Texan billionaire who had run as a third-party candidate for the presidency on an anti-NAFTA platform. Though I didn't agree with Perot's politics, I always get a kick out of talking with lively, opinionated, unorthodox characters—and he was certainly lively, opinionated, and unorthodox. Because his name sounds like Perrault, I began by joking that he might have some French-Canadian blood in him. "Maybe your ancestors were Cajuns from next door in Louisiana who had Americanized their name over the centuries," I said, "just as there are Chrétiens who moved to the United States and became Christians."

Perot congratulated me on my victory, and then he said—his thick Texan accent made harder to understand by his rapid way of talking—"Mr. Chrétien, if you manage to block NAFTA from going through, I will erect a huge statue to you here in Texas."

"Thank you very much, sir," I replied lightly. "But, you know, there aren't many votes for me in Texas."

Late on the afternoon of Tuesday, November 2, before I had even moved out of the Opposition leader's office on Parliament Hill, I asked James Blanchard, the U.S. ambassador to Canada, to come for a serious talk. A former Democratic governor of Michigan and long-time "Friend of Bill," Blanchard lived and breathed politics, had a bright and enthusiastic personality, and loved being the proactive insider who overcomes all obstacles to get things done. President Clinton, he told me, would be sending NAFTA to Congress the next day, the vote would be extremely close, and the American government wanted to urge me not to make the situation worse by calling for another round of negotiations.

I explained that the Liberals had opposed the FTA not because we were against free trade in principle, but because it wasn't a multilateral arrangement and didn't offer Canada secure enough access to the American market. Even Mitchell Sharp strongly opposed that particular deal. We were ready to sign NAFTA if we got the changes we needed to honour the promises set out in the Red Book. I also demanded that the American government make last-minute corrections to a few items that, by accident or design, had been arbitrarily altered en route to Congress. Canada wasn't going to accept what hadn't been acceptable to the Mulroney government.

"You haven't even formed your Cabinet yet," Blanchard said. "What happens if we work something out and your new trade minister won't go along?"

"Then I'll get a new trade minister the next day," I replied.

Not only did I not have a Cabinet, but I barely had any PMO or PCO advisers at hand. So, having already passed the ball to Eddie Goldenberg, who had been advising me on Canada-U.S. relations for decades as part of his job, I asked him to run it through the system as quickly as possible. He discussed various approaches and specific wordings with American trade officials according to my general instructions and supervised two trade officials, Al Kilpatrick and John Weekes, in working out the technicalities. On November 4, I appointed Roy MacLaren, a Toronto businessman and former diplomat, as minister for international trade to continue the negotiations. My thinking was that if the deal fell apart at the last minute, MacLaren's reputation as an ardent free trader and his connections to Bay Street would help reassure the business community that we had tried our hardest. In short order, however, he was able to get side letters on energy, culture, and water that didn't require reopening the agreement, as well as a joint statement to set up two working groups to seek solutions to the problems of subsidies and dumping.

I was often asked what I would have done if we had failed, but I never answer that kind of hypothetical question or spend much time thinking about it. Often you go to the edge knowing that you have to win or you'll have big problems, but that doesn't mean you have the solutions to those problems until you actually have to face them. For me, it's meaningless to speculate about backup plans when you may not need any of them. Besides, I was optimistic. Nothing we were proposing was likely to be a deal-breaker for the Americans, and the odds were in Canada's favour. Bill Clinton had more to lose than I did because he had already spent a great deal of his time and political capital to get close to the end of the process in Washington. I was just beginning my term, and I had kept all my options open during the election campaign, including the option of not signing. Though some people argued that we should have held out for more, we got most of what the Red Book had promised, and that was good enough for me.

—

Late on November 18, 1993, I had my first face-to-face encounter with Bill Clinton, who had been up half the previous night over-seeing and then celebrating NAFTA's victory by a mere thirty-four votes in the House of Representatives. Our meeting took place in a hotel suite in Seattle, Washington, the site of the inaugural sum-mit for the leaders of the Asia-Pacific Economic Cooperation (APEC) group of twelve nations. I'll never forget arriving on the Challenger for this meeting, my first international conference as prime minister, having flown to Seattle from the opening of the new parliament of the Northwest Territories in Yellowknife via Vancouver. When Canada's little plane pulled up between the colossal Boeing 747s of the president of the United States and the president of the Philippines, I realized for the first time that I might have gone a bit overboard as Opposition leader in criticiz-ing Brian Mulroney's imperial style, which turned out to be quite modest compared to that of most heads of government.

My get-together with Clinton had been squeezed into a busy schedule for 8:30 at night and was little more than an introductory chat in which we touched lightly on a few issues while a dozen members of our delegations, seated in two rows of chairs, watched from the sidelines. Though Clinton was obviously exhausted by his long day of travel, I found him easy to talk to and quick to laugh. Still, I was leery about establishing the sort of coziness Mulroney had cultivated with Ronald Reagan and George Bush. While Canadians don't want their leaders to pick unnecessary fights with the U.S. president, they also don't want them to get too chummy either. "My ambition is not to go fishing with the president of the United States," I had joked on the campaign trail, "because I don't want to be the fish." Not wanting to look as though I was rushing to ingratiate myself with Clinton at our first meeting on American soil, I rejected the suggestion that I should announce Canada's support for NAFTA in Seattle. It took me months before I felt comfortable calling him by his first name.

"Mr. President," I said, "I have to tell you something. I don't want to get too close to you." He looked startled. I imagine it was a rare thing for a U.S. commander-in-chief to hear. "Canada is your best friend, largest trading partner, and closest ally, but we are also an independent country. Keeping some distance will be good for both of us. If we look as though we're the fifty-first state of the United States, there's nothing we can do for you internationally, just as the governor of a state can't do anything for you internationally. But if we look independent enough, we can do things for you that even the CIA cannot do."

—

Striking the right balance between partnership and independence was never simple. Though my initial meeting with Clinton was cordial and positive—more so, certainly, than it would have been if I had pulled the plug on NAFTA—we had a serious difference of opinion at our second meeting, which took place just a couple of months later at a summit of the North Atlantic Treaty Organisation (NATO) in Brussels in January 1994. (I was happy to see François Mitterrand there, accompanied by his prime minister, Édouard Balladur. I liked President Mitterrand from the many times I had met him over the years, and I admired his deep culture, his instinct for the right word, and his skilful manoeuvrings. It's true that he carried himself with a certain grandeur, but I also found in him a kind of humility—especially in comparison to the haughtiness of Mr. Balladur.) Two years earlier, when the Mulroney Conservatives were still in power, the United Nations and NATO had felt compelled to intervene in the brutal civil war taking place in the former Yugoslavia, and the Liberals had supported Canada's decision to contribute troops to the mission. It was our duty as citizens of the world to try to stop the ethnic cleansing that had already claimed so many lives on all sides; it was a signal of our commitment to the UN and NATO; and it suited our traditional role as humanitarian peacekeepers. Only the British and the French had larger contingents on the ground.

Though the Americans were reluctant, for domestic political reasons, to risk the lives of their own soldiers, they still insisted on dominating the strategic discussions at the Brussels meeting, and I took strong issue with a U.S. proposal to launch air strikes against the Bosnian Serbs. Air strikes, I believed, would only incite the Serbian forces to retaliate against the Canadian peacekeepers whom they had trapped in the "safe area" around the town of Srebrenica. "If you think air strikes are so necessary militarily," I told Clinton during the NATO meeting, "fine, but go try them somewhere else." I put it even more bluntly to the press when I said, "The Americans are willing to fight to the death of the last Canadian." In the face of my strong objection, the United States backed down, and we later joined France and the United Kingdom in preventing the Americans from lifting the arms embargo by threatening to withdraw our forces from Bosnia. Arming the Bosnian Muslims, we argued, would end any real hope of reaching a negotiated solution, destroy our neutrality, further threaten our forces, and probably draw Russia into the fray on the side of the Serbs.

Because of our troops, I spent a lot of time thinking about Bosnia, even though Canada had been left out of the high-level group that the Americans, British, French, Germans, and Russians had formed shortly after the NATO summit in Brussels to search for a political solution. In view of the fact that three of these nations had no soldiers in the field, I can't say I was pleased with the arrangement, but our diplomats kept working for peace on the front lines and behind the scenes anyway. In June 1994, as a sign of our commitment to finish the job we had started and also to show my personal support for our men and women, I made a surprise visit to Bosnia, flying with a small staff from Paris to Split and then, by helicopter, over the devastated farms and villages to the Canadian base in Visoko, near Sarajevo. There I could see for myself the challenges of the UN mission and the professionalism of our troops. I remember our commanding officer telling me how he had negotiated a ceasefire with the Serbs in the hills on one side of the river and the Muslims on the other and reopened a bridge that both could now use. I also remember how moved I was to meet three young men working together in the Canadian Forces' garage: one was a Serb, another was a Muslim, and the third was half Serb, half Muslim.

It was apparent how this intervention was a more complicated and dangerous kind of peacekeeping than we had experienced since Lester Pearson's day. In Cyprus, for example, the Greeks and the Turks in effect agreed to be separated by a wall, and our job over the decades was to make sure that no conflicts broke out between them. In Bosnia and Croatia, we were caught in the middle of the crossfire between two heavily armed factions. Though we had gone there for humanitarian reasons—to deliver food and medication to the civilian population—we spent most of our time defending ourselves and others. We weren't really peacekeepers but peacemakers, what I once described as "the Red Cross with guns." The purpose and the equipment were basically the same, but the level of active military engagement was much higher, as was the risk of casualties. To make peace, we sometimes had to fight terrible battles. It was a very difficult role to play, and very frustrating.

In July 1994, at the G7 summit in Naples, President Clinton asked for Canada's help in another trouble spot, Haiti, where Lieutenant-General Raoul Cédras had overthrown the democratically elected government of President Jean-Bertrand Aristide in September 1991. Thousands of innocent Haitians were being massacred under the military dictatorship, and more than forty thousand refugees had fled on boats to the United States. When the United Nations and the Organization of American States (OAS) failed to achieve a peaceful solution, Clinton came under mounting pressure to intervene militarily. His dilemma was that, with midterm congressional elections coming up in November, the idea of invading Haiti wasn't popular among the American people, including leading Republicans and even many Democrats. If they remembered Ronald Reagan's quick and relatively painless victory in Grenada in 1983, they also remembered the savage killing of U.S. soldiers in Somalia in 1993. They feared that getting out of Haiti might be a lot harder than going in.

Clinton asked me if Canada would be willing to join a U.S.-led, UN-authorized multinational force to oust Cédras. I replied that we didn't see deposing dictators as our role in the world. We preferred to try to make the economic sanctions work and, if an invasion proved absolutely necessary, to go into Haiti afterwards to help in its reconstruction with military engineers, tactical helicopters, communications experts, and security personnel during the second phase of the United Nations Mission in Haiti (UNMIH). "Indeed," I wrote to the president on August 29, 1994, "we will shortly start to train a new police force made up of Haitian expatriates here in Canada. This will be followed by our participation in UNMIH-II with members of the Royal Canadian Mounted Police (RCMP), and a possible contribution of experts to judicial and other administrative reforms critical to the establishment of the rule of law in Haiti."

As a result, Canada wasn't part of the large multinational force that intimidated Cédras into surrendering power in September and then backed up Aristide's tumultuous return from exile in the United States in October. True to our word, though, in March 1995 we participated, along with a smaller contingent made up mostly of American soldiers, in helping to restore peace and democracy. A year later, with his second election coming up, Clinton wanted to pull out of Haiti completely, in case the violence erupted again and waves of Haitians began showing up on the coast of Florida in the middle of the campaign. He asked Canada to take over command of the force from the United States by the end of March 1996. We agreed and sent 700 soldiers at our own cost as part of a UN peacekeeping force.

Haiti was, in my opinion, a classic example of how we could do something for the Americans that they couldn't do by themselves. Canada and Haiti were both members of La Francophonie; we were connected through the Quebec universities and the large Haitian community in Montreal; we were concerned with the political and social conditions of the underdeveloped world; and we were perceived by our many friends in the Caribbean as neutral peacekeepers rather than imperialist invaders, thanks in part to our having said no to the first phase of the mission.

Later, and on more than one occasion both privately and publicly, President Clinton expressed his deepest gratitude.

—

In December 1994, to my great delight, the United States government convened the Summit of the Americas in Miami, the first time all thirty-four countries of North, Central, and South America—with the sole exception of Cuba—had ever met together. Because Canada had been exceptionally vocal in our attempts to get Fidel Castro invited, I was picketed by demonstrators when I arrived and got into a few arguments with other delegates, but the heated exchanges were almost a relief given the cold blast of air conditioning in the Vizcaya Museum. One evening the driver and military escort assigned to Roy MacLaren lost their way while taking him to a dinner in honour of all the trade ministers. MacLaren ended up way out in the Florida countryside late at night, in a place so remote and so dark that both the driver and the soldier were too scared to get out of the car to ask for directions back to the city. By the time they returned to downtown Miami, three hours had passed and the dinner was over.

The main discussion concerned the establishment of a hemispheric free trade zone. Not only did I believe in the principle and benefits of free trade, but I also thought that, in an expanded NAFTA, it was in Canada's interests to have the more than 400 million people of Latin America as a strong counterweight to the economic power of the United States. The Americans usually preferred to make bilateral deals, one by one, so they would become the hub to which all the spokes were attached. The United States was ten times as large as Canada in terms of population in the Free Trade Agreement of 1989 and less than three times as large as the combination of Canada and

Mexico in NAFTA: the weighting would be even fairer if Chile, Argentina, or Brazil joined us in a hemispheric deal.

In those days, political and economic liberalization was an acceptable idea to most of the Latin American leaders. Though time was still needed to build up the institutions of elected government, constitutional procedures, respect for the rule of law, and free markets after a century or more of military coups, authoritarian rule, state ownership, and protectionism, it was clear that trade and development had strengthened this progress from dictatorship to democracy, which in turn had fostered further trade and development. The Chileans were particularly eager to join NAFTA. The Argentinians were interested. The Brazilians were somewhat more hesitant, in part because they were trying to strengthen their own customs union with Argentina, Uruguay, and Paraguay (MERCOSUR), and also because they were being lobbied to enter into free trade negotiations with the Europeans, who had their own historical links to South America. For me, that was merely another reason to push forward on our own pan-American agreement as fast as possible.

"Despite this progress," I wrote to President Clinton on May 24, 1994, in reply to his formal invitation to the Miami summit, "we must nevertheless continue to work to strengthen and consolidate these democratic reforms. I recommend therefore that democratic governance, human rights, cooperative security, and judicial and legal reform be important agenda items. There remain many serious social and environmental problems in the hemisphere. I believe that our two governments must reinforce our commitment to ameliorate the unacceptable living and working conditions of many people, to truly embrace sustainable human development. Such a commitment would include the alleviation of poverty, the moderation of endemic industrial and residential pollution, the reduction of chronic unemployment, and an attack on crime, especially the drug trade."

As an industrialized nation in the Organization of American States and as the number two in both La Francophonie and the Commonwealth, Canada plays a useful and important role in the hemisphere, especially among the smaller, poorer Caribbean and Central American countries that often look to us for advice or assistance. Whenever the standard speeches about their oppression under the colonial regime went on too long, I used to joke, "Relax, Canada is the expert on that. We had both the English *and* the French." Sometimes we even represented these countries at technical meetings or international agencies where they couldn't afford to maintain a delegation, and in 1998 I flew fifteen of their leaders on the Canadian plane from a Caribbean Community meeting in the Bahamas to the second Summit of the Americas, in Santiago, Chile.

Meeting with the Caribbean leaders on a regular basis in Canada and abroad was a great way to get to know their countries and their concerns. In Miami, at a breakfast meeting with the heads of all the Commonwealth nations of the Caribbean, I heard about the nature of their economic problems and the difficulties they could face in implementing free trade. I found it encouraging, however, that they were talking about trade, not aid. Patrick Manning, the prime minister of Trinidad and Tobago, later referred to me as the "Godfather" of the Caribbean Commonwealth nations. Similarly, I struck up a warm friendship with Cheddi Jagan, the colourful and controversial president of Guyana who had converted from Marxism to capitalism during the course of his long career and who had family whom he visited regularly in Canada. He sought my help in sending retired teachers to Guyana and in other development initiatives he was excited about, and I always found him to be intelligent, articulate, and good company. In 1997, after he became mortally ill, one of his last requests was to talk with his friend Jean Chrétien. I was deeply moved when his wife told me that. Every hour I spent with these and other leaders, chit-chatting about world affairs or local politics, paid off countless times in terms of trade and international clout, especially at the United Nations, where the Caribbean countries had a large block of votes.

The first Summit of the Americas was considered a success, mostly because it ended with a general determination to work toward a Free Trade Agreement of the Americas that would eliminate all barriers to trade and investment by January 1, 2005. I, for one, was extremely keen to make it happen. On the stage with Bill Clinton and Mexican president Ernesto Zedillo at the concluding press conference, I enthusiastically welcomed President Eduardo Frei of Chile as our fourth amigo. Within a month, I became the first Canadian prime minister to make an official visit to Santiago as part of an extensive trade mission to South America, and early in 1998 I led two hundred Canadian business leaders on a Team Canada trip to Brazil, Argentina, and Chile. When Clinton failed to get a mandate from Congress that would have allowed him to sign off on the entry of Chile into NAFTA, we Canadians went ahead and signed our own bilateral agreement with Chile in 1996.

All too quickly, unfortunately, the momentum to merge NAFTA and MERCOSUR into a vast hemispheric free-trade zone was lost because of the re-emergence of radical anti-American regimes in Latin America and the short-sighted, short-term protectionism of too many U.S. congressmen. In my experience, every U.S. president is always in favour of free trade. To get it, however, he has to fast track a negotiated deal through Congress; otherwise, every senator and representative has a finger in the pie and nothing ever happens. Whereas Canadian prime ministers rarely have any problem getting the agreement of the House of Commons (as long as they have a majority government), American presidents don't have the same control.

The United States Congress is basically made up of independent legislators rather than disciplined parties. Members of

Congress may meet in caucus as Democrats or Republicans, but a southern Democrat doesn't necessarily have the same views or interests as a northern Democrat, and a northern Republican is not the same as a southern Republican. Even a senator from a very small state can wield extraordinary influence by being a member of a key appropriations committee, and every vote is in effect a free vote. Impasses get even worse if one party is in the White House and the other controls Capitol Hill. U.S. presidents may be the most powerful people on the planet on defence and executive matters, but on many domestic and legislative issues they are powerless to get their way.

One morning in July 1997, while attending a NATO summit in Madrid, I was standing in a group with Helmut Kohl of Germany and a few other people, waiting for Bill Clinton to show up. Clinton was late, as was his habit, and everyone was already unhappy with him for having kept us all waiting for dinner with the king of Spain the night before. But we were having fun complaining about the Americans, and we started talking about their political system. "Congress operates by horse-trading," I said. "You scratch my back, I'll scratch yours. You give me an airport, I'll give you a bridge. In Canada we'd be in jail for that." And everyone laughed. A few minutes later I was in my seat beside Jean-Luc Dehaene, the prime minister of Belgium, and he asked me what was so funny. So I repeated what I had said, not realizing that the microphone in front of me was on and that my joke was being broadcast into the media room and then around the world on CNN. I let the dust settle for a few days and then phoned Clinton to apologize. I didn't mean to offend him, I explained—it was only a lighthearted comment that got picked up by mistake.

"Don't worry, Jean, the same thing's happened to me," he said generously. "We'll settle it someday on the golf course."

—

The division of power is one of the great frustrations of dealing with the government of the United States, and it's just as frustrating for the U.S. president. Even when you're able to talk to him about a problem and he agrees to fix it, he often can't deliver. That's the reality that lies behind so many of Canada's trade disputes with the Americans, NAFTA or no NAFTA. Take the perennial issue of softwood lumber. The fact was, the Americans hadn't expected free trade with Canada to cause so much trouble for their softwood industry; otherwise, they would have fought for the same sort of exemption we were able to obtain for water. We didn't say we would never sell the Americans any water—we just said that it's not included in NAFTA.

In the United States, most tree farms are privately owned. To offset the costs of buying the land, planting the saplings, and waiting forty years to harvest them, American timber owners need an adequate return, and they claim they can't compete against these damn Canadians whom they see as benefiting from a lower currency and a form of subsidy—by being able to cut on public land for a low stumpage fee. So this huge, powerful sector, influential in almost every region of the country, goes to its senators and its House representatives and complains that it will have to close its sawmills if free trade is applied to softwood lumber. The elected politicians say, wait a minute, forget about free trade with Canada, my constituents want import tariffs—and they slap billions of dollars of countervailing duties on Canadian softwood. I once had to listen to a lecture from a Republican senator from the South about why, even though the builders in his state loved Canadian lumber, the wood producers didn't—and later I discovered that his own family owned tree farms. When I mentioned this apparent conflict of interest to a U.S. government official, I was told that, under the United States constitution, all citizens have the right to defend their property.

I thought the Americans were wrong, and I believed they knew they were wrong (if only because the courts and the dispute panels kept telling them they were wrong), but they couldn't do anything else politically. Clinton even told me that the United States would never, ever agree to implement completely free trade in softwood lumber. In 1996, therefore, rather than giving in to cries that we should retaliate by restricting our energy exports to the United States or penalizing some imports from south of the border, which would have ended up hurting Canadians as much as it would Americans, I reluctantly decided to sign a five-year agreement that guaranteed us a third of the U.S. market. And when the agreement was about to expire in 2001, I argued in favour of asking the American government to renew it for another five years, with the hope that we could increase the quota incrementally from 33 per cent to 36 or 38 per cent, in the way that the Japanese had moved into the North American automobile market—climbing stealthily, backing down a bit whenever the complaints got too loud, growing and retreating until they finally secured a major share. But the provinces and the Canadian lumber producers wanted me to push the Americans for nothing less than 100 per cent access for Canadian softwood.

"Okay, you can try," I told Pierre Pettigrew, the minister of international trade at the time, "but you will fail. Sometimes perfection just doesn't exist in this world." Sure enough, the U.S. government refused to be bound by the dispute settlement process, and it took years of threats and acrimony before another—still unsatisfactory—agreement could be reached, in April 2006. When it comes to trade disputes, in my experience there's little that any president can do even if he wants to do something.

Bill Clinton frankly admitted as much in the sometimes heated dispute we had with the Americans over salmon fishing on the west coast. When I complained that the U.S. government was dragging its feet about negotiating a fair quota system to prevent the depletion of the stock, Clinton always gave me the same answer: "I'm sorry, Jean, but that's up to the states of Washington, Oregon, and Alaska, the Indian bands, the federal departments concerned, and Congress. With three or four dozen different stakeholders, I just don't have the power to do what perhaps should be done." It took a frank, undiplomatic argument between Vice-President Al Gore and Fisheries Minister Brian Tobin during a lunch at 24 Sussex in July 1994, the threat of a $1,500 licence fee for every U.S. fishing boat passing through Canadian waters, and the blockade of an Alaskan ferry by irate Canadian fishermen in Prince Rupert before an agreement was finally signed in 1999.

That's not to say that NAFTA is a failure—far from it. Bilateral trade in goods and services between Canada and the United States doubled between 1993 and 2003 to almost $2 billion a day, and no more than 1 per cent involved disputes. Many of those disputes were resolved to the satisfaction of both sides by the hard work of the ministers and officials whose departments were involved. In fact, according to my nephew Raymond Chrétien, a career diplomat who was Canada's ambassador to the United States from 1994 to 2000, the number of controversial files he had to handle each year actually decreased from 120 to 10 during his time in Washington.

It certainly helped Canada that Raymond was a pro with a vast amount of experience, a sharp mind, a loud voice, and a terrific personality. Lucien Bouchard, then leader of the Bloc Québécois, had nothing but praise for the appointment because he knew of Raymond's reputation as a distinguished foreign service officer in Europe, Latin America, Africa, and the Middle East, and at the United Nations. Though Raymond did his job through the appropriate departmental channels, I talked to him more forthrightly and more often than a prime minister normally does to a public servant, not only because he was my nephew, but because he was in the U.S. capital and was also an excellent political analyst. He had a profound understanding of the system in Washington and in Ottawa; he knew the senior bureaucrats in both capitals; and he suggested I ask James Bartleman, who had recently been Canada's ambassador to NATO in Brussels, to be my foreign policy adviser. Whenever Raymond phoned senior White House officials, I liked to joke, he always got through, because the switchboard couldn't tell which one of us was calling, and I was told he was the only foreign ambassador Clinton and Gore called by his first name. "Hey, Raymond, how's your old uncle doing?" the president always asked.

As important as personal chemistry and good communications may be in greasing the wheels of diplomacy, business is business and friendship is friendship. Even Brian Mulroney hadn't always got everything he wanted from his friends Ronald Reagan and George H.W. Bush. In fact, as I had told Bill Clinton from the start and demonstrated time and again, I wanted our relationship to be friendly yet professional. But Clinton proved a very hard guy not to get close to. We both came from modest circumstances, small towns, and rural areas. We frequently talked on the phone or exchanged letters. We got together several times a year at meetings of the G7, the UN, NATO, APEC, or working bilaterals. We played golf a dozen times. Though neither of us ever hesitated to confront the other in direct terms when the occasion called for it, we both preferred to score our points with humour rather than anger. One time, after protesting his administration's decision to limit the import of Canadian durum wheat, even though it was generally recognized as the best product for making pasta, I teased Clinton that he would lose the Italian-American vote trying to win the Midwest, and I threatened to repatriate Wayne Gretzky from the Los Angeles Kings in retaliation. He laughed, but he got the message too.

Most of all, we shared our love and knowledge of sports and politics. Like me, Clinton was nuts about every kind of game. Even now, in our retirement, if I ever feel like chatting, I know the best time to catch him is during an important football or basketball event on TV because I know he's watching it. On a couple of occasions, we've followed the game and talked politics over the phone at the same time. Talking politics is natural among all politicians—it's pleasant; it's our trade; it's what we have in common—but Bill Clinton really loved it. During breaks at summit meetings or after dinner on state visits, when the formal events were over and the official business was done, we wallowed in the strategic and tactical details of election wins and election defeats, and, like any two leaders who get together anywhere in the world, we vented our fury and frustration about the media. "Your private life is your own," I offered when he was going through a particularly difficult patch with the press. "You should just tell them all to go to hell. You're a good president, and the best thing you can do is keep doing a good job."

The more Aline and I got to spend time with Hillary and Bill Clinton, whether at international gatherings or during official visits, the more we saw that the First Lady was just as political as the president. She wanted to participate in important discussions; she wanted to talk about substantial issues; and whenever I was seated beside her at a state dinner, she wanted to know how I had handled the problems of health care or welfare reform rather than to hear stories about my grandchildren. She was interested, well briefed, and intelligent, as well as exceptionally pleasant. Watching her and Bill together, I was struck by how little disagreement there seemed to be between them. Sometimes she stated a different point of view or asked a challenging question, but I found they shared many of the same views and a common understanding of the world. She seemed neither to the right nor the left of him, and though Hillary wasn't the natural charmer that her husband was, she had a strong presence and an impressive personality in her own right.

Because Canadians tend to know much more about U.S. politics than Americans know about ours, Bill Clinton and I usually discussed what was happening in the United States, though he was remarkably knowledgable about Canada. Needing only a few hours' sleep at night, he was an avid reader. One day he mentioned that he had recently been comparing the administration costs between hospitals of similar size in Boston and in Toronto. He admired our policies on multiculturalism and our two official languages. He envied the way we were able to handle gun control, marijuana, and abortion without unleashing a right-wing backlash. And he admired our moderation, our tolerance, and our social programs. When an American magazine called him "a closet Canadian," because of his progressive views and programs, he said he took it as a compliment.

"In a world darkened by ethnic conflicts that literally tear nations apart," President Clinton told the House of Commons on his first official visit to Ottawa in February 1995, "Canada has stood for all of us as a model of how people of different cultures can live and work together in peace, prosperity, and respect."

Neither he nor I could have guessed at the time how important those words and sentiments would be for the future of Canada before the end of the year.

FOUR

ONE DAY AT A TIME

I am a rather orderly man, a trait my wife says I inherited from my father and passed on to my son Hubert. I like to keep an orderly schedule, just as I like to keep an orderly tool box, and I view punctuality as the politeness of princes. Most mornings at 24 Sussex I was up by seven o'clock, took a shower, did some exercise, and hastily downed a glass of juice, a piece of toast or a bowl of Raisin Bran, and a single cup of coffee or hot chocolate. Some days I went for a swim in the indoor pool; otherwise I headed straight to my study to read documents or sign letters until nine o'clock, when I left for the quick drive to Parliament Hill.

Unlike my predecessors, I almost never used my office on the second floor of the Langevin Block, the fortress-like building across Wellington Street where the Prime Minister's Office and the Privy Council Office are situated, and I eventually gave it to

Jean Pelletier, my chief of staff. I much preferred my corner suite on the third floor of the Centre Block of the Parliament Buildings, in part because I liked to feel close to the action of the House of Commons even when it wasn't in session, but mainly because I didn't need a second office and didn't feel twice as important for having two. Since the room felt elegant enough, with its warm panelling, high ceiling, and tall windows, I kept it sparsely furnished: Laurier's desk and a portrait of him on the wall, family photographs, a few Inuit carvings, and a series of paintings by the great Quebec artist Jean-Paul Lemieux, based on a novel set in the West by the Franco-Manitoban novelist Gabrielle Roy. I liked the symbolism of two French Canadians interpreting scenes from Prairie life.

My first meeting of the day was normally at 9:30, with Jean Pelletier and the clerk of the Privy Council, of which there were four during my time: Glen Shortliffe, Jocelyne Bourgon, Mel Cappe, and Alex Himelfarb. This meeting—dubbed the "triangulation" by David Zussman—allowed me to receive political and bureaucratic advice at the same time and to get a dialogue going between my two most senior advisers. For half an hour or so, we reviewed what had happened the day before, what policy problems were coming up through the bureaucracy, or what difficulties and disputes were occurring in the Cabinet committees. The clerk would give me an oral report; Pelletier would discuss the political implications and the reaction of the caucus, the ministers, the press, or individual citizens and organized groups; and I would sum up with my views and instructions. On Tuesdays I met with the Cabinet from ten until noon; on Wednesdays, with the Liberal caucus. Most other mornings I tried to keep my schedule free for meetings with any ministers, officials, advisers, or staff members who had particular matters to discuss.

Visitors who came into my office were often puzzled, even astounded, to find that there was not even a single piece of paper on my desk. The truth is, I hate seeing reports and correspondence piled up around me. For me, order leads to decisiveness. Most people keep documents on their desk because they don't know what else to do with them. Trying to keep a clean desk is an incentive to make a decision, even if that decision is only to put a folder away in the proper drawer. Besides, the clerk and my chief of staff both made certain that everything coming up to me was worth my time, and they knew me well enough to realize that I wasn't going to pay much attention to issues I had already made up my mind to ignore. Most of the problems that reached my desk were the big problems that nobody else could solve, yet they had been studied and discussed by enough people to make the solution more or less evident to me. After all, people don't normally bother a prime minister with half-baked proposals.

Still, every head of government runs the risk of being drowned in paper when what is most needed is time to reflect. To allow me to get to the heart of an issue quickly, I asked the officials to summarize their documents in two or three pages and attach the rest of the material as background information. I soon discovered that this was a problem only for those who didn't really know what they were talking about. Though I always wanted to be able to consult the whole file, I had been a minister in so many departments for so long that I often knew the subject inside out or had seen the same data repeated over and over again. Rarely would I put a decision aside for very long. On the contrary, my habit was to deal with a problem immediately—search for its essence, analyze the options, and either scribble my initials at the top of the document, if I was satisfied, or add a question mark, if I wanted more. The clerk, seeing a question mark, would return with the document; we would discuss what I had found wanting or wrong; the clerk would go away and return sometime later with a new draft, and, if it answered my concerns, I would approve it.

I generally preferred to deal with people face to face. Sometimes, of course, I wrote letters to friends on personal matters, but on government business I suggested a response to my staff, made a few comments at the bottom of a page, or left the composition to them for my approval. If the matter required a carefully worded reply to a foreign leader or a provincial premier, I first discussed it with my chief of staff, my policy advisers, or the experts in the relevant area. Needless to say, the vast majority of the letters—and, later, the emails—I received every day were repetitive petitions or minor issues, and I simply delegated them to the PMO's correspondence section to answer on my behalf. Even so, I was given an awful lot of letters to read and sign, and I often paid attention to any good advice or thoughtful ideas.

Most days I went home for a quick lunch at 12:15, with guests or alone with Aline, and three or four times a week I was back in my office by 1:30 to meet with my legislative assistant, my press team, and my parliamentary secretary in order to prepare for Question Period at 2:15 in the House of Commons. Sometimes, if I needed to be more fully briefed on a specific topic, we were joined by a minister or an official. As a matter of courtesy, I almost always responded myself to the questions from the other party leaders, and because there were four of them, that often took up half an hour out of the forty-five minutes allocated for Question Period. I have to admit that I had trouble restraining myself from leaping to my feet to answer every question. My staff used to tell me to leave a few for my ministers—they had to be given a chance to perform, they needed to be seen on the news, and so forth. I fully agreed, and once in a while I would even let ministers reply to the first couple of questions in order to demonstrate that they were on top of an issue. The problem was, I enjoyed Question Period too much and loved the challenge it provided. Far from being a dreaded burden, it had become an exciting part of my life: opposition members attacked me, I fought back, I won or lost or held them to a draw, and the next day we did it all over again.

At three o'clock I sometimes stopped to meet the press on the way up to my office, though if there wasn't any urgency, I preferred to answer their questions once a week after the Cabinet meeting. I thought it was more respectful of Parliament to let the reporters work with what they had heard in the House. Back in my office, for about half an hour I received MPs—including members of the opposition parties—who might have a brief matter to discuss or wanted to bring in their relatives, constituents, or distinguished visitors for a photograph with the prime minister. These sessions were necessarily short, but I thought it was important for as many people as possible to feel they had access to me. For the rest of the afternoon I generally met with civil servants, foreign diplomats, party officials, ministers who might have a particular problem, and caucus colleagues who had a serious issue that required more time to resolve, many of whom weren't inscribed in my daily appointment book.

———

From time to time, of course, a crisis would interrupt the regular routines and schedules, but I urged my staff and ministers to continue doing their jobs as though everything was business as usual. The real difference at such times was that I had to take a more hands-on role, because only a prime minister can make these types of decisions. "That's why I'm paid the big bucks," I used to joke.

On March 8, 1995, for instance, I received a visit in my office from Brian Tobin, the minister of fisheries and the senior Newfoundlander in the caucus. He was an energetic minister and an excellent communicator, talkative, colourful, full of fun, and hot-tempered, and on this day he was in a rage about what was happening in his province. After decades of overfishing, the important and historic northern cod industry had been virtually destroyed. In December 1993 the Liberal government had no choice but to extend the moratorium Prime Minister Mulroney had imposed the year before, and we paid out hundreds of millions of dollars to those who had lost their livelihood at sea or in fish factories—more than 25,000 working people in Newfoundland alone—even though we were in the middle of our battle against the federal deficit. That was seen as a contradiction at the time, but we felt we couldn't abandon fellow citizens who were suffering through no fault of their own.

The greater problem was how to rebuild the fish industry while huge industrial trawlers from other countries, most notably Spain and Portugal, continued to harvest tons of under-sized or endangered stocks in the "Nose, Tail, and Flemish Cap" of the Grand Banks, just beyond Canada's two-hundred-mile territorial waters limit. During the election I had promised Newfoundlanders that I would put a stop to this situation, no matter what, and in spite of the legal and political objections of the European Union, the government amended the *Coastal Fisheries Protection Act* in May 1994 to give Canada the authority to take the appropriate action. Now, after more than a year of agreements, quotas, threats, and intense negotiations between Canada and the EU, Spanish fishermen were still netting small cod and more than their established share of turbot, the last commercial food fish remaining in any quantity.

"That turbot is a Canadian natural resource even if it happens to swim beyond our two-hundred-mile limit," Tobin argued. "We have to take action, damn it!" And he banged the top of my desk with his fist. Specifically, he wanted me to give the order to arrest the Spanish trawlers on the high seas and to inspect what they had caught, using armed force if necessary.

Though the Cabinet had supported his position in principle and though I had already issued a diplomatic warning to the EU members, it obviously wasn't a simple matter to attack a foreign vessel—one belonging, in fact, to a NATO ally—in what were widely perceived as international waters. The ministers of both foreign affairs and national defence were extremely reluctant to see Canada engage in this type of high-stakes drama. The clerk of the Privy Council, Jocelyne Bourgon, my foreign policy adviser, Jim Bartleman, and my senior policy adviser, Eddie Goldenberg, were all urging caution and had already had several heated exchanges with Tobin. I wasn't interested in getting into loud arguments or declaring winners and losers. As far as I was concerned, no one won and no one lost. I listened to both sides, made up my own mind, and decided to back Tobin, though I also kept him in check when I felt he was trying to go too far.

I wanted to be proactive. One, I saw the conservation of the stock as part and parcel of Canada's continual efforts to protect the global environment for all humankind. Two, my minimum offer of a sixty-day truce and a new round of negotiations had been ignored or rejected as a bluff. And, three, I wanted the world to know that Canadians could not—and would not—tolerate the impoverishment of our fishermen while allowing those from other nations to come and harvest the catch, even if they were technically beyond our boundaries. We had always been in the forefront regarding the Law of the Sea, pushing the territorial boundaries from three miles to twelve miles to two hundred miles. Now Canada was to take one of the toughest stands in its history in defence of our rights outside the two-hundred-mile limit, on the just grounds that there's no border crossing out there with security guards and flashing lights to welcome the cod and the turbot to Canada.

On Thursday, March 9, two Canadian patrol ships, armed with machine guns, manned by fisheries inspectors and RCMP officers, and accompanied by a Coast Guard vessel and surveillance aircraft, set off on a four-hour chase through thick fog and high seas to catch and arrest the leading culprit, the Spanish trawler *Estai*. I stayed in my office and followed the developments from there. Bourgon and Bartleman reported to me hourly. I also kept in regular communication with the ministers and bureaucrats involved. Fortunately, it took only four machine-gun bursts and no casualties for the *Estai*'s captain to surrender and agree to be escorted back to St. John's.

Not surprisingly, the Europeans weren't happy with Canada. We were accused of piracy and threatened with economic sanctions, and our embassy in Madrid was pelted with eggs and rocks by protesters from the fishing ports of Galicia. Worse, the Spanish government authorized the return of ten more trawlers to the Grand Banks a couple of weeks later, this time accompanied by a patrol ship of its own.

On Friday, April 14, Aline and I had returned to Ottawa from a fundraising swing through British Columbia and Alberta. We were exhausted, and she was looking forward to a few days of rest over the Easter weekend. "Maybe not," I said, "because I'm starting a war against Spain tomorrow morning." Poor Aline—she didn't sleep the whole night.

I couldn't blame her. The Cabinet's decision to use force and risk lives had not been taken lightly, but we felt we had no choice. Acting on a smart suggestion from Jim Bartleman, I now sent in an icebreaker—just as the Icelanders had done in similar circumstances against British fishermen in 1976—to join our small navy of three Fisheries Department patrol boats, two Coast Guard ships, a supply vessel, and two military frigates. When you're in a fishing trawler and there's an icebreaker bearing down on you, you don't need any guns to motivate you to get the hell out of there. At the last minute, with both sides staring down the barrel of a gun, Spain blinked.

I ordered Tobin back from the brink, and everyone agreed to return to the bargaining table.

It was a difficult, exciting time, and I was sustained in my decision by receiving a lot of good advice from our officials and a lot of moral support at home and around the world. When Royce Frith, Canada's high commissioner in London, visited ports up and down the British coast, he was cheered by fishermen waving Canadian flags, thrilled that somebody at long last had dared to take on the Spanish. And when Tobin took the *Estai*'s captured nets to the United Nations to give the international media proof that the poor little ugly turbot didn't have a hope of survival, Emma Bonino, the EU's commissioner for fisheries and a woman with a fiery Italian personality, was so ridiculed for her misrepresentations and evasions that she fled on the next plane home. Peter Jennings, the respected Canadian-born anchorman for ABC television news, later told me that Tobin's campaign was probably the best public relations stunt he had ever seen in politics.

A month later, in May 1995, when I was in Moscow for a ceremony to commemorate the fiftieth anniversary of the end of the Second World War, John Major urged me to come and shake hands with the Spanish prime minister, Felipe González. Though it was all very civilized, I must admit that González and I never regained our personal friendship, and he later confronted me in the corridors of the United Nations to express his country's displeasure. Yet there was no serious retaliation or long-term bitterness toward Canada, perhaps because the EU itself had second thoughts about supporting the hard-line Spanish government in the negotiations that eventually led to a settlement. As well, because of the warm relations I had been developing with other leaders, we were able to maintain the channels of communication and goodwill, even with those who hadn't agreed with what we had done. Everybody seemed to have forgotten all about the crisis by the G7 meeting in Halifax in June. We succeeded in putting a better international regime in place because of our forceful action, and relations with Spain had returned to normal by the time I attended the NATO summit in Madrid in 1997. I'm very proud, I must say, of how the government solved this problem.

—

At 6 p.m. each working day, I was given a briefcase full of red folders, documents, and signature books to take home, and Bruce Hartley usually dropped off another stack when he left the office around eight o'clock. If I wasn't hosting a reception or dinner at 24 Sussex and didn't have to go out to a formal event, I liked to have a quiet dinner with Aline before going back into my study for another couple of hours of work at the heavy, square desk Lester Pearson had used when he was Canada's ambassador to the United States. Sometimes I read a few more pages late at night, sometimes I read an entire report early in the morning, and sometimes I skipped from bit to bit during the drive to work, but all the documents were marked by the time I reached the office. None of my staff or officials ever knew exactly what I had or had not read in detail, and I liked to keep them on their toes by referring to an obscure fact or incidental statistic buried in one of the annexes. "Test me," I often said, just for the sport of it.

When I got tired of working, I went up to the second-floor sitting room and read a book—most often a history or biography in either French or English with an American or European subject, since anything to do with Canada seemed too close to my job to be relaxing—or I closed my eyes and listened to classical music, preferably orchestral or piano, by any of the great composers from Bach and Mozart to Beethoven and Chopin. On weekends, if I was autographing pictures by the dozen or signing routine correspondence, I had the crazy habit of watching a game on TV and listening to a CD at the same time. I didn't really need to hear the football play-by-play, since I knew the names of all the key players, and half the others seemed to be called Smith anyway. If I missed something exciting, I could catch it on the replay. I loved watching every kind of sport—Canadian football, American football, hockey, baseball, basketball, golf, soccer, tennis, anything. Most nights I was in bed by eleven. I never watched the evening news, which was probably why I slept so well.

FIVE

THE PHONY WAR

K eeping Canada united is the single most important responsibility of every national government and every prime minister. For me, as for so many people I have met around the world, Canada is a shining example of tolerance, diversity, and equality of opportunity, and I have spent a lifetime working to make sure that Canadians from every region and background can be full and active partners in this magnificent country that spans a continent from sea to sea to sea. Though a sense of alienation and discontent has arisen everywhere in Canada at various times, from Nova Scotia just a few years after Confederation to Alberta a hundred years later, only in my own province of Quebec did it evolve into a deeply entrenched political movement that captured control of the provincial government in more than one election and created a determined and ongoing effort to secede from the federation.

Canadian federalism is more than a form of government. It's also a system of values that allows different people in diverse communities to live and work together in harmony for the good of all. Will independence bring a better form of government for the people of Quebec? In my opinion, no. Will it bring more peace? No. More prosperity? No. More justice? No. Even a better chance for the survival of the French language and culture in North America? Again, no. The fact that Quebec is a part of Canada makes a big contribution to Quebec—and to Canada as well. If Quebec ever were to separate, I think it would be very difficult for the rest of Canada to resist being pulled into the United States, and only a matter of time, after that, before the small and isolated republic of Quebec would follow along.

Can anyone realistically expect a French-speaking senator to get very far in demanding French-language rights in Washington when there are already five times as many Hispanic Americans who haven't got anywhere with their own rights? Or Quebec to gain quick and automatic admission into NAFTA when Chile couldn't? Or Quebecers to enjoy the same level of economic security and international clout without access to the Pacific Rim, the Alberta oil sands, the Commonwealth, or the G7 industrialized democracies (which became the G8 when Russia officially joined in 1998 only after a great deal of delay and debate)? And, in 1995—when the francophone minority held the offices of the prime minister, his chief of staff, the governor general, the chief justice of the Supreme Court, the clerk of the Privy Council, the minister of foreign affairs, and the Canadian ambassador to the United States—how could anyone truthfully claim discrimination and oppression against Quebecers in Canada?

When I think back to the discrimination and disadvantages French Canadians faced when I first arrived in Ottawa in 1963, I find it incredible to realize how much progress we have made politically, economically, and socially. In Quebec in the early sixties, Liberal premier Jean Lesage brought the machinery of government, industry, and education into the twentieth century with the Quiet Revolution, while, across Canada, Lester Pearson's Royal Commission on Bilingualism and Biculturalism and, a few years later, Pierre Trudeau's *Official Languages Act* introduced meaningful reforms that finally made francophones equal partners with equal opportunities in Confederation. There was some negative reaction at first, but within a generation it became routine to expect that all English- and French-speaking Canadians should be able to deal with their national government in their own language and that all the major candidates for the highest offices of the land should be able to communicate in both languages. When Trudeau began appointing French Canadians to senior positions, everyone talked about "French Power" in Ottawa. By my time, though I appointed just as many or even more—not because they were francophones but because they were well qualified—nobody noticed or cared.

In May 1980, when the Parti Québécois government under René Lévesque held a referendum asking for a mandate to negotiate sovereignty-association with the rest of Canada, a solid majority of Quebecers understood how much had changed for the better in twenty years and voted a resounding no. Even so, to fulfill the promise he had made during the campaign, Trudeau launched a historic initiative to entrench French-language rights in a Charter of Rights and Freedoms. At the same time, after more than fifty years of effort and failure by successive Canadian governments, he was able to sever Canada's last important colonial link to Great Britain by "patriating" control of our constitution from the British parliament with the consent of every province except, ironically, Quebec.

Of course, the separatists would never—could never—sign any constitutional deal to improve the federation without losing their reason for existing. However, that didn't prevent them from shouting that Quebec had been stabbed in the back by Ottawa, betrayed by the other premiers, and left out of the Constitution—none of which happened to be true. Ottawa had acted only in accordance with the rules of law and convention laid down by the Supreme Court of Canada. It was René Lévesque who had betrayed the Gang of Eight—a makeshift alliance of eight provinces whose intention, for their own various reasons, was to block the constitutional initiative—when he agreed with Trudeau's suggestion to hold a referendum on the Charter in Quebec without consulting any of his fellow premiers. And, signature or not, Quebec was undeniably part of the Constitution. Robert Bourassa applied the Charter's "notwithstanding" clause to defend his language law against the claims that it violated the Charter's freedom of speech clause, for example, and a Parti Québécois government would later use the new amending formula to change the denominational character of the provincial school system as it had been set in 1867.

Despite the PQ's best efforts to organize mass demonstrations and legislative protests, most Quebecers were ready to turn the page and get on with the real concerns of their lives: their jobs, their families, and their future well-being. Lévesque, as realistic as he was discouraged, gave up and retired in September 1985. Within three months, his successor, Pierre-Marc Johnson, was defeated by Robert Bourassa, the Liberal premier from 1970 to 1976 who had returned to politics in 1983 and regained the leadership of his party. Not only did Bourassa win an overwhelming majority in December 1985, but, four years later, he won a second term.

All was quiet on the constitutional front, in other words, until Prime Minister Brian Mulroney, whose Progressive Conservatives had been elected in 1984 with the support of the nationalists in Quebec, decided to try to solidify that support by making a deal with Bourassa. Under the terms of the Meech Lake Accord, which Mulroney and all ten premiers signed in June 1987, subject to ratification by all provincial governments within three years, Quebec would be given five significant concessions in exchange for its signature on the *Constitution Act* of 1982. Four of the concessions were relatively uncontroversial: a veto over most future constitutional change, more power over immigration, financial compensation for any province that decides to opt out of new federal shared-cost programs, and a provincial say in the appointment of federal senators and Supreme Court judges. The fifth, which recognized Quebec as a "distinct society" within Canada, proved to be political dynamite.

Quebec is obviously a distinct society for all kinds of reasons, from its French-speaking majority to its Civil Code. The problem was that nobody knew what "distinct society" meant in substantial terms or what impact it would have if it were entrenched in the Constitution. On the one hand, it played to the emotions of those Quebecers who were investing their collective aspirations in these two words. On the other, it aroused the emotions of Canadians who feared that it was going to give Quebec extra powers and a special status in the federation. Even Mulroney, who had vigorously defended the inclusion of this recognition as absolutely essential to the accord, was claiming by the end of the ratification period that it would have no real effect—a reversal that must have come as a bitter surprise to those in Quebec who had fought so hard for what now appeared so little.

Having barely survived the battles over patriation and the Charter of Rights as Trudeau's minister of justice, I thought Mulroney was wrong to have reopened the constitutional file. In general, I felt that changing the Constitution is a distraction from dealing with the practical issues of the day, something to be undertaken only when all other options have failed. The Constitution is the basic law of the land, the law of reference, and fiddling with it will not grow potatoes in northern Quebec, as the union leader and Trudeau Cabinet minister Jean Marchand used to say. In this particular case, moreover, I felt that the Meech Lake Accord was more symbolic than real, but no less problematic because of that. Tampering with symbols can often ignite deep passions without solving any real problems, because people attach their hopes and fears to them. Few Canadians pay much attention to the Senate, for example, and the appointment of a senator is seldom an important issue for many people beyond the appointee's family and friends, but just try to reduce the number of Senate seats to which a province has been tradition-ally entitled or give one region a few more seats because of a change in demographics, and what might seem a reasonable reform will explode into a matter of grievance or pride. That's exactly what happened during the three years between the sign-ing of the Meech Lake Accord and the final deadline for its ratifi-cation on June 23, 1990—which by a fateful coincidence was also the date selected for the federal Liberal leadership convention.

At first, campaigning hard across the nation and preoccu-pied with gathering delegate support, I saw the Meech Lake Accord as less my problem than Mulroney's. I hadn't wanted to touch the Constitution after 1982, after all, and I was still in my temporary retirement from politics at the time. It became a prob-lem for me, however, once my opponents in the race, Paul Martin and Sheila Copps, came out in favour of Meech and used my reservations about the distinct society clause as an instru-ment to win Quebec delegates. After Robert Bourassa failed to talk his friend David Peterson, the Liberal premier of Ontario and an enthusiastic signatory of the Accord, into running against me, Bourassa's organizers divided themselves between Martin and Copps. Liberal members of the Quebec National Assembly who were friends of mine weren't allowed to speak up on my behalf. Even the member from my own riding, elected by the same voters in Shawinigan, fled in the opposite direction when asked if he was supporting me.

One of the lowest moments of the campaign came during the final leadership debate in Montreal in 1990, when Martin supporters began yelling that I was a sellout and a traitor to my people. Some of them had been brought by bus from Ontario and couldn't even pronounce *traître* or *vendu* properly. It stung, I must admit, but if I lost some delegates because of my stance on Meech, I probably gained some too.

Even some of my supporters who were strongly opposed to Meech began wishing that the Accord be implemented, if only to end the division within the Liberal Party and settle the whole issue of Quebec's place in the Constitution before we got to power. Perhaps they were right, but it's equally possible that the implementation would have opened a Pandora's box of new troubles that would have made running the federal government much more difficult. I consulted widely; I listened to the arguments; I tried, through intermediaries, to help work out a compromise. In the end, however, when the Meech Lake Accord died on the same day that I won at the convention in Calgary with almost 57 per cent of the votes, it was beyond saving. Lucien Bouchard had already quit the Conservative government because of Mulroney's mishandling of the file; Mulroney had dug his own grave by prematurely bragging in the press that he had gambled Canada's future on a roll of "all the dice"; and Meech was killed by its defeat in the Manitoba Legislature and a last-minute decision by the premier of Newfoundland not to put it to a vote.

In the aftermath, nevertheless, the Conservatives and the separatists found it to their political advantage to demonize me in the province of Quebec. For the Tories, a personal attack was a way to pull votes from the federal Liberals. For the separatists, it was a way to attack Canada. As the late Pierre Bourgault, the well-known separatist and essayist, stated in 1990 in his book

Aline and I watching the election results in Shawinigan with our son, Hubert, our daughter, France, and our four grandchildren, October 25, 1993.

The day before the 1993 election, the pundits proclaimed I was going to be defeated in my own riding.

With my senior advisers Eddie Goldenberg and Jean Pelletier on the victory flight from Shawinigan to Ottawa, October 26, 1993.

Celebrating with my family at 24 Sussex, November 4, 1993.

With Mitchell Sharp, my mentor and "dollar-a-year man."

In my office with Marcel Massé, the minister responsible for our unprecedented program review.

A light moment with three former prime ministers—Kim Campbell, Joe Clark, and Pierre Elliott Trudeau—October 1994.

The Chrétien clan on the front lawn at 24 Sussex, June 1995.

First and foremost, a member of Parliament.

At a Cabinet retreat with my colleagues, June 1994.

Addressing the Liberal MPs at our weekly caucus meeting in the Reading Room of the Parliament Buildings.

An impromptu pep talk in the Government Lobby on our way into the House of Commons.

Finance Minister Paul Martin with his crucial second budget, February 1995.

A typical evening reading documents while listening to music in the upstairs study at 24 Sussex.

A rare moment of quiet.

Now or Never, "Jean Chrétien? He can still cause us a lot of trouble. People say he's finished and powerless. They're wrong. He is still the most popular politician in English Canada, and, even in Quebec, he can count on support which, without being considerable, is nevertheless important." No matter how many books, articles, and documentary films chronicled the fact that I had not spent the wee hours of November 4, 1981, roaming around Ottawa trying to organize a plot among the nine premiers to leave René Lévesque out of the final agreement that led to the patriation of the Constitution and to the Charter—that I was at home and out of communication the entire night, that Lévesque had abandoned his provincial allies before they abandoned him, that Quebec never intended to sign any constitutional deal with Trudeau—the myth wouldn't die, partly because it's hard to kill a myth, partly because it was in the interests of my political opponents to keep it alive. Not so long ago, for instance, one of my grandsons got into an argument in his high school class because the textbook, authorized by the government of Quebec, presented a false account of what had happened. It wasn't just a different interpretation of history—it was factually wrong.

Similarly, in 1990, I was portrayed as the villain behind the collapse of Meech even though the Parti Québécois and Lucien Bouchard's newly formed Bloc Québécois were adamantly opposed to any accommodation with Canada. Indeed, when Mulroney and Bourassa managed to get the premiers, the territorial leaders, and Aboriginal representatives to agree to a second, last-chance constitutional deal in Charlottetown in August 1992, and it was put to the people for approval in a nationwide referendum that October, I supported the compromise, but the separatists in Quebec and Ottawa worked to kill it as well.

The Charlottetown Accord tried to be all things to all people by tinkering with the composition of the Senate, the House of Commons, and the Supreme Court, with the distribution of power between Ottawa and the provinces, and with future constitutional amendments—all with unpredictable practical implications. To be honest, I wasn't totally happy with everything in the proposed compromise. But the Liberal Party, the Liberal caucus, and I had suffered enough trauma with Meech, as had the whole country, and though Charlottetown still recognized Quebec as a distinct society, it did so within a general clause that also recognized the principles of equality and diversity for all Canadians.

My greatest concern was that my position in support of the Charlottetown Accord would be publicly attacked by my friend and esteemed predecessor Pierre Trudeau, who remained convinced that any mention of distinct society would mean an entrenchment of Quebec's special status in the Constitution, create a lever for more power for Quebec, and take the province one step closer to separation. When Senator Jacques Hébert warned my chief of staff that Trudeau was planning to come out hard against Charlottetown in a speech at the Maison Egg Roll in Montreal on October 1, 1992, Pelletier urged me to meet secretly with the former prime minister and iron out our differences. Trudeau was reluctant at first, but he finally agreed to have dinner with me in a suite at the Royal York Hotel in Toronto.

Our discussion, which lasted about two and a half hours, was always respectful but very vigorous. Mostly we discussed the meaning and implication of the term "distinct society." Trudeau claimed that it meant something in law, in which case it might allow the Quebec government to use it to overrule the Charter of Rights or to grab more powers through the courts. I still claimed that it meant nothing.

"Jean," Trudeau replied, "there are no words that mean nothing."

"I don't know too many," I admitted, "but these two mean nothing."

The very fact that Trudeau and I, the closest of allies on most constitutional issues, could disagree about the meaning of those two words from radically different points of view demonstrated what a confusion Mulroney and Bourassa had sown. By the end of the evening, over coffee, Trudeau and I could agree only to disagree. But though we were never going to be on the same page about the Charlottetown Accord, he promised to refrain from undermining my authority in public, and he said he would ask his admirers in the Liberal caucus to do the same. "You're the leader now, not me," he concluded, "so you have to live with some political realities that I can afford to ignore."

Even so, some of my advisers cautioned me against helping Mulroney. If he were able to achieve the unanimous agreement that Trudeau had failed to achieve in 1982, they argued, he could use it to his advantage in a run for a third term. In politics, however, if you proceed only on the basis of logic, you don't go very far, and often you have to make compromises. "But let me give you some political advice," I said to Mulroney when I agreed to come onside. "I'm not going to campaign much for it in Quebec. On most issues, I'm okay in Quebec, but because of my image in the press, people don't like what I have to say about the Constitution. Perhaps, because of some of your own image problems, you shouldn't take too high a profile in the campaign either." I thought he agreed, but he quickly drew fire for calling the opponents of the agreement "enemies of Canada" and ripped up a piece of paper to demonstrate what would become of Quebec's just demands if Charlottetown were to fail. Quite a dramatic intervention, I thought, for a guy keeping a low profile.

On October 26, 1992, Mulroney lost the Charlottetown Accord in the referendum. A year later his party lost the support of all those Canadians, in every part of the country, who had had enough of the subject. "If you want to talk about the

Constitution," I said during the 1993 election campaign, "don't vote for me."

The federal Liberals won a significant victory anyway, but Brian Mulroney had done enormous damage to the cause of Canadian unity by choosing a low road to get his deals. He catered to the nationalists' myth that Quebec had been, as he put it, "left alone, isolated, and humiliated" in 1982, and he linked the fate of Meech and Charlottetown to the fate of Canada. Not only did the Bloc Québécois win enough of the seats in Quebec to become the official Opposition in the House of Commons, thanks to the collapse of the Tories under Kim Campbell and the concentration of the Reform Party's votes in the West, but the Parti Québécois, under hard-line separatist Jacques Parizeau, was given a new lease on life in Quebec. If the PQ won the next provincial election, Canada was going to be facing another gut-wrenching referendum before too long.

SIX

"I WANT CLARITY!"

—

There's no doubt in my mind that Robert Bourassa, given his support for the Meech Lake Accord and his friendship with Brian Mulroney, would have been happier if the Progressive Conservatives had been returned to power in Ottawa rather than made to suffer a victory by the Liberal Party under Jean Chrétien. While all provincial politicians of all stripes struggle to advance and protect the best interests of their province, there's usually a mutual interest and common understanding between federal and provincial members of the same party. In Quebec, however, because the nationalist argument cuts across every debate and campaign, there can be federal Conservatives in the Quebec Liberal Party and provincial Liberals supporting the Bloc Québécois. In fact, although it's absolutely normal for the Parti Québécois to support the Bloc Québécois in Ottawa, for the Bloc to support the Parti

Québécois, and for the federal Liberals to support the provincial
Liberals, it's almost a sin for the Quebec Liberal Party to be seen
to be undermining its autonomy by supporting the Liberal Party
of Canada in a federal election.

In January 1994, just two months after I had taken office,
Bourassa retired as premier of Quebec because of ill health and
was replaced by Daniel Johnson Jr., who had represented the
province a few weeks earlier at my first federal-provincial conference. In many ways, Johnson was as close to the Tories as Robert
Bourassa had been, maybe even more so. He came from a very
bleu family. His uncle Maurice had been a Conservative MP
under John Diefenbaker. His father, Daniel Sr., had been a Union
Nationale minister under Maurice Duplessis, and became premier
after beating Jean Lesage in 1966. When the Union Nationale dis-
solved, the younger son, Pierre-Marc, became a member of the
Parti Québécois and succeeded Lévesque as premier. Whatever
their party affiliations, the Johnson clan remained tight with the
tiny crowd of Quebec Conservatives who clung together in
Montreal following the dispersal of the Union Nationale, the
defeat of John Diefenbaker, the ascendancy of Pierre Trudeau,
and the devastation of their party after Brian Mulroney. In fact,
Daniel Jr. may have been the first Johnson in generations ever to
vote Liberal—and only because he was an ardent anti-separatist.

Initially there weren't any major issues between us, except
for the closing of the Collège Militaire Royal and a few of the
other budget measures that were affecting the other provinces
just as hard or even harder. Johnson and I spoke on the phone
regularly, and Ottawa responded quickly and decisively in
February 1994 when he requested our help to deal with the
problem of tobacco smuggling across the Canadian border from
the United States. The price difference was making it so attractive a business that the RCMP and the provincial police were
incapable of stopping the flow, particularly when it passed

through First Nations reserves. Despite the wrath of most of the other provincial governments, the anti-smoking lobby, and our own Department of Health, we reduced the federal tax on cigarettes, effectively eliminating the illegal trade overnight.

When Johnson called an election for September 12, 1994, I wanted him to win—no doubt or discussion about it—and I did all I could to help without making him appear too close to Ottawa. Unfortunately for him, for Quebec, and for Canada, he was defeated by Jacques Parizeau. Still, the Parti Québécois was elected by only 44.7 per cent of the electors (a virtual tie, in fact), and many of them had voted PQ simply to get rid of an unpopular nine-year-old Liberal government. Don't give this problem to a political theorist, but the reality is that some people will vote for a local candidate regardless of party affiliation; other people will vote for different parties at different levels because they don't like to put all their eggs into one basket; and, while the dyed-in-the-wool separatists will never vote for the federal Liberals, a lot of soft nationalists and disgruntled federalists will frequently vote for the Parti Québécois. I knew that, and I knew that this result had nothing to do with how Quebecers would vote in a referendum.

I was especially infuriated by Parizeau's declaration on the night of his victory that Quebecers wanted to become a "normal people in a normal country." Presumably he was referring to the antiquated and impractical idea that every ethnic or language group should have its own independent state. But was it "normal" in today's world to want to split up a country that had been built on respect for values such as tolerance, generosity, and openness? To separate from a country that had allowed people of different ethnicities and languages to live together in a peaceful, democratic, and free society? To give up on a country that the United Nations had put first in terms of quality of life? To walk away after four hundred years of struggle and achievement from the prosperity and potential of a country that extends all the way from the Atlantic to the Pacific, from the North Pole to the American border?

"When Mr. Parizeau and Mr. Bouchard speak of becoming a normal country," I said in a speech to the Canadian Chamber of Commerce in Quebec City on September 18, 1994, "they imply that Canada isn't a normal country. It doesn't happen very often, I admit, but this time I'm in agreement with them. Canada isn't a normal country. Canada is an exceptional country. Canada is a formidable country. Canada is the best country in the world."

—

Early in December 1994, while I was en route home from a meeting in Budapest of the Organization for Security and Co-operation in Europe (OSCE), I received word that Lucien Bouchard had been rushed to hospital with a rare bacterial infection that claimed his left leg and almost took his life. It was a personal tragedy, particularly given his age and young family, but it turned out to have important political consequences as well.

Up until then, for all his gifts as a well-read, intelligent, and articulate politician, Bouchard had seemed uncomfortable to have found himself leader of Her Majesty's Loyal Opposition. As I knew only too well, there's not much satisfaction in a job in which your daily task is to criticize, attack, find fault, and be negative, especially after you have experienced the gratifications and complexities of getting things done for the public good on the government side. Moreover, as a separatist, Bouchard couldn't take much interest in long-term national goals. His primary focus, after all, was to use the House of Commons as a platform from which to denounce all the bad things the federal government was supposedly doing to Quebec.

There was a large element of theatre in it all. Even if the Bloc wanted to be as disruptive as the Irish nationalists had been in the British House of Commons in the late nineteenth century, rule changes had eliminated many of the filibustering tactics of the past. Because the Liberals had a majority, and because none of the other parties was interested in letting the separatists make a mockery of the Parliament of Canada, the government was always able to put a procedural roadblock to a vote and get around the Bloc. Besides, Lucien Bouchard was a rather civilized guy, even though he had a short fuse and could be extremely nasty in his speeches.

There were times, I'm embarrassed to admit, when I couldn't resist replying in kind. One day, during a Commons debate about independence, I really let him have it. "It's all right for you," I said. "Both your kids have dual citizenship because their mother is an American. So if things don't work out so well for Quebec, I guess they can always move to the United States. So it's pretty safe for you, but your buddies in Lac St-Jean don't have the same flexibility." Bouchard was so furious that he stormed out of the chamber. I had been too tough, perhaps, but what I said was true, which may have made it hurt even more.

His near-death experience, the amputation of his leg, and his remarkable recovery became the stuff of legend. At one point he wrote a note to his doctors that read, *"Que l'on continue, merci."* Though it was an instruction for them to keep operating as the flesh-eating disease advanced up his body, the nationalists interpreted it as an appeal for the people of Quebec to keep working for independence. God has spared his life, they claimed, because he had been chosen for a great historic purpose, and his reappearance on Parliament Hill the following February was compared to the resurrection of Jesus Christ. Even the way he walked with his cane kept the myth alive in the consciousness of Quebecers.

For the first half of 1995, however, most of the activity and attention of the separatists wasn't focused on Lucien Bouchard in Ottawa but on Jacques Parizeau in Quebec, as the PQ premier plotted and manoeuvred to prepare the ground for a referendum victory that would open the doors to full independence. He went to Paris to try to draw the French into his game. He spent millions sending a commission around the province to drum up support for his cause. And, on June 12, his PQ formed a common front with the Bloc and Mario Dumont's l'Action Démocratique du Québec, even though Dumont was opposed to separation and wanted to use a Yes vote only as a tool to get more powers for the province. Their agreement promised to negotiate a totally fanciful treaty between Quebec and the rest of Canada in which the two partners would manage the government and the economy jointly, like some two-headed animal. It assumed that Quebecers would be able to hold dual citizenship, work from coast to coast, retain the Canadian currency, access the Canadian common market, and remain in NAFTA, as though the government of Canada would have no say in the matter. And after one year, no matter what the results of these negotiations, Quebec's National Assembly would be able to declare sovereignty.

From where I sat, Parizeau's tricks looked like a distracting sideshow to the fundamental economic and social problems that Canada was facing. Paul Martin presented a particularly tough budget in February; Brian Tobin fought the Fish War in March; I hosted the G7 leaders in Halifax in June. Though we were concerned about any negative impact our program cuts, social security reforms, and transfer payment reductions might have on Quebecers, we believed that delivering good government, restoring confidence in the political system, creating jobs, and putting the finances of the nation on a solid footing would impress the voters more than trying to buy their support with reckless promises. Indeed, according to the polls, the federalists were in a stronger position in 1995 than we had been heading into the 1980 referendum campaign, which we ended up winning with 60 per cent of the vote.

Nevertheless, Preston Manning kept pushing me to come up with a Plan B in the event of a Yes victory, which he argued would be legitimate if the separatists won 50 per cent plus one vote. But for me, the way for the No side to win was to go out and win, not to spend half our time planning and debating what we would do if we lost. There were just too many possible scenarios to know how events would unfold. That didn't mean there was no Plan B or C or D. I was aware of all the options that had been considered by a group that Trudeau had put in place before the 1980 referendum (though I had told him that I wasn't going to waste a minute of my own time playing with disaster scenarios instead of battling for victory), and I presumed that the ministers were getting their departments ready to meet any and every eventuality: Paul Martin the financial and budgetary consequences, Allan Rock the legal and judicial possibilities, André Ouellet the diplomatic and treaty implications, and so forth. These weren't unusual measures—they were routine precautions for any government.

As for speculating on the size of the majority, I felt it was both inconsequential and irresponsible for Manning to try to play this sort of sport: inconsequential, because nobody inside Quebec paid any attention to what he was saying, and he could therefore say whatever he pleased; irresponsible, because it was crazy to argue that one vote is enough to break up a nation. Suppose one guy went home without voting because he had forgotten to bring his reading glasses. The Roman Catholic Church, not the most democratic organization in the world, requires two-thirds of cardinals to elect a pope; most corporations and unions require a two-thirds majority to change their charters; even the

Reform Party required a two-thirds vote to transform itself into the Canadian Alliance. Certainly, while Trudeau always spoke strongly in favour of democratic rights and respect for the will of the people, he and I had never entered into any abstract speculations about the size of the majority the separatists might need to achieve their goal. My suspicion was that Manning knew he could never become prime minister of Canada because of Quebec and, consequently, that he wouldn't have been terribly sorry to see it leave the federation.

—

On September 7, in the National Assembly, Jacques Parizeau announced the date of the referendum—October 30, 1995—and unveiled the question along with a bill asserting the sovereignty of Quebec. Instead of asking Quebecers whether they wanted to separate from Canada, yes or no, he decided to go with a question that was even trickier than the one Lévesque had presented in 1980: "Do you agree that Quebec should become sovereign, after having made a formal offer to Canada for a new economic and political partnership, within the scope of the bill respecting the future of Quebec and of the agreement signed on June 12, 1995?"—as though every voter in the province knew what bill it was referring to or what the hell was in the fine print of the deal Parizeau had signed with Bouchard and Dumont.

Whatever Parizeau's arrogant delusions and secret ambitions might have been for a quick, irreversible, and unilateral declaration of independence, he had obviously been persuaded by Lucien Bouchard and the polling numbers that he wouldn't be able to get a majority with a clear-cut question. Some of his strategists no doubt argued, as they had in the past, that the best alternative would be to try to sneak toward independence step by step in the same way that Canada had severed its ties from

Great Britain, grabbing one power after another, a bit at a time, until there were almost no links left at all. But those who wanted to move faster and more dramatically believed that the only way to secure a majority was to try to hoodwink the people.

That's why the separatists had replaced the scary words "independence" and "separatism" with the fuzzy notion of "sovereignty." Overnight the *indépendantistes* and *séparatistes* were transformed into *souverainistes,* and, except for a few foolhardy souls who weren't ashamed of their dreams for an independent Quebec, the separatists took offence every time anyone called them what they really were: separatists. In fact, the word *souverainiste* doesn't appear at all in the 1977 edition of the Grand Larousse dictionary, and in the *Grand Robert,* 2001, it is defined as an adjective or noun, originating in 1974, to describe *"au Canada, partisan de la souveraineté du Québec."* When that didn't fool most of the voters, the separatists qualified sovereignty with the promise to negotiate a pie-in-the-sky economic and maybe even political association with the rest of Canada, including the retention of the Canadian dollar, Canadian passport, Canadian pension, and Canadian army.

Jacques Parizeau's proposed partnership was no different from René Lévesque's sovereignty-association. Both were intellectually dishonest and pragmatically dysfunctional, though they had the virtue of allowing the separatists to hide their real intentions behind a veil of words.

In my judgment, they made a mistake in trying to be too clever by half. They would have been better served if they had been frank with the people from the very beginning. This notion that Quebec could, at the same time, divorce Canada yet remain married to it was obviously ludicrous, and it demonstrated the separatists' own lack of confidence in what they were proposing. I even heard one of them say on TV, "Sure, we want the best of both worlds, so why not ask for it?" For me, that was like a man asking his wife if he could take a mistress during the week and still come home on weekends. The odds of her saying yes weren't great.

—

Going into the campaign, my advisers had convinced me that I should limit my participation, even though a low-profile strategy ran against my political instincts and my competitive personality. I reluctantly went along, in large measure because I didn't want to get as wrapped up in the emotions of the battle as I had in 1980, and I rationalized my limited role by remembering that Pierre Trudeau had given only three major speeches during the first referendum, so why should I need to give any more? Besides, Daniel Johnson had made it perfectly clear that he didn't want me around too much.

The No team, an umbrella organization led according to the PQ's rules by the provincial leader of the Opposition, Daniel Johnson Jr., wasn't using the federal Liberals well, if at all. Many of our strongest and most effective organizers kept complaining to me that nobody had invited them to participate in any way; Jean Pelletier and Eddie Goldenberg felt they had to compromise more often than they wanted at all the meetings they attended; and when I went to shake hands with the volunteers at the No headquarters in Montreal, I was surprised to find how few I knew. The place was full of provincial Liberals and federal Tories. In fact, Johnson gave more prominence and attention during the campaign to Jean Charest, the Conservative leader in Ottawa, than to Lucienne Robillard, the prominent provincial minister whom I had persuaded to run for the federal Liberals in a by-election the previous February, rushed into the Cabinet as minister of labour, and selected as the federal representative on the No team, all at Johnson's urging. His staff wouldn't even give her his daily schedule.

When I shared the spotlight with Johnson and Charest at a No rally in Shawinigan on October 6, I wasn't very impressed by the arguments I heard—there was even a fuss because the organizers didn't want "O Canada" to be played—but I wasn't permitted to do anything except growl. It was very frustrating, especially when I had to take the rap for not doing enough.

One of the biggest hurdles for the separatists to overcome was the very real issue of the partition of Quebec. Logically, if Quebec can separate from Canada, why can't the English-speaking regions or the First Nations territories of northern Quebec choose to stay in Canada? And, logic aside, it would have been tough for the international image of the separatists if 90 per cent of the province's small, isolated minority communities begged the world to be allowed to remain Canadian. In fact, even though Parizeau had cancelled the Great Whale hydro-electric development the previous November in an attempt to get Aboriginal support, the Indian and Inuit communities of northern Quebec organized their own referendum and voted overwhelmingly in favour of Canada. I had been pleased, in truth, when the minister of Indian affairs, Ron Irwin, had courageously raised the subject in public in May 1994. "The separatists will have to live with that truth, Ron," I said to reassure him. "What is this notion that we can divide Canada, but we cannot divide Quebec? Remember, the Quebec of 1867 was only a small part of the Quebec of today. Ottawa gave it the northern territories, which had belonged to the Crown, in 1898 and 1912, so logically they belong to Quebec only as long as Quebec is a part of Canada. Quebecers have to be shaken out of their state of denial and made to think twice about the consequences of separatism."

Naturally enough, the Yes side refused to accept or discuss these implications, in the hope that ignoring the issue would make it go away. But even Johnson's team considered it too provocative to raise during the campaign, just as it wanted to hide the Canadian flag and keep any mention of Canada to a minimum. Though the strategy bothered me, I found comfort in the fact that the 55 to 45 per cent spread in Canada's favour was holding steady. Some federalists were claiming that we might win with as much as 65 per cent of the vote. More than three-quarters of Quebecers were tired of the subject; 84 per cent thought there were more important issues to worry about; and almost a third of those who intended to vote Yes in a second referendum also said that they would vote yes to remaining in Canada. We were helped, certainly, by the fact that Jacques Parizeau had none of the warmth, charm, or oratorical skills of René Lévesque. Though Parizeau could be pleasant enough in person, he came across on TV or on the platform as proud, puffed up, and extremely pompous. By nature he was more a technocrat than a politician, more an aristocrat than a man of the people, and it showed.

—

All that changed, and the world turned upside down on Saturday, October 7, the day after our rally in Shawinigan, with the surprise appointment of Lucien Bouchard as the "chief negotiator" for the new partnership with Canada that the referendum question was promising to achieve. In effect, as everyone immediately recognized, Jacques Parizeau had been pushed aside as the leader of the Yes forces by a rival who was more eloquent, more charismatic, and much more popular. At first, I admit, I didn't read that move correctly. I assumed that replacing a leader in the middle of a campaign is always a public admission of desperate trouble and likely to lead to an even worse defeat. In 1988, when some powerful backroom Liberals approached me to step in and take over the helm of the party halfway through the election campaign, I had refused, in part because I didn't like the idea of leading a mutiny, but also because I thought it would be an impossible task to turn around a sinking boat in midstream. And so, in my wildest dreams, I never imagined that Parizeau's public humiliation could be anything other than positive news for the No camp.

I could not have done anything to predict or control the bizarre phenomenon that was soon unleashed. Bouchard returned from Ottawa to Quebec like a prophet descending from the mountain to lead his people to the promised land. It wasn't rational or even credible, but crowds came forward to be in his presence and ask him to bless the flag of Quebec. The miracle of his recovery, coupled with his demagogic oratory, lent him an aura that no logic or fact could penetrate. He got away with declaring in a speech that Quebecers are "one of the white races that has the fewest children," an ethnocentric statement for which any other politician in Canada would have been clobbered. He held up the magic of a quick and easy partnership with the rest of Canada as though it were practically a done deal. Few reporters paused to reflect what it all meant or whether it had any substance because they were having so much fun with this fresh, dramatic story, and the sudden prospect of the breakup of Canada was selling a lot of newspapers. Meanwhile, my second intervention in the campaign, a speech to the Chamber of Commerce in Quebec City on October 18, got almost no publicity in the province, while a caution from Paul Martin about the negative impact of a Yes victory on jobs in Quebec was dismissed as exaggerated fear-mongering.

The next evening I received a phone call from John Rae, telling me that an overnight poll showed a dramatic reversal of fortune: the Yes forces were now in the lead, 54–46, and the No side was in freefall. No one had a clue how to stop it.

—

On Saturday, October 21, just nine days before the vote, I had to go to New York to attend the fiftieth anniversary of the United Nations. There, sitting in Canada's seat in the General Assembly, I received a call on Bruce Hartley's cellphone. It was from John Rae, informing me that the Yes lead was holding and we had dropped seven points in a week—a loss of more than a quarter of a million voters. That same day Daniel Johnson made matters worse by telling a reporter that he would welcome a constitutional change on the distinct society issue. When I was asked about it as I left a bilateral meeting with the president of Poland, I replied, as usual, "We're not talking about the Constitution; we're talking about the separation of Quebec from Canada." Despite Johnson's prompt retraction, the media jumped on his mistake as a sign of both division in the No camp and Ottawa's intransigence in the face of a desire for change.

To many of the delegates at the United Nations, it was both a mystery and a tragedy that an industrialized and progressive nation such as Canada, one that had ranked consistently at or near the top of the UN's list of the best countries in the world in which to live, should be on the verge of breaking up. If, with our history of tolerance and diversity, we couldn't survive, what hope was there for countries that had been built on centuries of religious or ethnic conflicts, dozens of different languages and cultures, and millions of people living in poverty and despair? Some of the leaders weren't just bewildered, they were angry. Instead of being a model toward which other societies should strive, Canada was in danger of becoming an example of the futility of imagining a more peaceful and harmonious world. And for what? To overthrow the shackles of oppression, injustice, or persecution? It was impossible to explain without drawing looks of disbelief and impatience.

Later that day, I met up with Bill Clinton at a reception, and he asked me how the campaign was going. "It's getting pretty tough," I said, and I explained my frustration at being prevented from doing what I thought needed to be done.

"You know, Jean," he said, "it would be a terrible tragedy for the world if a country like Canada were to disappear. Do you think it would help if I said something?"

I was sure it would be helpful because I knew how well respected and well liked Clinton was in Canada, especially in Quebec.

Four days afterwards, Clinton replied to a question that had been planted with a Canadian reporter at a televised press conference in Washington. "This vote is a Canadian internal issue for the Canadian people to decide, and I would not presume to interfere with that," he said. "I can tell you that a strong and united Canada has been a wonderful partner for the United States and an incredibly important and constructive citizen throughout the entire world. Just since I've been president, I have seen how our partnership works, how the leadership of Canada in so many ways throughout the world works, and what it means to the rest of the world to think that there's a country like Canada where things basically work."

Unfortunately, the president of France wasn't quite so helpful. Regardless of the referendum question, it had been Parizeau's secret scenario, if Yes were able to win 50 per cent plus one vote, to move rapidly toward some sort of unilateral declaration of independence, and he was counting on France's immediate recognition of a free Quebec to convince the Americans and the rest of the world to follow. In January 1995, with that strategy already in mind, he had managed to get a cordial meeting with the mayor of Paris, Jacques Chirac. Since it was normal for a Quebec premier to try to get his picture taken with as many French dignitaries as possible, and since Chirac didn't say anything particularly new or offensive, I simply dismissed their meeting when I was asked about it during a trade mission to South America. Referring to the fact that Chirac was far behind Prime Minister Édouard Balladur in the race to succeed François Mitterrand, whom I knew to be a good friend of a united Canada, I said, "There's no more chance of him winning the presidential election than of the separatists winning the referendum."

Jean Pelletier, my chief of staff, was furious with me. He and Chirac were long-time friends who had met while Pelletier was mayor of Quebec City between 1977 and 1988, and he had been working ever since then to pull Chirac away from the false arguments and devious tactics of the Quebec separatists. He had persuaded Chirac not to say a word during the 1980 referendum, had reasoned with him that the French fact in North America was better protected with Quebec inside Canada rather than independent, and had secretly gone to Paris twice a year after I became prime minister "to water my plants," as he liked to phrase it. Pelletier had even persuaded me to meet with Chirac at the Paris city hall in June 1994 despite my reservations about the French mayor as a right-wing Gaullist. So he saw my little barb as a setback to all his efforts, especially after I was proven wrong. Chirac did indeed win the presidency in May 1995.

Now, on October 23, in reply to a question from CNN's Larry King, Chirac said, "Well, yes, of course we would recognize the fact" if Quebec were to vote to separate. He did not say that France would recognize an independent Quebec. He merely said that France would take note of the reality of a Yes vote. So what? I too would have taken note if the separatists had won a very slim majority on a crooked question, but that would have been the beginning, not the end, of a long and difficult debate about what it really meant. Whatever Parizeau's fantasies might have been, the French would have thought twice before giving their blessing to a gang of separatists. After all, France has its own internal divisions, as do Great Britain, Germany, Spain, and almost every other country in Europe. What moral right would allow any of them to say no to their own separatists if they had said yes to Canada's? Nevertheless, coming as it did at our darkest hour, Chirac's ambiguous statement seemed insensitive at best and provocative at worst.

When I met up with him a few weeks after the referendum, in early December, at the Francophonie summit in Benin, it wasn't the most pleasant encounter he and I were ever to have. He was rude, arrogant, and unhappy with Canada over a number of commercial and diplomatic issues; I was rude, tough, and extremely frank with him about Quebec. "How would you like it if I showed up in Paris and shouted 'Long live a free Corsica!'" I asked, standing right in front of him and throwing my hands in the air in a victory salute as Charles de Gaulle had done in Montreal in 1967. Poor Pelletier was somewhat taken aback by the force of our argument, but he hoped—and half-expected, knowing the two of us as well as he did—that some good might come out of the no-holds-barred airing of our pent-up anger. He was right. Chirac and I became—and have remained—the best of friends from that moment on.

Skipping forward a few years, I believe that Jacques Chirac was finally converted to the virtues of Canadian federalism by the Francophonie summit in Moncton in September 1999. The existence of an old and vibrant French-speaking community outside Quebec was an eye-opener for him and the other leaders, all of whom were genuinely surprised by and impressed with the story of the Acadians. Even more moving was the visit to Iqaluit Chirac and I made together after the meeting. Chirac had a great personal love for indigenous art. He collected it, studied it, and ultimately built a beautiful new museum dedicated to it on the banks of the Seine as a cultural monument to his presidency. He was so thrilled to visit the North that he even tried to learn a bit of the Inuit language in preparation for his trip, during which he was also going to meet the French-speaking residents, inaugurate a French-language website, and drop in on a francophone community centre. One night, while we were having dinner, I looked out the window and saw the most beautiful northern lights I have ever witnessed in my life. We stopped eating and went out on the balcony. The celestial dancing was dazzling, unbelievable, breathtaking.

"You know, Jacques," I teased, "*this* is a federal responsibility."

Afterwards we flew to Cape Dorset, where he was excited to meet the artists and picked up some Inuit carvings, which I later saw in his office, and then on to Auyuittuq National Park, which I had created in 1976 when, as minister in charge of national parks, I had found myself in awe one day, flying over the spectacular beauty of its fjords and glaciers. When Chirac and I landed in a dry river bed in the middle of nowhere in a giant military helicopter, we saw a tent sitting all by itself, so we went over to say hello to the campers. They turned out to be a mother and daughter from Saskatchewan. Were they ever surprised to find the prime minister of Canada and the president of France standing there! And then, near the end of the day, with the sunset casting a golden glow on the snow, we flew over a huge, perfectly flat block of ice that jutted out in mid-air from the wall of a steep glacier. It would have been impossible to imagine a more beautiful or peaceful scene.

"Do you know what the Inuit call this place, Mr. President?" I said. "They call it the Seat of the Gods, and you may be the first modern European ever to see it." He seemed very touched. "And do you know something else? It belongs to us Quebecers as well as to the Inuit and every other Canadian."

Chirac immediately understood what I was saying. If Quebec ever separates from Canada, it will be separating itself from this splendour and from all the other privileges, benefits, and natural wonders of Canada. By coincidence or not, he soon became a supporter of federalism. Unfortunately, however, that came too late to be of any help during the 1995 campaign.

—

With the referendum now just eight days away, I returned from New York eager to move fast and hard to turn the separatists' lead around. At last I was going to act on my basic instincts and plunge into the campaign. The increasingly desperate No committee had already decided over the weekend to ask me to get more involved. They knew I could attract more media attention than anyone else simply because I was the prime minister, and, ultimately, no one else had the authority or position to hold out the hope of meaningful change. It was time to speak to the hearts of Quebecers rather than to their wallets; time to make the 20 per cent of soft federalists and undecideds wake up to the fact that Canada was at risk.

I spent most of Monday evening with Eddie Goldenberg and Patrick Parisot, planning and writing the critically important speech I had already been scheduled to give the next night, Tuesday, October 24, at a large rally in an arena in the Montreal district of Verdun. In 1980, Trudeau had used his final intervention to make a dramatic and remarkably personal pitch to the voters. I decided to adopt a more low-key tone in order to concentrate on two substantial issues. First I would assure Quebecers that their province would have a veto power over any future constitutional changes. This had been in the constitutional deal that Pierre Trudeau had reached with all the premiers in Victoria in 1971, before Robert Bourassa returned to Quebec and reneged on the agreement. Though René Lévesque had bargained the veto away when he sealed his pact with the Gang of Eight in their attempt to derail the patriation process in 1982, I had tried to get it inserted into the amending formula at that time, and I had supported its inclusion in the Charlottetown Accord ten years later.

The second issue, the recognition of Quebec as a distinct society, was more fraught with difficulty. Most Canadians were still highly suspicious that "distinct society" meant special powers for the government of Quebec, and though I remained more concerned that these words might lead to disappointment by meaning too little in practice, there was also a risk that, by addressing the issue now, I might look as though I was undergoing a deathbed conversion, out of weakness or despair. The phrase had become an important symbol for many Quebecers, however, and if it was what they needed to feel more respected and comfortable within Canada, it wasn't much of a problem for me to offer it to them.

When I phoned on Monday to warn Pierre Trudeau about what I intended to say, I found him as nervous as every other federalist about the polls. Though there had been a plan to get all the living prime ministers of Canada together to make a pitch for national unity, the No committee didn't want to use Trudeau, Mulroney, or any of the others in any way whatsoever. Trudeau was deeply alarmed and puzzled by the reluctance of the federalist side to stand up for Canada boldly and proudly, but no more than I. "Is it true that we're losing, Jean?" he asked.

"Yes, we're behind and it's going to be close, but I'm confident we can turn it around if we work hard," I replied. "I may have to say something you won't like about distinct society and the veto."

"You're in charge," he said. "Do what you think you have to do."

The traffic heading to the Verdun Auditorium was so heavy that Aline and I decided to get out of the car and walk the last few blocks, despite the drenching rain and crowded sidewalks. By chance we met up with Jean Charest and his wife, and all along the route people were on their balconies and porches waving and cheering their encouragement as we passed. Everyone knew it was to be a crucial night, full of high-stakes drama and high-octane emotions. At one point John Rae began to soothe our nerves by whistling the "Colonel Bogey March," and the rest of us joined in as though we were a small army marching bravely into a crucial battle with the odds against us. I regretted that I was going to have to stick closely to the written text, since many of my best speeches have come when I've been inspired by a historic occasion to speak passionately without any notes, but the content of this one was too important for me to risk flying without a net.

"I know that some people are considering voting Yes because they think it's the best way to bring about changes within Canada," I told the loud, flag-waving crowd of seven thousand federalists, with an equal number outside the packed arena in the downpour. "They think it would create new leverage. They think the only thing the Yes proponents want is a mandate to negotiate within Canada. I'm telling them that they're making a mistake. To all those who think they can vote Yes and stay in Canada, I ask you to listen closely to Messrs. Parizeau and Bouchard. For them, there is no question of renewing federalism or obtaining recognition of Quebec as a distinct society. What they want is a separate country. The country they are planning is not an improved Canada, it is a separate Quebec. Think it through before you vote."

The next morning I addressed a very emotional caucus meeting. Some MPs started to cry because they knew of my love for Canada. I too choked up when I reflected on the indecency of being called a traitor to my people, especially by someone like Bouchard, who had changed parties four or five times in his life. Though I still believed that the federalists had time to regain the lost ground and win the vote, there was a lot of scepticism and agitation inside the caucus and the Cabinet. There was even some whispering that I would have to resign if we lost the vote because, as a French Quebecer, I couldn't be expected to represent the best interests of Canada. I wasn't offended when I heard about this chatter. Everyone has the right to debate anything in a democracy, and it's natural for ministers to speculate about politics and government whenever they get together for dinner or a drink. However, I had won the majority of seats outside Quebec and three times as many as any other party. I would still have been the legitimate prime minister of Canada, elected across Canada by the people of Canada. I would still have had all the powers of the office. Nor did I think that any of the ministers, even the most ambitious or panic-stricken ones, would have confronted me in person or been in any better position to handle this difficult situation.

Nevertheless, I sympathized with those MPs and ministers who felt they were being forced to stand by and watch their great country fall apart without being able to do anything about it. They shared the desire of grassroots Canadians to find some way to demonstrate their affection and concern to their fellow citizens in Quebec. As a result, when Brian Tobin came up with the idea of organizing a gigantic pro-Canada rally in conjunction with one already being planned in Montreal for the Friday before the Monday vote, I told him to go ahead. Tobin and countless others immediately began working the phones and arranging the buses, planes, and logistics.

On Wednesday afternoon I taped a televised address to the nation, to be broadcast at seven o'clock that evening. I again promised to recognize Quebec as a distinct society and affirm its veto power over constitutional change, but I also made a pitch that would speak to the hearts as well as the heads of the people. I was in a very difficult position. On the one hand, I wanted to sway the soft nationalists and the undecideds into voting No by alerting them to the very real risks behind the question. On the other, I had to be careful not to trap myself into having to accept the referendum as a step toward inevitable separation if Yes were to win. I decided it was more important to set aside the unknowable consequences for tomorrow by doing all that I could to secure a No victory today.

"The end of Canada would be nothing less than the end of a dream," I said, "the end of a country that has made us the envy of the world. Canada is not just any country. It is unique. It is the best country in the world. Perhaps it is something we have come to take for granted. But we should never, never let that happen. Once more, today it's up to each of us to restate our love for Canada—to say we don't want to lose it. What we have built together in Canada is something very great and very noble. A country whose values of tolerance, understanding, generosity have made us what we are: a society where our number-one priority is the respect and dignity of all our citizens. Other countries invest in weapons; we invest in the well-being of our citizens. Other countries tolerate poverty and despair; we work hard to ensure a basic level of decency for everyone. Other countries resort to violence to settle differences; we work out our problems through compromise and mutual respect. This is what we have accomplished. And I say to my fellow Quebecers, don't let anyone diminish or take away what we have accomplished. Don't let anyone tell you that you cannot be a proud Quebecer *and* a proud Canadian."

According to the polls, the Verdun speech and the TV address halted our decline and pushed the No side back toward 50–50. We were also helped by the fact that Bouchard's TV speech, which followed mine, diminished his reputation in the eyes of many undecideds. Even I was shocked by how low he stooped when he suddenly held up the front page of a nationalist newspaper from November 1981, showing Trudeau and me laughing at a joke during a break in the constitutional talks, and then dared to say that we had been laughing at Quebec. It was totally unfair, completely untrue, and absolutely the worst kind of demagoguery. It was the crudest stunt I had ever seen in Canadian politics.

A few weeks later, on the afternoon of December 13, during the first one-on-one meeting Bouchard and I had ever had in my office, I told him bluntly that he was a man of better quality than his personal attacks on me had suggested. "You should be ashamed as an educated person of having distorted history in a way you must have known was not true," I said.

"Sometimes," he admitted, by way of apology, "it's easy to go too far in the heat of the moment."

On Thursday, with only five days remaining until the vote, I appeared on *Mongrain,* the popular supper-hour TV show that went directly into the kitchens and living rooms of ordinary Quebecers. On Friday I attended the pro-Canada rally in Montreal, surely one of the most extraordinary events in Canadian history. Though the organizers had initially planned for 10,000 people and the separatists tried to claim that 35,000 showed up, the actual number was more than 100,000. People from all parts of the city, the province, and the country packed the streets around Place du Canada to demonstrate their love and solidarity, cheering loudly and waving tens of thousands of Canadian flags in the strong, chilly wind. A few pundits argued that, far from having a positive effect, the rally backfired on us by arousing the fury and energy of the Yes forces, but I don't believe so. The No side had to catch up by that point, and the best way to lose was not to be present. Pro or con, the rally was the talk of the media for the next two days—and another reason for Quebecers to take a moment to reflect about the possibility of losing Canada.

The separatists were so cocky and self-satisfied that they began organizing their victory party for Monday night, but we kept working. All weekend the No team, by now reinvigorated and united in a common cause, never let up in its efforts to dominate the news and mobilize the organizers across the province to get out our voters. If we hadn't done that, I'm certain we would have lost. On Sunday I addressed a last-minute rally in Hull, where ten thousand people turned out to wave the Canadian flag despite the icy winds. On Monday morning I voted in Shawinigan, then flew straight back to Ottawa. We were all nervous, but also fatalistic. I felt optimistic that we had picked up the momentum to propel us over the top. I assumed that most of the undecideds were No supporters who had been intimidated into silence; I thought that the Bouchard effect, which had been based on emotion rather than substance, had run its course; and I felt happy that we had done our best. Now we could only wait for the verdict of the people of Quebec.

I watched the results in the upstairs sitting room at 24 Sussex in the company of Aline, my daughter, France, and her husband, André Desmarais, while various members of my staff came in and out all evening. Some couldn't bear to watch the screen for more than a few moments before going off to pace the halls or find a quiet corner to be by themselves. As usual in times of extraordinary stress, I became quiet, introverted, almost cold. When the first results came in from the Îles de la Madeleine, a small riding whose shifting electorate I always watched in elections, we lost by a large margin. "We won there in 1980," I told my son-in-law. "This is going to be tighter than we think. We'll win by one or two points."

The No side was behind for most of the evening, at times by as much as eight points, but when Montreal, the Eastern Townships, and the Gatineau Valley started to report, we began to edge back up. For a long while the numbers were almost exactly equal, tipping back and forth between a Yes and a No victory. Finally, at 10:30, it was announced that we had won by

50.6 to 49.4 per cent—fewer than 55,000 votes. Though it was a close call—much closer, certainly, than I had ever imagined going into the campaign with Parizeau as my opponent—I was happy and relieved. We had come from behind and regained seven points in the last nine days, and we had won.

While I was preparing to speak to the Canadian people from my office on Parliament Hill, Jacques Parizeau appeared on TV and blamed his loss on "money and the ethnic vote." That finished him, and he resigned the next day. I don't know whether he was pushed out or quit in a huff, but he must have felt doubly humiliated after being replaced by Bouchard as leader of the campaign and being denied his lifelong ambition to become the first president of the Republic of Quebec. That's why, whenever I am asked to give a talk about the virtues of political democracy, I always advise candidates for elected office to prepare themselves before the final vote in two ways: one, to get ready to say that they accept the decision of the people; and two, to prepare what they're going to say in case they're defeated tomorrow, even if they're certain of winning today. Over the years, I have seen too many politicians ruin their careers because they could not accept defeat graciously. In my own case, I had a concession speech ready, just in case, but fortunately I did not have to take it from my pocket.

I did not debate—and never will debate—what I would have done if the Yes side had won. Though the narrowness of the vote came as a shock to many Canadians, and though the country was clearly in no mood for a victory celebration, neither the people nor the pundits understood that even a loss would not have led quickly or inevitably to the breakup of Canada. No matter what tricks Jacques Parizeau might have held up his sleeve, the reality was that the crooked question had not asked for a mandate to separate. Events would have been chaotic, emotions would have run high, but a very slight majority for the Yes side could not have been interpreted as irrefutable proof that the majority of Quebecers wanted to sever their historic links with Canada. Resolving the problems would have taken a long, long time, without any certainty that the separatists would triumph in the end. In Cyprus, for example, the negotiations between the Greeks and the Turks had been going on for forty years, and they aren't over yet.

If Parizeau had been able to grab power back from Lucien Bouchard and had proclaimed independence unilaterally without the support of the people, he would have had to act on it. He would have had to establish borders and take control of federal institutions in Quebec. And he would have had to face a hell of a fight from Jean Chrétien.

—

The moment the referendum was over and won, I personally took charge to put the close call behind us, now and forever. The first task was to fulfill the commitments I had made in the Verdun speech. On the morning of Thursday, November 2, in Toronto for a fundraising speech, I arranged to have a secret breakfast meeting with Premier Mike Harris in order to get Ontario's support for constitutional amendments that would recognize Quebec as a distinct society and give it a veto on any future amendments, along with Ontario, Atlantic Canada, and the Western provinces, according to the formula that had been unanimously accepted by Trudeau and the ten premiers in Victoria in 1971. I assumed it was probably a futile effort, but I felt I had to try, if only because I had promised to try. Harris and I had got along well, despite our different views, since his election the previous June. He had attended the Canada rally in Montreal, and Ontario had traditionally enjoyed the role of a broker between Quebec and the rest of Canada when it came to matters of national unity. At this meeting in the Westin Harbour Castle Hotel, however, I found him in a grumpy mood, sick with a cold, and totally uninterested in reopening the Constitution.

Given that constitutional amendments were just about the last thing I wanted to spend my time on anyway, I immediately abandoned that course of action as dead in the water. Without Ontario and Quebec on board, I knew I would never be able to achieve the 50 per cent of the population required by the 1982 amending formula. I decided instead to ask Justice Minister Allan Rock to prepare a bill on the veto and a resolution on distinct society for presentation as soon as possible to the House of Commons. These two initiatives may not have been entrenched in the Constitution, I argued, but they made it almost impossible politically for any future government to stand up in Parliament and say it was going to ignore the provinces' veto or Quebec's distinct status. Bouchard and the Bloc voted against both of these proposals, yet another indication that they would never accept any accommodation with Canada.

As it happened, my greater problem was the people of British Columbia. They let it be known through their elected representatives in Victoria and Ottawa that they didn't like being lumped in with the other Western provinces under the old formula and demanded a veto of their own, based on the increasing size and importance of their province in the federation. I had no real objection to the idea. It had always been my desire to make the Constitution as difficult as possible to amend, because too many politicians want to make constitutional reform—like foreign affairs—an escape hatch to avoid dealing with the hard, practical problems of the day. But once we had tabled the legislation, I was reluctant to give in to the pressure from British Columbia. I was concerned that everyone else would demand concessions as well, and the whole process would start to unravel. My stubbornness turned into an unnecessary headache in the caucus, the Cabinet, and my own office, and after a few days I did what I should have done in the first place: the bill gave British Columbia a veto of its own.

On a second front, I set up a ministerial working group on unity, under Marcel Massé, to analyze where the country stood in the wake of the referendum, to integrate the veto and distinct society legislation into a comprehensive and coherent strategy, and to advise on any short- or long-term responses other than constitutional reform. In many ways, this committee was a natural extension of Massé's Program Review Committee, though charged by the crisis atmosphere and with different members, because it undertook a thorough examination of all the options to see what powers and programs could be, or should be, decentralized—not only to achieve cost-savings and efficiencies but also to promote national unity. Beginning almost immediately, the working group met at least once a week, and the debates became extremely vigorous between those who wanted to give in to the provinces' demands for more power or money and those who wanted to maintain strong national links or standards. I let it be known to Massé in very clear terms that, while I was more than ready to get rid of bureaucratic overlaps and contested jurisdictions, I wasn't interested in any plans for large-scale devolution. After all, Canada was already one of the most decentralized federations in the world, and national unity depended on a certain amount of national programs, national standards, and national sharing.

The Unity Committee reported to Cabinet by early February and got its principal recommendations into the Speech from the Throne later that month. We pledged restrictions on the federal spending power; withdrew from forestry and mining; pulled back from labour training; strengthened our partnership with the provinces on environmental management, social housing, tourism, and freshwater fish; and vowed to protect and promote Canada's economic and social union, including labour mobility and internal trade. We also took note of the committee's recommendation that we should raise the visibility of Canada in Quebec.

In the meantime, I had thought I needed some fresh new faces from Quebec in the Cabinet, as a way to show younger people and the opinion makers that we weren't stagnant. Watching the panel discussions on TV during the referendum campaign, Aline had been impressed by the strong views and cool rationality of a young Université de Montréal professor named Stéphane Dion. "That guy has a lot of guts," she told me, "and he's not afraid of anything. You know me, Jean, I like people who don't run away from a fight."

One evening, less than a month after the referendum, we were at home alone when she suddenly called me to come into the sitting room. Dion was being interviewed on television. The more I watched, the more I became as impressed as Aline had been by his firm, intelligent defence of Canadian federalism. It was something of a surprise because his father, Léon, a political scientist at Laval University, had famously advocated using the threat of separation as a "knife to the throat" to wrest more and more powers for Quebec, without ever thinking about the consequences for the viability of Canada. "He's very solid," I said to Aline. "What would you think if I asked him to join our government?"

"I think that would be a very good decision," she replied.

"I'll do it," I said, and I picked up the phone and asked the PMO switchboard to track Dion down.

The operator reached his wife, Janine Krieber, at their home in Montreal. When Janine was told that the prime minister was on the line, she was so bewildered that she blurted out, "What prime minister?" When she told her husband, he dismissed it as a student prank.

"Mr. Dion," I said after I finally reached him, "this is Jean Chrétien. I just saw you on a television show, and I'd like to have a chat with you. Do you ever come to Ottawa?"

"As a matter of fact," he said, "I will be there tomorrow." He didn't tell me that he was coming to give a speech in which he would be highly critical of the performance of the No team's leaders, including me.

So, without confiding in anyone—not even Pelletier or Goldenberg—I invited Dion to come to 24 Sussex on Saturday morning, November 25, 1995. He arrived on foot in a snowstorm and had to be escorted by a friend, or else he wouldn't have found his way to the house. When he showed up wearing heavy boots and a toque, covered in snow and carrying a knapsack on his back, I thought to myself, "Oh my God, what have I got myself involved with?" But we had a long and interesting discussion in the sunroom overlooking the garden and the hills beyond the Ottawa River. At one point Aline interrupted us to ask if Mr. Dion would like to stay for lunch and, in an aside, she asked me how our talk was going. During lunch I offered him a post in the Cabinet—the first and only time I ever made such an offer to anyone who hadn't yet decided to run for office—and not just any post, but minister of intergovernmental affairs in charge of the unity file. His first response was to say no, thank you very much: his life's work was to be a professor, not a politician. But I kept pressing, and he asked for some time to think about it. He also raised the idea of my inviting his friend Pierre Pettigrew, an international business consultant and former government adviser in Quebec City and Ottawa, perhaps remembering that Pierre Trudeau had not entered federal politics in 1965 without the safety of the two other "wise men," Gérard Pelletier and Jean Marchand.

About a month later, on December 21, Bruce Hartley went to the Ottawa bus station to pick up Dion and drive him to meet me at Harrington Lake. We talked some more, but still he wouldn't commit. It wasn't until after the holiday season, on January 6, 1996, that he finally said yes. Then, on January 25, he and Pettigrew were sworn into office, in the first major Cabinet shuffle since my taking office. Dion replaced Massé in Intergovernmental Affairs and took charge of the Unity Committee's report; Massé became president of the Treasury Board and continued his excellent work with Program Review; and Pettigrew was named minister of international cooperation. In March, Dion and Pettigrew got themselves elected to the House of Commons in by-elections created by the appointment of Shirley Maheu to the Senate and the retirement of André Ouellet from politics.

Poor Dion was barely a day in the job before a Montreal newspaper went after him for writing in one of his old academic essays about the possibility of the partition of Quebec. As we took a quick walk around Parliament Hill, with the media ready to pounce, he was obviously feeling the flak for moving from a university classroom to the front lines of politics.

"Stéphane," I asked, "did you write it?"

"Yes," he said.

"Did you believe it?"

"Yes," he said.

"Well, if you wrote it and you believed it, tell the press that you wrote it and you believed it. That's all."

Before long, I became closer to him than to any other minister. I had always followed Trudeau's example of never showing preference for any one colleague or clique in the Cabinet, because those preferences create jealousies and complications. But Dion proved an exception. For one thing, his job threw us together during an intense period when national unity was at the top of my agenda and we were both feeling under siege from the nationalists in Quebec. As well, he and his wife, Janine, became good friends with my daughter, France, so I often saw them together in a social setting. I used to invite Stéphane to come out to Harrington Lake because he shared Aline's love of fishing. Perhaps, too, I felt some personal responsibility to take him under my wing and teach him a few of the tricks of the political trade. To my enormous pleasure, he learned very quickly and became a star with a series of public letters he wrote to Lucien Bouchard and other separatist leaders in reply to their myths and distortions. His letters got attention because of their irrefutable logic and fearless honesty, though Bouchard never replied to them, saying that, for him, Stéphane Dion did not exist.

Ever since Trudeau's retirement in 1984, it seemed, too many federalists had been reluctant to speak up and cheer for Canada in Quebec. Brian Mulroney, like Joe Clark before him, figured that the best way for the Tories to defeat the federal Liberals in the province was to cozy up to the nationalists, many of whom had been the rural conservative base of the Union Nationale or the Créditistes. On the advice of the part-time federalists and avowed separatists who got important positions in his Cabinet and ministerial offices, not the least of whom was Lucien Bouchard, Mulroney went out of his way to attack the 1982 constitutional reforms (even though he had supported them at the time) and to cater to the politics of humiliation. All of a sudden there were no more Canadian flags on Quebec post offices or in its immigration courts—apparently to prevent some irate immigrant from striking the judge with the pole. Ottawa began doling out money to the provincial government without requiring the tiniest bit of public thanks or acknowledgment in return. Canada virtually disappeared in Quebec for a decade.

As soon as I got into office, I was determined to change that state of affairs. The taxpayers of Quebec had a right to know that their federal government was paying for half the cost of a road or a museum, and it seemed only fair and proper to order the Canadian flag to be flown on every public building or project that we were helping to finance. Of course, the separatists called us bullies when we threatened to cut off the funding if they did not fly the flag, the press accused us of seeking publicity for the sake of votes, and the right-wingers said we were simply wasting money. However, raising the visibility of Canada in Quebec had to be done, for the sake of national unity.

The situation got worse with the election of the PQ government in 1994. A draft bill on independence was sent at public expense to every household in Quebec. Millions and millions of dollars were spent to advance the separatist cause through direct sponsorships and subliminal advertising at public expense. Nobody questioned it then or later, but when the federalists tried to counter fire with fire, we were accused of unfair play or violating some law. After we almost lost the referendum in 1995, many of these same armchair critics began to shout that we hadn't done enough, we hadn't been emotional enough, we hadn't touched the hearts of Quebecers. Given how close the result had been, I tended to agree with them. Never again, I said—particularly after Bouchard took over from Jacques Parizeau as premier of Quebec in January 1996 and promised to hold yet another referendum as soon as the "winning conditions" were present.

In 1996, acting on the Unity Committee's report, I gave new purpose and $50 million a year to an established program in order to raise Canada's visibility and boost the profile of the federal government's support for all sorts of institutions and events in every area of the country. Like it or not, government sponsorship, whether municipal, provincial, or federal, is the lifeblood of many social and cultural organizations that are of enormous benefit to Canadians. Without this funding, there would be a lot fewer orchestras, museums, art galleries, ballet companies, and sports events. Even the Bloc and Reform members of Parliament used to complain if their ridings didn't get their share. As well, we wanted to match what the PQ was doing by backing events and projects that were the pride and joy of local activists. If the leaders of a small town or regional organization understood that Canada was with them, the message would gain additional authority and credibility.

In the program's first two years, for example, only a third of its funding went through Public Works and Government Services Canada for advertising and special events. The rest went through the Heritage Department and the Canadian Information Office to support, among other activities, Canada's athletes at the 1996 Summer Olympic Games in Atlanta, Canada Day events, arts awards, the Terry Fox Centre, the Council for Canadian Unity, a conference on federalism, sports teams, car and bicycle races, music festivals, tennis tournaments, youth exchanges, the promotion of Canadian culture abroad, and a host of tourist attractions across the country.

Though the program did much more than just show the flag, there's nothing wrong with showing the flag. Flags are an important way of fostering a nation's pride and spirit. If Canadians spent half the money per capita on the Maple Leaf that the Americans do on the Stars and Stripes, Quebecers, in particular, would realize that their national government doesn't just collect taxes from them but is directly present in their communities in all kinds of ways. For generations, when Montreal was the industrial and financial metropolis of Canada, the rest of the country benefited from the prosperity of Quebec. Now, when so much wealth has shifted to Alberta (thanks to God and the Canadian Constitution), the wheel of history turns and Quebec gets to share in the prosperity of the rest of Canada. That's the Canadian way, and that's why Quebecers have to see every day that they live in Canada as well as in Quebec.

The money came from one of the reserves that every government sets aside for unforeseen emergencies or unpredictable expenses—a drought in the summer, a flood in the spring, an ice storm in the winter, a union settlement, a court judgment. The reserves are like an insurance policy, except that Ottawa is both the insurer and the insured, and they are included in every annual budget drawn up by the minister of finance, approved by the prime minister, and passed by Parliament. Nor did I invent the idea of establishing a national unity reserve: Trudeau and Mulroney both had one. Spending it in Quebec during a period of budget surpluses to let Quebecers know about the greatness of Canada seemed like a reasonable price to pay to counteract the cost of potentially breaking up the country. If we hadn't spent anything and the separatists had won later on, I can only imagine the fury of the opposition, the media, and the Canadian people at a prime minister who had failed to take every measure possible to preserve the federation.

My instructions, such as those dated December 7, 1999, could not have been clearer, stricter, or any more in accordance with the normal rules: "Public Works and Government Services Canada through the Communications Coordination Branch will ensure that the creative services and/or media buys, sponsorships, promotions and any other marketing initiatives conform with established Treasury Board policy and guidelines and that they provide added value to the Crown. In addition, the Communications Coordination Branch will continue to ensure that all communications services, including advertising and public opinion research, are competitive as required and, subsequently, that appropriate contracts are issued."

Once I had established the spending priorities for the reserve, the president of the Treasury Board would be responsible for allocating the money to the appropriate departments. The ministers passed it on to their deputy ministers, who passed it on to their officials for contracting out to the ad agencies, the event organizers, and the various institutions. In the case of advertising, for instance, the minister of public works, Alfonso Gagliano, delegated the distribution to his deputy minister, Ranald Quail, who delegated it to Charles Guité, an experienced bureaucrat. As Guité later testified before a parliamentary committee looking into spending irregularities in the advertising program, the specific contracts were his to negotiate, supposedly under the supervision of his deputy minister. Certainly no one in the PMO or the PCO had the power to make decisions of that sort, and if Guité had ever felt he was under pressure to do something he should not do, he had the right and the duty to raise the matter with his deputy minister, who in turn had the right and obligation to raise it with his minister. Furthermore, because deputy ministers are appointed by the prime minister, they can always go over the heads of their ministers, if and when they think they're being dealt with unfairly, and come directly to the top. That didn't happen very often, but when it did, I invariably agreed to a meeting. In this case, I never received even one phone call concerning any sponsorship matter from the deputy minister of public works. As long as I was assured that the money was being used to advance the cause of national unity—and nothing else—I obviously didn't have any time or any reason to go through the program's hundreds of contracts myself.

I believed then, and I believe now, that the intent of the sponsorship program was a necessary component in our comprehensive strategy to defend national unity, conceived in good faith, noble in its objectives, and well executed on the whole by honest, professional public servants. I regret that a very few unscrupulous individuals were later found to have broken the rules and betrayed their colleagues, their government, and their country for personal gain, but I would have much more regret if Ottawa had not done all it could to preserve Canada.

—

By far the most important part of our multifaceted post-referendum strategy—greater than the sponsorship money or Dion's letters, the distinct society resolution or the veto bill, the limits on the federal spending power or the devolution of mining and forestry to the provinces—was my fixed determination to end the madness of phony referendum questions. Countless times, whether on long overseas flights or sitting on a chairlift, consulting with advisers or alone with my thoughts, I had reflected on how much these questions bugged me. Everybody knew that if the separatists ever had the honesty and decency to dare to ask a straightforward, seven-word question—"Do you want to separate from Canada?"—they would lose, and lose big. Should they ever win a clear majority on a clear question like that, I would say, "Okay, the people have spoken clearly. It's a crying shame and will set us back twenty years, but it's not the end of the world." However, I didn't think Canada should have to put up with the deceit and irrationality of sovereignty-association or fictitious partnerships a moment longer. But how could we stop the subterfuge fairly and responsibly?

A solution presented itself early in 1996 when Guy Bertrand, a disillusioned separatist, invoked his right as a citizen to go to the Quebec Superior Court to get a decision about whether Quebec had the right under international law to secede from Canada unilaterally following a Yes victory in a referendum. At first, because Bertrand was viewed as a controversial figure in Quebec, we were reluctant to associate Ottawa with his case. In April, however, when the government of Quebec intervened by trying to get the case dismissed, on the grounds that the courts were not entitled to interfere with the powers and privileges of the National Assembly, I felt that the federal government had no choice but to intervene as well. As Allan Rock put it to me, Quebec's attorney general was basically claiming that the Canadian Constitution had nothing whatever to do with the process by which Quebec would become independent—a stand that was both intolerable and nonsensical. I wanted to establish once and for all that separation was a legal issue, not just a political one, subject to the Constitution of Canada. I especially wanted to clear away the separatists' myth that Quebec had the right to self-determination under international law. In fact, the right to self-determination is recognized only in situations where a people are suffering extreme oppression or colonial subjugation, neither of which could be applied by any stretch of the imagination to the people of Quebec.

Lucien Bouchard took strong objection. "If you go to the courts with the Bertrand case, Prime Minister, I will call an election," he said to me while we were sharing the stage at an official ceremony in Montreal on May 6, 1996.

"Monsieur Bouchard," I replied, "if you call an election, what will happen? Either you will win or you will lose. If you lose, I'm all right and my problem is solved. If you win, you will be the premier, I presume, and I will still be the prime minister of Canada, I presume, and I will still go to court. So call your election. I don't give a damn." We turned our backs on each other and a photographer caught the anger in our expressions.

On August 30, the Quebec Superior Court released its judgment and agreed completely with the federal government's position that the Constitution was central to any talk of separation. It also allowed Guy Bertrand to proceed with his case. Rock worried that the process could drag out into years of uncertainty and confrontation. One afternoon in mid-September, he and Dion came to see me at 24 Sussex to recommend that we refer the matter to the Supreme Court ourselves, with our own questions and our own timetable. While aware of the possible objections and risks, I agreed without a moment of hesitation. It's the prime minister's duty to make sure that everyone respects both the rule of law and the fundamental laws of the land; otherwise, he does not deserve to occupy the office.

By the end of September, with the enthusiasm and expertise of Rock and his officials, Stéphane Dion had drafted three related questions to the Supreme Court of Canada. One, under the Constitution of Canada, does the government of Quebec have the right to secede from Canada unilaterally? Two, under international law, does the government of Quebec have the right to secede from Canada unilaterally? And three, if there is a conflict between the Constitution and international law, which prevails in Canada?

"We have to be very clear that we are not preventing a future referendum in Quebec," I explained to my Cabinet colleagues the next day. "Nor do we dispute that the Quebec National Assembly has the power to ask a question of its own choosing. Our message also has to indicate that if a clear majority of Quebecers vote on a clear question to leave Canada, the country will not be held together by force. However, they cannot expect to ask a confused question and think, on that basis, that the rest of Canada is obliged to negotiate the breakup of the country."

Two years later, on August 20, 1998, the Supreme Court was ready to announce its decision. I was with Jean Pelletier in his office in the Langevin Block when the decision came at 9:45 in the morning, and we were ecstatic. We couldn't have hoped for more. The judgment was wise, eloquent, and sensitive, and it should be required reading in every university in the country. In brief, the court ruled that a unilateral declaration of independence is contrary to Canadian law, nor is it supported by international law. To become independent, Quebec—or any other province—would have to take into account the rights of Canadians who live outside the province as well as those who live within it, the rights of the other provinces, and the rights of minorities. Everything would be on the table in any negotiations to separate, including the division of the national debt, existing boundaries, the protection of linguistic and cultural minorities, and the rights of Aboriginal people. Moreover, the referendum result would have to be "free of ambiguity, both in terms of the question asked and in terms of the support it generates." In other words, the question would have to solicit "the clear expression of a clear majority of Quebecers that they no longer wish to remain in Canada." Even then, for the results of a referendum to have any legitimacy, the secession of a province would require more than a simple majority.

Despite all the calls for an immediate reaction, I chose to wait to hear what Bouchard said first. I feared—and expected—he would do what Quebec governments had invariably done. Whenever the Supreme Court rules in the province's favour, the premier is quick to praise the judges for their wisdom and learning. Whenever it rules against the province, the premier is just as quick to denounce them as federal pawns and declare, as Duplessis used to, that the Supreme Court is like the Tower of Pisa, always leaning in the same direction, and therefore has no legitimacy or credibility in the eyes of Quebec. To my great joy and surprise, however, Bouchard seized on the one section that said, yes, under certain circumstances, it could be legal for Quebec to secede from the federation. For me, the fact that he had accepted part of the judgment meant that he had accepted the legitimacy of it all. I banged my desk and startled everyone by shouting, "Aha! I've got him!"

"The ruling yesterday by the Supreme Court of Canada is of extraordinary importance," I told Canadians the next day. "It is not a victory for governments or politicians. It is a victory for all Canadians. It protects the legal and democratic rights of citizens of our country for the future. It establishes the legal framework in which democratic decisions are to be taken. It sets out clearly the principles under which Canada has grown and flourished: federalism, democracy, constitutionalism and the rule of law, and respect for minorities."

That was the moment I began to contemplate a law or some other form of intervention that would set down the legal and democratic framework by which a province would be allowed to secede. At first, given the possibility that Bouchard might lose the upcoming provincial election, I decided that there was no need to take further action right away. But when the Parti Québécois won another term three months later, on November 30, 1998, though with a smaller percentage of the popular vote than the Quebec Liberals and absolutely no mandate to pursue independence, I concluded that the separatists' tricks and deceptions were not going to go away by themselves. The "winning conditions" that would prompt Bouchard to trigger another referendum could come at any time. The Supreme Court decision had made it explicit that it was now up to the elected politicians to determine what constitutes a clear question and a clear majority.

At first, among the small group of advisers I let in on my thinking, only Jean Pelletier and my press secretary, Patrick Parisot, were completely and immediately in accord. Eddie Goldenberg feared that such a move would be an unnecessary and ill-timed provocation, coming as it would when support for sovereignty was slipping in Quebec and everyone was sick and tired of talking about it. Stéphane Dion wanted more time to continue to engage the people of Quebec in a constructive dialogue about the virtues of Canadian federalism and to build up public support in the opinion polls. In my experience, whenever people want to stop or slow down something that the prime minister thinks is a good idea, they always argue that he's either four years too early or four years too late. Rather than confront the substance of the issue head on, they fuss about the timing or the process. By August 1999, however, I had made up my mind, though I still wasn't completely sure what kind of initiative I wanted to take or whether it would be kept in reserve for the time being.

Instead of proceeding by the usual route through the Justice Department, where Anne McLellan had succeeded Allan Rock as minister in June 1997, I asked Dion to lead a top-secret committee with a select group of officials from both the PCO and the PMO to help me draft a law. The more involved they became in the exercise, the more enthusiastic they became about the idea. A preliminary outline, dated October 6, came back to me for consideration, and I sent it on to the Department of Justice to be turned into legal language.

First, with regard to the clarity of any referendum question, the draft stipulated that the question had to make clear that a Yes vote would mean independence. But if the question asked only for a mandate to enter into negotiations, the lawyers thought that such a restrictive interpretation of the Supreme Court ruling could be challenged by the separatists, so we dropped it. Second, on the definition of "majority," we considered whether the federal government should have the *obligation* to negotiate if the Yes side won 60 per cent or more on a clear question, and the *option* of deciding whether to negotiate if the Yes side won, say, 53 to 55 per cent. This issue triggered the greatest debate. Though Dion and Mel Cappe, the clerk of the Privy Council, argued for some such threshold, the Justice Department countered that it ran contrary to the spirit of allowing the House of Commons to interpret the result according to the circumstances of the time. Third, we debated whether the bill should wade into the controversial issues of borders, Aboriginal rights, the division of assets, and the terms of secession. Dion was in favour of their inclusion; Cappe cautioned against. The October 22 draft that came back from Justice put those issues into a preamble, but Dion still wanted to include a provision that made sure they were dealt with before any secession went ahead through an amendment to the Constitution.

From November 7 to 20, 1999, I was overseas for official visits to Senegal and Nigeria, the Commonwealth conference in South Africa, and an OECD meeting in Turkey. On my return, Cappe briefed me on what had happened. "In discussions with Minister Dion," he wrote, "concerns have been raised about earlier approaches for the legislation. The latest draft of the legislation moves away from a numerical threshold and avoids a simple yes-no on the clarity of the question. It instead provides for the House of Commons to review and pronounce on the clarity of the question before the referendum (but not necessarily approve or disapprove it), and after the vote consider, if the question gets a majority, whether there has been a clear expression of a will to secede according to a number of factors."

I agreed. The breakup of a country is not a single, ordinary, mechanical piece of legislation: it's a radical transformation that is difficult to achieve peacefully. Therefore, the government of the day has to be able to interpret what constitutes the majority based on linguistic, regional, and social factors. If there were a territorial division of the vote, for example, the southern part of Quebec would probably vote to stay in Canada, and the eastern part of Quebec would vote to get out of Canada. That would have to be taken into consideration, along with the position of the Aboriginal peoples in the north and the split on the island of Montreal.

One day, I remember, when Aline and I were having lunch with a senior member of the French government and his wife at the French embassy in Ottawa, he said, "Mr. Chrétien, I would like to ask you a question that bothers me. Is it true that you said it will require 80 per cent of the votes to bring about separation?"

"No, sir," I replied. "I never said that. I have never declared what majority will be necessary, because you have to interpret the majority according to linguistic lines, regional lines, socioeconomic lines."

"So all you're asking for is a qualified majority?"

"Yes," I said. "And what's wrong with a qualified majority?"

"Absolutely nothing, Monsieur Chrétien." Then he turned to his wife and whispered, "We've been lied to." Obviously the separatists had been up to their old tricks in Paris.

However, the next paragraph in Cappe's memo showed there had been some nervous backsliding during my absence. Rumours had started circulating, and there weren't many people within the party, the caucus, or even the Cabinet who were applauding the idea of tackling the separatists head on at this time: "While the new approach addresses a number of important issues, it does not bring clarity before a referendum and it is open to attack both as provocation and as not being tough enough. Given the difficulty in using legislation to advance the government's objective of bringing clarity to the secession debate, consideration might be given to examining alternatives that would still achieve our objective."

I was determined, however, to proceed as planned. On November 23, during a particularly intense Cabinet meeting, Stéphane Dion presented the latest draft to his colleagues for the first time and invited their comments. Very few were in agreement. Most, including Paul Martin, feared it would be seen as a red flag in Quebec. No one, of course, spoke up in favour of ambiguity—how could they?—so their arguments focused on Bouchard's reaction and on when to move. Finally I said, "There is a large consensus here that we should do something about this problem, but nobody seems to know what to do. So I will do it for you."

I thought it prudent to try to get as many ministers as possible on board, so I sent the draft to a Cabinet committee for changes to the wording, but not to the design. Eddie Goldenberg and Allan Rock, a member of the committee though no longer minister of justice, worked with a small team of officials over the next couple of weeks to make the barriers and complexities involved in breaking up the country much clearer than they had been in the earlier drafts.

Even Pierre Trudeau was worried about possible repercussions from the legislation, though he never debated the substance with me. "People are telling me that this is very dangerous, Jean," he said over the phone. "Are you sure it won't wake the sleeping dog?"

"No, I can't be sure, Pierre. But I am sure that this has to be done, and it's better to do it when things are calm. If it fails, I guess I will have to resign and go practise law with you in Montreal."

"I'll back you up," he said at the end. "And good luck."

To my disappointment, many of Trudeau's former advisers weren't as supportive, even though the proposed legislation was in many ways tougher on the separatists than anything Trudeau had ever done. Senators Serge Joyal, Jerry Grafstein, and Michael Pitfield, among others, wanted me to go even further and correct what was, in their minds, Trudeau's original mistake at the time of the 1980 referendum of not declaring Canada indivisible. While it's true that there aren't many countries that have set down the terms for their own dissolution, Trudeau and I shared the view that a province was legally and democratically entitled to separate from the union as long as certain explicit conditions were met—precisely the view that had been articulated in the Supreme Court's decision.

The new version was prepared by December 8, a few words were changed, and I asked Dion to introduce Bill C-20 in the House of Commons on December 10. I was in my office with a few of my staff when I received the final draft for review. The first thing that struck me was the length and complexity of the bill's legal title: *An Act to Give Effect to the Requirement for Clarity as Set Out in the Opinion of the Supreme Court of Canada in the Quebec Secession Reference.*

"Nobody will be able to understand what this means," I fumed. "It's supposed to be about clarity, after all, so it has to be clear. I want clarity! Who can fight clarity? Nobody can get up and say, 'I don't want clarity—I want confusion. I don't want a clear question—I want a tricky question.' Why don't we just call it the *Clarity Act?*"

If I was determined, I was also nervous. One reason I asked Dion to introduce the bill in December was that that's the month we have both snow and exams in Quebec. Even the radicals don't like to take to the streets in a blizzard, and the university students are either hard at their books or home for the holidays. By the time they returned, the debate was over, despite Bouchard's best efforts to stir Quebecers into a fury. He made a few speeches and got a unanimous resolution in the National Assembly against it, but nobody paid much attention. In the Commons, of course, the Bloc and a few Tories voted against the bill, and I wasn't very happy when some Liberals and Tories tried to delay its passage in the Senate with amendments, but I was immensely pleased when it became the law of the land on June 29, 2000. I was even more pleased when, in a subsequent poll, 60 per cent of Quebecers expressed their support for it.

Pierre Trudeau had been right to say, in his farewell speech in 1984, that Canada had at last entered its adulthood. But the Canada I found nine years later was still a young adult in the throes of an adolescent breakdown. The constitutional brinkmanship of Meech and Charlottetown had shaken our identity; the fragile economy and fiscal mismanagement had caused us to doubt our future. Though far from having done it by myself, I am proud to say that my team and I overcame that identity crisis, got rid of the deficits, restored jobs and prosperity, and revived the hope and happiness of Canadians. In ten years the young adult matured into a well-established, well-balanced person, vigorous, responsible, productive, prosperous, and ready to compete with the best of the world. And I am convinced that the *Clarity Act* played a determining role in that transformation.

Following the 1995 referendum, as the economy continued to improve and as tens of thousands of new jobs were created, the separatists came to accept their defeat, and Canada regained its hope and confidence. Most Quebecers wanted a clear question and a clear majority. They were fed up with the uncertainty, the tricky questions, and the separatists' games. And so were most Canadians.

A happy people has no history, or so the expression goes. Perhaps that's true, but, like most Canadians, I prefer quiet success to tales of blood-soaked heroics. While the passage of the *Clarity Act* may not have been the kind of dramatic event that historians love to exaggerate, it was done in the way that Canada does so well: calmly, collectively, with peace, order, and good government. As for my own role, I am reminded of a quote from Voltaire, who was so hated by the good priests who had taught me in my youth: "I did something, and that was my best work."

SEVEN

SECURITY DETAILS

On the afternoon of Saturday, November 4, 1995, just five days after the Quebec referendum, I was informed that Yitzhak Rabin, the prime minister of Israel, had been assassinated. The sad news brought back warm memories of the times I had spent with him during his visits to Canada, where we had shared the kind of survivors' camaraderie that exists among politicians who have dedicated their lives to public service.

The threat of assassination haunts every political leader, and every nation has to devote a lot of money and effort to protection. That unfortunate fact of modern life had been made real for me on my first official visit to Mexico in March 1994. At the end of a day of ceremonies and meetings, while getting ready to go to the state dinner that President Carlos Salinas was to host in my honour, I was informed that Luis Donaldo Colosio, his party's candidate in the presidential election to succeed him and, therefore, the front runner, had just been assassinated in the northern city of Tijuana. It was obviously a traumatic moment for Salinas, who kept being called to the phone after I arrived at his official residence, and we agreed that he should cancel the dinner. So we shook hands with the guests, who had already assembled for drinks, explained the situation, and said goodnight.

The next day, after most of my scheduled appointments had also been cancelled, I decided to go and pay my respects to Colosio, whose body had just been brought back to the party headquarters in Mexico City for public viewing. Though I had never met him, I thought it was an appropriate gesture, so I headed off with my RCMP bodyguards. The street was jammed with a loud, hysterical mob, their faces full of sorrow and shock, all pushing and shoving to get to the door. My guards tried to clear a path for me through the crowd, telling them I was the prime minister of Canada and so on, but I kept getting pushed and shoved. As was my style, I pushed and shoved back and managed to make my way to the front with a lot of difficulty. There I was told that, because of the size and press of the crowd that had gathered, the decision had been made not to let anybody inside. I suppose I could have insisted, but I didn't want to cause anyone any more trouble. Instead, I squeezed round by the back of the building and left. I don't think I was ever in any danger, but it was quite an experience to feel so much unleashed emotion up close.

Even a relatively peaceful and stable country like Canada has had its share of such tragedies, from Thomas D'Arcy McGee in 1868 to Pierre Laporte in 1970, and there are always rumours of some plot or threat. It was police policy not to tell me about them, and I didn't want to know anyway, though sometimes I could see my guards watching more keenly or out in greater numbers. I never asked why—there was nothing I could do about it. I also knew that I couldn't take my safety for granted. Aline and I came to accept that our privacy had disappeared with the job. Now whenever she and I slipped out to see a movie at a local theatre, one of our favourite pastimes, we had to have the RCMP sitting in the row behind us.

At first Aline found it hard being constantly followed. Just after the APEC meeting in Seattle in November 1993, I remember, she and I were invited to visit some old friends of ours who were then living in California. When we went out to play a game of golf, we found half a dozen Canadian bodyguards and twenty or more Americans waiting to protect us. It may have made no sense in our case, but the United States has always been much more concerned with the safety of its prominent politicians, even after they leave office. Aline was too embarrassed to play golf with so many people watching her, so we made a deal to reduce their number to the bare minimum whenever we were on the golf course. Once in a while, as a joke, the bodyguards would hunt for a ball I had sent flying to the left or right and I would find it sitting on a tee in the woods. At other times I got a nod of approval if I was doing well—except when I played against my grandsons, because the RCMP always cheered for them and took their side in any argument about the rules.

In order to attend Rabin's funeral, I was told, I would have to depart on Sunday, November 5, a day earlier than I had been scheduled to leave for the Commonwealth meetings in New Zealand, for a stop in Jerusalem en route. So on the Saturday night, Aline and I left a pleasant dinner with friends in a restaurant near Harrington Lake early, without lingering for dessert and a coffee, and we got back to 24 Sussex by 9:30 to prepare for the trip. It was going to be an unusually long and busy one; I was still exhausted by the emotional stress of the referendum and its aftermath; and because I felt I had a cold coming on, Aline gave me a pill to help me sleep. She herself stayed up until midnight, laying out her wardrobe in the corridor and figuring out what she would need to take with her for the next two weeks.

A few hours later, shortly before three o'clock, she was awakened by footsteps on the floor above us. Disoriented and assuming it was the staff coming in early to help us pack, she got up to tell them to keep quiet so as not to disturb me. Instead, after passing through our bedroom and her small office on the second floor, she confronted a man, wearing glasses and a toque, standing in the corridor. He was in the midst of putting on a pair of gloves.

"Who are you?" Aline asked.

The man didn't say anything but gave a strange smile and looked down at the long knife he was holding in his right hand. Later he told the police, "I didn't want to harm Madame Chrétien. I just wanted to cut her husband's throat."

Aline kept her cool. She shut the door while taking care not to cause the loose key to fall to the ground, locked it, and ran back through her office into our bedroom. She shook my foot as she passed our bed, but kept running to bolt the main door to the second-floor hall. Then she dashed over to the side table and pressed the panic button to arouse the RCMP in the security booths at the gates. "Come right away!" she shouted into the phone. At last she was able to shake me awake. "Jean," she said, "there's a stranger in the house."

"Come on, Aline," I said, groggy from the medication. "You've had a bad dream. There can't be a stranger in the house. We're surrounded by security."

"No, Jean, I saw him. He was wearing a toque and holding a knife. He looks just like Forrest Gump." As she sat next to me on the edge of the bed, she started shaking like a leaf.

I finally realized how serious it was. And then we saw a shadow moving in the gap at the bottom of the door to the hall. I picked up a heavy Inuit sculpture of a loon by the neck, ready to use it as a weapon if the intruder broke in. He must have heard Aline wake me up; he may have suspected I was armed; and he certainly knew he was trapped. Without even trying to open the door—which was probably a lucky thing for him, given that the carving might well have killed him—he silently walked over to a bench at the top of the staircase, sat down, and waited for the guards to arrive. And so did we. Aline phoned them a second time: "Come right now! We're afraid!" Later we learned that they had arrived at the front door of the house without a proper set of keys.

At last, after a ten-minute delay, we heard voices, and I opened the door just as the Mounties were hauling the man away. Ever curious, I hurried downstairs in my bathrobe to have a look at him in the back of the police car. He gave me a funny look— that was all. "He came to assassinate you," one of the guards said. On my way back to the bedroom, I saw that the guy had left on the floor his toque, his gloves, and a brand-new jackknife with a blade long enough to have done quite a job on a sleeping man.

His name was André Dallaire. He had a degree in political science and a job in a corner store, was considered mentally unstable and socially maladjusted, and had decided to kill me because of his disappointment in the referendum result. His initial plan had been to attack me on Parliament Hill on Monday, but when he heard I was leaving for Israel a day early, he decided to act at once. He came along the escarpment above the river, climbed over the fence, and moved across the lawn to the side door. The two RCMP constables at the gates assumed that the moving figure they saw on the closed-circuit TV monitor was a third officer out patrolling the grounds. At that moment, however, the third guard just happened to be playing cards, I was told, with one of the governor general's troop.

After smashing a small window on the ground floor to get into the house, Dallaire went looking for our bedroom. But instead of turning left where he broke in and going through the living room to the front hall, he turned right, walked through my office, and found himself at the bottom of the back stairs. The stairs brought him to the hallway outside Aline's office, and so he assumed we were asleep on the third floor. Up he climbed, and that's why Aline first heard him overhead. If he had gone in the other direction initially and taken the main staircase up to the second floor, he would have arrived directly outside our bedroom, found the door unlocked, entered with his knife, and discovered me immediately in front of him, sound asleep.

In time, Dallaire was found not guilty of attempted murder by reason of mental illness. He ended up living in a group home in Ottawa, not so very far from me.

After the Mounties had taken him away, I couldn't get back to sleep, so even though it was still the middle of the night, I called my daughter in Montreal and a few of my closest advisers to tell them what had happened. Because the RCMP felt obliged, for their own obvious reasons, to play down the incident as minor, we decided I would tell the whole story to the press before getting on the plane to Jerusalem. Even so, the reporters didn't seem to treat it with any great seriousness. Certainly the Quebec media didn't leap to the conclusion that God had spared my life for a great historic purpose. For Aline and me, however, it had been a very traumatic experience. The night after we returned to Canada from New Zealand, she woke up at precisely 3 a.m., as though an alarm clock had gone off. At first she attributed it to the time change, but the next night it happened again and she realized she was looking at the door to her office. For a few days she slept at Harrington Lake or at France's house in Montreal, until she felt rested and the reaction passed.

One of the first things I had done as prime minister was to cut the size of my security detail as well as the staff in the PMO and at 24 Sussex. I thought there were more bodyguards than necessary, and I wanted to set a personal example at a time when I was asking Canadians to accept budget cuts in every government service. The RCMP had gone along with my request at the time, but now they thought it had been a mistake. Philip Murray, the commissioner of the RCMP, came to me and said, "Mr. Chrétien, security is not your business. Security is my business. If you're killed, I will be blamed, so I will do my job and will not take orders from you in regards to security. You will have to accept the bodyguards we'll put around you. It's our responsibility." From then on he put specially trained agents around me and installed more barriers, electronic surveillance, and alarm systems around the house.

—

Just a few months later, on Thursday, February 15, 1996, there was another incident, albeit a less dramatic one, that raised the security issue again. Following our victory in the referendum, Heritage Canada wanted to organize a ceremony across the Ottawa River in Hull on the day that had officially been set aside to honour the Canadian flag, and Sheila Copps invited me to drop by and say a few words. I was worried that it might be seen as a provocation by the separatists, but the organizers assured me it was only a small affair, mostly for schoolchildren—a decent crowd with no protesters. It was a short trip, the House wasn't sitting that day, and I liked the idea of celebrating the flag with a bunch of kids in Quebec, so I ignored my hunch and agreed to go. I even checked with the police on the way to the event and was told that all was quiet. As soon as I arrived, however, a couple of dozen protesters came out of hiding, blowing air horns and chanting slogans.

I have been in crowds all my life, so they don't make me panicky. Usually they're made up of a lot of friendly supporters who simply want to see me or shake my hand. Occasionally some demonstrators will yell something unpleasant, but they're quickly told to shut up by everyone else or are controlled by the police. This time, however, I was unhappy that the organizers and security people hadn't done their jobs properly by preparing me for what was to come. I gave a short speech and headed back to my car. My bodyguards and I were besieged by children, all wanting me to sign their flags, and since it looked as though the protesters had left at the end of the ceremony, I stopped to give a few autographs. Suddenly two guys rushed into the kids, swore at them, pushed them aside, and started hurling insults at me through a steel bullhorn. In my surprise and anger, I grabbed the nearer one with my two hands and flipped him to the side, though I don't remember the exact sequence. It had been only three months since someone had tried to assassinate me, so my reaction was instinctive and probably angrier than it would have been otherwise. Then, in a fraction of a second, I pulled the bullhorn away from the other demonstrator, because I was afraid he might use it as a weapon, and the police became all excited and flipped him too.

When I got home, Aline immediately recognized that something was the matter. "Didn't it go well?" she asked.

"Just a little incident," I said. "I pushed some guy."

"Will it be on the news?"

"Maybe."

But the news was big, and the news was bad. The separatists declared that I had finally lost my mind, that I had grabbed an innocent bystander from a crowd and almost killed him. The press even found psychiatrists willing to speculate that I had snapped under the distress of almost losing the referendum. And though the English-language coverage wasn't quite so wild, the TV clips and newspaper photographs looked pretty damaging, not least because the sunglasses I had been wearing at the time made me look like a mobster. My relatives phoned, some in tears, asking what had happened to me. Poor Aline was upset. She was always the one who had to manage the bad news with friends and family, and there's often bad news when you're married to the prime minister. "You might have to apologize, Jean," she said at one point.

"Perhaps," I said, though I didn't think I had anything to apologize for. Aline and I never fought or argued with each other; we discussed things.

Shortly afterwards, Peter Donolo, my director of communications, phoned me at home to give me the latest news. "Prime Minister," he said, "the *Toronto Star* has a front-page article about the public's reaction to the incident."

"Is it good or bad?"

"I won't tell you, Prime Minister, because if I do, you'll go out and grab someone else by the neck!"

Aline heard me laughing all the way up to her second-floor office. "Jean Chrétien," she said, standing at the top of the stairs, "if you can find something funny in that story, I'd like to know what it is." So I told her, to her enormous relief, that the *Star*'s polls were mostly in my favour. The overwhelming majority of the callers to one English-language radio station in Montreal had applauded what I had done because, in the words of the station's program director, "It's about time we have a prime minister who isn't a wimp."

I laughed even harder when Donolo told me that Bill Clennett, the so-called victim of what my RCMP guards called "the Shawinigan handshake," had claimed at a press conference that I had broken his dental bridge and should pay for it. "Don't worry, Prime Minister," Donolo said, "we'll cover it through the infrastructure program."

Three weeks later, at a meeting in Grenada with the Caribbean leaders, I could feel a kind of discomfort around me at the first dinner. A video clip of the incident had been broadcast around the world on CNN and everyone obviously knew about it, but it took a while before someone mentioned it. "The separatists in Quebec said I almost killed him," I said, "and the rest of Canada wondered why I did not kill him." They all laughed. A few months later, at a meeting in Vancouver of former world leaders at which Pierre Trudeau was the host, a former prime minister of Japan asked me what had happened. "In Japan," he said, "they say that the prime minister of Canada is a very strong man."

Working a crowd became a kind of instinctive collaboration between the bodyguards and me. Since they all had their own techniques, their own reactions, and their own understanding of how I moved and behaved, I found the system worked best when there wasn't a constant turnover. For example, I don't think that I would have been hit in the face with a cream pie by another protester, as happened during a visit to the Charlottetown Civic Centre on Prince Edward Island on August 16, 2000, if the local officers had been more familiar with my habits or had noticed that the guy was wearing a winter overcoat in the middle of summer.

The officer in charge kept apologizing over and over again until I finally said, "Forget it, you did your job, both of us were taken by surprise, and it didn't hurt. It didn't even taste that bad. And don't be worried—if I had seen him coming, I would have given him the Shawinigan handshake."

Later on, during a reception at Lawrence MacAulay's farm, I said, "Gee, you guys in PEI are strange. Here you serve the pie before the soup!" When the pie-thrower, a young man from Nova Scotia, was sentenced to a month in jail for assault, he was roughed up by his fellow inmates—fans of mine, apparently, who hadn't appreciated his abuse of the island's famous hospitality.

—

Personal security is no laughing matter, of course, and many world leaders take it extremely seriously. President Suharto of Indonesia, for example, threatened not to come to the APEC summit that Canada was to host in Vancouver in November 1997 if we couldn't guarantee that there would not be any protests against his government's actions in East Timor. I couldn't guarantee that, but I did promise that we would assure his personal safety as best we could. Because the meeting coincided with the collapse of the currencies of Korea, Thailand, and Indonesia and the economic problems facing Hong Kong and Japan, I felt it was important to have all the key players there, dictators or not. We had to show the world that we were not panicking in the face of the Asian financial crisis.

Still, we couldn't stop the demonstrators who came out to protest against the forces of globalization, nor did we want to stop them. They probably got closer to the leaders than at any other summit meeting in recent times, and they were given plenty of room and opportunity to express their views, however unhappy that might make President Suharto. We even gave funds to the People's Summit, a coalition of more than one thousand non-governmental delegates who were planning to gather in Vancouver just before the APEC meeting.

Everybody has the right to speak up in a democracy. We would be in trouble as a society if there wasn't a constant pressure to make reforms and to be just. Sometimes as prime minister, when I was caught in a really loud demonstration, I used to say to myself that I deserved it because of all the demonstrations I myself had organized as a student against Duplessis. I understood the anti-globalization protesters even when I didn't agree with them. For me, anti-globalization is often just another form of protectionism: people don't want to lose their jobs at home to someone somewhere else. At the same time they say they want to help the poor in Africa, Latin America, or Asia. That's a contradiction, in my view, because the very consequence of protectionism is to deny others the opportunity to produce and sell more goods. The reality is that the lowering of trade barriers has meant more jobs and more wealth around the world, no doubt about it, and as a result, there are more people than ever who can feed their family or get an education.

Maybe so, say the protesters, but the system has produced an unjust distribution of the wealth, exploitation of the powerless, and child labour. They're right, and there's no easy solution, but those were precisely the kinds of problems the leaders were tackling at the APEC summits, the G7 summits, or the Summit of the Americas, by trying to reform the international financial institutions, regulate the currency speculators, and establish global stability. In a fiscal crisis, after all, it's always the poor who pay the biggest price. They're the first who lose their jobs or entitlements, the first who go hungry, and the last who can tap into a savings account.

As chair of the Vancouver summit, I told the other APEC leaders that I wanted to stick to the agenda and have a joint communiqué ready by four o'clock on the last afternoon, not a minute later, or else the press would start speculating that we were having trouble reaching an agreement. I cut off any speaker who went on too long. I even asked Bill Clinton to stop talking at one point. Hard at work inside the magnificent Museum of Anthropology at the University of British Columbia, with its huge Haida sculptures, its breathtaking view of the sea and the mountains, and its garden-like setting, we didn't know what was happening out on the streets, where the RCMP had decided to use aggressive tactics, including the deployment of pepper spray, to break up a human blockade across the only road leading to and from the university grounds—and the only exit in the case of an emergency.

After the leaders agreed on the final communiqué and the conference wrapped up on schedule, I went to meet the press. I

Playing with President Clinton, Halifax, June 1995.

Working with President Clinton, Washington, April 1997.

"The Four Amigos"—Clinton and I with President Eduardo Frei of Chile and President Ernesto Zedillo of Mexico at the Summit of the Americas, Miami, December 1994.

Conferring with Caribbean leaders, April 1998.

Defending Canada during the Quebec referendum campaign, Shawinigan, October 6, 1995.

Daniel Johnson Jr. and I congratulate Jean Charest after his speech at the Verdun Auditorium, October 24, 1995.

Some 150,000 people gather in downtown Montreal to show their love for Canada, October 27, 1995.

Keeping in touch with my constituents in Shawinigan.

With Stéphane Dion, who took charge of the national unity file early in 1996.

After my confrontation with Lucien Bouchard, Montreal, May 1996.

Re-enacting the break-in at 24 Sussex with TV comedienne Mary Walsh.
Bruce Hartley, my executive assistant, is on the left.

Behind-the-scenes preparations for the 1997 campaign.

An unusual scrum with the Ottawa press, Rio de Janeiro, January 1995.

A veteran campaigner's favourite activity.

Meeting with our brave peacekeepers, Bosnia, May 1998.

A surprise party for Ontario's Mike Harris as the premiers and I head home from our Team Canada trade mission to Latin America, January 1998.

was feeling pretty good, I must admit, about how our agenda had been completed without a hitch. All at once everybody began shouting something about pepper. Because of my bad ear, I always have trouble hearing when there's a lot of noise in the room. "Pepper?" I joked. "I put it on my plate." If I had known what they were yelling about, I might have sounded less light-hearted, though it still wasn't exactly the massacre of the inno-cents. Nevertheless, the police behaviour led to complaints that led to an inquiry that led nowhere, and the press turned it into a little home-grown scandal of the day.

Calling the inquiry certainly wasn't my idea. I had learned my lesson with the Somalia Commission of Inquiry, which I had demanded in opposition and therefore felt obliged to create after I became prime minister. Instead of sticking to the allegations that a few soldiers with the Canadian Airborne Regiment, serv-ing on a United Nations mission in 1993, had tortured and killed a young prisoner, the three commissioners started investigating what happened before the tragic incident, what happened after, who reported to whom, whether this dossier was complete or not—any and every digression they could imagine. Their investi-gation dragged on for two years while the costs skyrocketed to above $15 million. When the name of another soldier or civil ser-vant was mentioned in passing at a public hearing, the govern-ment was often obliged to pay yet another legal bill. Then there was all the unnecessary expense of going on a fishing expedition through hundreds of thousands of pages of documents, requiring millions of dollars of taxpayers' money for a host of bureaucrats to gather, copy, and present them all. It was like going into the homes of ordinary citizens to hunt through their letters and chequebooks and then interrogating them about a note they had scribbled on a piece of paper ten years ago.

In these sorts of inquiries, the lawyers are paid by the hour and not by the case, so the more they keep asking for more and more documents, witnesses, and time to prepare and question, the more money they make. I remember asking one lawyer I knew why he was wasting so much of his valuable time on the Somalia file. "Because they pay me," he answered. No wonder there was so much bitterness when I decided to wrap it all up.

Of course, if you examine enough documents in an organization of over 325,000 people for enough years, you can always find mistakes, but the Somalia inquiry had simply taken on a lucrative life of its own and developed into a nasty intra-departmental fight. So when it became obvious that the inquiry was having a negative effect on the morale of our troops and leading nowhere, I closed it down, with the strong support of the minister of national defence, Doug Young. There were a few negative editorials for a week, then nobody ever mentioned it again. And I never appointed another commission of inquiry.

With regard to what the press took to calling "Peppergate," the Commission for Public Complaints against the RCMP, an independent civilian-review body established by an act of Parliament in 1988, was required by law to investigate any accusations of police brutality. But instead of proceeding quietly and efficiently as usual, its chair, Shirley Heafey, and not the federal government, decided to set up a public hearing. Sure enough, the whole business soon turned into a media circus, and there was even a fiasco around the composition of the panel, whose three members eventually quit and were replaced by Justice Ted Hughes. One day the CBC announced it had fresh evidence. Wow, I thought, fresh evidence, I'd better watch—and on came an interview with an Aboriginal leader who had been invited to say a prayer at the start of the APEC meeting. I remembered her quite well because I had had to prevent her from turning her prayer into a speech. Now here she was on TV saying that she had seen Mr. Chrétien giving orders to the Mounties. It's true that I was running the show. As the leaders arrived one by one, for example, I made sure that no one was left standing alone while I greeted the others at the door, and I was constantly issuing instructions, usually in French, to my staff to make sure that everything, even the small things, went smoothly. And because most of these guys were as big as bodyguards, and because the poor lady didn't know French, she must have thought she had seen Chrétien personally involved in putting down the demonstrators.

In August 2001, three and a half years following the event and after 170 days of hearings, 153 witnesses, and 40,000 pages of evidence, Justice Hughes's 453-page report found errors, inadequacies, and some inappropriate conduct by certain members of the RCMP, but certainly no malice or enough blame to justify having spent $12 million, including the fees to those unemployed student lawyers who were paid by the federal government to make faces at witnesses.

For the opposition parties, calling for a public inquiry is usually an easy way to dig up dirt or keep a hot issue on the front burner after they've exhausted their own supply of facts and questions. For the government, giving in to the calls is often a mechanism to do nothing, to dodge responsibility, or to postpone a controversial decision until after the next election. Very few of these inquiries in my experience have ever been of much use, and those few were valuable only because they didn't turn into television soap operas. If there's a problem, you should face up to it and make a decision. If you need more information, you can always ask the department to give you a full report. If you need an independent point of view, you can ask someone to carry out an investigation without a lot of fanfare, as happened when I asked Robert Nixon, a former treasurer of Ontario, to look into the circumstances around the Tories' deal to privatize Toronto's Pearson International Airport, which had been an issue in the

1993 election campaign. If you want to examine a broad social issue, you can set up a royal commission, as we did with health. But it is in the nature of public inquiries to get turned into show trials, kangaroo courts, and political entertainment. The rules of evidence don't have to be respected as they are in a court. There's not the same right of due process or even the same process to protect the innocent during the investigation into a possible wrongdoing. Scores of reputations are shattered for no good cause; people lose their jobs merely because their names happened to be mentioned in passing; and the entire public service is tarred by gossip and innuendo. Nor can an inquiry prosecute the guilty, since a prosecution is done traditionally in Canada by a provincial government acting on the evidence of the police.

—

On the whole, the RCMP officers really tried not to hem me in too much, and I became quite friendly with many of them, such as Pierre Giguère, a big, taciturn, very professional guy who also happened to be from my riding. Though the others didn't get to know me as well as he did, we all had a lot of laughs together. Once, I remember, one of them, a francophone, found himself alone with the Turkish ambassador to Canada. By way of making small talk, he asked His Excellency, "Are there many Turkeys like you in Canada?" We teased the poor guy for months about it.

Most of the bodyguards and I also shared a love of sports. Whenever I needed a golfing partner, I used to play with them, and when I went downhill skiing, I had to go with a team that was specially trained to protect me on the slopes. One morning I was booked to fly by helicopter to Mont Tremblant, Quebec, on government business and, given the glorious winter day, I decided to stay on to enjoy an afternoon on the hills. "I'm sorry," I said to the bodyguard, who had been off duty until summoned at the last minute to come with me because he was a skier. "I hope I'm not ruining your weekend plans."

"Yes, Prime Minister, it's terrible what you've done to me," he said. "Here I am, it's sunny, there's fresh snow, we never have to wait in line for the lift, and this was my day to stay home with my three daughters. Instead, my wife gets to stay home, I get to have fun skiing with you, and I'm being paid double-time. It's really a tough life, Mr. Chrétien."

Not all of them had such a wonderful time. During a Christmas holiday in Colorado with my four grandchildren at the end of 1997, one RCMP officer broke a leg and another broke her wrist trying to keep up with me on the slopes. I was supposed to travel from there to Mexico for a trade mission through Latin America, but when the famous ice storm devastated parts of Quebec and Ontario, I rushed back to Ottawa to help manage the crisis, which brought down trees and hydro wires, and left four million Canadians without power, some of them for a month. More than sixteen thousand Canadian Forces personnel were called out to cope with one of the greatest natural disasters in our history. Conditions were still treacherous when I landed for an inspection tour of eastern Ontario, and a couple of RCMP officers were at the bottom of the ramp to make sure I didn't slip on the runway. "Don't be worried about me," I told them. "It's probably more dangerous for you. You know, two of your buddies are in hospital right now because they couldn't keep up with the old man."

There were occasions, I admit, when I was overtaken by an uncontrollable urge to escape from my security detail. Trudeau liked to jump into his Mercedes and leave his guards in hot pursuit, I was told, and I sometimes had the same impulse for freedom that had caused me to run away from the school where I boarded as a young man when I was courting Aline. Having figured out a way to get under the fence that surrounded the property, I used to sneak downtown to see her and sneak back in when the priests were between their routine patrols.

In May 1998 I was at the G8 summit, which was being held in an enormous old country house outside Birmingham, England, surrounded by beautiful gardens, fields, and woods and heavily protected by security. Clinton and I were out at the back of the house, exchanging ideas as usual, this time about Fidel Castro and my recent trip to Cuba, when I suddenly realized that there weren't any bodyguards to be seen. "Bill," I said, "let's make a run for it." We rushed into the woods, as excited as two boys running away from their teachers, and went for a long walk by ourselves, coming back across a meadow and around a small lake about an hour later, to the enormous relief of Clinton's frantic agents. Beside the house was a stone wall with a ramp leading up to the terrace, and I immediately saw an opportunity for a little competition.

"Come on, Bill, let's see who can get to the top fastest." One, two, three, and I was up the wall in an instant. When I turned around, there was President Clinton, a dozen years younger but more than a dozen kilos heavier, struggling. One of the bodyguards rushed over to help him up while my photographer, Jean-Marc Carisse, snapped a picture, which was never printed in any American newspaper, me with a big smile of satisfaction and triumph on my face. Clinton had his revenge when, as the result of another wager we made, I had to wear a Washington Capitals jersey after their win over the Ottawa Senators in the Stanley Cup playoffs.

My other Great Escape took place in July 2001 in Italy, where Aline and I and our fifteen-year-old grandson, Philippe, were staying on the top floor of a very comfortable hotel, a quiet place beside a little river near Florence. We had just flown from Moscow, where I had met with Vladimir Putin and lent my support to Toronto's bid for the 2008 Olympic Games, and we had a couple of days to rest before going on to the G8 summit in Genoa. Everyone was on edge with warnings of mass demonstrations by anti-globalization activists and of terrorist threats—even two months before the al Qaeda attacks on New York and Washington—and the Italians had made plans to put the delegations on two cruise ships that could sail off into the Mediterranean at the first sign of trouble.

One evening, however, I got restless. "Come on, Philippe," I said. "Let's see if we can get away without being caught." So we jumped from the balcony onto a roof, then another roof, then a third one, until we were standing above a courtyard filled with Italian policemen. Philippe wanted to slide down a drainpipe and make a dash for the road, but I warned him that these were the type of guys who shoot first and ask questions afterwards. We climbed back to devise another exit strategy.

"Philippe," I said, "there's a bodyguard out in the corridor. Fake as if there's a knot in your shoelace that you can't undo and ask him for help. When he comes into your room, I'll go out of mine and I'll meet you at the end of the corridor downstairs."

It worked perfectly. When Philippe showed up, we walked through a gate in a fence, then through a tall, thick hedge, and then—sky! road! liberty!—we were out. For a half-hour or so we enjoyed a lovely stroll through the narrow streets of the nearby village and, gee, we had fun. Bruce Hartley had been having dinner with an RCMP inspector in a local restaurant when they got word that I had escaped. "The PM has left the room!" came the frantic phone message. "The PM has left the room!" They rushed back to the hotel and were in the middle of a powwow about what to do when we came sauntering into the courtyard, hands in our pockets, whistling a happy tune. The next morning, and from then on, there were six big Italian guys keeping a constant eye on Philippe's every move.

EIGHT

TALES FROM THE NINETEENTH HOLE

T here's a good reason why so many politicians like to play golf. Even more than the exercise, it gives them a rare opportunity to put down their briefing books, get away from their telephones, and have some quiet time in which to think. It's also a relaxing walk in a park with people who probably don't hate them, and a comfortable way to get to know what's on people's minds. In fact, I played more frequently when I was prime minister than after my retirement, not because I had more idle hours on my hands, but because I had more need of peace.

On Saturday mornings I used to golf in French and on Sunday mornings in English with a few regulars, not all of them Chrétien supporters or even Liberals. We had a lively time, and if anybody ever mentioned politics, I blamed them for causing me to slice my drive or miss my putt, and they would quickly

change the subject. Sometimes I used to startle people by showing up alone at the Royal Ottawa Golf Club, looking for a game.
One American visitor couldn't believe it when the pro asked him
if a fourth guy could join his threesome, and he found himself
playing with the prime minister of Canada.

I often played with Aline as well. One summer morning
she went off for a round with some friends, leaving me behind
in a meeting with officials in my study at 24 Sussex. An hour or
so later, the butler interrupted us to say that Madame Chrétien
was on the line and wished to speak with me at once. That was
extremely unusual for Aline. What was the emergency? Was she
in serious trouble? But, as I walked toward the phone, I somehow guessed correctly what she was going to tell me. "Jean," she
said, "I just had a hole in one!" The story got out and made the
news that night.

"So, Mr. Chrétien," I was asked at my next press conference, "is your wife better than you?"

"Yes," I had to concede, "on that hole." And, try as I did,
I was never able to match her achievement.

One of the most enjoyable games I ever played was at St.
Andrews in Scotland with Prime Minister Goh Chok Tong of
Singapore and his younger buddy, Sitiveni Rabuka, the prime
minister of Fiji. The Commonwealth leaders had been taken
there by train from our conference in Edinburgh in October
1997 and given an afternoon off to play a round on the famous
old course. The last two holes were by a road, so a number of
people were watching us. I was really nervous. Goh was quite
a good golfer, perhaps because the official residence he had
inherited from the old British Empire came with its own private course, and, my God, could Rabuka ever hit a ball. The
seventeenth hole was notorious for the very deep bunker where
Jack Nicklaus and many other great golfers had met their
doom, but I managed to avoid it. On the eighteenth I had a

good drive and followed it with a nice shot with a 5 wood right to the green. I missed a birdie, but not by much, and I was happy with my par. Though Goh and I were no match for Rabuka most of the time, I think—or prefer to think—that I beat him on that last hole. It was one of those spectacular finishes a golfer rarely has in front of a crowd. Maybe I was pumped up by the fear of embarrassing myself, or maybe it was because of the cheers of a couple of Canadians waving a big Canadian flag. A month later, at the time of the APEC summit in Vancouver, I had another match with Prime Minister Goh, and our partner on this occasion was Bill Clinton. Despite the torrential rainstorm that drenched us to the bone, Clinton lit a fat cigar and just wouldn't give up.

After Clinton's retirement, I invited him to play at the Desmarais family's private golf course in Quebec. We were joined by my son-in-law, André, my twenty-one-year-old grandson, Olivier, and his younger brother, Philippe. It was a cool, rainy day, and we were dressed in wet gear more appropriate to deep-sea fishing. When we reached the eighteenth hole, Clinton took from his bag a brand-new driver he had been given by Australian champion Greg Norman, and he used it to send the ball 260 yards down the middle of the fairway.

"Olivier," he said, "if you can do better than that, I will give you this club."

"Come on, kid," I said, "knock the hell out of it."

Olivier concentrated with all his might and drove a perfect shot more than 300 yards. Clinton asked to be given three or four chances to beat it, but he simply couldn't. After a while, Olivier said to me, in French, "Give him a bucket of balls, it doesn't matter. He's lost that driver." And now we have a marvellous souvenir of a great day with Clinton and my family.

—

In October 1999 I played Clinton at a resort in Mont Tremblant. Stéphane Dion, as minister of intergovernmental affairs, had asked me if I would invite the president to be a guest speaker at the international conference on Federalism in an Era of Globalization being organized by the Forum of Federations. "Do you have any idea how busy he is?" I said. "He'll never accept." But Dion is stubborn by nature, and so, to get him off my back, I mentioned the idea to Clinton during a recess at the G8 summit in Cologne that summer. "Please think about it, Bill. You can come in the morning and open the new American Embassy in Ottawa, we'll fly you over to Mont Tremblant by helicopter, you'll make a little speech, and then we'll play a game of golf. It could be fun." To my astonishment and delight, he agreed.

I had a bit more trouble persuading Mexican president Ernesto Zedillo to come and join us, not least because he required parliamentary permission every time he wanted to leave the country. If I had needed such a thing, I probably wouldn't have gone anywhere in ten years. On a visit to his home, however, I had noticed that he owned a collection of CDs by the beautiful Canadian jazz singer Diana Krall. "Ernesto," I said to lure him to the conference, "I'm so hoping you'll be able to come. I've arranged for Diana Krall to be there to perform all your favourite songs, just for you." A short while later he got his parliamentary permission and came. Zedillo was in heaven when he and his wife were serenaded by the singer in the living room at 24 Sussex after the lunch we held in their honour. It was one more proof of the benefits that the arts and culture can contribute to a society, even in the realm of international politics.

Just before Clinton was about to speak, he leaned over, asked me about a couple of people, jotted down their names, and glanced through his binder. Then he stood up and delivered a long, thoughtful speech about federalism without once reading from his text or turning a page. It was a truly impressive feat of learning and oratory. "It is especially fitting that this conference be held in Canada," he said. "A land larger than China, spanning five time zones and ten distinct provinces, it has shown the world how people with different cultures and languages can live in peace, prosperity, and mutual respect. In the United States we have valued our relationship with a strong and united Canada. We looked to you; we learned from you. The partnership you have built between people of diverse backgrounds and governments at all levels is what this conference is about and ultimately what democracy must be about, as people all over the world move around more, mix with each other more, live in close proximity more."

Before the conference started, Lucien Bouchard had asked if he could speak in his capacity as the current chair of the annual premiers' conference, with the promise that he wouldn't talk about separatism. He also pressed for a private meeting with the president as premier of the host province. Though the Americans were reluctant to give the separatists any credibility, they agreed to ten minutes, as long as Bouchard stuck to certain neutral topics. When he used his speech as a platform to promote the cause of independence, they were so furious that they threatened to cancel his one-on-one with Clinton and wouldn't allow a photographer to be present. It was their battle, and Ottawa stayed out of it, but I can't say I was disappointed when the meeting was cut short because Clinton had to rush off to something he considered more important—his golf game with me.

The game started late anyway, and we ended up playing the final holes after sunset, with the lights of the utility vehicles illuminating the fairways, and security guards holding flashlights on the greens. It reminded me of my old story about how, when I was a boy, French Canadians were allowed to play at the very Anglo golf club in Grand'Mère only at night. No wonder my handicap is so bad, I joked. Now here I was, half a century later, the prime minister of Canada with the president of the United States as my guest, and I still had to play in the dark.

—

In June 2001, after a Canada–European Union summit in Sweden, Bruce Hartley and I were scheduled to fly back to Canada on one of the government's old Challengers. That plane, which I normally used on domestic trips, had seen better days, though there was never much publicity about all its mishaps and near misses. One time, I remember, on a flight from Quebec City to Ottawa with Gordon Giffin, the U.S. ambassador to Canada at the time, on board, it lost an engine—a mishap that was not only scary but hardly a good advertisement for a country that manufactures airplanes. On this occasion, the Challenger's decompression system malfunctioned at 27,000 feet. We lost cabin pressure, our ears popped, the plane plunged thousands of feet in mere seconds, and Bruce and I had to put on emergency oxygen masks to help us breathe. We hobbled back to Stockholm, and I managed to catch a ride to Quebec City on the Canadian Forces Airbus, which was soon to depart with the ministers of foreign affairs and international trade, the officials, and the media on board.

As soon as we landed, a military doctor rushed up to give me a medical examination. I didn't know it, but anyone who has experienced a lack of pressure on an airplane isn't supposed to get on another flight for seventy-two hours. The doctor examined me and said, "You're okay, just take it easy," and I continued on to Shawinigan by car. By this time it was morning and I found I couldn't sleep, so I called Bruce Hartley and invited him to play golf. Strangely enough, we both played the best game of our lives. If you want to play a really good round of golf, I've told my friends ever since, all you have to do is get somebody to try to throttle you just before the game so you're a bit short of oxygen.

—

Three months later, on September 5, 2001, at a pro-am event preceding the Canadian Open at the Royal Montreal Golf Club, I was invited to play a round with Tiger Woods. Nothing in the game of politics had ever been as nerve-racking as that game of golf. Not only did Woods take our round seriously, but we were followed the whole way by thousands of avid spectators and play-by-play radio reporters. Though I managed a decent drive off the first tee, I didn't play very well. The pressure was excruciating, and so was the humiliation. Even when I had a good shot, Tiger's was always a lot better.

Woods was nice to me and we chatted comfortably, though he obviously preferred to keep his mind on his game. His concentration was a wonder to behold: he wouldn't sign autographs or interact with the crowd, so it was left to me to satisfy them by shaking hands and making jokes. A few times, I had to rush back to my ball while Tiger waited a bit impatiently. On the seventh hole, just to keep the game moving, I broke a rule and picked up my ball after knocking it back and forth from one bunker to another trying to get it on the green. As a penalty, I was given a 7 on a par 3, but I could have been given 100 and it wouldn't have made any difference. "I'm playing okay," I joked. "It's the course that's crooked." In the end, I wound up with a 92 to Tiger's 64. I had all sorts of excuses and distractions, of course, but the plain truth was that I was only the prime minister of Canada. He was Tiger Woods.

NINE

BUT WHO WATCHES THE DOG?

O n April 27, 1997, three years and seven months into my first mandate, I went to Rideau Hall to ask the governor general, Roméo LeBlanc, to dissolve Parliament and call a national election for June 2. By law there must be a vote at least once every five years. In practice, most governments, unless they are in serious trouble, think about calling one after four years, mostly because the opposition parties and the media start making life very difficult as soon as the countdown begins. However, there was nothing under our rules and traditions to prevent a Canadian prime minister from holding a snap election at any time, except the risk of being punished for political opportunism, as happened to David Peterson in Ontario in 1990.

Though there has been some movement toward establishing American-style fixed terms, the idea conflicts with the fundamental parliamentary principle that a government has tenure as long as it has the confidence of the House of Commons. If a government loses that confidence and falls on a serious matter, then the fixed term is meaningless. Or if there's a major crisis in the middle of a fixed term, the government of the day may want to get a new and clear mandate from the people before it responds. In my opinion, therefore, such institutional reforms should never be promised rashly and must always be implemented with prudence.

Now was the appropriate time, I thought, to give Canadians a chance to judge what we had accomplished to date and for us to ask for a second mandate to lead the country into the new millennium. While we were still in the process of implementing our key promises in the Red Book, we had come a long way in achieving the three major priorities I had set for the government in the fall of 1993: keeping the International Monetary Fund from the door, maintaining our independence from the United States, and preserving the unity of the nation. Though some regions and sectors weren't happy with the reforms we had made in our struggle against the deficit, confidence in the national government had been restored and we had an impressive economic record on which to campaign. We were through the darkest days of the cuts and on the eve of a balanced budget, the first since 1969–70. We had the fastest-growing economy in the G7, including the United States. Almost 800,000 new jobs had been created since 1993, and unemployment was down to 9.6 per cent, the lowest in nineteen years. Interest rates were down and still falling. Our international competitiveness rating had jumped to fourth place from sixteenth in three years.

One of our government's most important achievements was to put the Canada Pension Plan (CPP) on a sound financial footing. When the plan had been introduced in 1966, there were eight working-age people for every retired person in Canada.

Thirty years later, there were only five. In another thirty years, according to the projections, there would be three. Given these numbers, you didn't have to be a mathematician to understand that the CPP fund would be exhausted by the year 2015 if current contribution rates and low returns on its investments were maintained where they were. However, Lloyd Axworthy, in his capacity as minister of human resources development, was vehemently opposed to changing the entitlement age. Paul Martin didn't have strong views about it one way or the other, and I concluded that there were only so many political battles we could take on for the moment.

It would have been relatively easy to dodge the long-term issue altogether and do what previous governments have done— nothing—but that would have been an abdication of this generation's responsibility to our children and grandchildren. We also rejected the advice of the Reform Party and its friends in the financial services industry to wash our hands of the problem and replace the public pension system entirely with some kind of super Registered Retirement Saving Plan. No matter how wise an RRSP may be as a private investment for those who can afford to bear the risks, the whims of an ever-fluctuating stock market couldn't give ordinary Canadians the security and predictability they feel knowing that their government is standing behind their hard-earned retirement income. "Canada isn't about the fittest—or the fattest," I used to argue in speeches at the time. "It's about pooling risk and caring for one another. It's about providing a basic minimum for those who have worked all their lives to build this great country." And so we sought the necessary agreement of the provinces, set up the CPP Investment Board in December 1997 with a mandate to generate a greater return on capital, and increased the annual premiums from businesses, government, employers, employees—everybody. We removed some of the sting by reducing the Unemployment

Insurance payroll tax, in stages, from $3.30 per $100 of earnings to $1.98 by 2003.

At a private dinner in Florida one evening, I listened while Peter Peterson, a leading American businessman who had been Richard Nixon's secretary of commerce, argued that all national pension programs were headed for bankruptcy because they were based on future payments that would be impossible to cover. We exchanged a few letters afterwards and, by the end, he had to admit that Canada was the first major industrialized country to make its public pension system actuarially sound for the next fifty to seventy-five years. This stabilization had been accomplished in the way I most preferred: without a lot of trumpets or controversy, even at the price of appearing easy and routine.

Meanwhile, Canada-U.S. trade continued to grow under NAFTA, and relations between the two countries were warm and respectful. Early in April 1997, I had paid my first official visit to the United States to meet with President Clinton. We discussed global affairs and the regular list of bilateral irritants: softwood lumber, Pacific salmon, durum wheat, and the impact of American magazines, television, and films on Canadian culture. The evening before the formal sessions were to take place in the Cabinet Room, during which members of our Cabinets would report on the progress being made in their various files, Clinton spontaneously phoned to invite me to drop in to the White House for a casual tête-à-tête at nine o'clock. Alone in his study in his private quarters for about an hour and a half, with portraits of U.S. presidents staring down from its dark red walls, we surveyed the political scene in our two countries in the comfort of two armchairs and ranged over a host of world issues from Bosnia to Haiti, from the upcoming G7 summit in Denver to the reform of the United Nations, from landmines to Cuba.

Because Clinton was so intelligent and well briefed, I rarely had to raise my voice or explain the same thing ten times over for him to get the point. He immediately understood, for example, the problem we were facing when American magazines such as *Time* or *Sports Illustrated* could print an extra edition for pennies a copy, fill it with cut-rate Canadian advertisements, and dump it north of the border with little or no Canadian editorial content. It threatened not only our magazine industry but our cultural identity, which was why we had pushed so hard to be allowed to protect our cultural industries under NAFTA. Despite enormous pressure from the very powerful American media lobby, Clinton took the rare step of basically ordering his officials to come to an acceptable compromise with Canada.

The only mishap occurred at our final press conference, when I was asked about a reported increase in the amount of drugs coming across the border. Because of my bad ear, I heard "trucks" instead of "drugs." "No problem," I answered, "it's more trade."

I thought Clinton was going to die laughing. "I'm glad we clarified that," he said. "Otherwise you'd have to delay calling the election!"

Back in Ottawa, the opposition was divided and in disarray. Reform and the Tories were still a long way from merging, and neither party was in a credible position to criticize us for not cutting the deficit enough. The NDP under Alexa McDonough, however pleasant she was as a person, was still a captive of the unions' fiscal and protectionist policies and out of sync with the public mood, as demonstrated, in Ontario, by the defeat of Bob Rae's government by Mike Harris's very conservative Common Sense Revolution in 1995. The Bloc Québécois was wounded by the loss of the referendum and by Lucien Bouchard's subsequent departure from Ottawa to succeed Jacques Parizeau as premier of Quebec. According to the opinion polls and my own instincts, there might never be a better moment for the Liberals to win a second majority, especially if the typical four- or five-year cycle began to turn downwards, the stock market got jittery, and the period of growth we had been enjoying came to an end.

The only thing that gave me hesitation was the flooding of the Red River, which, in late April, had wreaked havoc on a large area of southern Manitoba and threatened to drown the city of Winnipeg. In hindsight, I should have postponed the election for a month. Tens of thousands of people were still evacuated from their homes, campaigning was virtually impossible in parts of the province, and we weren't even sure that the voters in one or two ridings would be able to cast their ballots. Not only did I appear insensitive by pressing ahead once my decision had been made and the electoral machinery set in motion, but I seemed cold-hearted and calculating when I showed up at the scene just before the election call and dropped a symbolic bag of sand on the hastily constructed dam. That one photo op undid most of the good work the federal government had done—sending in 8,500 members of the Canadian Forces from across the country, calling President Clinton to help with water management issues on the American side of the border, setting up assistance programs with the provincial and municipal governments, and offering to pay 90 per cent of the damages.

Otherwise, the Liberal campaign went quite well. Our second Red Book promised to keep us working toward a balanced budget, to put new resources into health care and child poverty, and to help Canada compete in the new global economy through grants to education, research, and advanced technology. Preston Manning simply didn't have a competitive agenda. Unable to fight us on the big issues of the deficit and jobs, he was reduced to the petty politics of trying to embarrass the Liberals on trivial matters, such as releasing a leaked copy of our platform in advance of its official launch, or he got sidetracked by his half-baked ideas about direct democracy and Senate reform.

Some of these ideas may have sounded reasonable enough on paper, but in practice made no sense whatsoever—not to mention the waste of time and energy required to get them enacted when so many other more important matters demanded attention. At first blush, for example, an elected Senate might seem like a desirable improvement over a Senate whose members are appointed by the prime minister and remain in office until the age of seventy-five. But suppose the House of Commons has a Liberal majority and the Senate has a Conservative majority, both elected by the voters of Canada. Which one is the legitimate representative of the will of the people? Which one should prevail in a dispute? Should the senators be elected at the same time as the MPs, and for how long? What powers should they have? Should the existing composition of the Senate be altered by a constitutional amendment? If so, are New Brunswick and Prince Edward Island ready to give up the seats they were guaranteed in 1867? Manning, in other words, was going to get himself into a political trap by tinkering, just for the sake of tinkering, with a complex system that had actually been working quite well. Those who live off the difficulties of government, I have noticed, often become great advocates of measures that would make the operation of government even more difficult, whereas logically they should be trying to make government function better.

I can't say I had gotten to know Manning well. We talked a couple of times in my office at the beginning; we said hello to each other at receptions; he said some positive things about my being a decent family man; I spoke to him about the career of his father, Ernest Manning, the former premier of Alberta, with whom I had swapped stories when he was in the Senate. But Preston was too much of a preacher's son for my taste. Like many of the holier-than-thou people who liked to lecture others about their high moral standards, he was also a bit of a hypocrite. For a short while, for example, he sat in the second row in the House of Commons to show his humility, but that act didn't last very long, and he used to make a big show of refusing the perks of office while quietly using his party's money, indirectly subsidized by the taxpayers of Canada, to buy suits and a car.

One of Reform's favourite tricks was to protest loudly against any increase in the MPs' pensions and then pocket the money when the public wasn't looking. Deborah Grey, a feisty and effective opponent, even showed up with a pig one day, and she and her colleagues wore buttons with a pig's face crossed out during a vote in the House. When they all started to oink, Doug Young shouted, "Hey, I didn't know you guys were bilingual!" It was the quickest, funniest retort I ever heard in all my years in the Commons. Aline later told me that she heard the roar of my laughter off-camera while watching the session on TV. "Okay," I finally said. "From now on, if you want your pay raise, you'll have to sign a piece of paper to get it." They were furious, of course, because it meant they would be caught breaking their vow to their constituents. Almost all of them eventually signed, including Deborah Grey. The next time Grey stood up to attack the government, I simply countered, "I'm sorry, Mr. Speaker, I'm afraid I cannot reply to somebody who has lost all credibility." She looked as though she wanted to kill me. The truth was, though, I had a lot of admiration for her. She did her job well; she was a gutsy fighter; and she knew she would have pulled the same trick on me if she could have. We used to see each other in the corridors afterwards and always had a civilized exchange.

Manning's biggest problem was that Reform couldn't build on its Western-centred, populist base and also attract conservative voters in Ontario and Atlantic Canada. He tried, but with limited success. If I had been him, I would have moved heaven and earth to take over the Progressive Conservative Party as quickly as possible. The Tories were down and out, with virtually nothing left but their history, so it would have been easy for Reform to take control from the inside by buying up the memberships riding by riding, electing the local executives, nominating the convention delegates and party candidates, and making sure that whoever became the next Tory leader was a friend ready and willing to merge with Reform. I don't know why Manning didn't do that. Perhaps he had come to hate the Tories too much for what he saw as their betrayals of true conservatism. Perhaps he thought that his right-wing Western supporters would never accept the kinds of compromise that Brian Mulroney had made with the Ontario Red Tories and the Quebec nationalists for the sake of power. If so, it was a mistake. Though Jean Charest, who had replaced Kim Campbell as Tory leader following the 1993 rout, was having trouble holding onto the right while moving toward the centre, he was still strong enough to split the right-wing vote—which allowed the Liberals to come up the middle.

Take gun control, for instance. It had emerged as a social issue under the Conservatives in the wake of the Montreal Massacre on December 6, 1989, when a deranged man killed fourteen female students in a senseless shooting spree. The Liberals' first Red Book promised to strengthen gun control, as most of the world's industrialized democracies had already done; our policy convention in May 1994 called for the licensing of all gun owners and the registration of all firearms; and, after extensive consultations, we passed legislation by November 1995 that required over two million owners to register their firearms and keep them secure in their homes. After all, if many Canadians already have to register their dogs and bicycles, it's hardly an infringement on their basic freedoms to require them to register their guns. Unfortunately, in the face of the well-organized and well-financed gun lobby, a lengthy and useless constitutional challenge by several provincial governments in the Supreme

Court, and the complexity of the regulation, implementing the law proved even harder than passing it—and much more expensive than originally projected.

The extra costs had little to do with registering the guns. A federal handgun registry had existed since the 1930s, after all, and was already costing the taxpayer about $30 million a year. The real expense came with licensing the owners, because that required elaborate, costly, and time-consuming background checks, advertising and information packages, financial-incentive programs, and new information technology. Allan Rock, one of my ablest ministers, got the blame for the overruns, and it may have cost him his leadership aspirations later on, but that wasn't fair to him. Though he had introduced the legislation, I moved him from Justice to Health after the 1997 election, by which point very little money had been spent on the program. Nor was it fair for the auditor general in her 2002 report to ignore the costs of the existing registry, confuse it in the public's mind with the licensing process, and come up with the attention-grabbing total of $1 billion only by running the projections ahead to cover a ten-year period.

As poll after poll demonstrated, gun control remained a popular policy, especially in urban ridings, not only as a deterrent against crime but as a core value that helped define the difference between Canadians and Americans. Anecdotally, I remember, a police chief told me how important it was for his officers, when approaching a house, to know beforehand whether the occupant owned a gun. If there's no gun, he said, we can enter more gently, and there's less likelihood of an explosive situation that might put the life of an innocent citizen at risk. And the results were clear: the United States had seven times more murders by guns per capita than Canada and fifteen times more murders by handguns; the rates of death from firearms were higher in rural Canada than in urban Canada because of the higher rate of gun ownership; and the rates of accidental death, suicides, and domestic killings involving firearms dramatically decreased with the program. Between 1991 and 2002, five hundred fewer Canadians per year were killed by firearms; the number of homicides by rifles and shotguns declined by 64 per cent during roughly the same period; and more than nine thousand people were either refused licences or had them revoked.

As I told the students at Michigan State University in East Lansing on May 7, 1999, "Our belief in the need to balance individual rights with the responsibilities of shared citizenship explains our decision to introduce anti-hate laws, which, we believe, place reasonable limits on the right of free speech. This is also why we have adopted a much tougher approach to gun control. We have one of the toughest gun control laws in the world, and Canadians want to keep it that way. I may be a big supporter of free trade, but, believe me, the National Rifle Association is one export Canadians will never buy. Charlton Heston should know that when it comes to his gospel on guns, Canada is not the promised land."

Personally, I remained a strong supporter of the program. Though I have gone on hunts from time to time, I've never liked guns and have never bought one. I'm afraid of them, in fact, and don't really find much sport in killing birds or animals. Still, coming from a part of Quebec where hunting is almost a cultural tradition among farmers and sportsmen, I fully appreciated how unpopular gun registration was in rural Canada. One of my long-time supporters told me he wasn't going to vote Liberal the next time because of it, even though he could well afford the licence fee. In fact, quite a number of Liberal MPs were worried about losing their seats over the issue.

That presented me with a tricky problem. If I had let all of them vote against the legislation, it would have failed. If I had let some of them vote against it, I probably would have had enough NDP and Bloc votes to win, but that wouldn't have been fair to those in the caucus who had stayed loyal to the party policy. Suppose there were two Liberal backbenchers whose ridings adjoined each other in northern Ontario. What would happen if I forced one to support the bill while I allowed the other to do the popular thing? The first MP would probably be punished by his constituents for looking like a sheep and would feel angry at the second MP for getting to enjoy all the advantages of being a Liberal candidate with none of the downside. That's exactly what happened. When I turned a blind eye to the three members who had lost the argument but voted nay on the bill's second reading, the others were immediately on my doorstep to accuse me of not being tough enough and to demand that I kick the traitors out of the caucus. I compromised by removing them from their committees.

"Two things," I explained at the time. "First, leadership is a question of judgment. Sometimes it's wrong to be too rigid. Sometimes you have to take the pressure off the MPs and show a bit of understanding and flexibility. Second, don't be worried—gun control is good for you even if it's unpopular in your riding. I'll tell you why. Every one of you is running against Reform and the Conservatives. Reform will feed on the fact that the Tories are taking a more ambiguous position in order to get votes in the cities and, therefore, it will get the votes of the hard-line opponents of gun control. So this issue divides them, and any issue that divides them will make your life easier."

The lowest point of the 1997 campaign was reached when Reform stooped to running advertisements that essentially asked Canadians if they wanted to have francophone Quebecers in power forever. It's a dangerous road to start judging Canadian politicians by anything other than their merits. In 1984 I had fought the notion that John Turner deserved to become leader of the Liberal Party simply because it was time for an anglophone, and in 1990 I had refused to argue that I should be his successor simply because I was French-speaking. The best person should win, no matter what his or her mother tongue, ethnic background, or province of origin. Fortunately the Reform ads backfired, perhaps because they had been aimed against two Quebecers who had taken so much flak in their own province for being too Canadian.

With Bouchard gone to Quebec City, it was Gilles Duceppe's first campaign as leader of the Bloc Québécois. Duceppe had won the Bloc's very first seat, in a Montreal by-election that took place in the emotional turmoil following the collapse of the Meech Lake Accord in the summer of 1990, but, far from being a star candidate, Duceppe was seen as just an ordinary, radical union organizer who happened to be the son of a famous Quebec actor. Even after he became leader, he clearly didn't have Bouchard's charisma or experience, and he soon suffered bad luck when the press made fun of him for wearing a plastic hairnet during a visit to a factory. In my judgment, however, he grew into the job. Leadership makes or breaks a person. Some people are enlarged by it; others are diminished. That's why it's always dangerous for a politician to ride into office on a wave of media adulation as a saviour, a miracle man, or a genius. There's no such thing as a genius in politics, or at least I've never met one. There are only human beings, some better than others, who rise or fall on the challenges they meet. Duceppe arrived with nothing except his intelligence, was undersold at the start, and surpassed everyone's expectations during the campaign.

While I was attending rallies across the country and preparing for the leaders' debates on TV, the Bloc was trying its best to unseat me back home in Shawinigan. Its candidate was Yves Duhaime, Jacques Parizeau's successor as provincial minister of finance in René Lévesque's PQ government and a committed separatist. Though I had known his family as long-time

Liberals in the riding and had once helped Duhaime himself get a job as a lawyer, we had sparred in some fierce arguments after he went over to the other side. Now he fought so hard against me that everybody thought he might actually win. I wouldn't have been the first party leader to be defeated in his home riding. It had happened to, among others, Mackenzie King, René Lévesque, and Robert Bourassa. But it was an unpleasant thought as well as a distinct possibility.

I couldn't be in the constituency very much; it was in one of the poorer parts of Quebec, which had been hit by our social security reforms and spending cuts; and Parizeau, Bouchard, and Duceppe all showed up to campaign for the Bloc. Duhaime's organizers were using every old trick in the book. While the unions and the PQ were sending hundreds of people to knock on doors for him, the Bloc protested that Senator Philippe Gigantes, an eloquent and perfectly bilingual friend of mine, was working on my behalf without including his time and all his expenses on my return. I had to call Gigantes and say, thank you very much, Senator, but get out of there or else they will take me to court and I'll be disqualified as a member of Parliament. It was a very tough battle, but I managed to win anyway by more than sixteen hundred votes.

The Liberal Party won too. Despite the loss of 22 seats in a slightly enlarged Commons, we won a second majority in a row for the first time since 1953, taking 155 ridings out of 301. In Quebec we went from 19 to 26 seats and, with the Tories, pushed the federalist vote to almost 60 per cent. We lost a couple of seats in Alberta, partly because the West voted Reform in order to kick the Bloc out of the Opposition leader's office (which it did), and partly because Albertans were getting rich— and I've seldom met a rich person who isn't mad at the government. Atlantic Canada was unhappy because of our spending cuts, the tighter conditions we imposed on Unemployment Insurance claims, and the impression I had created of being too callous about the impact of our battle against the deficit on both seasonal workers and the hinterland.

That's a good illustration of the unforgiving nature of politics. When the Liberal government decided to hold the G7 summit in Halifax less than two years earlier, it helped put the city's name on the world map. The leaders couldn't believe how friendly and beautiful the city was. Some of them hadn't plunged into a crowd for years because of security concerns, but here they felt comfortable shaking hands and chatting with the people who welcomed them on the street. They had a ball, in other words, because there's nothing a politician loves to do more than meet people. And though we had selected Halifax for the good of Canada, I admit to having had some expectation that Nova Scotia would reward us by once again giving the Liberals all eleven of its MPs in the next election. Instead, we lost every single seat, even in Halifax. Let that be a lesson to any politician who believes voters who say, if you do this or that for me, you will have my support forever. The reality is, while you might please some people today, you shouldn't expect them to remember it tomorrow.

—

In the aftermath of the 1997 election, with the economy booming, the deficit shrinking, and employment on the rise, the opposition parties found themselves with no important issues with which to undermine the Liberals' steady popularity, so they had to settle for a small scandal. Boy, was it ever small. In fact, it would have been completely trivial, hardly worth recounting, if it hadn't hijacked Question Period for months, wasted time and energy that could have been put to better use debating and tackling much more substantive problems in

Parliament, and threatened to reverse all the successful efforts we had made to restore the confidence of Canadians in the integrity of their democratic institutions.

In 1988, when I was out of politics, presumably forever, I had heard that the Grand'Mère Golf Club was for sale and I managed to persuade two well-to-do friends, Louis Michaud and Jacques Marcotte, to join me in buying it, more for my love of the game than for any profit. It was a beautiful course, built in 1910 for the anglophone owners and managers of the local mills and frequently described as the most Scottish of all the golf courses in Quebec. It amused me to think of it now belonging to three French Canadians. We even kept on the English-speaking pro and found ourselves the proprietors of the Protestant cemetery. Down the road from the club was an old, rather dilapidated hotel, Auberge Grand'Mère, which was owned by Consolidated Bathurst. The company asked us if we would be interested in taking over the operation of the hotel, not as a purchase but as a lease. How much? A dollar a year. Since none of us had the time to manage a hotel, we spent about $200,000 on new furnishings to bring it up to date and then subleased it to others. And so, as I was to repeat hundreds of times to no effect, I never, ever owned even one share of the Auberge Grand'Mère.

Five years later, in 1993, before becoming prime minister, I sold my interest in the golf course to a Toronto real-estate developer, and my partners and I gave over the lease on the hotel to a local businessman, Yvon Duhaime—no relation to my political opponent Yves Duhaime—who repaid us for the furnishings in cash. Subsequently he was able to purchase the Auberge from Consolidated Bathurst, and he made plans to renovate and expand it, creating about twenty new jobs in the process. For that, he needed money. One thing that many Canadians can't appreciate is how difficult it was for many Quebec businesses to borrow money in the early 1990s. The big banks and insurance companies would never admit it publicly—they always had some fancy excuse or other—but the threat of separation made them extremely reluctant to lend to small ventures outside the Montreal area. Though Canada as a whole has been well served by its six major banks over the years, Shawinigan was not.

That's one good reason, if I may digress, why I was opposed to bank mergers and didn't believe that bigger was necessarily better. The banks claimed they needed to be bigger in order to be more efficient and more competitive. "But the biggest banks in the world are Japanese," I replied, "and they all seem to be on the edge of bankruptcy." Then they argued that they needed to merge to serve the nation better. "Fine," I said, "I'll agree, but only if you first demonstrate your good faith to the public by announcing that none of your directors or executives will exercise the stock options that are going to be worth so much more because of the mergers." Of course, there were no takers. I had been a minister of finance, I had been on a bank board, and I suspected that the banks' real incentive was to push up their shares in the short term so the CEOs could retire rich and leave the consequences to their successors. And one way to push up the price was to cut back on loans and close branches in rural areas, not just in Quebec but across the country.

Given the banking situation in rural Quebec, it was normal for a Grand'Mère entrepreneur to seek funds for his hotel expansion from alternative sources. In fact, he succeeded in securing loans from two independent financial institutions, the Caisse Populaire and the union-based Fonds de Solidarité, which demonstrated that his venture wasn't entirely without merit. He also approached the Business Development Bank of Canada (BDC), a Crown corporation designed to help small businesses assemble enough financing to create jobs and boost regional growth, for a $615,000 loan from its Tourism Fund. The problem was that BDC was taking its time signing off on the loan.

Though I knew Duhaime socially and used to attend receptions at his hotel, he wasn't a close pal of mine, nor had he ever given one cent to the Liberal Party. He was nothing more or less than a constituent who was trying to do something beneficial for my rural riding and who needed help.

As far as I remember, I had met François Beaudoin, the president of the Business Development Bank, on only one occasion, when he came to a reception at 24 Sussex with other business leaders, introduced himself, and asked if he could have his picture taken with me. "If I can ever do anything for you," he said at the time, "just give me a call."

So now I gave him a call. "Look," I said, "I'm phoning you in my capacity as the member of Parliament for Shawinigan, not as prime minister. The Caisse and the Fonds de Solidarité are on board with this project, and they're waiting for you to decide. So, yes or no, please decide." That was it. No undue pressure to approve the loan had been applied, no big favour received. Nor, as Beaudoin charged, did I have anything to do with his later resignation as president. In fact, I had even renewed his mandate, despite the advice of the minister in charge.

Prime minister or not, I felt it was my duty to take care of this problem personally. When you're the member of Parliament for a riding with 19 per cent unemployment, you're constantly thinking about jobs, and I saw no reason why my constituents should be punished simply because their MP also happened to be the prime minister. As long as politicians obey the law and abide by the rules, it's their responsibility to help their constituents with a government program or a piece of advice; otherwise, every decision would be made by unelected bureaucrats. At one time, I remember, I put that argument to Trudeau, when he asked me to make a decision as a minister that I felt was contrary to the interests of the people of my riding. "Don't force me to choose between my job as minister and my duty to my electors," I told him, "because I will always pick my electors. They're the ones who elected me here, not you."

In fact, by the time I retired from politics, I was extremely proud to be able to say that unemployment was down to 10 per cent in my riding because of new jobs in the tourist sector, the wood industry, some high-tech enterprises, and other small businesses. Even the local PQ member of the National Assembly came to my defence. "I find it deplorable," Claude Pinard told the press, "that rocks are being thrown at Mr. Chrétien for his having worked within government programs."

So there you have it, the perfect Canadian scandal: no sex, no violence—and I even lost a bit of money on the transaction.

—

Shawinigate, as it was called, lasted much longer and played with much more intensity than the usual parliamentary cut and thrust because of rivalry for media attention between the Reform Party and the Progressive Conservatives. In November 1998, when Jean Charest left federal politics to take charge of the Quebec Liberal Party, Joe Clark returned to public life as Tory leader, and he found his party in worse shape than it had been when he had retired from public life in 1993. It had only twenty seats, it was in fifth place behind the NDP, and it was locked in an ideological and political fight to the finish with the Reform Party for the support of conservative Canadians. In addition, Clark himself didn't seek and win a seat in the House of Commons until a by-election in Nova Scotia in September 2000. It didn't take him long to realize that the best way— perhaps the only way—to get any attention was to outdo Preston Manning in throwing accusations and insinuations at the Liberals. Clark became downright nasty and would say almost anything for the sake of a headline. At one point he even tried to get the RCMP to launch a formal investigation into my dealings with the Auberge Grand'Mère.

Clark's antics infuriated me. I had always considered him a friend. I had urged him to run in the Tory leadership race that he was to win in 1976. I had followed through when he asked me when I was minister of justice to appoint his brother to the bench. More important, I felt that Clark should have known better, as a veteran parliamentarian and former prime minister, than to launch this type of personal abuse. The overwhelming majority of MPs on both sides of the House of Commons are honest people. Most of them make a financial sacrifice to be there, especially if they've been successful professionals or business people. Even those who might be earning a bit more are certainly not getting rich on an MP's salary. How many MPs, after all, have had to face criminal charges in the recent past for illegally filling their pockets with the taxpayers' money? None, in my memory, but that's not what the public thinks or what the press implies. Too often, however, politicians are tempted to attack the honesty of their opponents in order to win a few votes or ingratiate themselves with the press, little realizing that if they choose to play that game, their turn to be attacked will come round someday. "Those who throw mud," Lester Pearson used to say, "only lose ground." Moreover, by trying to damage the reputation of another politician, they end up damaging the reputation of all politicians, including themselves, in the eyes of the people.

The irony was that no government had ever done more than ours to reinforce the importance of ethics in public life, by establishing the office of the ethics counsellor and strengthening the regulations concerning lobbyists and ministerial conduct. Of course, as happens in every large organization, whether in the public or the private sector, people sometimes made errors of judgment. When David Collenette, the minister of national defence, felt obliged to resign in 1996 after contacting the head of a refugee board to permit the husband of a dying woman to come into Canada, his only mistake was not to have talked to the minister of immigration instead. When Andy Scott, the solicitor general, offered his resignation in 1998, it was because he had been overheard talking too freely about the APEC inquiry on an airplane. In fact, I was extremely proud to be able to say at the end of my tenure that none of my ministers—or their staff, for that matter—had been forced to leave under a cloud for profiting personally from their high positions.

—

No sooner had Joe Clark begun to compete with Preston Manning for headlines than an equally vicious competition broke out in the media for advertisers and readers. In October 1998 Conrad Black launched the *National Post* and triggered an unprecedented newspaper war with the *Globe and Mail*. As a result, both right-wing parties and Canada's two national newspapers shared, along with their basically pro-business political agenda, a life-or-death incentive to dig up sensationalist dirt about the Liberal government, so they all kept on about Shawinigate. It was as though the Canadian right's envy of all things American now extended to envying the Republicans' attempts to destroy Bill Clinton by getting a special prosecutor to spend $50 million trying to prove that he and his wife might have made some money on a land transaction before he became governor of Arkansas.

It's odd, I mused later, how these same conservatives, usually so vigilant to expose corruption in government, showed such a strange lack of curiosity about the fact that U.S. vice-president Dick Cheney had been the CEO of a huge corporation that was getting hundreds of millions of dollars in military contracts without bids, while in Canada they had exhausted themselves endeavouring to prove an unfounded smear against a Liberal prime minister who had been trying to help his constituents find work. But when you're a well-paid reporter or columnist in Toronto or, even better, a media tycoon with residences in London, New York, and Palm Beach, I suppose you don't have to concern yourself too much with the plight of the unemployed in rural Quebec.

Though the *National Post* began with a competitive energy that benefited readers, reporters, advertisers, and the industry in general, the newspaper soon degenerated into a highly partisan, extremely negative scandal sheet whose sole agenda seemed to be the destruction of the values, institutions, and traditions of liberal Canada. To that end it had at least one reporter working full-time on the Shawinigate file, and its founder-proprietor was quoted as saying that by the time he had finished with Jean Chrétien, what was left would go through an eyedropper. The bottom was reached in an editorial on March 27, 1999, in which it was suggested that I might have profited personally from federal government assistance in my riding.

"I respect those who disagree with decisions I have made as prime minister," I replied in a letter to the editor on April 9. "I welcome honest debate about the policy directions set by my government. But I will never countenance unwarranted attacks upon my personal ethics and honesty."

Why the witch hunt? I don't know, though I suspect it had a lot to do with Conrad Black's thirst for influence, his conservative ideology, his pursuit of profit, and what I perceived as an arrogant contempt for me. Previously I hadn't considered Black a personal enemy of mine. He wasn't the type of fellow with whom I spent a lot of time, true, but we had been friendly enough over the years. He was smart and amusing, spoke fluent French, and for a while was a partner with the Desmarais family, when Hollinger and Power Corporation co-owned the Southam newspaper chain. Black invited me to be a guest speaker at one of his famous black-tie dinners in the days when John Crosbie and I used to insult each other with jokes and wisecracks for the entertainment of the after-dinner crowd; I visited with Black a few times in his fancy offices in downtown Toronto when I was a minister; I came across him now and then in London; and he occasionally dropped by 24 Sussex to discuss politics.

He was wrong, I told him, to support the Reform Party. "You should support the Progressive Conservatives," I explained. "If you want to transform them into a bunch of right-wing fanatics, fine, that's up to you, but you cannot destroy the party of John A. Macdonald." I was speaking in good faith. Though I felt secure as prime minister, I knew that my party was bound to lose someday. That's the reality in a democracy. If so, I thought it was much more likely that the country would go to a middle-of-the-road alternative like the Tories—on the right but not the radical right—than to Manning's Reform, because Canadians like moderate parties. From the way Black reacted, however, I could tell that he suspected me of deviously trying to get him to stop doing what he was doing because it was hurting me. So instead of taking my advice, he went off and backed a unite-the-right movement that didn't last very long because it was too extreme and too ideological. As a result, he probably helped the Liberals stay in power longer than we might otherwise have done.

On Thursday, June 17, 1999, I was in Vienna, the first Canadian prime minister ever to visit Austria while in office, to discuss bilateral trade, address a gathering of the Organization for Security and Co-operation in Europe, meet a number of business leaders at a private dinner organized by Frank Stronach, unveil an Inuit sculpture at the university, and help secure an exhibition of Klimt paintings for the National Gallery of Canada. Around lunchtime, Bruce Hartley received a call from Conrad Black, obviously in a fury and demanding to speak with me. I was busy, but I told Bruce to tell Black that he could phone me later that afternoon in Cologne, where I would be arriving for the G8 summit.

For several months, without my knowledge or consent, Prime Minister Tony Blair, acting on a recommendation from William Hague, the leader of Britain's Conservative Party, had been planning to ask the Queen to elevate Conrad Black to the British House of Lords. In the process, however, some official in Buckingham Palace raised a concern. Why was Conrad Black allowed to become a peer of the realm when other prominent Canadians such as Roy Thomson and Garfield Weston hadn't been? Thomson had been required to give up his Canadian citizenship in order to become Lord Thomson of Fleet, while Weston had turned down a title so he could remain a Canadian.

In Black's case, messages had flown back and forth between London and Ottawa for several weeks until finally, on June 10, the Department of Foreign Affairs advised the British High Commission that the Canadian government was against the honour, in keeping with Canada's long-standing policy that Canadians should not be given titles. Either Blair never received the message or he assumed that Black's hasty acquisition of dual citizenship—achieved in a record two weeks—had resolved the problem. On Monday, June 14, he told Black that his name would be on the Queen's list, to be announced the following Saturday. When I heard about it, I phoned Blair to ask him what was going on, and he confirmed the reports.

I was at a desk in the hotel suite overlooking Cologne's magnificent cathedral when Black called shortly before six o'clock. "Mr. Black," I said, "I don't know all the details about your specific case, but I gather there's some question about Canadian citizens accepting foreign titles."

"But I had my lawyer look into that," he replied. "I don't believe it's against any federal law, regulation, or convention. I'm a permanent resident of Britain, I'm a British citizen as well as a

Canadian citizen, and I assume that the government of the United Kingdom has the right to recommend to Her Majesty the Queen that a British citizen be honoured for his services to the United Kingdom, which it will do if you withdraw your objections immediately."

"Well, it's now Thursday, I don't know what I can do before Saturday. I'll have to have my officials look into it. I guess you'll just have to be patient. This is an important issue involving principle and precedent. It isn't something I can decide right away."

I presume his celebration party was all organized, the champagne was in the fridge, and he was afraid of looking humiliated in front of his friends. This had been the lifelong dream of a man who had never been denied anything he had ever wanted, and it's tough to break the dream of an adult. He sounded increasingly desperate. "If you say yes," he said, "I owe you a big one."

"You owe me nothing, Mr. Black. I will look into it. If it's possible, I'll do it, but you might have to wait six months or so until the Queen's next list."

Then he said something very surprising: "I can understand how this might cause you a problem, Mr. Prime Minister, a perception problem, but there's a solution. You could allow me to become a lord in England and at the same time make me a senator in Canada. I'd serve in both. I'd even be willing to sit as a Liberal."

I had never heard such a strange idea and, despite myself, it made me laugh out loud. "I'm sorry, Mr. Black. But I'll check and get back to you if there's anything I can do."

And I did look into it. Assuming I would be blamed if Black were denied his peerage, I asked Herb Gray, the deputy prime minister, to chair a special committee of ministers to study the matter. It didn't take him long to report back that it had been the established policy of the government of Canada, whether Liberal or Conservative, that titles are incompatible with the democratic traditions of our country. In 1919, when Robert Borden was prime minister, the House of Commons passed the Nickle Resolution, which asked the King to discontinue the practice of bestowing titles of honour on Canadians. "The Prime Minister is firmly of the opinion," a background report to the governor general stated in March 1918, "that the creation or continuance of hereditary titles in Canada is entirely incompatible with the ideals of democracy as they have developed in this country." In the early 1960s, John Diefenbaker didn't let his love of British institutions or his political friendship with the media owner Roy Thomson make an exception to the rule—despite a personal appeal from a young Tory at the University of Ottawa who was a protegé of Thomson's from northern Ontario and would become Conrad Black's future media partner, Paul Desmarais. In 1968 Lester Pearson passed a regulation that stated, "Approval is *not* given to accept an order or decoration which carries with it a title of honour or any implication of precedence or privilege." Twenty years later, Brian Mulroney reiterated that policy: "The Government of Canada *shall not* grant the approval . . . for an award, (a) that is at variance with Canadian policy or the public interest; (b) that carries with it an honorary title or confers any precedence or privilege."

Of course, Canadians can accept an honour from Great Britain or any other nation; many have done so. But being a British lord is different from receiving, say, the *Legion d'honneur* from France because a British lord is a member of the United Kingdom's parliamentary system. And though Black's dual citizenship raised a new issue, I did tell him that the government might be able to address it when we came to update the *Citizenship Act*. Instead, after suing me for $25,000 for "abuse of power" and losing in the courts twice, he decided that becoming Lord Black of Crossharbour was more important than remaining a Canadian citizen. It wasn't the choice I would have made myself—and, for him, it may have been a serious error in judgment in light of his subsequent troubles with the U.S. justice system—but it really had very little to do with me.

—

I can't say that my relationship with the *National Post* improved dramatically after Black sold control of it and the Southam newspapers in 2000 to Israel Asper, a card-carrying Liberal, a former leader of the party in Manitoba, and an old friend of mine. Though Asper hadn't supported me for the leadership in 1984, he was on my bandwagon in 1990, and we always shared a lot of laughs whenever we got together. I was told that he had wanted to make his newspapers more moderate, but Black's ideologues were still in command of the newsrooms and, because Asper was a well-known Liberal, his smallest interventions raised cries of alarm from the same people who had never lifted an eyebrow when Conrad Black used the op-ed pages to promote his views—perhaps because Black had bought their loyalty and then left Asper to clean up the financial consequences.

Of course, rich Liberals tend to be right-wing Liberals, and Izzy was certainly very conservative fiscally, very pro-American, and very pro-Israel. Still, he had a lot of respect for our party's record of human rights, immigration, and multiculturalism; he thanked me for balancing the nation's books; and he felt comfortable with the openness of the Liberal Party. That's not to say he was always happy with me, but at least he wasn't a sworn enemy. Ironically, about a week before he died in October 2003, Asper said he wanted me to become the chair of his media empire once I got out of politics. I took it as a jest, but he made the statement at a dinner table in front of other people, and his family later told me he had been serious.

Having a newspaper owner as a friend or getting a nice editorial before an election may be pleasant, but it usually makes no difference in the end. After the Liberals won the 1980 election, I remember, a survey showed that, out of 105 editorials, 101 had asked Canadians to vote for the Tories and only 4 had supported us. When I showed it to Trudeau, he said, "We missed, Jean. They weren't all against us."

My own son-in-law, André Desmarais, was the chairman of the company that owns *La Presse,* the most important French-language newspaper in Canada, and it probably caused me more harm than good. The journalists went out of their way to prove that they weren't being influenced by the Desmarais family's connection to me, to the point where my daughter, France, became so fed up with the headlines and editorials that she refused to have her husband's newspaper in their own home. Two of his newspapers, *La Presse* in Montreal and *Le Nouvelliste* in Trois-Rivières, had even come out with headlines, the day before I won my riding in the 1993 election, announcing my probable defeat.

That's just a fact of life with the media corporations today. They want to increase their audiences; they want to sell more advertisements or commercials; and they will rarely let the facts get in the way of a catchy headline. Nobody feels obliged to ask you anything before rushing to print. Reporters are under constant pressure to produce a fresh story every fifteen minutes— true or not, no matter—and they no longer have any time for research or fact-checking because of company cutbacks and chronic understaffing. Meanwhile, the owners seldom care because they know that few politicians have the deep pockets to challenge the big media companies in court. It's rarely worth the hundreds of thousands of dollars in legal bills needed to correct a false story, even if you manage to win. Once your temper has cooled down, you realize that the more important thing is to be able to live with your own conscience. Today they write something good about you; tomorrow they write something bad about you. So what?

Besides, I used to console myself, the muckraking was actually a sign of the good health of the nation, not of our political or social decay. It was because Canada was enjoying a robust economy, a balanced budget, growth in jobs, and a peaceful society that the opposition parties and the media were desperately devoting so much of their attention to "Peppergate" and "Shawinigate." Some of the ministers used to thank God for that, because it distracted the press and the public from criticizing the really serious problems we were facing in health care or UN peacekeeping. During the 1998 ice storm, I remember, one French-language reporter begged us to do something really stupid. "Please," he wrote, "I have nothing but ice to chew on."

However, the media coverage did do great damage to our public life and our public institutions. In the frenzy of round-the-clock television news and tabloid journalism, scandal sells newspapers and commercials. Just check how many times the word "scandal" is used during the course of a day, and about what. Whenever something goes wrong, it's a scandal; if it's proven not to be a scandal at all, it's never mentioned again. In 2000, for example, everybody across Canada heard about the "billion-dollar boondoggle" that hit Human Resources Development Canada and caused a major headache for Jane Stewart, who hadn't even been the minister at the time when the hundreds of millions of dollars were supposed to have gone missing. Yet very few people got the news, as eventually reported by Hugh Winsor in the *Globe and Mail,* that HRDC officials had found only about $85,000 that couldn't be accounted for—less than three one-hundredths of 1 per cent of the total funds dispersed by the department in a year.

That's not to say there is never any abuse in government or corruption in politics, and a free press plays an important role in democracy as a watchdog. But who watches the dog? If the dog bites an honest citizen who happens to be strolling down the street minding his or her own business, it's no longer a guardian of law and order. In most cases, the best way to curb abuse and corruption within the public sector is simply to let the police do their job. Not only do they resent political interference, but they are completely within their rights to oppose it. That's why I didn't intervene one way or another in the RCMP investigation into the so-called Airbus scandal, in which a German lobbyist named Karlheinz Schreiber was reputed to have paid bribes to members of the Mulroney government to secure Air Canada's purchase of thirty-four new Airbus planes for $1.8 billion in 1988. I didn't order the investigation. Nor did I try to stop it when I heard about it through a reporter's question at a scrum during an APEC summit in Osaka, Japan, in November 1995.

The RCMP wanted access to certain bank accounts in Switzerland as part of its investigation and, as a matter of routine, it asked the Department of Justice to send a confidential letter of request to the Swiss authorities. The wording of the document, which included Mulroney's name, didn't state clearly that what the police were investigating were only allegations—an unfortunate mistake—but Solicitor General Herb Gray, Justice Minister Allan Rock, and I were not aware of the letter's contents until the letter had been mysteriously leaked to the press. Indeed, Gray was known for his integrity and discretion; Rock, an extremely well-respected lawyer and twice head of the Law Society of Upper Canada when I asked him to run as a candidate in 1993, hadn't even been in politics when Mulroney was prime minister; and I felt awful about what had happened. Though Mulroney and I had had our share of battles over the years, he had been elected by the people of Canada with two majority governments, he had done a number of good things as prime minister, and he had suffered enough humiliation when his great party had been reduced to two seats in the wake of his retirement. As far as I was concerned, he didn't need to be hit with anything else.

I saw very little of my predecessor other than at a few social functions and, though always polite, we rarely spoke about current issues. Shortly after I became prime minister, I recall, a small problem arose concerning Mulroney. At the time of the national referendum on the Charlottetown Accord, Robert Bourassa had insisted on conducting his own referendum in Quebec, but he later wanted the federal government to pay the bill of $47 million—an estimated $13 million more than Ottawa would have spent to organize it in the province. Logically enough, both Mulroney and Kim Campbell had refused to pay Bourassa's bill, and now the problem landed on my desk. So I phoned Mulroney to find out what the deal had been, for which there didn't appear to be any documentation, and, before we hung up, we agreed to keep the call confidential. Minutes later Jean Charest was on his feet in the House of Commons asking me questions about it. Because there were only two possible sources for the information, and I knew I wasn't one of them, I hesitated before consulting Mulroney again.

Occasionally I used to hear rumours that the former prime minister was saying negative things about me around Montreal or had taken offence at not being invited to some official function or other, but I never let it bother me too much. He can't have been happy to see someone he looked down on succeed in so many areas where he himself had failed. Still, when Mulroney showed up in Ottawa on November 19, 2002, for the unveiling of his official portrait in the Parliament Buildings, we were able to share a few jokes. "I'm happy to be hanging Brian Mulroney in this corridor," I told the assembled guests, "just as I'm sure he's happy that I'll soon be hanging here too. I read the other day that he's thinking of coming back into politics. Well, if he's coming, I'm staying. And I guess that will make two more bachelors in Ottawa." Aline and Mila laughed and nodded in agreement.

When Mulroney decided to sue the federal government for defamation and sought $50 million in damages, I thought it would hurt him, the police, and the reputation of all our public institutions and officials. So I was relieved when the government settled out of court in January 1997. Though we agreed to pay him $2 million for his legal costs because of the bureaucratic error, Mulroney accepted that the Airbus investigation had been started by the RCMP on its own and conducted without any political interference. Of course, I was as mystified as every other Canadian when Mulroney later admitted to having received $300,000 in cash payments from Schreiber after leaving office. However, as I told my officials, the only proper thing to do was to accept the word of a former prime minister of Canada.

———

The slurs on my character didn't succeed, I think, because the public felt they knew me to be an honest person. When people have seen you on TV for forty years, they know in their hearts whether they can trust you or not, and most Canadians continued to believe that I was working hard for the good of the country and was not in politics for the bucks. In my experience, there's usually a big gap between what the press is writing and what the people are thinking. The politicians and the press gallery live and work side by side in a very small community in Ottawa, and they share the opinion that what they're doing is of all-consuming interest to the people of Flin Flon, Manitoba, or Cornerbrook, Newfoundland. In fact, I don't remember many people ever mentioning all the nonsense about hotels and golf courses that filled the newspapers for a year, and I received only a few letters on that subject, mostly from those citizens who like to write abusive letters to their prime minister. People generally understood that I was simply trying to help my riding.

Though I received a certain number of newspapers at home, I rarely read them thoroughly. Aline always got up early, and she used to look at the morning news on TV, read the main stories, and talk by phone with France in Montreal. When I came down for breakfast, I used to joke, I received my instructions for the day from my wife and daughter. If the headlines were bad, I put them out of my mind and got down to work. In the office, of course, I was briefed on anything of political importance by the PMO staff whose job it was to research the day's problems for Question Period, and if someone wrote something serious relating to a serious issue, I paid attention. However, I wasn't very interested in all the gossip about who should or should not be in the Cabinet and when the prime minister might retire, and I found most editorialists and columnists unreliable messengers because they tend to pronounce one truth today and exactly the opposite tomorrow.

Near the end of my term in office, a reporter apologized for all the nasty articles he had written about me during the past year. "Don't worry," I told him. "I never read you." He didn't like it.

I rarely complained to the press, as I had in my letter to the *National Post*. Sometimes I used to ask my press people to answer questions, clarify issues, or correct mistakes, but I wasn't one of those politicians who are always on the phone screaming at reporters or currying their favour. They did their job, I did mine. If they wrote that I was nuts, I consoled myself that I was nuts enough to have been elected prime minister of Canada. Imagine if I'd been intelligent! And, in the end, the only judgment that counts is the judgment of the people on voting day.

From time to time, however, a little tactical intervention could produce wonderful results. Early in 1991, for example, shortly after winning the by-election in Beauséjour, New Brunswick, and being sworn in as the leader of the Opposition, I went for a routine medical examination, during which the doctors found a small spot on my lung that might or might not have been cancer. Taking no chances, they operated on me at once and gave me the all-clear. Cancer would have made a better story for the press, of course, and I used to joke that some of my rivals were already practising sympathetic looks in the mirror and thinking about buying huge bouquets of flowers for my funeral. For months afterwards, whenever I took a couple of days off to go to Shawinigan or on holiday, the rumour mills worked overtime to fabricate reports that I was undergoing secret treatments somewhere and possibly was at death's door. So how could I prove I wasn't sick?

I met with a few of my closest advisers to discuss what to do. Saying that I was in good health was obviously useless, since no one would believe it. What about showing it by doing something physical? Every politician knows the truth of the old saying that a picture is worth a thousand words. Trudeau pirouetting behind the Queen's back, Stanfield dropping the ball, Duceppe with the hairnet, I with an army helmet on backwards in Bosnia— we all have had to recognize the press photographer's power to make us look like heroes or fools.

"I could go bungee-jumping," I said.

"If you go bungee-jumping," they laughed, "people will think you're really sick. Sick in the head." Pelletier didn't think it was funny. He told me that I could get myself another chief of staff if I was going to be so irresponsible.

John Rae suggested I invite a Canadian Press photographer, Ryan Remiorz, to come to Lac des Piles and watch me waterski. It was a gamble, of course, because if I fell, Remiorz was frank in telling me, that would be the picture he would use. But my brother-in-law André Chaîné had trained me well and I had had a lot of practice, with the result that he took a fabulous picture of me with a big grin on my face and the sun shining through the perfect arc of water in my wake. That one photograph, coming before the 1993 election, put a stop to all the speculations about my health.

I played a similar sort of game when I was prime minister and just about to turn sixty-five. On holiday north of Montreal, my grandchildren persuaded me to try snowboarding for the first time in my life. On the way home in the car I had an idea and phoned Peter Donolo. "Peter," I said, "tomorrow I'm going to turn sixty-five and all the papers are going to write that I'm now eligible for the old age pension and all that jazz. Perhaps we can give them another story. Why don't you let them know that, at sixty-five less a day, I took up snowboarding?" So he did, and that became everyone's angle the next day. No surprise, really, except for the fact that no one ever questioned it. I mean, at least one editor might have said, well, there were no witnesses except for his own grandchildren, maybe he's just bragging. But this was one case in which they all believed me. Just as well, because I never snowboarded again. I had fallen too many times to enjoy it and was keenly aware how long it takes for a senior citizen's broken bones to heal.

Both the press photographers and the television cameras love an action shot, and I was usually happy to give it to them. Most days I ran up the stairs to my office when I arrived on Parliament Hill or left the Commons. Some cynics suggested that I did it only for the show, but in fact I've virtually never gone up a flight of steps one by one, always preferring to take them two at a time and very quickly. I found it an easy form of exercise and it charged my energy, getting my heart pumping fast enough that I didn't sit down at my desk like a dead weight. Even as a boy I used to go with my dad from the church or post office in La Baie up hundreds of steps to our home, and he always said, "Come on, little guy, let's run." He also liked to walk at a rapid pace all over town, so I guess I inherited that habit from him too. Once, when the press kept bugging me with questions about when I was going to retire, I joked that I would resign the day Sean Durkan, a heavy-set reporter with the *Toronto Sun,* beat me in a race up to my office. The next day his colleagues ordered him to the gym, but I think I'd still be in office if I had waited for that day.

On one of my official trips to China, I was visiting the Great Wall when, just for the hell of it, I started to bolt up a steep set of very rough stairs, with the cameramen struggling to keep pace with all their heavy equipment. Later, coming out of a meeting in Shanghai to go to another, I saw that the street was full of people riding bicycles. "Why don't we go by bicycle?" I asked my hosts. "No time," they replied. But when I emerged from the second meeting, they had a bicycle waiting for me. So I jumped on it and took off for a couple of blocks, with the bodyguards and media corps all running and laughing behind me. It even made CNN Live. Aline was with me on the trip but at a hairdresser's at the time, and she looked up to see me riding a bicycle on TV. "Hey, that's my husband, what's he doing?" she shouted, but nobody spoke enough English to explain it to her.

These spontaneous photo ops wouldn't have worked if the media had thought they were being manipulated. Take the case of Stockwell Day. Shortly after beating Preston Manning to become the first leader of the Canadian Alliance on June 24, 2000—a new face and a new label for the old Reform Party—he tried to show off his youth and vigour to Canadians by riding up to a lakeside press conference on a jet ski. Unfortunately for him, he looked rather odd in a black wetsuit, and his machine was made in Japan. The media, no doubt annoyed by how dumb he must have thought they were to try to dupe them with such an obvious trick, didn't hesitate to make him a figure of fun.

Many Liberals considered Day quite a threat, however, and his appearance on the scene gave fuel to the idea that it was time for me to retire. In truth, I had absolutely no intention of running for a third term. Two terms as prime minister were demanding enough, the country and the party were in very good shape on the eve of the new millennium, and I knew how tired the public can become of seeing the same guy on the television screens day after day after day. Even business changes its advertising frequently because it knows that people stop buying until they get a new angle. It's particularly difficult for a modern politician to remain in the limelight in this age of instant communication and twenty-four-hour news. That's why, as high as the government's standing in the opinion polls continued to be, I assumed that my good run couldn't last forever.

The truth was, I was working so hard in those days that I had no other ambition than to spend most of my time in a beautiful part of my riding, commute into Montreal now and then to do the odd job, or perhaps get a small apartment there in the winter months and simply enjoy the rest of my life with Aline. As usual, my life didn't evolve quite as I expected.

TEN

POWER BEHIND THE THRONE

A line was, is, and always shall be my Rock of Gibraltar. She is my closest confidante and my most trusted adviser, and, of all the people in the world, it is she who knows me best. Meeting her when I was eighteen and she sixteen was the greatest, most important moment of my life.

My mother loved her from the start. The two of them used to take the bus to Trois-Rivières to visit me at boarding school, and Mum would leave us alone for a couple of hours so we could take a walk in a park or hold hands on a bench. She knew that Aline would be a good influence on me. Not that I was a bad student, but I was involved in too many things outside the classroom, and I didn't pay much attention to regulations and timetables. I enjoyed being different, liked having fun, and needed to act up, perhaps because I had been sent away from home to a rigid, oppressive environment when I was only five. If it was a study period, I played baseball. If it was a sports practice, I went to bed. Aline helped change all that with her love, her ambition, and her sense of discipline. I started to read more and study harder. Though my mother died when I was only twenty, I think she was content to see that Aline had already got me to settle down and do well.

Aline has always been a hard-working person. She got her first job as a secretary at the age of sixteen to help support her family, and she kept working to help put me through university even after our first child was born. When I was a backbencher and a minister whose job kept me either at my desk or on the road, she represented me at weddings, funerals, and events all over the riding. She acted as my local assistant when I didn't have one. She knew everyone, listened to their problems, and brought me their views, and though she hated making speeches or giving interviews, she presided at ceremonies whenever I couldn't. Almost every weekend, in every kind of weather, she drove with the children and the dog between Ottawa and Shawinigan—four and a half hours there on Friday evening, four and a half hours back on Sunday night. Whenever I could, I joined them, because those nine hours were often the best opportunity we had to talk as a family.

After twenty years of that demanding routine, Aline was delighted when I got out of politics in 1986, even though I frequently had to go to Toronto or Montreal on business. When I decided to go back into the game four years later, she swallowed her disappointment—she understood that we owed it to our parents, our children, and our grandchildren to leave an even better country than we had inherited. "If you go back," she told me, "I will be there to help you do your job and do it right, but don't come looking for pity from me if you have a rough day." Well, of course, I did have a few rough days. One evening Aline found me sitting in the living room of 24 Sussex, licking my wounds and feeling sorry for myself. "Jean," she said, "I know I said I wouldn't pity you, but I guess I pity you a little bit."

Aline liked to say that she never would have married me if she had known I was to become prime minister—she would have been too scared. Shy by nature and reluctant to call attention to herself, she nevertheless performed her role as mother of three, political wife, and model for young people with outstanding elegance and quiet dignity—whether representing Canada at Mother Teresa's funeral in Calcutta, delivering a speech in Italian during an official visit to Italy, serving as the honorary chair of the Royal Conservatory of Music's national advisory council, or presiding in French, English, and Spanish at the annual Conference of Spouses of the Heads of State and Government of the Americas that was held in Ottawa. She's beautiful, poised, experienced, and an excellent judge of politics and people.

Many times she kept me connected to the day-to-day realities of life and the feelings and needs of ordinary people. Politicians of all stripes are always in danger of looking at every problem from an abstract point of view or being briefed by officials, academics, or economists who know every science but the science of human nature. Besides following what the newspapers and TV commentators were saying more closely than I did, Aline kept in touch with a network of her own friends who weren't in politics or government, especially in the riding. And while I was the extrovert who made the speeches, worked the room, argued too loudly, and talked too much, she chatted with people on the sidelines, studied the mood of the crowd from the stage, observed the body language, and read the scene very carefully. We were partners, a good team, and I really appreciated her constructive criticism, because if she didn't tell me I had made a mistake or was on the wrong course of action, who would?

Over the years I came to place a high value on her advice about everything, from pension reform to Stéphane Dion. She rarely loses her temper, and it has never been our style as a couple to shout at each other, but she always let me know in her firm way what she thought. Often she didn't realize her influence. One Saturday in December, to give a small example, she called my attention to a book she was reading. "According to this, Jean," she said, "when you feel you're too old to do something, that's the time to do it." As it happened, I woke up very early the next morning and it was freezing outside. Go back to sleep, I said to myself, a guy of your age shouldn't be going skiing on a day as cold as this. But then I remembered Aline's advice, so I got up and went. I'm not sure whether she was more surprised that I had gone skiing or that I had actually been listening.

Being the wife of a prime minister is a full-time job, and it wasn't made easier for Aline when, as cost-saving measures, she voluntarily gave up Mila Mulroney's office and secretary and cut the staff at 24 Sussex. There were countless events to organize, letters and phone calls to answer, and official functions to attend; there was the constant travelling across Canada and around the world; and even during vacations and weekends she was always expected to be on show if we went to a restaurant or concert. Worse than the fatigue was the emotional toll. Though Aline didn't feel we had any right to complain about anything, since we had chosen to enter public life, had won the trust of Canadians, and could always leave if we weren't happy, few people are aware of the stress that a politician's family has to endure. The family are the ones who bear the full force of the rumours, worries, jokes, and headlines, because they're often as much in the dark about the true situation as the average citizen is. In Aline's case, I put her through eleven general elections, one by-election, two leadership campaigns, and two bitter referendums.

While there were many aspects of the job she liked, she was happiest having an ordinary day. "Are you served breakfast in bed?" an envious friend once asked Aline, and the question made her laugh. Awake most mornings at 6:30, she was usually in the kitchen before anyone else was up, and she often prepared breakfast for the bodyguards who arrived at 7:30 to join her for a one-hour, six-kilometre power walk beside the Rideau Canal. The RCMP liked to assign the heaviest officers to Aline to help them lose weight and get into better shape. In bad weather she worked out on a machine; in winter she went cross-country skiing a few times a week. Besides French and English, she picked up Spanish and Italian and took regular lessons to maintain her fluency. She loved to read a book in the solitude of Harrington Lake or Lac des Piles. And, having learned to play the piano extremely well after the age of fifty, she practised religiously. To prepare for her higher-level exams, she used to bring a keyboard with her whenever we went overseas.

We shared a love of music. The house was alive with Chopin or Schubert, and many of our best parties ended with everyone singing tunes around the piano in the living room. When I was a student at boarding school in Joliette, I discovered I could get off early from study hall if I attended music lessons. So I started playing French horn in the band and orchestra—not well, but enough to learn how to move my fingers, control my breath, and read music. When I was kicked out of Joliette for being a bit too mischievous, the lessons stopped and that was that. After I became prime minister, however, Aline decided that playing a musical instrument would be a good way for me to relax and something we could do together. Without telling me, she found a trumpet through a friend, bought a basic how-to book, and gave them to me one weekend at Harrington Lake. By morning I had learned "Love Me Tender." Suddenly Aline, who was upstairs, heard me playing it for her from below. "Jean," she said, "I never thought I'd live to see the day when I'd be serenaded by you."

A while later, during a caucus Christmas party on the Hill, I picked up a German trombone while the True Grit Band, made up of Liberal MPs, was playing. Its pistons being similar to those of a French horn, I blew a few notes, just to make the crowd laugh. I guess they couldn't hear the mistakes above all the noise, because they gave me a big round of applause. The next year I played again, and they gave me another enthusiastic reception. The year after that, as a Christmas present, they gave me my own German trombone. Eventually I managed about a dozen tunes on it. Clinton and I used to joke about starting a trio, with him on saxophone and Tony Blair on guitar, and on one occasion I even put on dark glasses and joined Dan Aykroyd as a Blues Brother.

The sad truth was that I really wasn't much good, as became apparent to everyone when I agreed, just for fun, to do a solo of "When the Saints Come Marching In" at the Liberal convention in 1998. Poor Jean Pelletier, he was always trying to discourage me from looking "un-prime-ministerial," but it was more important for me to remain close to the people than to appear reserved or aloof. I was the prime minister, after all, so I was what a prime minister looked like. This time, however, I really regretted not taking his advice. Once in a while, alone in my office at the end of the day and really tired, when I was absolutely certain that no one could hear, I found that five or ten minutes of standing up and blowing into the trombone was a wonderful way to unwind. And in the privacy of my own home, I enjoyed accompanying Aline, on the piano, joined sometimes by Bruce Hartley on the violin.

Aline's greatest pleasure was being with our children and grandchildren. Our daughter, France, her husband, André, and our four grandchildren—Olivier, Maximilien, Philippe, and Jacqueline—came frequently from Montreal for a weekend visit or over the holidays, almost always for Canada Day, Halloween, and Christmas. Michel, our youngest child, visited regularly for a few days or weeks from wherever he was then living, out in the West, in the United States, or up North. But Hubert, our middle child, who lives in Ottawa and is single, was in and out of the house all the time. The staff doted on him because he was an entertaining storyteller. As a hobby, while working for a high-tech company, he started teaching paraplegics and quadriplegics how to scuba dive, and he often brought them to the pool at 24 Sussex for lessons. Later, in fact, he left his job and started a foundation to turn his hobby into his life's work.

Though Aline had come from an even more modest background than mine, she never let all the trappings of high office either intimidate her or go to her head. She tells a funny story about the time she was persuaded to perform a piano recital before twelve hundred senior citizens in Trois-Rivières. Waiting backstage to go on, she met a fellow performer who was more jittery than she was. He took a sip of cognac to calm his nerves and offered her one, saying, "You know, the prime minister's wife is going to be here." After the concert, when she was formally introduced to him, he was full of embarrassment and apology. "That's okay," she said. "It's not as if it's written on my forehead."

In May 1995 Aline and I were in the Netherlands to help celebrate the anniversary of its liberation by Canadian troops. The towns and countryside were full of Canadian flags, and I felt very proud to be the prime minister. Just before the official ceremony, Queen Beatrix invited us to visit her, and we had a very friendly, informal chat, just the three of us. She even served the coffee herself. Later, when we went outside to the cemetery where the Canadian dead lay buried, Lawrence MacAulay, the secretary of state for veterans, offered us a coffee or tea in a tent set up for the ceremony. "No, thank you," Aline said, putting on the voice of a *grande dame,* "I've just had coffee a few minutes ago with the Queen of the Netherlands, and I'm going to have another with the Queen of England tonight." It was so unlike Aline, and so funny, that I roared with laughter. That evening, after we flew over to London for a formal dinner at Buckingham

Palace, I toasted Aline from across the table with a coffee cup and we laughed again. Her Majesty caught us sharing the private joke, but she hadn't a clue what it meant.

—

I would never claim to be a personal friend of Queen Elizabeth, but of all the Canadian prime ministers, I was probably the one she knew the best. I had been around for so long and had accompanied her on many of her trips to Canada as far back as 1970. I first saw the Queen in my new role as her prime minister in January 1994, when she invited Aline and me, along with Jean Pelletier, to lunch at Sandringham with other members of the royal family. It particularly pleased me to discover that the Queen Mother, like the Queen herself, spoke excellent French. In fact, she said, she enjoyed any occasion to speak French, so that's what we did all through the meal. She told me a couple of amusing stories about her first visit to Canada in 1939 with her husband, King George VI. At dinner one evening with Camillien Houde, the colourful mayor of Montreal, she remarked on the fact that he wasn't wearing a chain of office, as most of the other Canadian mayors had been. "Oh no," Houde said. "I wear it only on very special occasions." She thought that was very funny. And when he rode in the open car with the royal couple, waving at the cheering crowds that lined the streets, he said to King George, "You know, a few of them came out for you, sir." At the end of the lunch, when the Queen and I left for an official meeting, the Queen Mother took Jean Pelletier aside and taught him her secret recipe—a mixture of Dubonnet and gin.

Less than six months later, in June 1994, Aline and I were invited to attend a large reception at Buckingham Palace to commemorate the fiftieth anniversary of D-Day. All of a sudden a butler came over to me and announced, "Her Majesty would like to see you, sir." So, without saying anything even to Aline, I slipped away after him.

"Prime Minister," the Queen said, "I have a problem and I'd like you to help me. Mr. Bolger, the prime minister of New Zealand, would like me to go to all the Maori villages and apologize to them personally for their treatment under the colonial regime. What do you think?"

"Well, Your Majesty," I said, "I have a problem with that. If the government wants to apologize, fine, that's for the government to do, not the Queen. It would set a very dangerous precedent because, if you do that in New Zealand, I will have to ask you to do the same thing in Canada. But I warn you, we have more than six hundred First Nations bands, so you'll be on your knees for quite a long time."

She laughed and thanked me for my advice.

When I returned to the party, I saw Aline standing with Prime Minister Bolger and his wife. I put a hand over his shoulder and told him what I had just told the Queen. "Come on, Jim," I said, "you'll create a problem for Australia, for Canada, and for Her Majesty. There'll be no end to it, and I don't think that's her role anyway."

Just then the Queen herself appeared in front of us and saw me with Bolger. She looked at me and gave me a big wink. My wife, who had wondered why I had disappeared, made a good story out of it, and Bolger withdrew his request.

In November 1995, when we reached New Zealand for the Commonwealth conference after stopping in Israel for Yitzhak Rabin's funeral, the Queen had heard about the break-in at 24 Sussex. Having had to deal with an intruder of her own in Buckingham Palace one night in 1982, she went out of her way to show her concern, and both she and Prince Philip congratulated Aline for having acted so bravely in saving my life. Her Majesty and I also shared a laugh about a prank that had taken

place a couple of weeks before, when a radio comedian managed to get through to her on the phone by pretending to be me.
The conversation had been bizarre, to say the least. I split my
sides laughing as I listened to it, perhaps because, as one of the
few funny things that had occurred during the referendum campaign, it helped to break the tension I felt in those fraught weeks.
The Queen herself wasn't quite so amused, though she had handled the incident graciously. "I didn't think you sounded quite
like yourself," she told me, "but I thought, given all the duress
you were under, you might have been drunk."

—

In April 2002, Aline and I decided that it was important for us
to represent the Canadian people at the funeral of the Queen
Mother, even though it meant interrupting a series of important
meetings on African development to make a long detour from
Pretoria, South Africa, to Addis Ababa, Ethiopia, by way of
London. There we discovered that the organizers had chosen to
do things in the old imperial way, and, according to protocol, the
five "colonial" prime ministers were nobodies. First we were
told we would be taken to a side door of Westminster Abbey on
a bus. After some negotiation, we were permitted to arrive in cars,
subject to two conditions: our national flags were not to be flying
on the hood, and we were not to enter by the main entrance,
which was reserved for real big shots such as the wives of the
presidents of France and South Africa. Then we were seated in a
row at the back of the church and off to the side, far behind the
grand old families of Britain, the royal households of Europe
(even those who no longer had a throne to sit on), and all the
republican presidents, no matter how small or new the republic.
We were so well hidden that the CBC camera crew couldn't find
me in the crowd for the news report they were sending to Canada.

"We, the people," I joked with John Howard of Australia, an avowed monarchist who had fought a serious political battle to preserve his country's ties with the Crown—but he was furious. Helen Clark of New Zealand seemed to have had her Labour Party biases against the British upper class confirmed, while I thought the whole show was amusing at one level and completely unacceptable at another. At a reception afterwards I complained a bit to Tony Blair, who, I noticed, had managed to get himself into a special gallery near the front even though he too wasn't part of the official pageant, but he said there was nothing he could have done about it. Surrounded by the heads of Great Britain's most ancient noble families, all decked out in what looked like their great-grandfathers' ermine robes, Aline observed, "It smells like mothballs around here."

—

Unlike the president of the United States, who is both the head of state and the head of government, the Canadian prime minister is only the head of government. The Queen is Canada's head of state, with the governor general as her representative. As a result, even though I had to greet foreign dignitaries, preside over important ceremonies, open major events, and attend the weddings and funerals of VIPs, the constitutional role of the governor general spared me from having to perform hundreds, if not thousands, of other duties, from handing out honours and awards to giving speeches to worthy associations across the land.

Whenever there was a visiting head of state, the governor general hosted a dinner at Rideau Hall, at which I might be present but would not give a speech, and then I hosted my own lunch or dinner later. Similarly, while the governor general formally received the accreditation of foreign ambassadors to Canada, I met with them on particular issues and hosted an annual party for the diplomatic corps in the Parliament Buildings before Christmas. This hospitality was important, I thought, because many of these people would return home to more senior positions, and if they left with a strong knowledge and good impression of Canada, they could become useful allies someday in resolving any bilateral problems that might arise or in forging a common purpose in multilateral organizations.

The significance of the governor general means that the prime minister has to be particularly prudent about putting the right person in that position, someone who can speak about Canada with authority and ease in both official languages to kings and commoners alike and, should complex constitutional crises arise, deal also with those. The position also serves as an inspiration to our young people—and that was why I asked Jean Pelletier to suggest to my first choice, Roméo LeBlanc, that he marry his partner, Diana Fowler, if he wanted to be offered the job. My second appointee, Adrienne Clarkson, must have picked up the hint. When her name began showing up in the press as his possible successor, she casually let Pelletier know she had recently married John Ralston Saul.

Both LeBlanc and Clarkson were highly qualified individuals. He had been a journalist, Cabinet minister, and Speaker of the Senate. She had been a television broadcaster, book publisher, and Ontario's agent in Paris. Each choice had a symbolic significance as well. LeBlanc became the first Acadian ever to hold the office, which sent a message to all Canadians about the vitality of the French-speaking community outside Quebec, while Clarkson's personal history as a refugee from Hong Kong who settled in Toronto and learned to speak beautiful French was a living testament to Canada's diversity and opportunity in a global age.

"Over the last hundred years," I said at her installation ceremony on October 7, 1999, "this country has been built and enriched by immigrants, by people from all over the world who came to our shores, made a life for themselves and their children, and made Canada the extraordinary country that it is. At the turn of the last century, overseas immigrants came almost exclusively from Europe. Today we are on the eve of what many predict will be the century of the Pacific. How fitting it is that the remarkable woman who now occupies the highest office in the land is an immigrant from the Pacific—Chinese-born; a refugee who came here as a young child with her family; a woman who has made a major contribution to the cultural life of her adopted country. One hundred years ago, Mr. Speaker, who would have predicted that a woman immigrant from China could one day become governor general of Canada?"

Madame Clarkson, often accompanied by her husband, an author and a well-known personality in his own right, worked hard, articulated a clear vision of Canada in her many speeches, and travelled extensively across the country and abroad on behalf of the national interest. I certainly encouraged her to make as many trips as possible overseas. Her words, her story, and her image were enough to demonstrate to the world that Canada is a very special place, and she was able to establish useful connections to government, business, science, and the arts in countries I had no time to visit myself.

There was one problem, however, though it had nothing to do with her personally: few foreigners understood the constitutional role or colonial title of the governor general of Canada. If the governor general were called the president, everybody would have grasped at once the significance of this person, regardless of the fact that a president in a parliamentary system, as in Germany, Italy, Ireland or Israel, has much less authority than a president in a republican system, as in the United States or France. To get around the confusion, I toyed for a while with the notion of taking the existing title of president of the Privy

After eluding our bodyguards, Clinton struggles to keep up with the old man, Birmingham, England, 1998.

Showing French president Jacques Chirac the natural beauty of the North, September 1999. On the left, in white, is Nunavut premier Paul Okalik.

A tough assignment for the security detail.

Enjoying a friendly hockey game at Rideau Hall.

Shooting pool in Shawinigan, 1995.

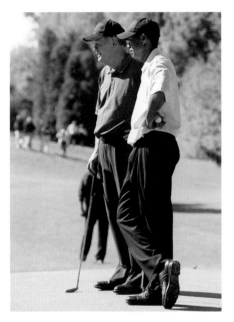

A nerve-racking game with Tiger
Woods, Montreal, September 5, 2001.

When in China, do as the Chinese do.

Always eager to get to work.

At the memorial service for those who died on September 11,
with Governor General Adrienne Clarkson, John Ralston Saul, Aline,
U.S. ambassador Paul Cellucci, and his wife, Jan.

Reassuring Canada's Muslim community at a mosque in Ottawa,
September 21, 2001.

An aspiring Blues Brother joins Dan Aykroyd in the living room at 24 Sussex, April 1999.

Diana Krall plays for one of her biggest fans, Mexican president Ernesto Zedillo, October 6, 1999.

A proud grandfather introduces Jacqueline, Philippe, Maximilien, and Olivier to Her Majesty Queen Elizabeth II, August 1994.

Aline and I honour the war dead, St. Petersburg, October 1997.

A chivalrous Jacques Chirac charms my Aline, June 1999.

Aline welcomes delegates to the Conference of
the Spouses of Heads of State and Government
of the Americas, Ottawa, October 1999.

Council, which is currently held by a member of the Cabinet, and giving it as an extra honour to the governor general. Over time, while all the powers and laws would remain the same, everybody would start referring to the governor general as Mr. or Mme. President, and the problem would disappear gradually. I didn't push forward with the idea, however, because, particularly as a Quebecer, I didn't want to stir up a hornet's nest about the fate of the monarchy or the Americanization of Canadian institutions. In many parts of the country, British traditions and symbols were still vitally important. I already had enough trouble on my hands with the separatists of Quebec, and I didn't want to take on the monarchists in the rest of Canada too.

———

Adrienne Clarkson was just one of the many women who contributed so much to their country during my time in office—to name but a few, Deputy Prime Minister Sheila Copps, Minister of Justice Anne McLellan, Clerk of the Privy Council Jocelyne Bourgon, Chair of the Canadian Broadcasting Corporation Carole Taylor, Chief Justice Beverley McLachlin of the Supreme Court, eight provincial lieutenant governors, and countless senators, MPs, and public servants. In fact, my first director of appointments was a woman, Penny Collenette, as were two of her three successors, Manon Tardif and Nikki Macdonald, and they were determined that good women should receive good jobs.

I used to get regular reports in which the appointments were systematically broken down into the proportion of women, of francophones, of visible minorities, and so on, in order to ensure that the government was being fair and proactive among excellent candidates with more or less equal qualifications. If one group seemed to be slipping behind, I used to urge my staff to do better. It was a kind of voluntary affirmative action, if you will, because I thought it essential for all Canadians to feel that they have an opportunity to participate in the governing of their country.

The same attention was brought to the appointment of the Cabinet and the nomination of Liberal candidates. Though many party workers didn't like the new rule introduced in 1992, giving the leader the right to select a riding's candidate in certain exceptional cases, it was done as much to increase the number of women running as Liberals for a seat in the House of Commons as to prevent single-issue groups from abusing the nomination process. Obviously it's a power that has to be used sparingly and with great tact, but it helped to break the pattern in which women either couldn't get nominated or got nominated only in ridings where the party didn't have any hope of winning.

Even as a young MP, I had earned the wrath of many old-time Liberal organizers in my riding for naming Rachel Bournival as my assistant. They thought it unacceptable that a woman should be given the important role of being my eyes and ears in the constituency. And, as minister of justice, I had to fight Trudeau to get him to appoint Bertha Wilson to be the first female justice of the Supreme Court of Canada. She was qualified, popular, and on everybody's list, but Trudeau had made up his mind to select another equally distinguished candidate—a man. Usually that would have been the end of the story, but I was convinced enough to take my case directly to the Cabinet. "I'm having a little disagreement with the prime minister," I told my colleagues in a matter-of-fact way, so as not to sound offensive. "I want to name Bertha Wilson, and he wants to name someone else. It's not often that I disagree with Mr. Trudeau, but what do you think?"

"We think you're right, Jean," came the unanimous answer. "She's great, and it's about time that a woman was on the Supreme Court."

If a minister had pulled a stunt like that on me when I was prime minister, I probably would have hit the roof. Trudeau, however, gave in.

Early in 2000, with the retirement of Antonio Lamer as chief justice, I had no hesitation about appointing Beverley McLachlin to succeed him. I had named her to the Supreme Court of British Columbia in 1981; I knew she had been an excellent judge since her elevation to the Supreme Court of Canada in 1989; and, following a francophone from Montreal, it was a happy coincidence to have an anglophone from Western Canada. She turned out to be a first-rate chief justice, and she has made me very proud of that decision.

In fact, I used to say, Canada was run by three women: the governor general, the chief justice, and my wife.

"When are you going to call an election, Mr. Chrétien?" the reporters always wanted to know.

"Whenever Aline says it's the right time," I always answered.

ELEVEN

NOT THE RETIRING TYPE

A line found it odd that less than a day after winning the second majority government in 1997, I had been asked how long I was planning to stay. If there's one thing the press likes more than anything else, it's a leadership fight, and all through 1998, 1999, and into 2000 they kept saying that it was time for me to go.

Even my older brother Maurice was trapped into agreeing with them. Maurice always loved an argument for argument's sake. If you said something was white, he'd say it was black, and vice versa. So when a reporter asked him why I should retire when everything was going so well, Maurice's habit prompted him to take the opposite position and declare that I had been in public life too long, had done enough, and now owed it to my family and myself to retire. If the question had been put the other way, he no doubt would have answered it to the contrary. Poor

Maurice, he was almost ninety, in failing health, and really upset by the headlines that resulted from his comments. He didn't sleep that night and was in terrible shape for weeks, worrying that he had somehow hurt me. I was his godson, after all, and he had practically raised me like a second father.

"Don't worry," I told him. "It wasn't fair to put you on the spot like that, but I've seen it all my life and I'm used to it."

I sympathized with all those media types who make a living out of writing negative stories. Though the government had its normal share of problems and crises, the late nineties were a very good time for me, my party, and the country. No matter how vicious the attacks, the Liberals maintained a strong lead in the polls, and the people of Canada continued to think we were doing the job they wanted done. The size of the deficit, the support for sovereignty in Quebec, and the number of trade irritants with the United States were all melting away. The economy kept growing year after year; unemployment kept going down. In 1998 the federal government balanced its books. We were paying down the national debt, cutting taxes, and investing in health, research, and higher education. The *Clarity Act* became law in June 2000 and received the approval of a substantial majority of Quebecers. Relations with the provinces were generally smooth and professional. President Clinton and I continued to enjoy a good working relationship. Canada was elected to the United Nations Security Council for a two-year term starting in January 1999; we were trying to bring peace to Kosovo with our NATO allies; and we were building a unique economic and diplomatic relationship with China and the other APEC tigers.

No wonder Aline had to slap my wrist for crowing about the government's standing in the opinion polls. Moreover, because I had passed the leadership review at the party convention in March 1998 with more than 90 per cent of the vote, I didn't need to be afraid of anything or anybody. We were also bringing in a lot of money at Liberal fundraisers, to fulfill my goal of leaving the party in a strong financial condition and ready for the next election.

Everything was going so well, in fact, that quite a few people were telling me to stay and fight for a third majority. A part of me liked the idea. I still had the energy, the interest, the ability, and the popular support, and there never is any end to the important, exciting, and unforeseen challenges of governing. There's always another good program to implement, another hard decision to make, another social problem to tackle, another sudden crisis to face, and I was confident that I was still as competent as anyone else to do the job. But I had made a pact with Aline not to run again. She had sacrificed years of her own peace and happiness for the sake of my career and she was tired of the demands of public life, and I fully intended to keep my commitment to her. In 1999, the year I turned sixty-five, she and I finished building a beautiful retirement home next to our old cottage on Lac des Piles. Nobody builds a large, expensive house with the intention of leaving it vacant for five years, and Harrington Lake was already at our disposal if we were looking for a place to go in the summer.

Besides, it's always a good rule in politics to quit while you're ahead. Two terms were enough. Indeed, many countries, including the United States, don't even allow a third term. I had survived the deficit cuts and the Quebec referendum, I had done my duty to my country, I didn't want to push my luck, and it was time to give someone else a chance at the top. In my mind, I would serve four of the five years for which I had been elected in 1997, lead Canada into the new millennium, announce my retirement in the fall of 2000, and leave the country and the party in excellent shape to allow my successor to win another Liberal majority government.

Everything went along according to plan until the spring of 2000. On the eve of the party's biennial convention in March, stories began to circulate that a couple of dozen Liberal MPs and organizers had held a secret meeting in a Toronto airport hotel to plan how to stop me from running a third time. I was aware, of course, that some of the ministers and their supporters were actively interested in the leadership. Ambition is a natural thing in politics, and it was understandable if ambitious people were starting to get anxious that their chance to win the brass ring might be slipping away. Paul Martin was working particularly hard, but Brian Tobin never hid his interest, John Manley was waiting in the wings, Allan Rock told me he was thinking about running, and Sheila Copps was probably going to try again. They each raised the subject with me at one time or another, or I teased them about it in public at the annual Press Gallery dinner. Even members of my own staff in the PMO were known to be speculating about whom they might support once I left.

One day when I was playing golf with Mike Robinson, an unabashed Martin organizer and a lobbyist with Earnscliffe Strategy Group, he hit a ball that narrowly missed my head. "Mike," I joked, "you don't have to kill me. There's other ways to make sure that your guy becomes prime minister."

As for the caucus, I found nothing offensive or abnormal in MPs' talking among themselves about the leadership. When I was a rookie with Pearson, Liberals were always getting together after hours over a few drinks to muse about the succession or to test the waters for their favourite candidate. The same happened under Trudeau. No leader remains for eternity, and if someone can gather future support, good for him, good for her. Far from being bothered, I knew for sure that I wasn't going to be staying for a third term, and I took it as a compliment that so many worthy candidates were eager to take my place. An exciting convention like the one at which Pierre

Trudeau had triumphed in 1968 could only be good for the party and for democracy. So I let them all organize quietly on condition that their campaigning didn't get out of hand in the media or interfere with their responsibilities as members of the Cabinet. I also warned them to be especially careful that their money-raising efforts didn't cause a conflict of interest—or even the perception of a conflict—with their departments.

As isolated as everybody thinks a prime minister is, I had many grassroots contacts throughout the party, I had a few ministers who never hesitated to give me the bad news along with the good, and I had some reliable members of Parliament who would tell me what their colleagues were up to because they were worried about the negative consequences for the Liberal Party and, by association, for their own electoral success. Whereas most people in most professions have a limit to how many people they deal with in the course of a week or a year, a politician gets to meet an endless stream of people from all walks of life, day after day. Experience makes you very astute at picking up on their behaviour and judging them accordingly. Whether in caucus, Cabinet, or the Commons, while seeming to be writing a note or studying a text, I listened, I observed, and I read the signals. Human nature being what it is, those who were badmouthing me behind my back always kept their distance from me in a room or avoided looking me in the eye. If I did something nice for one of them, bingo, he moved closer to sit with my friends, while the others kept whispering behind their hands over in the corner.

Still, the news of that meeting in Toronto took me by surprise, as did the sight on TV of Paul Martin scrambling down an escalator in order to flee from reporters' questions about what was going on. Not that I didn't know what he had been up to ever since I beat him at the 1990 convention. I well understood his thirst and impatience to be the boss before his hour passed and his age caught up with him. But he knew from me, from Eddie Goldenberg, and from Jean Pelletier that I did not expect to run a third time. The way things stood, he had reason to think he had a very good chance to win. He had only to be patient and to do his job well, and victory would fall into his lap.

I was hurt by his betrayal. I felt he owed me, at the very least, the decency of letting me retire on my own terms and some respect for the Liberal tradition—one of our greatest strengths—of supporting the leader. Hadn't I convinced him to become minister of finance and to accept the deficit-cutting strategy that he had adopted as his own as soon as it turned out to be a success, and bolstered his reputation by supporting him through thick and thin, all the time aware of the games he was playing to try to undercut my authority? If people were happy with the budget cuts, Martin accepted their thanks. If people were unhappy, he blamed the prime minister. Fair enough. It's normal for every minister to try to pass the buck, and in the end, to paraphrase Harry Truman, the buck did indeed stop with the prime minister. Canada was going through a very tough period early in our term during which we had to resist everyone's demands for more money, and I cared only that Martin was dealing with the government's number-one priority in the way I had established. Most times, I reasoned, if my finance minister looked good, I would probably look good too. Even so, it used to bother me to get reports that he was telling people he had taken their side in Cabinet or in an argument with me when I knew as a fact that he hadn't.

If there was a conspiracy afoot, I figured it would backfire badly. There was no mechanism to oust me until after another election; there had been no resignations from the Cabinet or uprisings in the party, except when John Nunziata voted against the 1996 budget and was expelled from the caucus; and Martin wasn't strong enough to orchestrate a coup. As well, though the antics of Martin's supporters grabbed the headlines, they didn't take away from the sense of pride and celebration the party was feeling. Sure enough, when I walked into the Liberals' biennial convention at the Ottawa Congress Centre on Saturday morning, March 18, 2000, hundreds of Young Liberals began to chant "Four more years! Four more years!"—and that became the slogan for the entire weekend. Some of the more unruly of them even swarmed around Martin shouting "Four more years!" to embarrass him in front of the cameras. But while I was addressing the convention, Aline studied the crowd as usual and grew increasingly upset at the sight of the Martin supporters who sat on their hands when everyone else stood and cheered. She's a proud person, and knowing as she did that I was going to be leaving, she thought I deserved better.

Afterwards, at a small gathering in a suite at the Congress Centre, my staff members were in a good mood. The grumblers in the caucus had been discredited, and the enthusiastic support of the Young Liberals had reflected the true mood of the party. "Now will you stay and run a third time, Mr. Chrétien?" someone asked me. "You're still high in the polls, and the country is in great shape."

"All the more reason for me to leave," I answered. "Besides, I've promised my wife that I will not run a third time, and I will keep my word."

Just then Aline interrupted. "Excuse me, Jean, I must go. We have a delegation from the riding coming to the house and I have to get everything ready to receive them." She left the room, closing the door behind her. An instant later she reopened it and poked her head back into the room. When everyone looked her way, she startled us all by suddenly shouting, "Four more years!" She got a standing ovation, led by myself. I had been liberated from my promise.

I didn't stay because I wanted to cling to power, beat Wilfrid Laurier's record in office, or deny Paul Martin his dream. I stayed because I loved the job and I had a mandate from the

Canadian people to complete the Liberal agenda. To be very frank, now that Aline had removed the only impediment to my staying, I was damned if I was going to let myself be shoved out the door by a gang of self-serving goons. By trying to force me to go, they aroused my competitive instinct, ignited my anger, and inadvertently gave me the blessing I needed from Aline to fight for a third term. For that, ironically, I owed Paul Martin a great deal of thanks.

Though there was some chatter that Martin, unhappy with the turn of events, might not stick around for the next election, he never discussed it with me and certainly never offered his resignation after the convention. And though I was annoyed enough for a day or two to think of removing him from Finance, firing the conspirators on his staff, and cancelling the government contracts with his friends and advisers at Earnscliffe, I was talked out of it by Jean Pelletier and Eddie Goldenberg, who were concerned about the financial community's reaction. Both were to regret their advice, and I soon regretted my decision to keep him.

—

Canada entered the new millennium full of optimism and success. With three balanced budgets under our belts, the government was ready and eager to embark on a new agenda. Figuring out what to do with a surplus is a nicer problem for a politician to have than wrestling with a deficit, but we wanted to be strategic in our new spending and to avoid the pitfalls of the past. I remember Norway's conservative prime minister, Kjell Magne Bondevik, telling me that distributing a surplus had caused him more political difficulty than reducing a deficit had—and, sure enough, his coalition government fell apart in 2000. Why? Because when there is a surplus and the economic trends all look positive, it's extremely hard to resist the pent-up needs and desires of the people.

Canadians wanted and deserved their just rewards after so many years of cutbacks and sacrifice. Some wanted their taxes reduced; others wanted more social programs. Some wanted the debt paid down; others argued that it was coming down automatically as a percentage of GDP and was already getting the unspent reserve. Just as I had decided on the 3 per cent target as party policy in the first Red Book in 1993, so I had decided in the second Red Book in 1997 that we would split the surplus evenly between new programs and a combination of tax relief and debt reduction. Predictably, whether inside the Liberal Party or among the opposition, the left wanted more for the former and the right wanted more for the latter, but I thought that 50–50 was a perfect balance between social justice and fiscal responsibility, the so-called Third Way.

Though the concept has often been attributed to Tony Blair, I had first heard the term at an informal session with Bill and Hillary Clinton and President Fernando Cardoso of Brazil during the Summit of the Americas meeting in Santiago, Chile, in 1998, when the four of us were discussing the idea of bringing together progressive leaders from around the world to talk about mutual problems and to share possible solutions. Though the idea became a reality a year later, Canada wasn't invited to the first conference on progressive governance because the host, Massimo D'Alema, the prime minister of Italy at the time, was a former Communist who clung to the European view that a liberal is really a conservative. Clinton regarded that as a mistake. Before the second meeting, which was to be held in Germany in June 2000, he told Gerhard Schröder that Chrétien had to be included or else he himself wouldn't attend. "His Liberals are to the left of my Democrats," Clinton explained, "and Canada is an important country and a member of the G8." In fact, Clinton often told me that he thought Canada was practising the Third Way better than any other country.

While other countries were planning to celebrate the second millennium with gigantic monuments and extravagant parties, we chose to continue spending money on building a knowledge-based economy for the twenty-first century. As trade barriers continued to come down around the world, Canada had to position itself to compete aggressively for investments, jobs, and growth, and that meant helping our people acquire and hone the necessary skills.

Education had been of primary importance to my own parents. When my dad was in his nineties, I remember, a television interviewer asked him why none of his children had gone to work in the paper mill right next door. He worked there, after all, and it was the dream of most of his friends to see their kids land a steady job in the factory at the age of sixteen, have a nice life, and retire with a pension at sixty-five. "The grass is always greener for those with an education," Dad replied, "and that's what I wanted for my family." He had held three jobs concurrently in order to put us through school, and my mom had been even more determined to give us a solid education. That ambition set them apart in the blue-collar community, but if they hadn't shared that conviction, as well as a competitive spirit and an ethic of hard work, my brothers and sisters would never have included two doctors, a pharmacist, two nurses, two businessmen, and a social worker, and I certainly would never have become prime minister. True, I never earned as much in that job as the lowest-paid player in the National Hockey League, but a lot of people seemed to want to take it from me anyway.

Even when money was tight, the government had begun to invest in education and youth. We established a prenatal nutrition program and improved child-care expense deductions. We restored the National Literacy Program, funded the

Aboriginal Head Start program, and launched SchoolNet and the Community Access Program, which brought the Internet within reach of all Canadians and made us the most connected nation on earth by the end of the twentieth century. When I met with the progressive leaders in Berlin in June 2000 and showed them a video of children in Rankin Inlet communicating with people in Japan, Europe, and the United States, they were amazed. President Clinton referred to it in his closing press conference as a model for the world.

Next, for sound economic and social reasons, we committed ourselves to working cooperatively with the provinces, academic institutions, business, and labour to improve access to higher education. While there was plenty of work available for university graduates, there were fewer jobs for people without a high school diploma. There was also a need to reverse the "brain drain," in which so many of our brightest scholars, scientists, and students were being lured to the United States or Europe by greater financial incentives and better research infrastructure. We didn't announce these extremely important long-term programs with a lot of chest-thumping just to win votes. For one thing, scholars, scientists, and students aren't usually the sort to parade in the street to say thanks to their government. For another, the guys on a production line in Shawinigan might well wonder why bourgeois professors were getting so much cash. But I insisted that we make these investments because it was the right and necessary thing to do, and many people in the government, the PMO, the public service, and the private sector worked hard to make them happen.

In 1997 we created an independent corporation, the Canada Foundation for Innovation, to upgrade the research facilities in our universities, teaching hospitals, and non-profit research centres. After Scott Clark, the associate deputy minister of finance, convinced me of its benefits, we decided to give it an

$800 million endowment, and its phenomenal success earned it another $2.8 billion later on. In the 1998 budget we announced the Canadian Opportunities Strategy, designed to give every Canadian who wanted to learn the chance to learn. It included a new Canada Education Savings Grant to help parents save for their children's college and university educations; it allowed Canadians to make tax-free withdrawals from their Registered Retirement Savings Plans to upgrade their skills throughout their working careers; and it eased the debt burden on university and college graduates to give children in low-income families a fair start in life. In addition, as the result of an idea Eddie Goldenberg and Chaviva Hošek had developed in the PMO, we invested $2.5 billion in the Canada Millennium Scholarship Foundation, which would fund 100,000 scholarships a year for ten years for needy students—the single largest investment ever made by the federal government to help young Canadians attending universities, colleges, or professional schools.

In 1999, thanks to the persistence of Dr. Henry Friesen, the president of the Medical Research Council of Canada, and my brother Michel, a well-known medical researcher who kept writing me memos to push us to do better, as well as the passionate advocacy of Health Minister Allan Rock at the Cabinet table, the federal government agreed to invest $500 million over three years to help create a new, multidisciplinary organization, the Canadian Institutes of Health Research, to link the best minds in diverse fields across the country, establish priorities, and get results. And, in 2000, through the efforts of two prominent academics, Robert Lacroix of the Université de Montréal and Martha Piper of the University of British Columbia, we began to endow two thousand Canada Research Chairs across the country, at the cost of $2.4 billion over ten years. The purpose was to allow the universities to attract the best young researchers at a time when the baby-boomers were about to begin to retire and we were heading into an intense worldwide competition for high-calibre replacements. In a remarkably short time, these initiatives turned the brain drain into a brain gain. In fact, they were recognized by university presidents, politicians, and bureaucrats at home and abroad as one of the most innovative and useful social policies ever implemented in any country. As Aline once told me, "You know, Jean, if programs like these had existed when I was young, I would have been able to go to university."

The only sour note came from the provincial governments, especially the PQ government in Quebec. Education was a provincial responsibility, they complained, and Ottawa had no right intruding into their jurisdiction. For me, however, we weren't interfering in the operation of the universities and hospitals, nor were we hiring or firing or telling anyone what to do. We were simply using the federal spending power to help young Canadians, Canadian researchers, and the Canadian economy in an extremely important sector of our society, as Ottawa had done for decades through the Social Sciences and Humanities Research Council, the Natural Sciences and Engineering Research Council, the National Research Council, and the Canada Council.

"I have been in public life quite a while," I had told the Liberal convention on March 20, 1998. "One of the descriptions that I am proudest of is that I am a 'practical' politician. I like to think that is someone who gets things done, who seeks solutions. Some think it is no substitute for vision, whatever they mean by that. To them, I say, vision is not political rhetoric. It is a young child in Rankin Inlet, connected to the world through the Internet, through SchoolNet, who learns that others in Toronto, in New York, in Tokyo are fascinated by his Arctic life. Vision is not political rhetoric. It is a working single mother in Surrey, BC, learning that she has won a Millennium Scholarship and will begin a new life. Vision is not political rhetoric. It is a child in downtown Montreal born healthy because his mother benefited from a prenatal nutrition program."

Ten days later, Lucien Bouchard came to see me about the Millennium Scholarships and to demand the right to withdraw from the program with full compensation. We had a hell of a discussion. "You know, Mr. Premier," I said, "you're from Jonquière, I'm from Shawinigan. You've been lucky to go to university, I've been lucky to go to university. But, like me, you must have had good friends who never went to university because they had no money, and they could have had a very different life if they had gone to university. There will be 100,000 of those kids in the future who will receive money from the federal government. And there will be about 25,000 students from Quebec who will receive these bursaries every year because I made that move. And I want to tell you there is not one living soul who will stop me. I'm investing in the brains of the kids. That is our monument for the new millennium."

He never fought me again on that issue.

—

Disagreement between Ottawa and the provinces is normal in Canadian politics. On the whole, however, I think the premiers treated me fairly, and we never built up any personal animosities. Most times, I understood, they were just doing what politicians have to do. Besides, the more they criticized me, the more they strengthened the importance of the office of the prime minister. When you're a mayor and you have a problem, you say it's the fault of the provincial government. When you're a premier and you have a problem, you say it's the fault of the federal government. And since the federal government can't blame the Queen anymore, we blame the United States as much as we can, because it's the big shot. Similarly, when the provinces complain so much about Ottawa, they're in fact recognizing the importance of the federal government in the lives of the people.

One thing that made dealing with the premiers and territorial leaders easier for me was our eight trips overseas with Team Canada, plus three to different regions of the United States. The idea grew out of an early invitation from André Desmarais, one of the most active and best-connected Canadian businessmen in China, to attend a meeting of the Canada China Business Council in Beijing in November 1994. When Mike Harcourt, the premier of British Columbia, heard about it, he asked to be invited too, because of his province's importance in the Pacific world. Then some other premiers jumped on the bandwagon. In the end I decided to invite them all along, as well as the territorial leaders, five hundred business executives, representatives of municipalities and non-governmental organizations, academics, government officials, and the media. It was an all-star team, the largest and most senior foreign mission Canada had ever fielded abroad, and, by the end of the trip, the most successful. We spent almost two weeks together travelling to China, Hong Kong, and Vietnam, negotiating with government officials, signing close to $9 billion worth of commercial agreements, holding joint press conferences, attending official receptions, and working in common for jobs and investments. The mood was upbeat and productive. One entrepreneur, I remember, didn't sell anything abroad but had to create dozens of jobs to meet all the sales he made to other company representatives on the plane.

The Team Canada missions to Asia, Latin America, Russia, and Germany made a vital contribution to the growth of our economy, because so much of our economy depends on exports. In India in January 1996, for example, we signed deals totalling almost $3.5 billion. By the time we arrived in Pakistan, President Benazir Bhutto had calculated we needed to reach $2 billion worth of deals if her country was to beat India handily on a per capita basis. By lunchtime we were at $1.3 billion, and a major negotiation to supply the Karachi transit system had stalled over the price. Madame Bhutto began giving orders to her officials in her native tongue, rapidly and firmly. A short while later the log-jam was broken and we hit the $2 billion mark. Without Team Canada, the lawyers would still be arguing today.

Team Canada also had a beneficial effect on our domestic politics. Out on the world stage, the premiers were clearly Canadians first and foremost—even Lucien Bouchard and Bernard Landry—and they stopped undercutting each other, as was the habit back home. They came to recognize that a company with a head office in Toronto might have plants in Quebec or British Columbia as well, and it wasn't uncommon to find two or three of them working side by side on the same file without feuding over the precise allocation of the investments. We all shared a great deal of pride in Canada's reputation as a peaceful, tolerant, and reliable trading nation, and the sight of so many politicians and CEOs pulling together with such competence and enthusiasm only confirmed that reputation in the eyes of the countries we visited.

Away from the office and the telephone, there were always opportunities in an airport or a hotel room for the premiers to come to discuss their problems with me one on one or in groups, and we developed a warm, relaxed rapport, despite the fact that Jacques Parizeau had refused to come to China because he preferred to stay behind and plot the dismemberment of Canada. One night in the bar of Shanghai's Peace Hotel, Ontario premier Bob Rae entertained everyone with songs at the piano and Manitoba's Gary Filmon danced with PEI's Catherine Callbeck. And the fact that our spouses usually came with us added a warmth and family feeling. Aline, assisted by our daughter, France, at her own expense, worked extremely hard to organize events and show everyone a good time. Indeed, Aline was such a charming hostess that the wives of some premiers used to tell their husbands not to give me hell when we got back to Canada because they didn't want to risk hurting her feelings.

The Team Canada trips made it very difficult for any premier ever to say that he or she never had a chance to talk to the prime minister of Canada about the issues of the day, even though I called only seven formal First Ministers' meetings in the ten years I held office. It's in the nature of those meetings to criticize rather than to get things done, and I didn't want to put the country through the wringer of any more failed conferences. I was determined not to call any at all if I couldn't be reasonably certain, going in, that enough groundwork had been done to produce a successful result.

At my first federal-provincial conference, which took place behind closed doors in December 1993, Ottawa merely signed the infrastructure deal that the ministers and bureaucrats had already hammered out with the federal minister responsible, Art Eggleton. At the second, in July 1994, thanks to the preparatory work of Industry Minister John Manley, we were able to reach an agreement with all the provinces and territories to reduce internal trade barriers, the first such agreement since Confederation. It provided concrete changes, timetables, and a plan to help make Canada a true economic union with a freer movement of people, capital, goods, and services, which included a dispute settlement mechanism to resolve trade differences among the provinces, an open procurement process for all Canadian companies, and a code of conduct. Generally speaking, the provincial governments were in favour of lowering the barriers, but their professional groups, whether doctors, lawyers, architects, or engineers, as well as the trade unions, were protectionists who wanted a closed shop for their own self-interest. In one ridiculous case, a contractor in Hull had to replace Ontario bricks with Quebec bricks. In another, a young Albertan who had gone to study medicine in Ireland was forced to pass a test to prove he knew English when he returned to practise in his native province. That sort of nonsense is still going on, but the professional associations are sacred cows that no politician dares to attack.

While the opposition parties and the press kept looking for fights, Ottawa and the provinces kept working in close cooperation. We got an agreement to reform and sustain the Canada and Quebec pension plans. We signed a fishery agreement with British Columbia. We coordinated the management of environmental problems so that every level of government no longer had to send its own inspectors to carry out the same air and water tests. In 1998, in conjunction with every province, territory, and First Nation—except the government of Quebec—we introduced the National Child Benefit, which sent monthly cheques to low-income families, and I kept the pressure on Paul Martin before almost every budget to keep enriching it. In effect, it replaced the old welfare cheque, got rid of the shameful stigma of poor parents having to present themselves before some bureaucrat with their tales of misery, and relieved the provinces of a lot of the cost and responsibility for looking after children in poverty. It was an important step by which Ottawa became more present in the lives of the people, and it brought Canadians closer than ever to achieving the minimum annual income that had been the dream of Liberals for decades.

In February 1999, we signed the Social Union Accord with every province but Quebec, though Premier Bouchard took the additional money for health care and accepted the new conditions anyway. It set down the principles and procedures by which the federal and provincial governments would work together to devise and deliver social programs for Canadians. The federal government agreed not to introduce any new joint programs without the consent of at least six provinces, for instance, while the provinces agreed to give Ottawa credit for the programs and account for the use of the money. The accord proved, if proof were still necessary, that the federation could improve and adapt without changing a word of the Constitution.

—

No social program was of more concern to Canadians during my time in office than health care. Though it is primarily the responsibility of the provinces, Ottawa has been deeply involved in the issue ever since 1966, when the Liberal government of Lester Pearson introduced the *Medical Care Act,* updated by the *Canada Health Act* in 1984. Intended to ensure that Canadians receive good heath care because they need it, not because they can afford it, the act imposed a national standard based on five fundamental principles—universality, portability, accessibility, comprehensiveness, and public administration—in exchange for which Ottawa agreed to cover half the costs. The federal government also continued to look after the medical needs of the Aboriginal people for an annual sum that eventually exceeded the health budgets of some of the smaller provinces, developed a national strategy on AIDS, funded research into breast cancer and other diseases through the Medical Research Council, launched an anti-smoking campaign, set up the Centres of Excellence for Women's Health, endowed the Canadian Health Services Research Foundation, and underwrote a host of other health-related initiatives, including the National Forum on Health, Senator Michael Kirby's report, and Roy Romanow's Royal Commission on Health Care Reform.

Medicare is a complex system, involving doctors and nurses, bureaucrats and administrators, more and more patients, more and more technology, and never enough money to do everything perfectly. An ambulance might not arrive fast enough.

An operation might be delayed too long. A flu epidemic might cause frustrating waits. Revolutionary procedures for hip and knee replacements, heart transplants, or cancer treatments—all of them non-existent and unimaginable when the *Medical Care Act* was introduced, as I know, because I was there—might put an unbearable strain on the system's financial and institutional resources. And all the bad stories are kept in the public eye by the opposition, the media, and the unions, while the good stories seldom get told.

The truth is that our system, while far from ideal, remains among the best in the world, as Bill and Hillary Clinton often noted when they tried in vain to reform health care in the United States. The hospitals respond quite well in emergencies, and, where there are waiting lists for non-emergency illnesses or procedures, doctors have always had the legal right to work outside the public system—as long as they don't charge a dime to the government. It becomes a problem only when they want to be inside the public system and outside it at the same time, operating privately but still receiving money from the government. That's a form of double-dipping and it's illegal, which was why Diane Marleau, the federal minister of health, took the courageous step in 1995 of withholding a portion of the cash payments to Alberta for contravening the *Canada Health Act*.

Premier Ralph Klein wasn't happy about it, needless to say, though he and I had always enjoyed warm personal relations. He's the type of no-nonsense guy I like, and vice versa, I suppose, because when I ran for the leadership of the Liberal Party in 1984 and Klein was mayor of Calgary, he was quoted as saying he supported me and might even run as a candidate for the Liberals if I won. When it came to health care, however, he was ideologically committed to mixing the two systems, and I felt that Ottawa had no choice but to confront him. In a mixed system, the best doctors would invariably end up taking care of the richest patients, who would still want public hospitals to be available to perform all the really expensive procedures. Though Alberta could have afforded to go all the way and said, fine, we'll open up private clinics and not take a cent from the federal government, its private sector probably didn't want to pay the extra costs, and most ordinary Albertans would have been aghast.

In practice, medicare is a social asset that benefits all Canadians, whether as individuals, families, or corporations. There's a sense of both justice and security in knowing that no one will ever have to lose his or her house because someone in the family is sick. In Canada, unlike in the United States, where some 45 million Americans aren't covered by health insurance, we don't have to go into bankruptcy to pay the bills if our child needs three or four operations in order to survive. It's a good economic program as well. In the United States, for example, automobile companies such as Ford and GM have to spend more money on medical coverage for their employees than they spend on steel for their cars. As a result, it's cheaper and more efficient for them to operate in Canada, which is one reason why we manufacture 18 per cent of North America's cars and car parts even though we represent only 10 per cent of the market.

Because public medicine is now recognized as part of our national values, Canadians have been willing to pay higher taxes than Americans to protect and enhance it, though the difference isn't all that great if you factor in the thousands of dollars U.S. citizens have to pay each year for their private services. But our system is expensive, and when our fight against the deficit forced us to cut everywhere, we could not ignore the increase in salaries and prescription prices, the fiscal consequences of longer lives and more home care, the cost of new machines and procedures, and the billions of dollars Ottawa had to send to the provinces for health care every year. In 1993 the United States was spending more than 14 per cent of its GDP in health care, Canada was second at almost 11 per cent, while most of the so-called social-democratic states whose public systems we admired—Sweden, Norway, Denmark, Germany, and France—were around 9 per cent. Japan and the United Kingdom were below 7 per cent. If these progressive countries could manage to keep their costs under control, I assumed we in Canada could increase our efficiencies and savings as well, though we never set a precise target.

In October 1994 I met with the National Forum on Health, an independent body of twenty-four experts in the field, to consider how to trim and improve the system. Were we getting the best results for our $50 billion of annual public expenditures? Should we have been spending more in some areas and less in others? Were we taking full advantage of new opportunities in the health field? How could we learn from experiences within Canada and other countries? But the reality is, under the Constitution, the federal government doesn't have the job of micro-managing the hospitals on a daily basis, just as it doesn't have the job of telling a university president how many students should be in a classroom or ordering a mayor to pave a certain road in town. That falls under the jurisdiction of the provincial governments, and it's up to their legislators and electors to make sure that the right services are provided as cheaply and effectively as possible. And ever since 1977, when Trudeau decided to transfer the federal contribution in the form of tax points and unconditional block grants, Ottawa has not had the ability to monitor whether Ontario spent it on cutting taxes or Quebec used it to open foreign offices instead of training more doctors and nurses. All we could do was uphold the five principles of the *Canada Health Act* by means of the cash we handed over to the provinces every year.

Thus, while the federal and provincial civil servants worked hard on joint efforts to improve the system, the concern at the first ministers' level was always about the cash. Our second budget in 1995 pooled the federal transfers for health, education, and welfare into one block grant, the Canada Health and Social Transfer (CHST), and told the provinces to expect significant reductions in 1996 and 1997. I wasn't completely happy with the one-year delay, but Paul Martin had promised it to the provincial governments in order to give them time to adjust to the new levels and maybe get past their next elections. That didn't stop them from blaming us for downloading our deficit problem onto them, even though we had cut our own program spending deeper than we had cut our transfers to them. Nor did we cut the equalization grants to the poorer provinces, more than a third of which, on average, was spent on health programs.

As well, the provinces never figured into their calculations the tax points that Trudeau had given them in 1977. Ottawa reduced its income taxes one day, the provinces increased theirs at the same time, and the average taxpayer never realized that what he used to pay to the feds he was now paying to the provinces. In other words, the provinces were able to increase their revenues by hundreds of millions of dollars without having to suffer any political penalty. That's why, whenever they complain about the fiscal imbalance, they always want Ottawa to hand over tax points, even though there's nothing to prevent them from increasing their own taxes at any time. They prefer Ottawa to give them money without getting the credit for it, and who can blame them?

The provinces also never gave Ottawa any credit for the fiscal dividend they earned because we had balanced the books. Though we had to cut the transfers in order to accomplish that, the provinces certainly would not have been better off in the long run if we had given them more money at the start, continued to run annual deficits, and forced them to service their debt at the old rates. More important, the decline in interest rates led to an enormous boom in business investments, housing starts, and economic growth across the country, all of which poured new revenues into the provincial coffers, especially given the extra tax points Ottawa had conceded to them.

The problem we faced was to make sure that the cash portion always remained large enough to give us a stick by which to enforce the *Canada Health Act*. Thus, the moment we could afford it, we increased the health transfers, according to the recommendation of the National Forum on Health, by $1.5 billion in 1997–98 and $11.5 billion over five years in February 1999. But it was never enough for the premiers. The pattern had been for them to show up at meetings with the prime minister of the day, grandstand for the benefit of the TV viewers back home, and demand more money or power without ever offering anything in return. If they didn't get their way, they sped off to denounce Ottawa as a stubborn bully to their friends in the press, who, in turn, love nothing better than participating in the sport of fed-bashing. Enough of that, I said to myself.

At the outset of the First Ministers' meeting on health in September 2000, I informed the premiers that the game was over: what was on the table was all they would be getting, and Ottawa wanted something back. Acting on the excellent work of an ad hoc Cabinet committee, Health Minister Allan Rock, and a team of high-powered officials, I then offered the provinces $21.7 billion over five years, to be tied to a number of specific goals, from home care to drug costs, from hospital equipment to an annual progress report that would make their governments accountable to the public. Any province that didn't sign the agreement wouldn't get a penny. I even hinted that I might call a snap election on the issue if the premiers stood in the way of solving the number-one priority in the minds of Canadian voters. However, I must have felt confident of success because of all the groundwork that had been done, or I wouldn't have called the meeting in the first place.

When six of the premiers unexpectedly objected to the very notion of a conditional deal, even though their own health ministers had already approved the conditions in principle, I got up and walked out of the room. A short while later, once I had cooled down sufficiently, I returned, but only to deliver a short, clear message: no conditions, no money. Then I left again. Though I suspected there would be some movement, I wasn't going to go back to the table unless I could be certain of an agreement. By mid-afternoon, Eddie Goldenberg was able to work out a clever statement that got four of the premiers onside without compromising the federal position. The last two holdouts, Mike Harris of Ontario and Lucien Bouchard of Quebec, soon broke down and grabbed the money—after reaffirming their commitment to Ottawa's national standards and accepting our new requirements.

Now, with that important issue out of the way, I was ready to think about an election.

—

The buzz around Stockwell Day after his election as leader of the Canadian Alliance the previous June had made nervous Nellies out of the Liberal caucus. However, I had survived the same "shooting star" phenomenon with Kim Campbell in the summer of 1993, and I knew that Stockwell Day was no Pierre Trudeau, however much of a post-convention honeymoon he might have been enjoying in the media. In fact, the polls were still showing the Liberals around 40 points, with the Canadian Alliance in second place no higher than 20. "When I was with Trudeau," I reminded the caucus, "we used to feel pretty good with a 3-point lead, so relax." I also thought that Day made a big mistake by showing up at a $5,000-a-plate fundraiser held by the business community in Toronto. "Oh-oh," I said to myself, "it looks like Bay Street wants you, kid, and I don't recommend that to anybody." The cockier he became after winning a seat in the

Commons through a by-election on September 11, 2000, the more tempted I was to go to the polls.

The campaign team wasn't enthusiastic about the idea—with the sole exception of my press secretary, Patrick Parisot—when a dozen senior organizers and advisers gathered in the living room at 24 Sussex in early September to talk me out of calling an election too quickly. Though we had got away with it in 1997, some argued, three and a half years was too soon to go to the people. Day still had a personal bump in the polls, others said. Spring would be a better time. We needed a platform, an organization, star candidates, nomination meetings—and a very good reason for an election. I explained my thinking, which was really my gut instinct. One, the economy could turn down by the spring. Two, the right could be united by then. Three, by now I had had a chance to look into Stockwell Day's eyes directly across the floor of the House of Commons, and I just knew I could beat him on the hustings.

To those who said an election would inflict an unnecessary expense on the country, I responded that the expense would have to come some day, and Canada would be better off if there was stability for another four or five years. But what if we got only a minority? That didn't scare me. I had been in two very productive minorities with Lester Pearson and one with Pierre Trudeau, and though a majority would be nice, a part of me would have relished the intellectual fun of handling a minority. By the end of the meeting everyone was revved up and willing to go. It was only a matter of putting together a platform, preparing a mini-budget, organizing the party machinery, and waiting for the perfect moment to pounce.

Meanwhile, I pursued a few star candidates to bolster the party on the left, in Atlantic Canada, and out west. I tried to woo Roy Romanow, Brian Tobin, and Frank McKenna into running federally. McKenna, a former premier of New Brunswick, declined.

Though he told me he was concerned about his wife's health, I heard through the grapevine that he didn't think I was going to win again. Romanow was a moderate social democrat from Saskatchewan as well as a personal friend. In 1984, when I ran against John Turner for the Liberal leadership, I had nearly persuaded Roy to become a Liberal. He came to that convention in Ottawa as a television panellist, and when it was over, I heard that, in one way, he was happy I had lost to Turner because it meant he could return to Saskatoon as a New Democrat, not as a Liberal. Now, sixteen years later, I knew he was thinking about retiring as premier of Saskatchewan and might be interested in coming to Ottawa. As for Tobin, though he had quit the federal government to become premier of Newfoundland in 1996, he had been a popular minister, he was demonstrating good qualities as the leader of his province, and he made no secret of his wish to succeed me.

In September, when Tobin and Romanow were in Ottawa for the First Ministers' conference on health, I invited them to 24 Sussex, hoping that Tobin would lend his considerable persuasive powers to helping me convince Romanow to join our team. "Roy," he said, "I'm going to run, and you have to come too!" Tobin, swept up in his own enthusiasm, found he had committed himself almost by accident. As I remember it, Romanow more or less agreed but a few days later called to say he couldn't do it.

I also tried to recruit another prominent New Democrat, Bob Rae, the former premier of Ontario. I had known him a long time. The Raes were almost family to me. Bob's father, Saul, was a retired diplomat who had been close to Pearson in the Department of External Affairs; his brother, John, started as my executive assistant in 1967, became the organizer of both my leadership runs, and oversaw the Liberal campaigns in 1993, 1997, and now in 2000; and I had tried to convince Bob himself to work in my office when I was minister of Indian affairs and northern development. He was a bright, pleasant, well-read person whom I had got to know better on the first Team Canada visit to China in 1994. Though he was hit by his province's severe economic downturn and lost to Mike Harris in 1995, he remained more popular than his party, and I thought he understood Canada very well.

He gave serious consideration to my offer, but eventually decided against it. Leaving his political home in the NDP would have been hard, and, with his children still in university, it was the wrong time for him to re-enter public life. I knew from my own experience, having left politics in 1986 and come back in 1990, the dilemma faced by many former politicians who are torn between a desire to return to the service of their country and the happiness of those they love. Staging a comeback can seem even more of a sacrifice than the first dip into politics. Suddenly the wife or husband is back on the road, and the family is separated again. The extra cash that had helped pay for the kids' education or fund a winter holiday dries up overnight. And much of the fun of life away from the glare of the media cameras evaporates as the whole weight of the world is put back on your shoulders. I was both impressed and glad when Bob Rae later changed his mind, because of his concern for the future of his country and a change in his personal circumstances, but he likely would have been elected leader of the Liberal Party in December 2006 if he had joined us earlier.

On Monday, September 25, the moment I had been waiting for arrived at last. Stockwell Day got up to ask an innocent question about taxes and concluded by demanding an election. I almost crossed the floor to kiss him. He could hardly blame me for calling one after three and a half years when he himself had demanded it. Apparently I had a smile on my face when I rose to reply. "Mr. Speaker," I said, "two weeks ago he was for an early election. Over the weekend he was not for an early election. Now he is for an early election. This gentleman flip-flops so much that we are having fun on this side. I tell him that Canadians know the person I am, a politician who has served

Canada for more than thirty-seven years. I will never be afraid to go in front of the Canadian people with my record and the record of the Liberal government."

—

Three days later, on September 28, fate intervened. While flying from trade-related meetings with a group of Central American leaders in Guatemala to a Caribbean Community summit in Jamaica, I learned that Pierre Trudeau had passed away. He had been ill for a long while and his death was somewhat expected, but it came as an emotional shock nonetheless. One woman who worked in Foreign Affairs came forward to offer me her condolences but ended up sobbing. For the most part I was left alone with my thoughts and memories. Pierre and I had been companions-in-arms for thirty-five years, as strong federalists in the battle against separation, as centre-left Liberals in the caucus and the Cabinet, as shoulder-to-shoulder members of the team—the family—that is the party. We had shared most of the same values; he had made my career by putting his confidence in me to do the toughest jobs; and though we had different backgrounds, personalities, interests, and circles, and never presumed to be best buddies, we respected each other as professionals and as people. Indeed, during the days ahead, alone in my office or at home, I too shed a few tears at losing his friendship and his counsel.

Trudeau's personality was a huge factor in explaining his success. In many ways Lester Pearson had been just as modern and progressive in his ideas, and had more obvious warmth and charm as a person, but he didn't have Trudeau's extraordinary charisma. From the moment Trudeau arrived on the scene in Ottawa, he was the odd man out, unusual in his style, exceptional in his intellect, and unpredictable in his ways. I had been watching a football game on TV with Pearson, during a tour of his northern Ontario riding, when he told me that the union leader Jean Marchand, the journalist Gérard Pelletier, and the essayist Pierre Trudeau were going to run as Liberals in the 1965 election. "Marchand and Pelletier are great catches," I replied, "but Trudeau—I'm not sure where we'll be able to get a guy like that elected." In fact, we did have trouble finding him a seat. The Liberal MP in Outremont, Trudeau's home riding and his first choice, refused to step aside. A riding near mine didn't want to have anything to do with an intellectual millionaire parachuted in from Montreal. In the end Trudeau had to run in an English-speaking suburb, and even there he had to fight to get the nomination.

Once elected, however, and in the Cabinet as minister of justice, Trudeau's handicaps as a traditional politician were turned to his advantage. It was the 1960s, after all. Suddenly his jeans and his sandals symbolized a new generation. His rigid, hard-edged debating skills, which had been seen as arrogance or contempt, made him look principled and courageous when he confronted Quebec premier Daniel Johnson Sr.'s "two nations" theory on national television during a federal-provincial conference in November 1967. And his bachelor lifestyle, his Mercedes sportscar, and his beautiful women somehow corresponded to his political values of individual liberty, human rights, and a Just Society. To everyone's shock or amusement, Trudeau the man was transformed overnight into Trudeaumania, and though he still had difficulty winning the Liberal leadership convention in 1968, the adulation carried him to victory in the subsequent federal election.

The high, almost crazy expectations didn't help him as prime minister, of course. Instead of peace and love, he had to deal with inflation, joblessness, regional disparity, and all the usual problems that challenge every Canadian prime minister, not to mention the FLQ crisis in 1970. He almost lost his second election in 1972. He won a third two years later, but only at the cost of his credibility after he changed his mind on wage and price controls. He watched the Parti Québécois take power in Quebec in 1976. He suffered the pain of a failed marriage. He was defeated by Joe Clark in 1979. And though he managed to return to power in 1980, win the first referendum, bring home the Constitution, and entrench the Charter of Rights, he was much maligned by the time he left office in 1984. The Tories, the pundits, and even some Liberals blamed him for every failure, from the size of the deficit to the absence of Quebec's signature on the constitutional deal. The Reagan administration didn't care for his nationalistic policies or his peace initiative, and the separatists dragged his name through the mud.

I always found Trudeau philosophical about his critics and never obsessed with his place in history. There was little he could do about either of them was his attitude, and he wasn't going to be around to read the historians anyway. Though he rarely phoned me after his retirement, I sought out his views every once in a while and invited him to 24 Sussex on a few occasions, including a lovely dinner with some of his oldest friends in honour of his eightieth birthday in October 1999. He will always be remembered, I said then and still believe, as the first and greatest prime minister of the new Canada, the personification of modern Quebec on the federal stage, and our first international superstar. Wherever I travelled as prime minister, all sorts of people, from party officials in China to wine growers in Italy, used to ask me about Trudeau for several reasons: his reputation as an interesting thinker and long-surviving politician, the notoriety of his ex-wife, his standing among world leaders. Compared to Nixon and Reagan, he offered hope and inspiration to liberals everywhere. Compared to Carter and Ford, he gave excitement and copy to the media. He was the JFK of his time.

When it came to the government's own tribute to Pierre Trudeau's greatness, strength, and love for his country's natural beauty, I thought there could be no more appropriate memorial than our highest mountain, which had been named in honour of William Logan, the nineteenth-century founder of the Geological Survey of Canada. The largest lake in southern Saskatchewan was Lake Diefenbaker, after all, and Trudeau and I had once made plans to climb a Yukon peak that had been renamed following the assassination of John F. Kennedy. (When I proposed we take a helicopter most of the way up Mount Kennedy and hike the rest, just as Robert Kennedy had once done, Trudeau insisted we had to go entirely on foot. That was typical of him, in both the very exacting standards he set for himself and a certain lack of practicality as to how it might affect other people. But because we couldn't spare so much time, we never did it.) Unfortunately, those in Western Canada who still reviled Trudeau's name because of the *Official Languages Act* and the National Energy Program raised a commotion, and one of the few things I regret in my career is my decision to cave in to their pressure rather than give Pierre Trudeau the honour he deserved. In due course, however, my government named Montreal's international airport after him and contributed $125 million toward the establishment of the Trudeau Foundation, which awards scholarships and fellowships in his memory.

Millions of Canadians mourned his passing—some because of a nostalgia for their own vanished youth; some because he had been in the centre of their consciousness, through good times and bad, for fifteen years; some because of his vision of a Just Society and his achievement of the Charter of Rights; some because his economic and constitutional legacies didn't look quite so bad after ten years of Mulroney's deficits and the folly of Meech Lake. And so, to allow us all to pay a heartfelt tribute to both the man and the values he courageously stood for, I postponed going to the polls until the extraordinary outpouring of grief and affection had subsided.

Among the dignitaries at Trudeau's funeral, held on October 3 amid a crush of somber and teary-eyed Canadians standing outside Montreal's historic Notre-Dame Basilica, were Jimmy Carter and Fidel Castro. Apparently they kept their talk to baseball. Castro, wearing a dark pin-striped suit instead of his usual military uniform, also had a brief conversation with Stockwell Day. Afterwards, during my private meeting with the Cuban president, he said to me, "If I were you, I'd call an election."

——

The campaign, which was finally launched on October 22, wasn't so much about issues as it was about values. It was very difficult for the opposition parties to attack the Liberals from either the right or the left when most Canadians wanted their federal government to remain in the centre—balanced, to be more precise, between the right on economic issues and the left on social issues. Now, having undermined the divided right with our strong fiscal record and tax cuts, we could afford to move to the left with health care, education, Aboriginal reforms, the arts, and children. Indeed, it had long been my view—and someday it will happen—that the progressive elements in Canadian society shouldn't split themselves between the Liberals and the New Democrats. King, Pearson, and Trudeau had tried to bridge the chasm, and so did I. Not only did I want to absorb more NDP voters, but I wanted to finish my career where I had begun it: as a defender of social justice and equality of opportunity on the centre-left of the political spectrum.

I never felt I was in any danger of losing to Stockwell Day. He was in many ways a fresh and interesting personality, but he came from the religious right, which is dangerous ground in most of Canada, and his background as a Cabinet minister in Ralph Klein's government in Alberta raised suspicion that he had a hidden right-wing agenda. Nor was he a skilled campaigner. He tried to use Niagara Falls as a symbolic illustration of Canada's brain drain to the United States, until a reporter pointed out to him that the Niagara River actually flows from south to north. He became a figure of fun when his creationist beliefs prompted Liberal strategist Warren Kinsella to reply that *The Flintstones* wasn't a documentary, while Day's direct-democracy and anti-gay views inspired Rick Mercer to get hundreds of thousand of signatures petitioning him to change his name to Doris. During the leaders' debate, Day embarrassed himself by holding up a sign reading "No 2-tier healthcare" to try to put to rest the persistent rumours that the Alliance was going to destroy Canada's public system. Meanwhile, Progressive Conservative Joe Clark wanted to talk only about scandals and broken promises, Bloc Québécois Gilles Duceppe wanted to talk only about scandals and sovereignty, and New Democrat Alexa McDonough wanted only to be heard.

On November 27, we Liberals won our third consecutive majority and increased our representation in the Commons from 155 to 172 out of 301. We regained most of the seats we had lost in 1997 in Atlantic Canada. We stopped the Alliance from picking up more than two seats in Ontario. Best of all, in spite of the all-out efforts of Lucien Bouchard and the PQ organization, we took nearly half the seats in Quebec and beat the Bloc Québécois by almost 5 per cent in popular vote. Coming as the election did only eight months after the passage of the *Clarity Act,* the result was a tremendous setback for the separatists. In fact, it was Bouchard's Waterloo. Unable to ignite a popular reaction against Ottawa's move, unable to defeat me in my own riding, unable to foresee the winning conditions for another referendum, he announced his retirement from politics in January 2001.

On a personal level, perhaps what made me proudest was to be given the opportunity by the people of this great country to lead Canada into a new century just as my hero Wilfrid Laurier had done, with the same economic boom, the same social harmony, the same open arms, the same values of tolerance and liberty and hope. Like Laurier in 1900, I had no idea in 2000 how quickly and how severely we would be tested as a people and as citizens of the world.

TWELVE

NO TO WAR

———

Three weeks before our third victory, George W. Bush won his first presidential election in the United States, defeating the Democratic contender, Al Gore, by so small a margin that the result wasn't finalized until the middle of December. By way of comparison, an American television network had sent a reporter to examine our voting system. Canadians, he reported, vote by marking an X on a piece of paper; they count the ballots by hand, and they announce the results the same night. Our old-fashioned system is better than any new-fangled voting machine. Not only is it guaranteed to work, but there's something I find appealing in putting a mark on a piece of paper for the candidate of your choice, as opposed to pulling a lever as if you were gambling on a slot machine in Las Vegas.

Before Bush took office, I flew to Washington on December 2 for a farewell meeting with Bill Clinton. The White House was busy with volunteers putting up Christmas decorations, as well as a documentary film crew following the president for the day, and I got roped into putting ornaments on the tree before the camera. Though Clinton seemed relaxed and upbeat, wearing a sweater and telling stories, he gave me a remarkably detailed analysis of the American election—district by district, this poll captain here, that voter turnout there, this group that had switched, that organizer who had delivered the machine—and he concluded that Gore was the legitimate winner. And, he joked, as he had in the past, "When I was in high school, you were in Parliament. When I was in university, you were a Cabinet minister. Now I'm leaving the presidency, and you're still prime minister."

Though I was going to miss dealing with him, we would remain personal friends. In April 2003 we happened to be holidaying at the same time in the Dominican Republic and got together for a game of golf. Afterwards, over lunch, he delighted in the fantasy that, because Arkansas had been part of the Louisiana Territory in the days of the French Empire, he would be legally eligible to run to be president of France. "I have a proposition for you, Bill," I said. "I'll make you a Canadian citizen and then you'll be able to run to replace me as leader of the Liberal Party and become prime minister of Canada. I'm sure you would have no trouble winning the election, especially given your popularity in Quebec." Slapping his thigh with laughter and delight, he loved the idea of sitting across the table from George W. Bush and taking him to the cleaners on all the files he knew so well.

On February 4, 2001, I returned to Washington for my first meeting with George W. Bush. The media had tried to make a fight between us from the start. The previous summer, they had unfairly criticized my nephew Raymond, who was still our ambassador to Washington, for suggesting in a speech he gave in Ottawa that Canada was hoping for a Democratic victory, whereas he had simply stated the obvious fact that Vice-President Gore knew more about Canadian-American issues than the governor of Texas did. Then the comedian Rick Mercer caught up with Bush on the campaign trail and tricked him into referring to me as Prime Minister Jean Poutine. And then there was a fuss because President Bush had met with the president of Mexico before meeting me, as though that had been a deliberate insult to Canada instead of two neighbours getting together across the Texan border. In fact, I was the first foreign head of government to visit the new president at the White House, but if I had been the second or third, so what?

I found Bush to be cordial, meticulous, and extremely polite. We had in common the fact that we were traditional family men and had been underestimated our whole lives. We also liked to have meetings begin and end precisely on time. Unlike Clinton, who had loved long seminars and meandering debates, Bush kept to an agenda, knew what he wanted to say, expressed it clearly and succinctly, listened attentively, then went ahead and did whatever he wanted to do without really caring if you agreed with him or not. I began by telling him the same thing I had told President Clinton: Canada and the United States are the best of friends, close allies, and share many of the same values, but Canada is of much more use internationally if it keeps its independence than if it looks like the fifty-first state. "I don't want to offend you, Mr. President," I said, "but I think it's important for both countries that I keep my distance."

Far from being offended, Bush seemed curious, and I suppose he had been briefed about my long experience as a survivor in politics. He was full of good questions about a wide range of topics. He also followed every kind of sport, kept himself physically fit, and had a charming sense of fun. You could tell he had enjoyed some good times in his youth with frat brothers and cowboys. Though Bush and I never got into the nitty-gritty of domestic politics as I had with Clinton, we swapped a lot of stories and statistics about baseball and football between our official meetings, and I found he responded well if I coated a tough message with a light joke. One time, after confronting him in very strong terms about his government's decision to impose a $2.5 billion tariff on Canadian softwood lumber, I added, "You know, George, your baseball players love the bats that are made in Canada with good Canadian maple wood. I'll stop their export, and the Texas Rangers won't have as many home runs. Maybe that's your plan, because if your ball players scored less, you wouldn't have to pay them as much. Alex Rodriguez, your shortstop, is going to make $250 million in ten years just for picking up a ball or hitting it with a Canadian bat. I've calculated that you're going to have to be the president of the United States for four hundred years to earn the same amount of money." He laughed, though he clearly understood that softwood lumber was no laughing matter in Canada.

During a dinner in the White House dining room, with a dozen high-ranking Canadian and American officials sitting around the table, I told him and Vice-President Dick Cheney about the Alberta oil sands, and was surprised to discover that the two Texas oilmen weren't aware that Canada had reliable reserves potentially on the scale of Saudi Arabia's. "If I were to stop selling you Canada's oil and gas and electricity," I teased, "you Americans would need a hell of a lot of softwood lumber to heat your homes."

Cheney, knowing that Vladimir Putin had visited Ottawa a couple of months earlier, asked what I thought of Russia's new president, who had succeeded Boris Yeltsin in December 1999. "He's an intelligent guy," I said, "articulate, knowledgable, serious, always methodical and on topic. Pleasant to be with, though not as much fun as Yeltsin, of course. I was impressed by him. He has a hell of a tough job on his hands trying to change a political system with no decent bureaucracy and to bring a backward economy with no proper infrastructure into the twenty-first century—even considering Russia's vast quantities of oil at high prices."

"But wasn't he a KGB guy?" Cheney asked.

"Yes," I said. "I once discussed that with him. He had grown up in hard circumstances and, after graduating from university, needed a job. The KGB offered him one, so he went to work for it. It was as simple as that."

Bush interjected to make what I thought was a very smart remark. "Don't forget, Dick," he said, "Putin was never the head of the KGB. My father was head of the CIA."

Of course, I disagreed with Bush on a number of issues. I was a Canadian Liberal; he was a United States Republican. I was against capital punishment, he was for it; I was for gun controls, he opposed them; I supported freedom of choice for women, he was against abortion. However, since I wasn't an American voter, his social views weren't really my problem, and if I sometimes had disagreements with my ministers, my staff, or my friends about these and many other matters, that didn't mean we were enemies. As far as I was concerned, we had started out on the right foot. Bush must have thought so too, because he sent me a photograph inscribed, "Jean—the beginning of a great friendship." Maybe he realized I wasn't going to be such a difficult guy to work with after all, despite all he might have heard from Brian Mulroney, and Canada-U.S. relations were more important than our personal relations anyway.

Bush's first visit to Canada, a three-day stay in Quebec City to attend the third Summit of the Americas in April 2001, was also his first appearance at a major international gathering of heads of government. As the host and by now a veteran of these get-togethers, I went out of my way to introduce him to all the other leaders. Unlike some of them, Bush always arrived on time, stayed for the entire day, and listened attentively to each speaker.

He also appreciated how smoothly we ran the show in the face of the protest demonstrations, which were relatively peaceful compared to those that had disrupted the World Trade Organization meetings in Seattle two years earlier or the IMF and World Bank meetings in Prague the previous year. The only slight delay occurred when the opening ceremony started an hour late because the prevailing winds had come round and blown tear gas through the venting system into the hall where the thirty-four leaders were to gather.

The summit coincided with a small but irritating border dispute in which American potato growers managed to obtain a ban on imports from Prince Edward Island after the discovery of a harmless "potato wart" on the produce from one remote farm. So I gave instructions that PEI potatoes were to be served to President Bush at every meal. During the last lunch, at a NAFTA trilateral meeting held in the Citadel looking over the St. Lawrence River and north to the Laurentian hills, Colin Powell turned to Bush and, translating the French menu, said, "He's still serving us PEI potatoes."

"You see, George," I said, "you've been eating PEI potatoes for two days now, and you're still alive. So tell your guys in Washington that they're wrong." Apparently he did, because the problem was quickly solved.

———

Five months later, on the morning of Tuesday, September 11, 2001, I met at 24 Sussex with Lorne Calvert, Roy Romanow's successor as premier of Saskatchewan, to discuss agriculture, highways, equalization payments—all the normal Canadian issues. We had been scheduled to meet the day before, but the House wasn't sitting and it was also my wedding anniversary, so Aline and I wanted to be alone together. Calvert graciously agreed to rearrange the business appointments he had in New York City and come to see me instead. All of a sudden Bruce Hartley, my executive assistant, rushed into the living room to say that a plane had just flown into one of the World Trade Center's twin towers. A very unfortunate accident, I thought. A moment later, however, he was back with news that another plane had flown into the second tower. Premier Calvert left, though not for New York, of course, and I went upstairs to the sitting room in time to watch the towers fall. By now I knew, like everyone else, that this was a terrorist attack aimed at the heart of Wall Street, the United States, and Western civilization. "The world is going to be a very different place from now on," I remember thinking.

I began making a number of phone calls—to the chief of the defence staff, the commissioner of the RCMP, our ambassador in Washington—to get more information about what was happening and to organize our emergency response. I also tried to reach Paul Cellucci, the American ambassador to Canada, but he was in Calgary. Not wanting to bother President Bush himself in the midst of a crisis, I asked the U.S. Embassy to pass on Canada's condolences and offer whatever humanitarian help we could provide. Later, after all the commercial flights were cancelled, I sent a Challenger to bring Cellucci back to Ottawa. From 24 Sussex I could see a light aircraft taking off from the small airport across the river in Gatineau, Quebec. We didn't yet know who the terrorists were or what their next target might be, and that little plane suddenly looked very close and very threatening.

I wasn't afraid so much for myself as for Aline. As it happened, she was downtown at the Byward outdoor market, not far from the new U.S. embassy. She had just handed over a twenty-dollar bill for three dollars' worth of fresh corn when, before she could even receive her change, her bodyguard yelled that she had to leave at once and practically threw her into the back of the RCMP car. "Why don't you go out to Harrington

Lake?" I said to her by phone. "It will be safer for you there."
But she refused to leave my side.

Like everyone else, I spent the rest of the day not certain
what had occurred or what was coming next. However, I have
a tendency to become cool rather than panicky in crisis situations. Both my personality and my experience had led me to
adopt a low-key approach, to quietly and methodically solve
problems without making a drama out of them. It's the
Canadian way to do things—smoothly, informally, without a lot
of bragging and noise. When I heard on the radio, for example,
that tens of thousands of Canadians were donating blood, I
thought that was a good and practical thing to do, so I went
down to a clinic without any fanfare and gave a pint of my own.
Some Monday-morning quarterbacks suggested that I should
have closed down the government offices, sent all the bureaucrats home, sealed the borders, and rushed to console the nation
on TV. Perhaps, but as prime minister you have a responsibility
to remain calm, rational, and in charge when people are upset
and looking to you for leadership. There's little room for fear
or error, because the least sign of weakness or the smallest mistake can have terrible repercussions.

Without taking any chances or dismissing any dangers, I
didn't believe in my heart that the terrorists had targeted Canada.
They could have, just as they could have targeted London or
Paris, but it was soon evident that their focus this time was only
on New York and Washington. Instead of putting the government on red alert, with war rooms and emergency meetings, I
kept in contact by phone with my advisers, the clerk of the Privy
Council, and the various ministers who were most directly
involved, even if most of them hadn't yet returned to Ottawa for
the opening of Parliament. They all got down to work to figure
out how this tragedy might affect their departments—Eggleton
in Defence, Collenette in Transport, Martin in Finance, Manley

in Foreign Affairs, and so forth. They talked with their deputies, the deputies with their bureaucrats, the bureaucrats with each other. As long as I was being kept fully informed of what everyone was doing and knew that everything was under control, I didn't worry about not being able to hold a special Cabinet meeting until everyone got back to town. There were no collective decisions that had to be made, no controversial options that I wanted to test out on my colleagues. I had full confidence in the ministers and their officials. As for the House of Commons, the opposition could wait until Monday, as scheduled, to ask questions and have an emergency debate.

The most immediate decision that needed to be made was whether Canada should accept more than two hundred planes that had been forbidden to fly over or land anywhere in the United States. Collenette gave an immediate yes, without having had to consult me, and I fully concurred. Some forty thousand American passengers were welcomed, fed, and comforted for several days by thousands of Canadians, mostly in Newfoundland and Nova Scotia, who did their country honour by opening their homes, their hearts, and their wallets to strangers in distress. The town of Gander alone, with a population of ten thousand, took in more than twelve thousand people without missing a beat. Too often we Canadians don't appreciate how special we are. I've met or heard from dozens of Americans who claimed that their lives were changed by the kindness of Canadian families who gave them everything, even when those families themselves didn't have much. One letter, I remember, told me of an exchange between a Canadian host and his American guest. "Don't think about it," the Canadian protested, embarrassed by so much thanks. "You would have done the same for us." To which the American replied, "I only wish we would."

A more difficult decision came when an unidentified Korean Airlines 747 failed to respond to the control tower in

Anchorage, Alaska, and was heading towards Canada. There was some suspicion, I was informed by phone as I was being driven to the Hill, that it might have been hijacked by terrorists who could be intending to crash it into Vancouver or Edmonton. I gave authority for the plane to be followed by American jet fighters and, if necessary, shot down, though not without calling me first. It was a heavy responsibility, with hundreds of innocent lives at stake and possibly on my conscience, but I had been trained to make that sort of quick assessment, and there wasn't much choice given the potential risk to so many other people. Fortunately, no further action was needed.

The following morning I received a phone call from President Bush, who had already heard many reports of the sympathy and generosity of Canadians. He asked me to thank them on his behalf. I also talked with Prime Minister Silvio Berlusconi of Italy, in his capacity as the current chair of the G8, about what we might do collectively in response to this attack on one of our allies. Then I turned my attention to the national ceremony we were planning for the Friday to pay homage to the dead, two dozen of whom were Canadian. Over the strong objections of the RCMP and the Ottawa police, I decided to conduct it on the lawn in front of the Parliament Buildings, as a way of expressing our grief and support in a free and public fashion, reassuring the people of Canada that there was no cause for panic, and showing the world that we were not hiding in fear. It was the right thing to do, not least because the anticipated crowd of 15,000 turned into 100,000 people. I especially hadn't wanted the ceremony to take place in a church or be presided over by the different religious representatives who were already bickering about who should or shouldn't be invited and what prayers should or shouldn't be said. I didn't feel this was the time, for obvious reasons, to put religion and clergy front and centre. It was a time to come together as citizens and human beings to mourn, reflect, and fortify ourselves—

not in a sectarian cathedral surrounded by soldiers and police, as other nations were going to do, but in a collective three minutes of silence in which everyone present or watching on live television across Canada and the United States could offer a prayer according to his or her own faith. Governor General Clarkson, U.S. Ambassador Cellucci, and I were the only ones who spoke.

"At moments like this," I told the crowd that had gathered at noon on a beautiful autumn day, "we can only cling to our humanity and our common goodness, and, above all, to our prayers. At moments like this, what we feel and the gestures we make are all that matter. The wave of sympathy and support from Canadian men and women clearly expresses the feelings that have moved them to make such gestures. So, even when we cry for our own dead, the message we send to our American friends is equally clear: Do not lose courage. You are not alone in this. We are with you. The entire world is with you."

—

I have always made a sharp distinction between the role of religion and the role of the state. That goes back to the days when Liberals such as my grandfather and Wilfrid Laurier had to resist the interference of the Roman Catholic Church in the political affairs of the people. For me, the church is the church and the state is the state. The two are separate spheres of life, and part of my job as prime minister was to keep them separate. And though I consider myself a good Roman Catholic, it would have been wrong for me to try to impose my beliefs on a multi-religious society—not least because I wouldn't like to have someone else's beliefs imposed on me. Thus, when I became the leader of the Liberal Party, I had to step in before the 1993 election to prevent a number of our riding associations from being taken over by anti-abortion religious zealots. No, I said, you have the right as a

Liberal to be pro-life or pro-choice, and we can have a civilized debate about it, but you aren't allowed to turn the party into an instrument for an interest group with one specific agenda. In other words, while there undoubtedly were some Liberal candidates who were pro-choice, they had not been selected simply because they were pro-choice. When the bishop of Calgary declared that I was going to go to hell for tolerating the rights of homosexuals, my wife said, "If you go, Jean, I'm going with you."

In the United States, by comparison, the fundamentalist Christian churches had succeeded in hijacking the Republican Party for their own aims. I don't think that serves any society very well. On the contrary, making everybody feel equal is the best way to protect all religions. I am happy to see so many strong religious groups in Canada, and they're free to hold their own values and beliefs as long as they don't try to impose them on the whole society. That's why, on September 21, 2001, ten days after the attacks on New York and Washington, I made a particular point of coming to the defence of innocent Canadian Muslims who were experiencing the sting of an emotional and sometimes racist backlash.

"I have come here as your prime minister," I said in my speech at a mosque in Ottawa, "to bring a message of reassurance and tolerance. I know that the days since September 11, 2001, have been ones of great sadness and anxiety for Muslims across Canada. Because the cold-blooded killers who committed the atrocities in New York and Washington invoked the name and words of Islam as justification, many of your faith have felt constrained when expressing your sympathy and solidarity with the victims. This despite the fact that many Muslims also perished in the attacks. Worse, some of you have been singled out for denunciation and violence, acts that have no place in Canada, or any civilized nation, and have made me feel shame as prime minister. I wanted to stand by your side today and to reaffirm with you that Islam has nothing to do with the mass murder that was planned and carried out by the terrorists and their masters. Like all faiths, Islam is about peace, about justice, and about harmony among all people."

For some editorialists, the National Day of Mourning hadn't been enough. They wanted me to do something dramatic, perhaps jet to New York to be among the first to visit the site of the tragedy or show up in Washington to be seen at President Bush's side. It certainly wasn't that I didn't want to show my sympathy, but I didn't feel comfortable with the idea of orchestrating a photo op in front of that horrible mass grave or elbowing my way next to the president at the hour of his greatest trial, simply to please the press photographers. I felt it would be in very poor taste. The Americans had more substantial things to worry about than trying to organize a visit from the Canadian prime minister, and I had no personal desire to push myself forward, as some of the other leaders were doing. If Tony Blair wanted to be seen at Bush's side in order to strengthen his position in Europe as the United States' closest ally, that was his call, but it wasn't in my character to try to spin some political advantage out of the innocent dead. In fact, I agreed to go to New York only after the crisis had passed and in the company of the other federal party leaders. Even then, I much preferred the time when I joined the thousands of Canadians who went on their own initiative in early December to show their personal solidarity with the people of the city.

On September 20, when President Bush failed to include Canada in the list of allies he thanked during his address to Congress, many Canadians were outraged, considering that we had done more for the United States in its hour of need than any of those named, and the opposition used this omission as evidence that I had somehow offended the Americans. Perhaps the president should have remembered us, but every leader (or his speechwriter) makes that kind of accidental mistake once in a while, and I personally didn't read any bad faith into it. In fact, as Bush mentioned during our luncheon in the White House on September 24, I had been among the first international leaders who called to offer support and sympathy to him and his country.

"I didn't necessarily think it was important to praise a brother," he told reporters gathered outside in the Rose Garden afterwards. "After all, we're talking about family. There should be no doubt in anybody's mind about how honoured we are to have the support of the Canadians and how strong the Canadian prime minister has been. And not only his condolences, but his offer of support for the American people. I guess somebody's playing politics with you, Mr. Prime Minister."

A more serious matter was the wild and unsubstantiated rumour that some of the suspected terrorists had come from Canada. They could have, I suppose, because there was little that anybody could have done to prevent it, but the fact was they hadn't. Though our security system had been keeping a close watch on a number of terrorist suspects in Canada and contin-ued to do so, just as every other country in the world was doing, none of those suspects was involved in the attacks on New York and Washington. As it turned out, the nineteen perpetrators had been living within the United States for months, if not years. But that didn't stop the right-wing journalists who like to portray Canada as a haven for socialists, drug dealers, and international criminals from refusing to believe that these guys weren't Liberal organizers. The story that a few of them had come into the United States on a ferry from Nova Scotia to Maine, though absolutely untrue, was a convenient way for them to attack our social pro-grams, our cultural differences, and our immigration policies.

Blaming the "strangers in our midst" for every kind of social and economic problem has long been an excuse for those in Canada and the United States who dream of returning to an illusionary white, Anglo-Saxon, Protestant utopia of the past.

Unable to say so directly, given the politics and sensitivities of pluralistic democracies, they have to resort to indirect arguments and blatant fabrications to advance their ideas. And so they used the terrorist attacks to promote their prejudices, their anti-immigration policies, and their self-serving mythology.

Canada did respond to the call for tighter security, but first we needed to put in place the proper legal instrument to do the job. Trudeau had faced the same problem during the October Crisis in 1970, when there was nothing but the clumsy and outmoded *War Measures Act* to deal with the FLQ terrorists. In December 2001, when Anne McLellan brought in the *Anti-Terrorism Act,* it must have struck the right balance between public safety and civil liberties, because some people said it didn't go far enough while others said it went too far. If anything, we probably gave more weight to human rights than most other countries and even agreed to add a five-year sunset clause to force a review of its two most draconian measures—preventive arrest without a warrant and investigative hearings behind closed doors—once the heat of the circumstances subsided. At first the Cabinet didn't think a sunset clause was necessary and worried that it would create more work for everybody, but once it became an important matter of principle for a lot of Canadians, we conceded. Was that weakness? Perhaps, but I didn't think it was a bad idea to take a second look at laws that remained on the books long after they were needed. Even though my government never used the two powers in the new legislation, that was no guarantee that they wouldn't be abused by those in control in the future. In fact, thanks to the efforts of the Liberal opposition, they weren't renewed by the House of Commons in February 2007.

In the aftermath of September 11, Americans became understandably preoccupied with protecting their borders, and there was much talk of strengthening the defence and security perimeter around North America. For me, it felt more like a debate than like pressure. The idea of lowering the barriers between Canada and the United States had been floating around ever since the NORAD and NAFTA treaties had been signed. But Canadians have never warmed to the idea of tighter integration, and they didn't see the border as a big problem requiring a big solution. Nor were the Americans asking for a harmonization of our laws or a continental perimeter. Instead, Foreign Minister John Manley worked with Tom Ridge, the U.S. Homeland Security director, to reach the Smart Border Accord, which they signed on December 12, 2001. It used electronic technology, pre-authorized clearance, infrastructure investments, increased personnel, and other measures to improve border security without unduly disrupting the normal flow of trade.

As for the idea of building a missile defence shield around North America, that debate had less to do with its logic than with its practicality and consequences. On the one hand, if ever there were a missile attack on the United States, Canada would likely be a fighting ground whether we consented or not. We would certainly be in no position to ask a missile en route to New York to turn back or show us its passport, nor would the Americans have any choice but to protect us in order to protect themselves. On the other hand, there were genuine concerns about the cost of the shield, its technical feasibility, and its necessity in an age of under-the-radar terrorism, as well as diplomatic fears that it would destabilize the arms race and lead to the weaponization of space. Because those concerns and fears were not addressed to Canada's satisfaction by the time I left office, and there had been no pressure or urgency to make up our mind one way or another, I passed the decision of whether we should participate to my successor. And he eventually said no.

Ultimately, of course, the United States government and the American people would decide whether to go ahead with their missile shield, no matter what Canada or anyone else thought.

Once, when I was discussing it with Vladimir Putin, he remarked rather cryptically, "The Americans aren't building it against the Russians. They're building it against the Japanese." What he meant was that the United States has traditionally used its defence spending as a way of supporting its largest and most profitable corporations without being subject to international trade regulations. I agreed with him. By putting billions of dollars a year into the research and development of new technologies for the Defense Department and the space program, Washington is in effect giving its major industries a competitive advantage over companies in other countries that can't afford to keep pace. In fact, though no United States administration will ever admit it, the American military budget is the largest government subsidy on the planet and the most anti-free-trade instrument in existence.

Whether for national security or economic growth, every government is under constant pressure to spend more and more on defence. In our case the pressure came from the American government, which wanted us to carry more of the load in NORAD or NATO, as well as from the arms manufacturers and military lobbyists for whom no amount of money is ever enough. The Canadian Forces always claimed it needed more tanks and guns, more submarines and destroyers, more bombers and helicopters, but I wasn't always sure that its self-interest was the same as the national interest.

During the period of high deficits and major cutbacks, it was hard as a matter of principle, politics, and the heart to buy new equipment for the military while reducing assistance to the poor, the ill, and the old. Nor was it clear that the wars of the future would require the same equipment as the wars of the past. If a rogue nation chose to drop a nuclear missile on New York, if a stateless terrorist cell chose to blow up the Parliament Buildings, or if the United States chose to invade Canada, a few dozen more tanks or jet fighters wouldn't make much difference. One National

Defence document I read wanted the government to buy a very expensive nuclear submarine in part to prevent the North Koreans from coming up the St. Lawrence River. Given that I couldn't name one river in North Korea, I didn't imagine there were many North Koreans who had ever heard of the St. Lawrence, and there were probably even fewer who had any great interest in visiting Montreal by sea. Of course you have to be prepared for any eventuality, but you also have to be realistic about your priorities.

Our priorities were international peacekeeping through the United Nations or NATO, defending the boundaries of North America and the citizens of Canada, and fighting terrorism at home and abroad, and we adjusted our spending to reflect those priorities. I remember visiting our troops in Edmonton and being amazed, after all the complaints and demands I had been getting from the opposition and the U.S. ambassador, to see the quantity and quality of the new equipment they had. Though the minister of defence and the chief of the Defence Staff always asked for more as part of their job description, I never found them especially bitter about our cuts or reallocations. The $8 billion we put into security measures after September 11 was in effect new money for defence, though we never got the credit for that from the military establishment or the Americans, and we were able to increase the Defence Department's budgets once we were in the black.

Overseas, too, Canada had been the first to talk about the use of NATO's Article 5, which stated that an attack on one member was an attack on all, and in October 2001 we joined our NATO and Afghani allies in an operation led by the United States and Great Britain to go after al Qaeda in Afghanistan. Not only was this a multilateral undertaking in keeping with our commitment to NATO, but it made sense, because the fundamentalist Taliban government was undoubtedly in league with Osama bin Laden and his terrorist training camps.

Early in 2002, after the overthrow of the Taliban government, we agreed to position our troops to stabilize the situation, protect the new government and the Afghani people, and help keep the peace. By March, our soldiers fought alongside the Americans in the mountains of eastern Afghanistan. Even more than Bosnia, this operation was really about peacemaking more than peacekeeping, but the Canadians proved that they had been well trained to be mobile, intelligent, and among the very best. When I visited our troops there, the commanding officer said, "Prime Minister, I have to tell you that we are as well equipped for this job as anybody around here, including the Americans, and better fed too."

Towards the end of the year, NATO began seeking someone willing and able to assume command of the International Security Assistance Force (ISAF), which had been established by the United Nations Security Council in December 2001 to secure and help rebuild Kabul, the capital. In January 2003, while responsibility for ISAF was passing from the UN to NATO, I instructed John McCallum, the defence minister, to inform his U.S. counterpart, Donald Rumsfeld, that we were willing to take over from the Germans and the Dutch at the conclusion of their term in August. Even though the commitment would require on our part many more troops and a lot more money, we were going to get our soldiers into a more secure place where their assignment was closer to traditional peacekeeping. When ISAF's mandate expanded to include other regions of the country, I made sure that we remained in or around Kabul. In retrospect, it was a very good deal for Canada. Later, unfortunately, when my successor took too long to make up his mind about whether Canada should extend our term with ISAF, our soldiers were moved out of Kabul and sent south again to battle the Taliban in the killing fields around Kandahar.

—

On Saturday, September 22, less than two weeks after September 11, I was at home flipping channels on TV when I came across old Jesse Helms, the Republican senator from North Carolina and former chair of the Senate Foreign Relations Committee, being interviewed on CNN. In response to reports that the U.S. Defense Department was getting ready to attack Iraq in order to get rid of Saddam Hussein, Helms stated, "We're right close to it." Wait a minute, I thought to myself—Saddam isn't the Taliban or al Qaeda, so what does he have to do with the attacks on New York and Washington? "The first President Bush ought to have gotten rid of him," Helms went on, as if that were a sufficient answer. But Bush Sr. hadn't had UN support for extending the war into Baghdad, and his own generals had opposed the idea for strategic reasons. And hadn't the Americans once used Saddam against the Iranians, just as they had also used the Taliban against the Russians? So I began by being sceptical about an invasion of Iraq, and I remained sceptical.

Though President Bush called Iraq a part of the "axis of evil" in his State of the Union address on January 29, 2002, and accused it of hiding weapons of mass destruction from the eyes of UN inspectors, it wasn't on the agenda when I met with him in the White House on March 14 to talk about softwood lumber and the preparations for the G8 summit in Kananaskis, Alberta. If it had been, I would have told Bush that the key issue for Canada was whether such an invasion would obtain the blessing of the United Nations. At the time of the first Gulf War against Iraq in 1991, Mulroney had insisted on getting the UN's approval, and he was right. And in February 1998, I didn't hesitate to agree when President Clinton called me at home on a Sunday afternoon to seek Canada's support for a multinational military initiative to force Saddam to comply with previous UN Security

Council resolutions calling for nuclear, chemical, and biological weapons inspections. We had a debate in the House of Commons on Monday, and on Tuesday the Cabinet took the decision to participate in the mission with a frigate and two planes, but not to send combat troops. Now, as rumours about military buildups for an American invasion grew louder and more frequent, the Bush administration was arguing that the series of UNSC resolutions on Iraq gave the United States the authority to take unilateral and pre-emptive action, if need be, because Iraq had refused to allow the unconditional return of the arms inspectors.

On August 14, 2002, I received a confidential update from the clerk of the Privy Council, Alex Himelfarb, on the situation: "U.S. action against Iraq to implement regime change is a question of when, not if, using the justification that the Iraqi government is a sponsor of terrorism and a developer of weapons of mass destruction (WMD). Timing is unknown, but unlikely to be before the November Congressional elections. Allied support may be sought as soon as the end of August. The Arab world is opposed to an attack; France, Germany and Russia are calling for a new UN mandate before an attack; Australia supports the U.S. doctrine of pre-emptive strikes; and the UK is fully supportive of U.S. action. Canadian policy has centred on the return of UN arms inspectors to Iraq to resolve the disarmament question and to address the issues of terrorism when clear evidence is available. The integrity of Iraq and regional stability will be severely threatened if Saddam Hussein is ousted, particularly if Israel is drawn into the conflict." Not the least of the memo's reservations was "the enormous challenge of rebuilding a post-Saddam Iraq (the Iraqi opposition remains divided and no clear future leadership has been publicly identified)."

At the beginning of September 2002, I met up with Tony Blair at the World Summit on Sustainable Development in Johannesburg, South Africa. We went off to have a long, frank talk over a couple of beers in the hotel bar with a member of Blair's staff and Claude Laverdure, who had succeeded Jim Bartleman and Michael Kergin as my foreign affairs adviser. Since our last meeting, at the Kananaskis G8 summit in June, during which Iraq had not been a formal item of discussion, Blair had gone on a holiday in France, and by August there were diplomatic and press reports that he had decided to join the Americans.

"Okay, Tony," I said, "if we're getting into the business of replacing leaders we don't like, who's next? After all, we're both members of the Commonwealth—you're the number one, I'm the number two—so why don't we go in and take out Mugabe in Zimbabwe? He's part of the family, so to speak, so why shouldn't we settle the problem?"

"Jean, it's not the same thing," Blair said.

"Of course it's not the same thing," I countered. "Mugabe has no oil. And if it's democracy that the Americans want to establish in Iraq, why are they doing it with the support of the king of Saudi Arabia? Look, I want to be with you guys, but I can't go without a United Nations resolution—and neither can you, in my judgment. But it will be easy if we go in under the flag of the UN, as happened in the Gulf War. You're the only one who can persuade Bush to go that route. You're close to him, and he needs you."

Whether because of our conversation or because he hadn't in fact made up his mind about what to do, Blair agreed. "It's amazing," he had said to me. "You don't seem to be having any problems with this issue, whereas I'm having no end of problems." When he met with Bush at Camp David the following weekend, he persuaded the president to give the United Nations another try.

The next day, Monday, September 9, 2002, President Bush and I had a prearranged meeting in Detroit to announce new measures to improve border security at the Ambassador Bridge, but he used the occasion to make a personal pitch to get Canada onside regarding Iraq. He asked to meet with me alone—no advisers, no note-takers, nobody else—which was highly unusual. In fact, his national security adviser, Condoleezza Rice, had a fit when she heard about it. I didn't know what he wanted to tell me, but when he arrived he said he had made up his mind to address the UN and push for a new Security Council resolution.

"If you get a resolution, George," I said, "don't be worried, I'll be with you. But I have to tell you, I've been reading all my briefings about the weapons of mass destruction and I'm not convinced. I think the evidence is very shaky."

At one point, for example, I had been given an ultra-secret U.S. intelligence report based, apparently, on an intercepted telephone conversation between two Iraqi military officials. Hold on a second, I thought to myself, these guys sound as if they're talking about moving their grandmother's furniture from one place to another, not transporting weapons of mass destruction. Maybe they didn't have what they were claiming to have. Maybe they wanted the phone call to be overheard so that they could play a cheap and easy trick to frighten whoever was listening with talk of a threat. All I knew for certain was that I wouldn't have been able to convince a judge of the municipal court in Shawinigan with the evidence I was given. Indeed, when Colin Powell presented his government's case to the United Nations the following February, I knew he was on very thin ice indeed. From what I had read, I figured he had been sold a bill of goods.

"This is very serious, Jean," Bush said with all his sincerity. He even offered to send his intelligence experts to Ottawa to convince me.

"No, don't do that, George," I insisted. "Canadians will not accept that I've been briefed by American officials. If you have proof, send it to my analysts through the normal channels. They will look at it, and I will decide." It was spoken with no bitterness or anger. Besides, I didn't think that finding weapons of mass destruction would matter much if the United States got UN backing.

Oddly enough, both Bush and I were under the impression that our meeting was supposed to last an hour, not ninety minutes. So, with nothing else on the agenda, we spent the remainder of the time having a very pleasant chat over a cup of coffee about baseball, golf, and our families. He was in a jolly mood afterwards, telling reporters that I was "a plain-spoken fellow with a good sense of humour" who would make "a great Texan."

Three days later, on September 12, Bush went to the Security Council, and on November 8 he got UNSC Resolution 1441, which gave Iraq one "final opportunity" to disarm or face "serious consequences." Saddam agreed on November 13, and two weeks later a team led by Hans Blix returned to Iraq for the first time since 1998. Even though Blix's regular reports failed to find any weapons of mass destruction, the Americans kept preparing for war, in the face of strong resistance from France, Germany, Russia, China—and now Canada.

All that autumn I was under increasing pressure to back the United States all the way—from Washington, from the business community, from the right-wing press, even from those Liberals who were in favour of military action or who opposed everything I did because they were supporting Martin's leadership bid. But I had a strong view based on a clear principle, and I knew I would have no problem in getting my colleagues in the Cabinet or the caucus to support me, even if some of them thought I was wrong. To those who were particularly worried about the economic repercussions of Canada saying no, I replied, "Give me a list of all the goods and services that the Americans are buying from us just because they love us." I never got it.

Tensions were high by the time I met Bush at the NATO summit in Prague in the middle of November. Caught in the line of fire was Françoise Ducros, a former chief of staff to Brian

Tobin and Stéphane Dion, who had succeeded Peter Donolo in 1999 to become the first woman ever to occupy the post of director of communications in the PMO. As she later explained it to me, she had been talking off the record with a CBC reporter about the possibility of an invasion of Iraq. "If Bush does what you say he's going to do," Ducros countered, "you will have the right to say that Bush is a moron." Only the last four words were reported by a *National Post* journalist, whose paper was no friend to my position on Iraq, and the remark was quickly blown out of all proportion back in Canada. I was ready and willing to defend Ducros, but because she was already planning to return to a job in the federal civil service in a matter of weeks, she chose to leave early. After she resigned, she received flowers from all over Canada and the United States, and on a later trip to Mongolia she was startled to be congratulated for what she had said. She almost came to regret having denied ever saying it.

"The price of being the world's only superpower is that its motives are sometimes questioned by others," I said in a major address to the Chicago Council on Foreign Relations on February 13, 2003, the eve of Hans Blix's latest findings on Iraq's compliance with Resolution 1441. "Great strength is not always perceived by others as benign. Not everyone around the world is prepared to take the word of the United States on faith. Canada firmly supports the objectives of the United States. We have been close friends and allies for a long, long time. It is essential that the United States can count on support from around the world. Therefore it is imperative to avoid the perception of a 'clash of civilizations.' Maximum use of the United Nations will minimize that risk. And so how the United States acts in the days ahead will have profound consequences for the future. I am convinced that working through the United Nations, if at all possible, as difficult and as frustrating as it sometimes can be, will immeasurably strengthen the hand not only of the United States but also of those around the world who want to support it."

When it became perfectly obvious that Resolution 1441 was never going to be sufficient grounds for the United Nations to authorize an invasion of Iraq, the Americans—urged on by the British—tried to get a second, more explicit resolution, but they paid a heavy price for not having respected the United Nations enough. I often talked to Clinton and Bush about how short-sighted it was for the United States not to pay its annual dues year after year, for example, and though they claimed to be embarrassed, both presidents said they couldn't get what they wanted because full support for the UN was always blocked by the conservatives and isolationists in the Senate. I told them, in a somewhat jocular fashion, that the United Nations brought more than enough money into New York City, what with hotels, apartments, embassies, bureaucrats, restaurants, limousines, and tourism, to cover Washington's entire obligation. "If you don't want the UN," I said, "give it to Canada. I'll give it free land in Montreal and build it a new building, just like Rockefeller did, and we'll make billions in taxes."

It was vitally important, if the United States ever needed the United Nations, as it did now, to develop alliances and networks, to stay informed, and to talk to everybody all the time. Even though Canada's two-year term on the Security Council had expired in December 2000, we hoped to play the role of an honest broker between the United States and Great Britain, on the one hand, and France, Germany, Russia, and China, on the other. We drew on the good relations I had nurtured with Mexico and Chile, Africa and the Caribbean, China and Russia, and at the G8, the Commonwealth, La Francophonie, the Summit of the Americas, and so on, all of which were now divided between those who were with the Americans and those who were not going to join them in the war. I felt at ease whenever I went to the UN because I was

With two of Europe's greatest postwar leaders, Helmut Kohl and François Mitterrand, G7 meeting, Naples, July 1994.

Discussing the "Third Way" with Tony Blair and Bill Clinton.

Arm-wrestling with the other "polar bear," Boris Yeltsin, G8 meeting, Cologne, Germany, June 1999.

President Jiang Zemin enjoys a laugh at the APEC Summit, Seattle, November 1993.

Glad-handing in China, November 1998.

With UN secretary-general Kofi Annan, Lloyd Axworthy and I celebrate the signing of the Ottawa Landmines Treaty, December 3, 1997.

Welcoming Pope John Paul II, a living symbol of compassion and peace, to Canada, July 24, 2002.

With Israeli prime minister Yitzhak Rabin, my first official visitor at
24 Sussex, November 1993.

Lunch with PLO leader Yasser Arafat and his wife, Gaza, April 2000.

Cuban president Fidel Castro picks me up at the airport, Havana,
April 27, 1998.

Summit of the Americas, Quebec City, April 2001.

Taking a break from the Francophonie summit during one of my many trips to Africa, Benin, December 1995.

With Nelson Mandela, the great South African leader and honorary citizen of Canada, at the Commonwealth Conference, Edinburgh, October 1997.

Despite our disagreement over Iraq, George W. Bush was full of smiles and kind words, Detroit, September 9, 2002.

"Watch your back, Jean," Russian president Vladimir Putin seems to be warning me. "Your grandson Olivier may be plotting a coup." Kananaskis, June 2002.

My grandson Maximilien serves as a "peace bridge" between North America and Europe, Évian-les-Bains, June 2003.

An emotional moment with Aline at the end of my farewell speech,
November 13, 2003.

Aline and I walk away from Rideau Hall and into private life,
December 12, 2003.

among friends and people I could rely on, and whenever Canada spoke up to make a point, I noticed that the other delegates listened.

Though I spoke to Jacques Chirac a few times, mostly in relation to France's influence with the African countries, I talked much more with Tony Blair, who had made a commitment to help the Americans but who still seemed to be hoping for an exit. I would call him to suggest he change his draft resolution with this word and that date in order to give the UN inspectors more time. I also advised him to get Mexico or Chile, both of which had seats on the Security Council in 2003, to introduce the change, because it would have a better chance of success coming from them. But the British insisted on doing it themselves, which only antagonized their opponents, while the Americans kept pushing forward with their military plans anyway.

When it became clear that the second resolution was never going to fly, if only because France or Russia was ready to use its Security Council veto, Canada began working on a compromise that would delay any invasion until Blix had finished his work but would commit to war if he found weapons of mass destruction and Saddam refused to dismantle them. My hope was that if we could get an extra six to eight weeks, the U.S. military strategists would have to delay their plans long enough to give everyone more time to work out a diplomatic solution. I participated in negotiations, made a lot of phone calls, and was kept informed about what was happening in the corridors at the UN by Paul Heinbecker, our able and very active ambassador. I think we came close, because Canada was one of the few countries with the courage and credibility to try, but the clock was running out too fast. Though Mexican president Vicente Fox and Chilean president Ricardo Lagos were under an extraordinary amount of pressure from the United States, first to support the U.S. resolution, then to join "the coalition of the willing," they told me they wouldn't do either if Canada wouldn't as well.

So I felt I had a special commitment to them: this was the first time we "other" Americans, by sticking together, had a real opportunity to take a coherent independent stand and influence the United States on the global stage. Afterwards, in fact, both President Fox and President Lagos privately thanked me for helping them to say no.

Shortly after nine o'clock on the morning of March 17, 2003, we received a note asking whether Canada was willing to "provide political support for military action against Iraq," yes or no. Furthermore, the Americans wanted an answer by noon, because they were in the process of making a list of those who were with them and those who were not. The note didn't come from Bush himself or even from Washington, but from the British government. The president hadn't called me, so I didn't think I had to call him with my decision. Even more important, I wanted to inform Parliament and the Canadian people first. As I rose to address the Commons at 2:15, Claude Laverdure phoned his counterpart, Condoleezza Rice, to tell her what I was about to say.

At this point, knowing that the American government was looking for moral support even more than it was looking for military assistance, I could have said to Bush, "Yes, we're with you, we approve of your actions, but, as you know, our soldiers are fully committed in Kabul." That probably would have satisfied him and been enough to get Canada's name on the coalition of the willing, as happened with other countries. For me, however, it would have been politically and intellectually dishonest. As a matter of principle, we didn't approve of his actions because he hadn't convinced the United Nations of the urgent need to invade Iraq.

"Over the last few weeks," I stated in the House, "the Security Council has been unable to agree on a new resolution authorizing military action. Canada worked very hard to find a compromise to bridge the gap in the Security Council. Unfortunately we were not successful. If military action proceeds without a new resolution of the Security Council, Canada will not participate."

It can't have come as much of a surprise to the Americans. Four months later, in fact, at the wedding of Paul Cellucci's daughter, I had a discussion at the reception with Andrew Card, Bush's chief of staff, who told me that the White House had been disappointed but not angry. (When Aline saw that she was to be seated at dinner between Card and the archbishop of Ottawa, who had attacked me in a "confidential" letter on an anti-abortion website, she whispered to me as a joke, "I think I'll go home.") "Mr. Chrétien," Card explained, "you told us right from the beginning what you intended to do, and it was our mistake that we did not take you seriously. We assumed that, at the last moment, a practical guy like Chrétien would decide to come along. That was our fault. We should have believed you. Others may have double-crossed us, but not you."

Of course, all those who opposed Canada's decision—the right-wing opposition parties, the right-wing premiers of Alberta and Ontario, the right-wing editorialists, the right-wing CEOs, the right-wing think tanks, even some right-wing Liberals—sought to portray me as a reckless anti-American peacenik. The same people who accused me of muzzling my ministers and MPs now jumped on me for not severely punishing Herb Dhaliwal and Carolyn Parrish for a couple of imprudent comments they had made in the media. Then the press made a big fuss because I hadn't been invited to visit Bush at his ranch in Texas. In fact, he did invite me, though the events of 9/11 made it difficult for us to find a suitable date. I suppose if I had been as proud of my friendship with the Bush family as Brian Mulroney continued to be, I would have gone, but I never interpreted my not going as an insult. After all, I had never gone to Camp David with Clinton either. And though it's true that Bush's scheduled visit to Ottawa in May was cancelled, that was by mutual agreement. I didn't want to expose him to anti-war protests on the streets or even in the House, and I guess he didn't think it was the appropriate time to be seen patting my back in public.

In fact, relations between the United States and Canada were less frosty than were those between the United States and Great Britain, on the one hand, and France, Germany, and Russia, on the other. When the G8 leaders arrived for the summit in Évian-les-Bains, France, at the beginning of June 2003, the pro- and anti-war camps were hardly speaking to each other at the opening reception. As usual, Canada played the role of go-between to break the ice, though the method I used was highly unusual.

When my grandchildren grew older and my years in office began to draw to a close, I used to invite them to join me one at a time, at their parents' expense, at various international summits, starting with Olivier at the G8 in Okinawa, Japan, in 2000. It was an education for them, a pleasure for me, and, as it turned out, a useful way to relax the mood at the start of our sessions. Before the leaders got down to work, the kid would come in with my briefcase, be introduced to everyone, pose for a few pictures, and leave. At my last APEC meeting, which took place in Bangkok, there was a small crisis when I was told that no photographers would be allowed into the reception because the king of Thailand would be present. It seemed a pity that my granddaughter, Jacqueline, had come so far and wouldn't be able to go home with a souvenir album. So I put a camera in my pocket, walked into the room with Jacqueline, and took snapshots of her with each of the leaders. Her favourite was the sultan of Brunei, not only because he was one of the richest men in the world, but also because he was just her height. Without exception, the leaders were generous and amiable—it seemed like such a natural and down-to-earth thing for a grandfather to do.

In Moscow in 2001, Vladimir Putin even took Philippe on a private tour of the Kremlin, describing through a translator the history and treasures of the great palace. After half an hour, Putin said in Russian, "I'm sorry, but I have to go back to work now."

"I'm sorry, but I have to go back to work now," the translator repeated in English.

"Goodbye," Philippe replied, politely shaking the translator's hand. He was surprised when President Putin himself suddenly dashed away without a word of farewell.

In Évian, it was Maximilien's turn. As luck would have it, Maximilien's godfather was a very wealthy Texan whose wife also happened to be one of George W. Bush's most active supporters. So while President Bush and Maximilien were talking, I waved to Tony Blair and Jacques Chirac to come over for a photograph. With Bush and me on one side of Maximilien, and Blair and Chirac on the other, I declared Maximilien to be the bridge between North America and Europe, between the hawks and the doves. Before too long, the discomfort had melted.

"I know it's difficult, George," I said to him later while we were sitting side by side. "If it helps, Canada is willing to donate more than its fair share to help the people of Iraq rebuild their society."

"I appreciate that, Jean, but you're not the problem," he said, looking around the table. "It's these other guys who are the problem."

—

I'm still puzzled why the Bush administration decided to invade Iraq. If it was to establish democracy, that's a long shot, especially when you're supported by kings. Or was it, as I had suggested to Tony Blair, because of oil? Or was it that the Americans were under pressure from their generals and weapons lobbyists to use their expensive, high-tech armies? Or was it to defeat terrorism? If so, military might alone wasn't likely to succeed. The war against terror is not an old-fashioned war against an enemy state. It's against a group of fanatics from different continents who work, sometimes alone, sometimes together, to kill and destroy by stealth.

I remember Bill Clinton telling me in the days preceding the invasion that the war wouldn't last seventy-two hours. He was right in the sense that Saddam decided not to fight when it became evident that his army could never withstand the American forces in battle. Instead, Saddam dispersed his soldiers and told them to keep shooting guerrilla-style for as long as it took to pin down and drive out the invaders. To date, unfortunately, the U.S. occupation of Iraq has revealed that, with enough persistence, sacrifice, and resolve, the world's greatest superpower can be taken on and possibly beaten.

"When you're as powerful as you most certainly are," I used to say in private to Clinton and Bush or, in public, to U.S. audiences and reporters, "it's the time to be nice. Tiger Woods doesn't have to say he's the best golfer. You Americans don't have to tell the world that you're the strongest."

I believe that Canada's decision not to go to war in Iraq was one of the most important moments in our history. It proved to us and to the world that we are a proud, independent nation. Could we as a government and as a people stand up to the strong pressures coming at us from the United States, the corporate interests, and the ideological press for the sake of our traditions and principles? As I made very clear to President Bush in Detroit in September 2002, if the United States couldn't come up with a United Nations resolution and real proof of weapons of mass destruction, Canada wasn't going to war.

Not long ago I met a Toronto businessman who said, "You know, Jean, I was really angry with you about Iraq. I cursed you, I told everybody that power has gone to that son of a bitch's head and he's crazy. Well, today I would like to apologize. You were right and I was wrong."

It took quite a man to say something so generous, though by that time the polls were showing that over 90 per cent of his fellow citizens agreed with my decision. However, my real satisfaction came with knowing that we Canadians had held firm to our values as a keeper of peace through multilateral institutions, no matter how great the threats and uncertainties we faced.

THIRTEEN

FRIENDS AND ALLIES

N ostalgic observers like to lament that Canada had more influence in world affairs in 1945 than it has today. That may be true, but it's mostly because the world of today isn't the world of 1945. Having increased our international prestige with the size and significance of our voluntary participation in the Second World War, we were one of the very few countries to emerge from it with our domestic economy and infrastructure intact. In many ways it was our golden age by default. We could assume a major role in multilateral activities, whether in the founding of the United Nations or the reconstruction of Europe, because so many of the once-great powers weren't able to. It didn't take long, however, for even the losers to rebuild from the ashes and for whole new continents to begin to break the bonds of their colonial pasts. When I began in politics in 1963, nobody could have predicted the fall of the Berlin Wall, the disintegration of the Soviet Union, the globalization of trade and business, the impact of the Internet, or the rise of China, India, and Brazil as economic powerhouses—to mention just a few examples of the massive transformations that took place over forty years. That is the context in which we must place Canada today.

That doesn't mean we don't continue to play an exceptionally influential role for a country with a relatively small population. We are in the Group of Eight industrialized nations and are a highly respected member of the United Nations. We have a presence in Europe through the North Atlantic Treaty Organisation and the Organization for Security and Co-operation in Europe (OSCE), in Asia through APEC, in Africa and the Caribbean through the Commonwealth and La Francophonie, and in Central and South America through the Organization of American States and the Summit of the Americas. We share a border with both the United States and Russia, and we are linked to the Nordic countries through our common concern with the peoples and environment of the Arctic.

All these associations, as well as our ongoing bilateral relationships, require constant meetings all around the globe, creating the impression, sometimes, that the prime minister of Canada loves nothing better than to travel to exotic places at the taxpayers' expense. It's true that when a politician is in trouble at home or is bogged down in petty hassles, it can be a relief to get out on the international stage. One leader, who shall remain nameless, visited Ottawa during a tour of the world and asked me if he could stay an extra day, in order to postpone all the problems he knew he would have to face the moment he returned home. Indeed, he was defeated a few weeks later. But as far as I was concerned, travelling abroad was a lot of work and very little play. The preparations included days, sometimes weeks, of reading and briefings. The summits involved hours of talking and listening.

And the follow-up often required more meetings, more phone calls, more reports, and more decisions, all while I had to catch up on the backlog of work that had piled up in my absence.

I visited about sixty different countries during my years as prime minister—and I saw almost nothing of them. The pattern is invariably the same. You arrive at an airport that looks like every other airport. You shake hands with the welcoming party and inspect a guard of honour. You get into a big, black car that looks like every other big, black car. You sit in the back seat with a Canadian ambassador or foreign official, who briefs you non-stop all the way downtown about what's to come and seldom wastes the precious opportunity of having the ear of a captive prime minister to advance some idea or project. You're taken to the best hotel, where you're given the best suite, full of beautiful furniture and flowers and food, all paid for by the host government. You don't have a moment to sit down and enjoy any of it before you're told you have five minutes to shower and get ready for your first appointment. One meeting follows another for a day or two, and you're lucky if you can squeeze in a half-hour walk around the outside of the hotel. You never have any time to go into a shop or a home; you get to go to a theatre or a museum only if it's on the rigid schedule; and if you ever try to go out to a café or restaurant on your own, the bodyguards get nervous and the press wants to know who's footing the bill. And then you're taken back to the same airport in the same car along the same road and sent home, where the opposition accuses you of dodging the domestic issues and wasting money on some frivolous overseas holiday.

As every international business traveller knows, jet lag is a professional hazard, both going over and coming back. Some corporations even forbid their executives from taking any major decisions for forty-eight hours after a long trip. Heads of government rarely have that luxury. On the contrary, they're expected to hit the ground running. At one summit meeting I attended, one leader was so exhausted after a flight across the Pacific that he fell into a deep sleep, and all the documents on his lap crashed to the floor. Many times I returned to Ottawa at midnight after a series of intense, complicated meetings, was in my office the next morning, and had to be on my feet answering tough questions in the House in the afternoon. It was a dangerous gamble, because I knew that if I made a factual error or expressed myself incorrectly, neither the opposition members nor the media were going to forgive me just because I said I was tired. Usually, however, I rested on the plane and had the energy to bounce back quickly, in part because I was born that way, in part because I loved the job so much.

However arduous, the overseas meetings are essential to the well-being of Canada and the world. They often involve serious matters with vital consequences for the peace and prosperity of the planet, and they are the only way to get to know other leaders as statesmen, politicians, and human beings—and that helps enormously when there are bilateral issues to solve or multilateral alliances to be forged.

—

Canada was particularly fortunate to be invited to join one of the most exclusive clubs in the world, created in 1975 by French president Valéry Giscard d'Estaing as the Group of Five. The G5 was designed to be a forum where the leaders of the five largest industrialized powers—France, Britain, Germany, Japan, and the United States—could come together once a year to discuss current economic issues. Almost immediately, the agenda evolved into discussing political and military problems as well. When the Italians pressed to be included in 1976, U.S. president Gerald Ford said, all right, but if the Europeans get another member, the United States wants Canada. It was a friendly gesture, and probably a wise move on the part of the Americans too. In fact, in my several encounters with President Ford over the years, I always found him to be a bright, thoughtful person and, as someone from Michigan, well informed about Canada. "I'm a Ford, not a Lincoln," he used to joke. His down-to-earth approach to people and problems caused him to be underestimated by the press, but I know that Trudeau, for one, liked and respected him a great deal.

Over the years there have been many proposals to expand the group to fifteen, twenty, or even more members. In my opinion, the bigger it becomes, the less effective it will be. It's useful because it's basically a few people sitting around a table in a rather small room for two or three days of discussion without many formal statements or procedural wrangles. They talk candidly, even if it's through translators; they eat together; they chitchat between sessions; they get to test each other's mettle and become friends. A lot of those benefits would be lost if there were twenty delegations present. As APEC grew from twelve to twenty-one members, I observed, it became stiffer and less productive, with one prepared text presented after another and with less interaction among the leaders. Moreover, as far as Canada's self-interest is concerned, it's obvious to me that we would soon be pushed aside by all the newcomers with bigger populations, bigger economies, and bigger armies. Most times, your authority at the table varies with your power in the world. The more power you have, the more everyone pays attention, but when the leader of a less powerful nation gets too talkative, everyone starts looking at the ceiling. If Canada ranked seventh at the G7 in terms of size and influence, we would probably rank near the bottom at a G20. While the new members might be grateful for a while for having been admitted, it wouldn't take them long to start saying, shut up, little Canada, we're bigger than you and we want to speak first.

That said, from the very start of my time in office, I pushed hard to get the G7 to include Russia. First, I thought it smart geopolitics to bring Russia in from the cold, even though the former Soviet Union was still undergoing the turmoil of its economic and political changes. Second, I was worried that Canada might be kicked out of the group if the four European countries ever decided to speak with a single voice and reduce the G7 to a G3 of the United States, Japan, and the European Union. Though Britain, France, Germany, and Italy clearly weren't keen to surrender their national sovereignty and prestige, they were feeling a lot of pressure to act on the world stage as a unified economic and political bloc. An EU representative had already been showing up at the G7 meetings in an unofficial capacity since 1977 and had been allowed to intervene more and more frequently over the years. If Russia joined, I figured, Canada's seat at the table would probably be more secure. Third, there were a number of issues, particularly the Balkan wars, about which I thought it was crucial to keep Russia informed and onside, so it wouldn't feel either surprised or threatened.

In July 1994 Boris Yeltsin was invited to attend a political discussion at the G7 meeting in Naples, Italy, which also happened to be my first. Yeltsin was physically strong, intellectually tough, and surprisingly soft-hearted, and I always imagined him standing on a tank in front of the Russian parliament in August 1991, alone, unarmed, valiantly trying to prevent a coup by a gang of old, reactionary Communists. Like Nelson Mandela in South Africa or Fidel Ramos in the Philippines, he was one of those heroic figures who had the courage to put their lives on the line in defence of liberty and democracy, and as a result, he helped to change the course of world history. If it was Mikhail Gorbachev who made the first brave moves toward opening Russia up, it was Yeltsin who implemented it, not with some fancy words spouted from a bulletproof lectern or written in a peaceful university, but by his own fearless actions.

As host of the G7 meeting in Halifax in 1995, I took the initiative of allowing Yeltsin to sit at the table, and no one objected. He spoke at the leaders' dinner on the first night and attended every session except for the strictly economic one, because it didn't seem appropriate for a debtor nation to be at a meeting of its creditors, so to speak. Though he was totally committed to building a new Russia, it obviously wasn't going to be a quick or simple task. It takes a long time to convince a society that has been governed for centuries by emperors and dictators to accept democracy, and it's extremely difficult to carry off a rapid transition to Western-style capitalism without any of the necessary laws or institutions in place. Even the basic establishment of a fair and efficient taxation system can take years when there's no voluntary discipline and no means of enforcement. And democracy, as we in the West know it, is still a very young system in human history. Less than a hundred years ago, after all, Austria had an emperor, Germany a kaiser, and Italy a king.

One evening during the Halifax summit, Montreal's famous Cirque du Soleil put on a dazzling show for the leaders, during which an obviously inebriated Boris Yeltsin tried to join an act of Russian acrobats but found he was a bit too tired to climb onto the stage. Afterwards, during the outdoor fireworks, one of the performers came to me and asked if he might be introduced to the British prime minister, John Major. It so happened that this man's father had been a friend of Major's father during their days together in the circus. For a time, Major told me, his father had considered quitting show business and emigrating to Canada. "Gee," I said, "if that had happened, you and I might now be having a hell of a good fight across the floor of the Canadian House of Commons." What impressed me the most was that here we were, the son of a circus performer and the son of a factory machinist, prime ministers of our countries. Then I looked around the room and saw Bill Clinton, the stepson of an alcoholic car dealer; Jacques Chirac, the son of an ambitious bank clerk; Helmut Kohl, the son of a minor tax official; and Boris Yeltsin, the son of a construction worker. It brought home to me the enormous progress that ordinary working people have made over the past century. There wasn't a wealthy big shot or fine old family behind any of us, at least until George W. Bush showed up to represent the world's most powerful democracy.

Everyone loved Boris Yeltsin. He was funny, human, and canny. At the 1999 summit in Cologne, a year after the G7 had formally become the G8, he and I got into an arm-wrestling match at the conference table. "Look at the two polar bears going at it!" Clinton yelled. We remained friends even after his retirement. In February 2002, during a Team Canada trade mission to Moscow, Aline and I visited Boris and his wife, Naina, at their country home. He and I played billiards after dinner, and I was pleased by how fit and healthy he looked after swearing off alcohol.

That trip to Russia had been the result of my increasing closeness to Yeltsin's successor, Vladimir Putin. When Putin visited Ottawa in December 2000, I offered to escort him by foot to his hotel after the state dinner at the National Gallery. As we walked along Sussex Drive, stopping for a moment to shake hands with the startled drinkers in a bar, he invited me to bring the usual horde of premiers, business people, academic leaders, and journalists on a Team Canada mission to Russia. I spontaneously agreed, somewhat to the surprise and alarm of the Foreign Affairs officials, who thought it wasn't a useful priority. However, I thought it was important at that time for Putin to be able to demonstrate to the world that he was opening his country's doors to foreign investment and developing a market economy.

The trip in 2002, which included a stop in Germany, was a great success, in terms of both deals and diplomacy. For four days Putin opened the doors of his government to us, wined and dined us with the political and financial elites of the new Russia in a gilded hall of the Great Kremlin Palace, and spent more time with me than he had ever done with any other Western leader. During ten hours of talks, including a private luncheon in his Kremlin residence and a private dinner at his country dacha, we discussed investment, HIV/AIDS, corporate governance, the North, the International Space Station, hockey, federalism, terrorism, Iraq, the G8, and Kyoto. Sharing with me a love of music, Putin had his two daughters play the piano and violin after dinner. As enthusiastic skiers, we made plans to go on a ski trip in the Caucasus, though we were never able to find the time to make it happen. We even dreamed up the idea of getting together and raising a toast at our common Arctic border, where Siberia meets the Northwest Territories. We quickly developed a trust that would serve Canada well when I tried to find a compromise resolution on Iraq at the United Nations or to break an impasse at the G8 summit in Kananaskis over the costs and conditions of disposing of Russia's nuclear waste.

I remember, as an indication of that trust, an extraordinary bus ride I had in St. Petersburg in late May 2003, during the elaborate festivities Putin put on to celebrate the city's three hundredth anniversary. It was his birthplace and obviously still dear to his heart. Unfortunately, the weather was terrible for most of the three days—cold, wet, with piercing winds. At times Putin and I were the only dignitaries to show up on time for the outdoor ceremonies and remain for the duration. He appreciated it, I think, particularly since President Bush had flown in and out for one night—a stopover that Putin seemed to take as a personal snub for Russia's opposition to the Iraq invasion. At one point, the security people thought it would be safest to transport Putin, Chirac, German chancellor Gerhard Schröder, and me from one event to another by bus. The four of us sat on two benches in the front, with our translators sitting behind us and whispering into our ears, but no advisers or note-takers. For more than an hour I listened with complete fascination as the other three carried on a remarkably candid discussion about Europe and America, Europe and China, and the Europe of tomorrow.

While most of it must still remain confidential, because it concerned defence strategies or specific personalities, the gist was about how to link Western Europe and Russia economically and politically to build a countervailing force to the supremacy of the United States. What made the discussion so odd was that here I was, a prime minister of Canada, a North American, an outsider, and yet I was being treated as though I was one of them. The fact that I had been with them on Iraq was undoubtedly one reason; the fact that I spoke in French was probably another. I rarely said anything during this conversation, though at times, when someone revealed a misunderstanding of the American system or touched on an issue that affected Canada's interests, I felt compelled to interject.

At one point, for example, Putin brought up the difficulties—not unsympathetically, I should add—that the economy of the United States might face because of its dependence on oil from the Middle East. "In fact," I reminded him, "Canada's oil reserves in the oil sands and our gas deposits in the West, the North, and offshore in the East, secure and right next door, will make the United States much less dependent on the Middle East. Russia, too, will be in a stronger position to become a U.S. supplier."

—

One complicating issue affecting Canada-Russia relations was the lead we assumed in welcoming the emerging democracies of Central and Eastern Europe into the North Atlantic Treaty Organisation, which had been founded in 1949 as a joint defence alliance between North America and Western Europe. At the NATO summit in Brussels in January 1994, I had been alone in pushing hard for a large and immediate expansion. I felt particularly committed to three countries with which Canada had close ties: Romania, because its purchase of our CANDU nuclear reactors gave us a certain responsibility; Ukraine, because of the one million Canadians of Ukrainian origin; and Slovenia, on whose behalf I carried the brief at the urging of its prime minister, Janez Drnovšek, whom I knew and had liked since meeting him at a Liberal International conference in Iceland when I was still leader of the Opposition.

As I saw it, we in the West had a moral obligation to those countries that had been enslaved by communism to invite them under our umbrella for the sake of military security and economic stability. Most of them had become enthusiastic capitalists overnight. They were eager to join the European Union and NATO, and they were ready to make the necessary adjustments, no matter what the cost. I recalled meeting some young liberal politicians in Bucharest who had a paralyzing fear that their country would revert to its old ways if we didn't keep our word. However, almost all the other NATO leaders were afraid of Russia's reaction if we moved too fast to pick up its former allies in the Warsaw Pact, while the paper-pushing technocrats who had to justify their salaries were telling us that nothing could be done very quickly.

"Come on," I argued during the meeting in Brussels, "what's so complicated about using soldiers from the Czech Republic instead of from Canada? We made a commitment to take in these countries if and when they instituted democratic reforms and a market economy. Well, they're moving rapidly in that direction and there won't be any turning back. Now is the time to deliver. They're knocking at the door, waiting for our answer, and we should not make the same mistake of isolation that let these people fall into the clutches of Hitler and Stalin in the first place. If they're with us in the NATO club, they're less likely ever to be against us in the future. Besides, there will never come a day when the Russians are happy about the expansion of NATO. They will be just as angry in ten years as now, so we might as well do what will have to be done someday."

By the time of my second NATO summit, held in Madrid in July 1997, nine of the sixteen leaders were in favour of accepting five new members—Poland, the Czech Republic, Hungary, Romania, and Slovenia—while the rest, in particular the United States, were willing to take in only the first three. Though there's no vote as such at NATO summits, there is a custom that major decisions need unanimous consent, so I felt I had no choice but to admit defeat. But French president Jacques Chirac wouldn't go along. That evening, when I arrived for the official dinner at the Spanish prime minister's residence, I saw Chirac in a corner of the room engaged in what looked like a very serious and animated discussion in English with Bill and Hillary Clinton.

Afterwards Clinton called me over and said, "Jean, Chirac's causing me a big problem. We're in a bind. He just won't give in."

"So why don't you give in, Bill?" I asked.

"We can't and we won't. But we can't have a failure here either. Can you help me?"

I said I would think about it overnight and see what I could do. Chirac could be very proud and stubborn, I knew, so I would have to find a subtle way to let him back down from a position he had made quite forcefully in public and set down in the draft of the final communiqué. I had found that my long experience and pragmatic approach as a parliamentary legislator, a federal-provincial negotiator, and a former minister in Trade, Finance, and External Affairs served me as well on the world stage as it did in Canada, and I had learned that I could often be most useful by playing a quiet, supportive role.

I came up with a compromise in which NATO would agree to accept the first three countries right away, the other two in principle for a second round of expansion, and then more in due course. Then I suggested to Chirac that the French and English versions of the draft were different in a couple of significant places. "We should correct that," I said, "so that everybody can have a better understanding of what you and Clinton are proposing." When Chirac agreed, I asked Canada's foreign minister, Lloyd Axworthy, to work with officials during the lunch break to prepare a new draft based on the compromise. Chirac and Clinton both accepted it, and later they both made a point of crediting Canada for finding a way out of the corner into which they had painted themselves.

The fact that we are North Americans, next to and friendly with the world's greatest economic and military superpower yet independent of it, undoubtedly contributes to our usefulness. Like it or not, everybody recognizes the strength of the United States and the appeal of the American Dream. At the same time, everybody recognizes the brashness and insulation that are weaknesses in that superiority, and the poverty, racism, and inequality that are hidden behind its enormous wealth. To many peoples and governments, Canada offers a middle way between American individual enterprise and European social justice. We have fewer of the very rich, but also fewer of the very poor. We have delays and inefficiencies in our medical system, but also the fairness and security of universal health care. We have disputes and disagreements with the United States, but we also know them better than anyone else. We speak English, but we also speak French. Whether at the G8 or NATO or the UN, all those attributes give us a special voice at the table.

Of course, there's always a price to be paid for having a seat at the table. When the G8 passed the hat to help cover the billions of dollars it cost to dispose of nuclear waste in Russia or to clean up Chernobyl, Canada—along with the richer players—was obliged to put something into it. When NATO sent forces into

Bosnia, Kosovo, and Afghanistan, we were expected to be there. When the UN sent peacekeepers into Rwanda or East Timor, it would have been hard to say no even if we wanted to. Most times, however, Canadians wanted to participate in multilateral peace-keeping missions. They were practically a Canadian invention, after all, and the UN especially values our involvement because, compared to most countries, we have a very efficient system of decision making. While others have to take weeks or even months to discuss a proposal, the Canadian prime minister can meet with the ministers of foreign affairs and national defence within an hour, have a debate in the House of Commons within a day, and order the troops to leave as soon as they're ready.

In 2000, for example, President Abdelaziz Bouteflika of Algeria was mediating the conflict between Ethiopia and Eritrea in his capacity as chair of the Organization of African Unity and wanted UN observers to supervise a peace settlement. The Dutch were interested, but only if Canada agreed as well. Prime Minister Wim Kok and I discussed the matter and we decided that our countries would participate together, as we had in Bosnia. Both President Bouteflika and Kofi Annan, the UN's secretary general, were grateful that we were willing and able to move so quickly.

—

Canada has been able to maintain its international influence less by the success of its economy or the strength of its military than by the demonstration of its values. Wherever I went, I found other leaders looking up to us as a model of the type of society the world should emulate, primarily because of the values we have established over a long period of time—tolerance, generosity, harmony, and a concern for the environment. Again and again I was asked how we have managed to exist so peacefully with two official languages, ten diverse provinces, and three northern territories; how we have preserved the languages and cultures of our first peoples and our multicultural communities against the forces of assimilation and discrimination; and how we have absorbed so many immigrants so quickly without race riots or squalid ghettoes.

Immigration was a particularly important question for the Europeans, all of whom were dealing with the arrival in their midst of large numbers of labourers and refugees from other cultures, with other languages and religions. Politicians from both the left and the right looked to Canada for answers. I was frank with them. I told the Italians that their population was going to drop from 55 million to 40 million within fifty years—because "we Catholics don't have nineteen kids anymore," I joked—so they were going to need people to do the work, maintain the infrastructure, and pay into the pension programs. I told the Germans that it was wrong not to give citizenship to the Turks who had been living and working in their country for sixty years, while it takes only three years to become a full Canadian.

We do have our own problems, of course. There are some incidents of racism in Canada, and some difficulties with integration. Generally speaking, however, the biggest hurdle my government faced was how to meet our target of attracting 300,000 new Canadians a year, usually falling short by about 50,000. We couldn't afford to increase dramatically the number of officials required to speed up the process, and, despite a popular misconception that our rules and standards were too lax, we were often too strict in cases where strictness served no social or security purpose. After all, most of the immigrants in the past had come with no professional training or special skills, yet been able to build a decent life for themselves and their descendants because of their willingness to work their way up from the jobs that no one else wanted to do. It bothered me, too, that by demanding only the best and brightest, we were guilty of robbing poorer

nations of many of their own best and brightest. That was especially lamentable when a doctor or an engineer, trained at great
expense by a society that could hardly afford it, had to drive cabs
or scrub floors in Canada because of the closed-shop mentality
of our professional associations and regulatory agencies.

"We don't see immigrants as problems but as assets," I
explained, "so that gives us a totally different perspective. We
want them to become citizens because we need them. In many
cases, before an immigrant even steps off the plane, he's been educated somewhere else, so that costs us nothing. The first day he
buys food. The second day he rents an apartment. The third day
he buys furniture and clothes. Later he buys a car and a house.
He becomes a consumer, a worker, a taxpayer. So it's generosity,
yes, but it's also self-interest. That's why multiculturalism works
in Canada. Nobody gives a damn about a person's colour or religion. No party scores any political points for promising to cut
immigration quotas. On the contrary, we take pride in our tolerance and diversity. You have to look at it that way, and you have
to sell it that way."

Our values weren't just the standards we wanted to achieve
at home; they were the guidelines by which we intervened
abroad. It was no coincidence that Canada was a leader in the
world's diplomatic efforts to ban the manufacture, use, and
export of anti-personnel landmines. The success of this effort
was due to the work of many people, including Jody Williams of
the International Campaign to Ban Landmines, the late Princess
of Wales, the Mine Action Group, and Kofi Annan at the United
Nations. However, the Canadian government played a crucial
role in rallying the international community behind the initiative
from the moment Cornelio Sommaruga, the president of the
International Red Cross, first mentioned it to me during a visit
to my office in May 1994. Canada was alone in wanting to raise
it at the G7 summit in Naples two months later; André Ouellet

and especially Lloyd Axworthy gave it their highest priority at Foreign Affairs; and, as Axworthy generously recognized in his own memoirs, I spent countless hours on the phone or at gatherings with more than one hundred leaders to get as many of them as possible to sign a treaty by the end of 1997.

I remember putting the case in sentimental terms to Boris Yeltsin, who had lost the fingers of his left hand in a childhood accident while playing with a hand grenade. By now I knew he was a deeply emotional person, as was his lovely wife, Naina. She had wept in Aline's arms during a ceremony we attended in Moscow in May 1995 to remember the dead of the Second World War, among whom had been most of her family, and a month later in Halifax she was moved to tears by a rendition of "Evangeline," the lament about the deportation of the Acadians. "Boris," I said, "if we're crazy enough to start a war, fine, that's our choice, and we will have to pay the consequences. But what is unacceptable to me is that, fifty years from now, some boy will go into a field with his girlfriend, they'll step on a landmine, and they'll be killed or crippled for the rest of their lives because of this weapon we left there. They could lose a leg or an arm or—" (and here I held up my left hand and made a slicing gesture across it with my right) "—maybe their fingers."

It hit him hard. "But my generals don't want me to sign," he said. "They're telling me that we need landmines to protect our nuclear weapons storage sites from terrorists."

"That's permissible under the treaty. All you have to do is surround the danger zone with a fence and warning signs."

"Okay," he finally said, "if the Americans will sign, I will sign."

I worked especially hard on Bill Clinton. He was sympathetic, certainly, but his own generals were insisting, one, that the United States needed to retain landmines between North Korea and South Korea for the foreseeable future and, two, that their big anti-tank mines had to be guarded by a cluster of small anti-personnel ones. The first could probably get an exemption because of the special circumstances, I told him, and the second required only a new piece of technology. "There must be a way, Bill," I said. "I mean, if you guys can put a man on the moon, you can link a big mine to a small mine if you really want to."

My reading was that Clinton came close to signing the final version of the treaty being prepared in Oslo, Norway, in September 1997, but he was forced to back off at the last minute because his defense chief was threatening to resign over the issue. All I know for sure is that we spoke several times in the days before the deadline and all through the course of one night to try to find a compromise. Finally, around five o'clock in the morning, he informed me that his decision was no. When I persisted, he snapped back at me for badgering him, but for me it was normal for two civilized people to argue strongly about a difference of opinion. If he thought I had been pushy, he was right, because I wanted to see this treaty succeed. A month later, in fact, while flying back from Moscow after meeting with Yeltsin, I made one last effort. I wrote Clinton a note in my own hand begging him to reconsider. In the end, because the United States wouldn't sign, Russia and China didn't sign either, but on December 3, 1997, 122 governments did put their signatures on the Ottawa Treaty in front of a joyous crowd of 2,500 people from around the world. For me, it will always be one of the greatest achievements in Canada's diplomatic history.

"We will leave Ottawa proud of what we have done," I said in my speech that day, "but very conscious of what is left to do. There are still many nations that must join us. There are still hundreds of thousands of victims to help. There are still tens of millions of mines to clear. Certainly the commitment of the government of Canada does not end with hosting this conference. I am proud to say that, by unanimous consent, both Houses of our Parliament have ratified the treaty, and it has been proclaimed as law, making Canada the first nation in the world to ratify this historic convention. On behalf of our government, I am also proud to announce today the establishment of a $100 million fund to implement this treaty. This means bringing it to life, making it truly global, clearing the mines, helping the victims both with immediate medical care and with long-term help rebuilding their lives. I know other countries are making similar contributions. I call on all countries to put forward the resources needed to rid the world of these buried killing machines—once and for all."

Subsequently, in another demonstration of our values, a Canadian lawyer and diplomat, Philippe Kirsch, became one of the driving forces behind the establishment of the International Criminal Court in The Hague in 2002. Acting under the guidance of Lloyd Axworthy and me, and with a major diplomatic push by officials in Foreign Affairs and Justice, Kirsch overcame formidable resistance, not least the opposition of the United States government, and went on to become the court's president. No matter how often or how hard I tried to convince George W. Bush to change his mind, he refused to budge. "No American citizen will ever have to be dragged before an international court," he said.

"But, George," I argued, "if a country has a good legal system, the international court will have no jurisdiction. You can deal with a criminal under your own laws and your own constitution."

"Well, I'm not taking any chances," he said. "I'll never sign."

Once again, Canada and the United States stood apart because of our differences over multilateral solutions for global problems.

—

Human rights was another important area in which we worked hard to set our foreign policy in conjunction with our national values. In no case was that more sensitive than in our dealings with the People's Republic of China. For better or for worse, there was no stopping more than a billion hard-working people, and it seemed only a matter of time before China's economy would surpass those of the United States and Europe. Mature economies, including Canada's, simply couldn't match China's net growth of at least 10 per cent a year; we didn't have its sudden demand for new skyscrapers and high-rises, new schools and hospitals, new bridges and highways, new power plants and sewage facilities—almost everything, in fact, that we had taken over a hundred years to construct. From the moment I was elected, I made China a priority. My first international meeting as prime minister was the APEC summit in Seattle in 1993; my first Team Canada trip was to China a year later; and I met Chinese president Jiang Zemin so many times that he used to refer to me as his English teacher!

Compared to many Western nations, including the United States, we had a good base from which to build. Canada had sent one of its first trade officers to Shanghai in 1908, broken away from the constraints of the Cold War to ship wheat to China in 1961, and established formal diplomatic relations in 1970, when Pierre Trudeau was prime minister and Mitchell Sharp was secretary of state for external affairs. We enjoyed the advantage of having British Columbia as a gateway to the Pacific, with Vancouver's increasingly busy airport, the expanded port facilities at Prince Rupert, and a network of railway connections across North America. We were ready to sell everything from subway cars to CANDU reactors into Asia's colossal markets.

However important economics and good relations were in the relationship, so too were human rights. As was my style, I first tried to use a little sugar to help the bitter medicine go down. During the grand state dinner that Premier Li Peng, who had been raised like a son by the great Chinese premier Zhou Enlai, hosted in honour of the Team Canada visit to Beijing in 1994, with thousands of people seated in the Great Hall, I said to him, "In a democracy, you know, you have to get elected. To get elected, you have to be nice to everybody you meet, to say hello and shake their hands. It's tough. Come with me, I'll show you how we do it." We got up and started moving from table to table, shaking hands and making jokes. Everybody was laughing and applauding, they were so amazed. "Look how well you're doing," I said to Li. "You'd make a great street campaigner, though I guess it might be a big job if you have 700 million voters."

I was more explicit in a follow-up letter I sent to him on February 28, 1995, despite diplomatic warnings that the Chinese might retaliate against Canada in trade and investment or by blocking our bid to be elected to the UN Security Council if we didn't drop our co-sponsorship of a resolution about the situation in China at the UN Commission on Human Rights. "As you will know from my recent visit," I wrote, "I believe genuine dialogue, cooperation, and mutual respect are fundamental starting points for addressing differing perceptions concerning adherence to international obligations. I therefore welcome the commitment you have expressed to developing further our bilateral dialogue on human rights."

Nevertheless, Canada had to live with the reality that, however great we may be as a country, we're not a big, powerful player. You just have to go to Shanghai to understand at a glance that the entire population of Canada doesn't equal that of one Chinese province. One evening in March 1994 in Shediac, New Brunswick, I was tired and got trapped in a corner with some reporters who kept telling me what I should say to President Jiang about human rights. "Be realistic," I said. "I'm the prime minister of a country of 28 million people. He's the president of a country with 1.2 billion people. I'm not allowed to tell the premier of Saskatchewan what to do. Am I supposed to tell the president of China what to do? If you want me to try to run the whole world, fine, but don't criticize me if I don't get very far."

When Premier Li visited Canada in October 1995, we had to tread very carefully if we didn't want him to storm off early at the mere sight of protesters, as he had done elsewhere. As premier at the time of the Tiananmen Square protests in 1989, he bore the blame for sending tanks against the pro-democracy demonstrators, though the decision had probably been made by Chairman Deng Xiaoping. Deng remained popular everywhere, however, and Li was frustrated by what he perceived as his unjust depiction as a bogeyman in the eyes of the world. Personally I didn't mind if Canadian protesters wanted to wave signs and shout slogans at him, but the comparatively small group of demonstrators who showed up in Ottawa were out of Li's sight and earshot. That night, however, just before the grand formal dinner in his honour at the Sheraton Centre in Montreal, several hundred protesters arrived on the street, screaming insults and waving enormous cardboard tanks that were impossible to miss. Li Peng looked angry.

"Come with me," I said, and I led him over to the window, where I pretended to be able to read the writing. "Oh, they're protesting against me!" Fortunately, and against all the odds, Li found it funny. He still might have been upset, but at least he didn't leave ahead of schedule.

I had a closer relationship with his successor Zhu Rongji, whose daughter had studied in Canada. An engineer by education, an economist by training, and a former mayor of Shanghai, he was one of the brains behind the modernization of China, and an extremely nice person as well. We mostly talked about economic issues, and he was always curious about Canada's banking system or social programs.

But perhaps the greatest breakthrough came when President Jiang Zemin, another engineer by education, economist by training, and former mayor of Shanghai, visited Ottawa in November 1997 after the APEC summit in Vancouver. Human rights was customarily the last item on the agenda, and the dance was always the same. I would raise it, as he knew I had to. He would tell me, in the nicest possible way, to mind my own business. We would adjourn to meet the press. I would say we had discussed the issue; he would say, no comment. "I warn you, Mr. President," I said on the way to the press conference, "the Canadian reporters are going to ask you about human rights in China at our press conference. Why not simply make your case? I mean, you have a case to make. It may not be a convincing or comfortable one for Canadians, but make it anyway."

Sure enough, the first question was a very tough one from a reporter for the *Globe and Mail*. Instead of responding, I motioned to President Jiang and encouraged him to reply. "China accepts in general terms the principles of human rights," he said calmly, "but in each country, there are specific conditions relating to human rights." For example, freedom of assembly, already guaranteed under the Chinese Constitution, does not apply if it causes "complete chaos in government operations." And freedom of movement in China, while a lovely idea, would mean fifty million people in Shanghai within three years. Imagine the situation if seven million people suddenly turned up in Toronto over three years.

That marked, I think, the beginning of a new openness in Sino-Canadian relations. Some of our lawyers and professors worked to train Chinese judges and to advise on reforms in contract law, criminal procedures, women's rights, open trials, and legal aid. China signed the United Nations Covenant on Civil and Political Rights and affirmed the principle of the rule of law in its constitution. And, on November 20, 1998, in a speech to the students and faculty at Qinghua University, the unofficial training ground for China's future leadership, I became, I was told, the first Western leader ever to speak so bluntly about the importance of democratic principles and the rule of law in such an important public setting, with a question-and-answer period and the Chinese media in attendance.

"Some say that the right to eat is more important than the right to speak, that collective needs must always have priority over individual rights. This is no more true than the converse," I said. "You are, for example, building universal legal rights such as the presumption of innocence and the right to legal counsel into your traditional legal philosophy. This we applaud. But I would be less than frank if I did not say directly to you that many Canadians are disturbed when we hear reports from your country of restrictions on the right of free expression of different political views. And particularly when we hear of people being arrested or in prison for expressing political views different from the government."

As a sign of progress, it may not have been all that Canadians wanted, but it clearly demonstrated how far China had come in less than five years. Despite setbacks, I believe that such progress will endure, as China continues to grow economically, to receive television and the Internet from around the globe, to elect mayors and other officials, and to develop its legal system.

—

The issues were the same, though the repercussions weren't quite so threatening, with Cuba. In April 1998, when I went to Havana to meet with Fidel Castro, human rights were high on the agenda, despite the fact that he didn't like to talk about them. Canada had been practising "constructive engagement" with Cuba for almost forty years, but democratic reforms there had been few. Still, I thought that isolating the island with boycotts, sanctions, and threats of invasion had not helped. The reality is that a dictator is a dictator, whether of the left or of the right, and if you never do business with dictators, you wouldn't do business with a lot of people, including the Chinese and the Saudi Arabians. That's why Canada argued strenuously to have Cuba invited to the Summit of the Americas in Miami in 1994. That's why we have continued to recognize Castro's regime, to trade with his country, and to permit our citizens to go by the tens of thousands every winter as tourists. And that's why we vigorously objected to the *Helms-Burton Act,* an extraterritorial application of American laws that punished Canadian citizens by forbidding individuals or companies investing in Cuba from doing business in the United States. Not only was it bad foreign policy, as I kept telling Clinton, but it was against the liberalization rules of NAFTA and the World Trade Organization.

Cuba is a political problem of disproportionate importance in the United States because of the power, money, and numbers of the Cuban refugee community. In two states, Florida and New Jersey, Cuban Americans are concentrated enough to have real political impact, and they deliver their votes to anyone who promises to hold tough. The younger generation may be less obsessed than its parents or grandparents were, but every politician who ever dreams of being a senator or a governor is still afraid to suggest normalizing relations with Cuba. Though Clinton signed the *Helms-Burton Act,* I believe he had been moving toward a thaw until February 1996, when Castro shot down two small American planes whose civilian pilots had flown over Havana to distribute pro-democracy pamphlets. It was a disgraceful move on Cuba's part. Some people even claimed that Castro had done it as a deliberate provocation to prevent better relations with the Americans, though I later found him to be quite an admirer of Clinton.

"You know," I said in a speech to American business leaders at the Economic Club in New York on March 3, 1998, "the United States is the most powerful nation in the world. Never has a country been so powerful, ever. So it's the time to be benevolent, it's the time to be nice. And I don't think that *Helms-Burton* is very useful that way. You cannot dream of running all the countries of the world, because all the countries of the world will turn against you. That is something I believe very strongly. For example, you don't like Castro. Well, it's your choice. He's a dictator, yes, but you've dealt with other dictators before in that part of the world. And if you want to get rid of him, let the Americans go down there with their dollars. But don't do it too fast, because by the time you do it, you will be welcomed in Canadian hotels." They laughed, but later I was told my little joke was used by the U.S. Chamber of Commerce to put pressure on its government to change its policy.

A month later, I arrived in Havana. Though I was no fan of Castro's political and economic system, I couldn't help but be awed by him as a legendary figure and one of the most extraordinary personalities of the twentieth century. I remembered reading about his heroic revolution when I was still a student, and he had been in power even longer than I had been in politics. Aline and I had met him briefly once before, at the fiftieth-anniversary ceremonies for the United Nations in October 1995, and we found him a charmer. He chatted about his friend Pierre Trudeau, and he was very pleased when Aline spoke to him in Spanish. In Havana he greeted us like old friends, and I was soon teasing him about being the last living communist left in the world.

"Yes," he said, "and I'm proud of it."

"Mr. President," I said, "I understand that your father was a rich man and that you are a graduate of the Jesuits." Then I pointed across the room to Jean Pelletier. "And my chief of staff is from an old family in Quebec City and he's also a graduate from the Jesuits. So both of you are products of the bourgeoisie. That makes me the only product of the proletariat here."

My strategy was to put all the tough items on the table as soon as we got down to business before lunch. "Why not surprise the international community and make a move on human rights?" I asked him. "For example, you could sign the UN's Covenant on Economic, Social and Cultural Rights. There's nothing in there that you can't agree to."

It took Castro a few moments to absorb what I had said, and he obviously wasn't very happy about some of it, but he later brought out the text and started to discuss his problems with its details clause by clause. He didn't want to deal with the rights of unions, for example, because he was the head of all the unions, so there was no need to give them any more rights. "Gee," I said, "I'd like to be able to say the same thing in Canada. I guess you don't run much of a risk of having any strikes down here."

Castro loved to talk, and he talked for hour after hour at the dinner that began late that night and continued long after midnight. Despite my fatigue, I enjoyed it because he was so knowledgable. He was full of questions, too, sometimes grilling me like a prosecutor about the effects of NAFTA on Canadian workers or the impact of consumer societies on global poverty. The next morning he accompanied me to the airport in his own big Russian limousine and, stopping under a bridge to get out of the sun, he lectured me for another forty-five minutes about a fascinating array of subjects. The one thing that really struck me, however, was an offhand comment that the New York stock market had gone down that morning. Here was Castro, the last great communist, giving Chrétien, a "lapdog of Yankee imperialism," the latest Dow Jones numbers. I was to see him only once again, during our short meeting at Pierre Trudeau's funeral in Montreal, and the friendship between our two countries underwent a cooling off in August 1999 when he attacked Canada for not preventing the defection of almost a dozen Cuban athletes during the Pan-American Games in Winnipeg. But that was Castro, and he never changed.

—

Very few people in public life, in Canada or around the world, can ignore the situation in the Middle East, even if they wish to. The history of the Middle East, both ancient and modern, is universally known; its conflicts are thoroughly reported; its religions, its injustices, its poverty, its oil are subjects of endless debate. As MP, minister, or prime minister, every time there was another crisis in the region, I heard about it from all sides, from constituents and lobbyists, from caucus members and Cabinet colleagues. Many of them were well organized, well informed, and deeply passionate. As both a Canadian and a Liberal, I tried to keep a balanced point of view—not automatically on one side or the other of every UN resolution, for example, but reserving judgment until I had examined the facts of a particular matter at a particular time.

In 1992 Canada had been asked to chair the Refugee Working Group, a multilateral initiative to help improve the lot of more than four million Palestinian refugees who had been uprooted from their homes by decades of Arab-Israeli wars. The more I read about their lengthy ordeal or saw the atrocious condition of their camps on TV, the more I felt a responsibility to take action. I also wanted to promote trade and investment, encourage democratic values and human rights, visit our peacekeeping soldiers in the Golan Heights, and see if there was anything Canada could do to advance a just and lasting peace. In April 2000, therefore, I set off on a twelve-day trip to Israel, Egypt, Jordan, Lebanon, Syria, and Saudi Arabia, the most extensive tour of the region ever undertaken by a Canadian prime minister while in office. My predecessors had been warned off, I suppose, by the obvious risks. In fact, stones had been hurled at French prime minister Lionel Jospin in Ramallah a few weeks previously. But the greater risks were political, not physical, and I quickly understood how treacherous the terrain could be.

On the plane ride over, in a background conversation with the press, I talked about the possibility of the Palestinian Authority using the threat of a unilateral declaration of independence (UDI) as a bargaining chip. Not only were my speculations reported but they were twisted into a statement that Canada would support such a declaration, while the French-language journalists wondered, in that case, why Quebec shouldn't have the right to declare UDI as well—as though there were a comparison, in terms of international law and political reality, between the Palestinians and the people of Quebec.

I had barely touched down in Israel when the media, aware of the controversies surrounding the status of Jerusalem, wanted to know why I wasn't going to be meeting with Palestinian officials at their offices in East Jerusalem. The simple truth was that Chairman Yasser Arafat had invited me to come to his headquarters in Gaza. When the reporters kept pressing the point, I merely deflected it with a joke. "I don't know if I am in West, South, North, or East Jerusalem right now. I'm in Jerusalem." The next day's headlines back in Canada were that Chrétien didn't know his geography. I knew my geography—I just didn't want to answer the question.

While the media seemed determined to stir up trouble, all my meetings were trouble-free. When I met with the Israeli prime minister, Ehud Barak, he asked for my help in solving the refugee problem as an important step in the search for peace. Privately we explored a few ideas in what was clearly an extremely difficult and sensitive area. "Canada is in charge," he said. As a result, I later called the leaders of various nations to see if they would agree to take in more of the refugees as a humanitarian gesture. The next day, when I travelled to Gaza to have lunch with Yasser Arafat, he too thanked me warmly for the role Canada had assumed with the refugees and for the assistance we were providing through our trade and development programs. He even pinned a medal on me and said, through his interpreter, that he was welcoming me not just with respect and admiration but with a kiss.

Though the meeting itself was a matter of debate in some circles, I had already met Arafat in Ottawa and at the United Nations, he had been received by Clinton at the White House, he had been a co-winner of the Nobel Peace Prize, and there could be no hope for any solution to the conflict in the Middle East if everyone refused to talk with the leader of the Palestinians. He and I discussed the importance of human rights, for example, and the pace of the peace negotiations. When I stated the obvious, that the Palestinians will have their own state someday, the media accused me of insulting Israel. However, they didn't bother reporting that immediately after leaving Arafat, I went on to Hebrew University. There, before a large and enthusiastic crowd, I received an honorary doctorate, mostly for my contribution to the Canadian Charter of Rights, which had served as an inspiration for Israel's own charter.

"Canada was with Israel at the beginning, in 1947," I told the audience, "and we have been at your side ever since. Through your struggle to protect the rights of Jews everywhere, through your fight to reverse the deplorable Zionism and racism resolution at the UN. Through it all, Canada has staunchly defended the rights of Israel to live as a nation at peace and will never waver. Canada will always be a friend and a partner of Israel. We are also a friend to the Arab neighbours of Israel. That is why we have worked so hard to foster dialogue and understanding throughout the region, by taking part in every regional peace-keeping operation, through our leading role in the Refugee Working Group, where we are helping to improve living conditions for refugees and to develop ideas for longer-term solutions that respect human rights and ensure dignity."

In Cairo, I had commercial discussions with the prime minister and seven of his ministers, three of whom were graduates of McGill University, and then lunched with President Hosni Mubarak, who had already been my host at the international summit to promote peace and combat terrorism held at the Egyptian resort of Sharm el Sheikh in March 1996. Mubarak pleased me by singing the praises of Lester Pearson for his efforts in resolving the Suez Crisis in 1956. Now Canada and Egypt were often partners in UN peacekeeping missions around the world. In Beirut, I discussed Israel's withdrawal from Southern Lebanon and the plight of the 400,000 Palestinian refugees, mostly crowded into a dozen squalid camps, who weren't allowed to integrate themselves as Lebanese citizens for fear that they would unbalance the fragile social and political equilibrium among the Christians, the Shiites, and the Sunnis. In Jordan I talked about the refugee situation, the peace process, women's rights, and bilateral trade relations with King Abdullah II, whose friendly greeting really confused the press corps.

The year before, in February 1999, when the king's father had died, the Canadian media had made a tremendous fuss over the fact that I hadn't gone to the funeral, calling it an affront to Jordan and a setback for Canada's influence in the Middle East. I very much wanted to attend, not least because I had gotten to know and like King Hussein during his visit to Canada in April 1995 and on later occasions. Unfortunately, I was trapped in bad weather on a ski holiday in Whistler, BC, when I received word of King Hussein's death, and by the time I could get from Vancouver to Amman, the ceremony would be over. Three months later, when his young successor visited Ottawa, he dismissed my apology by thanking me for sending Foreign Affairs Minister Lloyd Axworthy, who had managed to arrive from Ottawa with only a half-hour to spare. In fact, King Abdullah II hadn't even heard about the rumpus, yet the Canadian reporters persisted in asking whether the Jordanians still had "their nose out of joint" about my not having been there.

On a visit to a Jordanian refugee camp, the photographers got a few good action shots of me throwing a basketball with some kids and even trying an impromptu dance with a group of men, but the media pack was still looking for failure. When asked about the Sea of Galilee, for instance, I said, "It's vitally important for the Israelis to keep this body of water" because it's the only freshwater lake they have. Since the Syrians laid claim to an access to the lake, the press wrote that I had insulted Syria and might not even be allowed to go there as planned. Imagine their surprise when I arrived at the airport in Damascus and was welcomed by a dozen or so senior ministers. Aline and I didn't have enough arms to carry all the flowers we were given.

Having read my briefing notes, I knew that Israel had been prepared to withdraw from the Golan Heights but that one of the sticking points was a very small piece of land at the northeast corner of the Sea of Galilee that had once been Syrian territory. Israel had taken control of it in 1967; Syria wanted it back. "There must be a practical solution," I said to myself, and I kept reflecting on what it might be, without consulting with any of our officials about it. Why not, I thought, make this little bit of disputed territory an international zone of peace? A third-party organization, funded by many nations, could lease the contested land for ninety-nine years from both Israel and Syria, so that neither would have to surrender its claims, and it could be turned it into a beautiful lakeside park for visitors from the surrounding countries and around the world, with theme pavilions built by a variety of nations. Canada, for example, could build one around the issue of landmines, though the details hardly mattered. The purpose was to remove a major impediment to a lasting peace settlement.

Though I wasn't ready to test the proposition on Prime Minister Barak, I mentioned it to Chairman Arafat, President Mubarak, and King Abdullah. (I also mentioned it to my old friend Shimon Peres, the former prime minister of Israel, who had driven all the way from Jerusalem to be with me at a moving reception I attended with Christian, Muslim, and Jewish students at a school in Nazareth.) They were intrigued. Mubarak even called for a large map, and he laid it out on a table for us to study. I was encouraged enough to raise the idea with Syria's President Hafez al-Assad, in the presence of his prime minister and foreign minister. Because he was quite frail, I had been told our meeting would last less than a half-hour. It went almost an hour and a half. He was friendly, focused, and very positive.

"Mr. Prime Minister," he told me, "I used to swim and fish in that lake when I was a kid. That piece of land belongs to Syria."

"If it's yours, fine," I said, "so lease it to me for ninety-nine years. After that, it will be someone else's problem, because there's a good chance I won't be around. And if the Israelis say it's theirs, fine, I'll lease it from them. The point is, instead of having a thorn in both your sides, you'll have an international tourist attraction, accessible to everyone."

In the end, I decided not to push the idea much further. Washington, which feels even more protective of the Middle East file than the Europeans do, was worried about anything that might distract attention from Clinton's efforts to secure a deal with Barak and Arafat the following July. Canada certainly didn't want to meddle where it wasn't invited, and it would have been presumptuous of me to suggest that I might be smarter or more powerful than the president of the United States when it came to Arab-Israeli relations. When Clinton's deal fell apart and Barak was defeated in 2001, the violence escalated once again. So it was more than enough for us to continue our work with refugees and human rights, maintain our peacekeepers on the Golan Heights, and try to achieve a balanced position at the United Nations.

In June 2000, two months after our meeting, President Assad died. As with Castro or Arafat, I believed that engaging him in dialogue had been better than isolating him, despite the many serious differences we had about foreign policy and human rights. His son and successor told our foreign minister, John Manley, that his father had said, shortly before his death, "The prime minister of Canada is a man of peace." As a direct result, I believe, through a letter I sent to him with Senator Pierre de Bané in July 2003, I was able to help secure the release and repatriation of Maher Arar, an innocent Canadian citizen who had been imprisoned and tortured by Syrian authorities after being delivered to them by the United States government as a terrorist suspect.

Though I had my fair share of run-ins with members of the parliamentary Press Gallery, I understood the pressures and constraints of the profession, and for the most part I was probably treated no better and no worse than every other politician. But the Middle East trip in 2000 was one time when the news being broadcast back home seemed to have nothing to do with the events on the ground. While our delegation was welcomed everywhere with never a word of criticism and laboured over a variety of important files—business contracts, terrorism, landmines, debt forgiveness, trade rules, health care, education, family reunification, high technology, agriculture, the environment, telecommunications, transportation, water management, air links, student visas, legal reforms, to name but a few—Canadians got the impression that the tour was nothing but a series of gaffes from beginning to end. It was as though the reporters had decided collectively, or been ordered by their editors, to bring their obsession with the petty scandals and succession squabbles of Ottawa on the journey.

I can't remember ever seeing my chief of staff, Jean Pelletier, so frustrated. When one of the journalists asked him how he thought the trip was going, he broke his own rule against speaking out. "Which trip?" he replied in cold fury. "Our trip or your trip? Our trip is going very well, thank you. Your trip seems to be going very badly, but I don't know what's the problem."

Near the end of the trip, the finance minister of Saudi Arabia spoke the truth. "Canada's traditional humility," he said, "is belittling the importance and the value of its role in the region." How I wish the Canadian people could have heard that message.

—

One of the great tragedies of the late twentieth century was how little attention the world paid to the millions of Africans who were dying from war, disease, and poverty. When ten people were killed in the Middle East, there were headlines everywhere. When ten thousand were killed in Africa, there wasn't a word. It was as though, in the eyes of the media as well as in the eyes of their readers and viewers, a human life in Africa didn't have the same value as a human life anywhere else.

In the spring of 1994 I learned with mounting horror about the brutal killing of hundreds of thousands of Tutsis, including the prime minister, Cabinet ministers, and the chief justice, by Hutu gangs in Rwanda, despite the presence of a small, ill-equipped, and hamstrung United Nations mission commanded by the Canadian general Roméo Dallaire. In April, while the rest of the world watched, either helpless or indifferent, Canada ordered two Hercules aircraft to Kigali to support Dallaire's mission and to evacuate over six thousand people at enormous risk to the crews. At the G7 meeting in Naples in June, I tried, without success, to get the other leaders to support the idea of sending a new international force into Rwanda. In July, when the United Nations finally acted, Canada was quick to contribute soldiers, medical teams, engineers, and supply units, but it all came too late to prevent the slaughter of as many as one million innocent Tutsis. This genocide was a dark blot on the history of the contemporary world. All of us in the West, not excluding Canada, could have and should have acted more quickly and with more force. I was determined that we would do everything possible not to allow this sort of tragedy to happen again.

One wet weekend at Harrington Lake in November 1996, I watched a disturbing television report. As a result of the Rwandan civil war, more than 725,000 Hutus, fearing revenge by the Tutsis, had fled for safety south and west into neighbouring Zaire, where they barely survived starvation, disease, and attacks from the tens of thousands of Tutsis who had settled there a long time before. A core of armed Hutu insurgents fought back with the help of the Zairian army; the Tutsis retaliated by shelling the refugee camps; and there was a serious risk that the local conflict would explode into a full-scale war between Zaire and Rwanda. As the battles grew more fierce, the living conditions more appalling, and the prospects for the peace negotiations taking place in Tanzania less hopeful, I decided that something had to be done.

After consulting with my nephew Raymond Chrétien, who had already been given leave from his ambassadorship in Washington to go into the region as the United Nations secretary general's special envoy to try to orchestrate a ceasefire and the return of the refugees, I now went to the phone and began calling a list of world leaders that Jim Bartleman had prepared for me. "We must all act at once on the UN's call for a military mission," I pleaded with them. "We just can't let this continue." Senegal had soldiers but no planes. Belgium had planes but no soldiers. Brazil had troops doing nothing at that moment in Angola and asked me where I wanted them to be sent the next day. The Europeans were willing to serve and, most astonishing of all, the Americans agreed to put their troops under the command of a Canadian general. Within days we had helped assemble an international force of about fifteen thousand soldiers and raised over $100 million to pay for it. However, while we were in the process of getting a Security Council resolution, the problem more or less resolved itself, when the Rwandan forces were able to move into the camps, drive off the Hutu militants, and persuade the rest to return to their homes in Rwanda. A major crisis had been averted—in part because Canada had moved quickly and forced a commitment from other nations, and also because we were ready to go as a group. That was very much a reflection of our values as a society.

—

Coming into office, I had assumed that the foreign-policy priorities of our government would be Asia and the Americas. There wasn't very much I could do in Europe, where our trade potential was limited in a developed market and the defence issues were being handled for the most part by NATO. Nor did I want to meddle in the United States' initiatives for peace and stability in the Middle East. Quite quickly and unexpectedly, however, I became absorbed in the issues of Africa, not least because all but a few of the African nations are members of either the Commonwealth or La Francophonie. The more I met with their leaders, the more involved I became in their agendas, the more I wanted Canada to help.

The social and economic challenges were compelling, even as statistics. Africa was the only region in the world where poverty and malnutrition were increasing, investment and saving per capita were decreasing, and life expectancy was on the decline. More than 300 million people in sub-Saharan Africa were living below the international poverty line of one U.S. dollar a day. More than 200 million Africans were without access to health services or safe drinking water. More than 140 million young Africans were illiterate. More than 25 million Africans were suffering from HIV/AIDS, and the number of orphans left by the AIDS epidemic was approaching the population of Canada. Meanwhile, sub-Saharan Africa's share of world trade had plummeted since the 1960s to less than 2 per cent; half the countries in sub-Saharan Africa were directly or indirectly involved in armed conflicts; and the continued marginalization of the continent from the benefits of the globalization process presented a serious impediment to the hopes for general prosperity, economic stability, and world peace.

From my very first G7 summit in Naples in 1994 I was constantly talking about Africa, raising its crises, and pushing for action. By the G7 in Denver in 1997, with the backing of Jacques Chirac and Tony Blair, I led the discussion on the political issues facing Africa and pressed the United States and the European Union to improve their preferential tariff regimes to help integrate the Africans into the global economy. So, when the G8 summit in Genoa in July 2001 decided to launch an African Action Plan, the other leaders asked me to pick up the file right away, even though I wasn't to take over the chair from Silvio Berlusconi until January 2002. The request was an honour and a surprise, and Berlusconi was very gracious in letting me proceed. Speaking French and English, being the number-two leader in both the Commonwealth and La Francophonie, and having an unusual amount of political experience were factors in my selection—or maybe they just thought that I wasn't as busy as they were.

My first step was to appoint Robert Fowler, our ambassador to Italy who had served as deputy minister of defence and Canada's ambassador to the United Nations, to be my personal representative on the G8's Africa file and Canada's chief "sherpa" involved in arranging the agenda, documents, accommodations, security, and declarations for the G8 summit in Kananaskis, Alberta, in late June 2002. As chair of these two key groups of multilateral officials, Fowler was able to coordinate and influence their negotiations to make sure that Africa remained at the top of the list of priorities.

The focus of the work was to figure out how the G8 could best support the New Partnership for Africa's Development (NePAD), a visionary initiative put forward by several progressive African leaders and endorsed by fifty-three members of the Organization of African Unity, to consolidate democracy and sound economic management on the continent, to promote peace and human rights, to foster education and health, and to introduce the legal and infrastructure requirements for sustainable growth. On trips to Morocco, Algeria, South Africa, Ethiopia, Nigeria, and Senegal, as well as at the United Nations and during meetings of the Commonwealth and La Francophonie, I spoke with NePAD's African leadership to build and maintain a consensus with regard to the G8's Africa plan, which eventually covered more than a hundred important areas, from peace to infrastructure, from the elimination of corruption to health, from education to agriculture, from environmental sustainability to child mortality, from gender equality to foreign aid.

I was impressed by what I learned during my travels. The African leaders had an enthusiastic commitment to move forward with their partnership. They understood the relationship between addressing their domestic challenges and attracting international investment, and most of them were taking meaningful steps towards democratic rule, honest government, respect for human rights, and tolerance for diversity. Their success in implementing these principles was going to be rated according to the transparency criteria of their own peers, which in turn would boost the confidence of the rest of the world to provide development assistance and, more important, to make investments. Moreover, everyone saw the value in more cohesion and better cooperation among north and south, east and west. Since most of the countries don't have the size, wealth, diversification, or infrastructures to go it alone, they can't implement the necessary solutions by themselves. For example, Nigeria used to burn off a lot of its natural gas because there were no pipelines to the poor Western African countries that were forced to import oil at high prices for their energy demands. So working together, maybe even in a federation, is fundamental to their growth and peace.

Kananaskis was a perfect site for the G8 talks and easier to secure than Ottawa or Banff, the other locations we had considered. The scenery was spectacular; the resort was so isolated that the only intruder was a roving bear, which was accidentally killed while the police were trying to sedate it; and though a couple of protesters mooned the leaders in Calgary, the summit was great publicity for the beauty and friendliness of Alberta. As host, Canada decided to devote a whole day to discussing Africa and the NePAD process, even though we knew that the Americans weren't comfortable with the subject. Though their contribution was large in terms of dollars, it was small in terms of GDP, and I didn't blame George W. Bush for not wanting to be beaten up for not doing enough. As usual, he was suspicious of multilateral solutions and wanted to go his own way bilaterally.

To keep my agenda, I let Jacques Chirac know that I was going to give him the floor to speak first. "Go ahead and put on the pressure," I said. And, boy, did he ever put it on. At one point he called the Americans "stingy," and I could see that Bush was offended.

"The translator made a mistake, George," I jumped in, resorting to my old trick. "I was listening to Jacques in French and the word he used doesn't mean exactly the same." That wasn't quite true, and everybody knew what I was doing, but it restored harmony. By the end, I am happy to say, the United States proved much more reasonable than anyone had expected. In fact,

Kananaskis was pivotal in bringing African issues to the forefront of the world's most pressing concerns and setting the bar high.

In March 2002, during the International Conference on Financing for Development held in Monterrey, Mexico, the Americans grandly announced that they were going to increase their contribution to foreign aid by $5 billion over three years. "That's very generous of them," I said, "but they're sending half the bill to Canada with the $2.5 billion tariff on softwood lumber that they imposed yesterday and the other half to Europe with their duties on steel." It got a big laugh, but the serious point was made as well.

Canada's moral suasion was strong only to the extent that we put our words into practice. I had deeply regretted having to reduce our foreign aid by 20 per cent in our first budget, especially since it had been Lester Pearson who set the target that every developed nation should dedicate 0.7 per cent of GDP to the needy recipients, but the federal government was virtually bankrupt and we had to treat all departments equally. Of course, it's always a domestic political problem to send money abroad when governments are running deficits and all kinds of social services have to be cut at home. In 2001, however, we stopped collecting debt payments from eleven poor countries that had shown a commitment to reform, and in the budget preceding Kananaskis we dedicated $500 million to a special African fund, which included $100 million for venture capital investment that was matched by the private sector. At the Monterrey meeting, much to the surprise of my finance minister, who happened to be sitting beside me at the time, I unexpectedly announced that Canada was going to double our overseas development assistance by 2010, with at least half earmarked for Africa. Not only did it serve as a spur to the other G8 members but it demonstrated my personal hope that we as a nation will reach Pearson's goal someday soon.

Too often, in my experience, Canadians have trouble feeling any personal connection to the results of their donations, whether through their government or the international agencies. When I was a law student, Père Georges-Henri Lévesque of Laval University had funded a French-speaking university in Rwanda, a particularly small and poor African country, and some people I know (including Bob Fowler) went to work there as volunteer teachers for a year or two because they knew it and felt it was somehow theirs. Similarly, I remember visiting a village in a very poor province of China where Canada had spent about $150 per family to build a tank system so that the women no longer had to walk fifteen kilometres twice a week to get drinking water. Our entire delegation—politicians, bureaucrats, even the media—was so taken by the value we saw in what had been given that we all fished into our pockets and handed over our cash to the villagers. A similar thing happened in Addis Ababa, Ethiopia, when we saw how grateful the people of an impoverished district were for the pump Canada had financed, so they no longer had to drink the same water as their animals. There was even a Canadian flag attached to the pump.

As I saw it, if the industrialized world were to open our markets to the Africans, they would be able to grow their market economies and eventually buy goods and services from us, as happened in Asia or Latin America, and thereby create more jobs and profits in Canada. The Scandinavians seemed to have already figured that out a long time ago. While they are extremely generous in their giving, they're also investing a lot of money in Africa and, as a result, they end up selling their own products there. It's one reason why Canada should welcome as many foreign students as possible. Just as Britain, France, Holland, and even Belgium maintained highly advantageous trade relations with their former colonies after independence, so people who study in Canada will go home with a good knowledge of what we make and how to get it. In the Seychelles one day I met a minister of agriculture who had trained in Nova Scotia, for example. In Pakistan I came across a man who was interested in importing beef from Canada because he had once been an engineering student here.

Putting money into Africa is not charity, therefore, but an investment. Africa is a huge continent with more than 800 million people, a wealth of resources, and an extraordinary potential to develop exports, tourism, almost everything. First, according to its own set of priorities, it needs roads, airports, seaports, electrical power, information and communications technology, and other basic infrastructure in order to seed its economic development. Then it needs access to markets for its products and natural resources to help lift it out of poverty. Then it needs practical education, good health care, and clean water to reduce the incidence of AIDS, malaria, tuberculosis, and other pandemic diseases. Now, thankfully, everyone from Bill Clinton to Bill Gates wants to help in Africa, and there's a new awareness of the problems that exist.

It's not just a matter of cash; it's also a matter of policy. Take agricultural products. Because of farm subsidies, I was told, the raising of a cow in France costs the state more than the education of a child, and I once met a billionaire from the southern United States who still received government money designed to protect the American cotton producer. Though cotton is one of the few things that the poor farmers in Burkina Faso can produce, they obviously can't compete against the United States treasury. I was astonished one day to discover that George W. Bush didn't even know how much his government was paying to the U.S. agricultural sector, most of which is owned by huge— and hugely profitable—corporations. "Maybe Clinton had to buy their votes, George," I once told him, "but you don't need to. They'd vote for you anyway, money or no money, because of their conservative views on social issues such as hanging, guns, and abortion."

Canada felt the power of the American agricultural lobby in May 2003, when a single case of "mad cow disease" was found in Alberta, and the United States immediately closed its doors to Canadian cattle. Though it was a legitimate health concern to some small degree, no Canadian ever got sick from eating Albertan beef, and it was used as a convenient excuse for the U.S. producers to remove a competitor, increase their prices, and make more profit for as long as they could get away with it. The fuss was just another example of how the Americans and the Europeans kept trying to get around free trade in agricultural products through non-tariff barriers, and I worked hard with Premier Klein to get that decision reversed by Washington.

In July, when former president Bill Clinton and I were attending a meeting of progressive leaders in London, a reporter asked me about the Canadian economy. "Ah," I said, "it's fantastic, we're doing very well. We have only one problem. We have one goddamn mad cow." Clinton laughed so hard. Afterwards he said, "Jean, you're the only one of us who can say 'one goddamn mad cow' on international television and get away with it."

"I'm French, Bill," I joked. "So what does 'goddamn' mean in English anyway?" Then I turned serious. "Look, this is hurting our farming community, we're having to pay a lot of compensation to our beef producers, and your own consumers are being hit."

In fact, that "one goddamn mad cow" cost the federal treasury billions of dollars without any flak from any other part of the country. It was a one-time emergency to help some of our fellow Canadians in their moment of need, and as such I saw it as a national responsibility rather than a form of subsidy, though no Albertan politician ever expressed any gratitude as far as I recall. It's probably a lucky thing that the cow didn't come from the Maritimes or I'd have had all those rich guys in Calgary yelling at me for tossing money to the East.

Generally speaking, though we were far from perfect when it came to protecting our own dairy and poultry producers, Canada kept working towards opening the world markets in accordance with the Uruguay Round of the World Trade Organization. The practical truth was, while the farmers in the United States and Europe still enjoyed tremendous political clout, in Canada the percentage of people working directly or indirectly in agriculture had dropped from 50 per cent to 3 per cent over the past sixty years, though this group remains of crucial importance in the rural ridings. By the time of the Kananaskis summit, we had eliminated the tariffs and quotas on all products from the least developed countries, thirty-four of which were African.

—

Of course, there can be no progress in development, investment, education, and health without creating a climate of peace, stability, and the rule of law. There is nothing more nervous than a million dollars—it moves very fast, and it doesn't speak any language. Many of the African countries had been put together artificially by the colonial powers without much sensitivity or reason. The borders usually suited some imperial purpose that had no relation to the needs of the local people, and different tribes had to compete for power within an inappropriate political system. Later, during the Cold War, the Americans and the Soviets played one corrupt government off against another in order to buy their votes at the United Nations or bind them to their ideological blocs. As a result, the continent was plagued for generations by boundary disputes, civil wars, brutal dictatorships, corrupt officials, and ethnic violence.

Thus, on our arrival in New Zealand in 1995, the Commonwealth leaders learned that Ken Saro-Wiwa, the author and human rights activist, was about to be hanged by the military regime in Nigeria. His son came to talk to me, and since none of the other leaders seemed willing, I decided to take up his father's case. I raised it in my opening speech, much to the fury of the Nigerian minister of foreign affairs, who shouted at me and came close to attacking me physically for interfering in an internal matter that had been the verdict of a court of law. Then I persuaded South African president Nelson Mandela personally to phone General Sani Abacha to try to stop the execution—to no avail, sadly. Saro-Wiwa was hanged while we were still meeting, and after a heated debate we decided to suspend Nigeria's membership.

Of all the political figures I have met in my life, none was greater than Nelson Mandela. In New Zealand he had been welcomed like a demigod by thousands of ordinary people who simply wanted to be in his presence. I'll never forget the sight of him standing erect in the sun during the Remembrance Day ceremony, with a fresh breeze blowing and the beautiful snow-capped peaks of South Island in the background, his posture almost majestic, his grey head proud and noble, the absolute centre of everyone's attention. Yet he turned out to be an easy man to talk with, courteous, charming, unpretentious, with a sharp mind and a wonderful laugh. In all the hours I was privileged to spend in his company, at bilateral and multilateral meetings, over dinner in Canada or at his home in South Africa, I never heard him express a moment's anger or thirst for revenge for the twenty-seven years he spent in prison during his fight for the rights and liberty of his people. I used to marvel at the eloquent words and soft rhythms of his speeches, but they didn't disguise the fact that he held very strong views, which he debated with great force, learning, and judgment. Most times, I'm pleased to say, we were on the same side of the issues. One day he called me looking for international support for an education project that was important to him. "I'm calling you first," he said, "because I need someone to get the ball rolling and I know that Canada won't say no."

In 2001, in Ottawa with his wife, Graça Machel, a charming and politically astute person in her own right, Nelson Mandela became the first living person to be named an honorary citizen of Canada and the first foreign leader ever to be decorated with the Order of Canada. From then on, whenever I saw him, he always greeted me with outstretched arms, saying, "I want to meet *my* prime minister."

In May 1999, less than four years after the New Zealand meeting, Olusegun Obasanjo was elected president of Nigeria by a democratic vote. He too had been jailed by General Abacha and sentenced to death, but the Commonwealth's strong response caused the Nigerian authorities to reverse the decision. "If Canada had not intervened," he told me, "I would not be alive today."

"Past human rights abuses and corruption are under investigation," I said in a speech in Abuja on November 9, 1999. "Economic policy is being reviewed. A universal education scheme and immunization program have been launched. This is progress that would have been beyond imagination just a few years ago. Just as Nigeria has taken a new path for the new century, so too are things changing for the better throughout Africa. Like Nigeria, more and more African nations are embracing democracy, the rule of law, and governance. The economies of almost all African countries are growing. African countries are increasingly applying solutions that are made in Africa."

Of course, as I frankly reminded my African audience, there was still too much corruption, poverty, and inequality, too many cases of AIDS, drug abuse, and disease, and too many regional conflicts. Indeed, when I went back to Abuja in December 2003 to attend my last Commonwealth meeting, we had a difficult debate about whether to expel Zimbabwe because of Robert Mugabe's brutal violations of democratic rights. When I ended up siding with those Africans who were seeking a less-humiliating solution, Tony Blair and Australian prime minister John Howard weren't very happy, and Commonwealth secretary general Don McKinnon and I had a serious argument with them in the middle of the conference hall.

"The Africans recognize that Mugabe isn't doing the proper thing," I argued, "but to them he was the first winner in the struggle against colonialism. He may be old, he may be unstable, he may be a thug, whatever, but he's still a kind of folk hero in their eyes, the one African freedom-fighter they looked up to before Nelson Mandela. So they do not want to kick him out, and the Caribbean will support them. Why? Because it's not a question of pure political logic—it's a question of brotherhood. If we put it to a vote, we'll lose, and that might even mean the end of the Commonwealth."

Though we were able to avoid a vote, Pakalitha Mosisili, the prime minister of Lesotho, led a final push to reverse a previous decision to suspend Zimbabwe from the Commonwealth's councils. "If you want to make a separate statement, fine," I said, "but if you make it here, everyone will say that Obasanjo's conference has been a failure. Why not wait until you get back home before releasing it?" Perhaps because Mosisili had attended university in Canada, he respected my point of view, and the world press didn't give any attention to the divisions within the Commonwealth when he eventually issued the statement from Lesotho. Obasanjo was so pleased that he personally accompanied me on the long drive to the airport. Though Canada was criticized in some quarters for not doing enough to bring down Mugabe, I didn't feel I could talk publicly about why we had had to settle for a weak compromise. Sometimes there's a political price to pay for discretion, but better to pay that price than lose trust, confidence, and effectiveness behind the scenes.

As I said in a CBC interview in 2002 on the first anniversary of 9/11, I think that part of the explanation for the terrorist attacks was the resentment caused in the rest of the world by the wealth and power of the West. I could feel it dealing with the African file. The rich were getting richer, the poor were relatively poorer, and the West was beginning to look too arrogant, selfish, and greedy. "And that," I said, "is what the Western world—not only the Americans—has to realize, because those other people are human beings too and there are long-term consequences if you don't look hard at what the reality will be in ten or twenty or thirty years from now."

FOURTEEN

VIVE LE CANADA

F
ollowing the election of the Liberal government in November 2000, I once again faced the question of my retirement. Even if party members and Canadian voters were willing to give me a fourth term, Aline certainly wasn't. Even more than in 1997, and for all the same reasons, I had absolutely no intention of staying. My plan, as before, was to hand over the leadership at the end of the third year of the new mandate. That would position my successor to govern for a few days with more or less the same Cabinet, call an election, win a majority, and start afresh with his own team, just as Trudeau had done in 1968.

In what should have been a clear signal to everyone, many of my oldest and closest advisers had moved on to other jobs or were about to. In 1999 Peter Donolo became Canada's consul general in Milan and was replaced as my director of communications by Françoise Ducros, who in turn was succeeded by Jim

Munson, a former reporter with CTV News. Late in 2000, Chaviva Hošek was named president of the Canadian Institute of Advanced Research, and Paul Genest ably assumed her responsibilities as director of policy and research. Though Jean Pelletier had told me of his wish to retire as my chief of staff in February 2000, after reaching the age of sixty-five, I convinced him to wait until the end of the Summit of the Americas, which was to be held in Quebec City in April 2001. Because Pelletier had been mayor of the city for twelve years and knew all the movers and shakers in town, I wanted his help in organizing the summit. Fortunately, he gave into my desire and agreed to stay another year, whereupon Percy Downe, a very steady and competant hand who had been a former executive assistant to PEI premier Joe Ghiz, took over as my chief of staff.

"I have asked a lot of Jean," I said when I announced his departure on May 4, 2001, "and he has never let me down. I believe his performance has set the standard against which senior aides in politics and government will be measured for years to come."

But Pelletier still had more to offer his country. In discussing his future, he had mentioned his long-standing interest in Canada's railway system. As mayor, he had re-established passenger rail service into the city centre, and in 1990 he had served as a member of the Ontario-Quebec committee set up by Premiers Robert Bourassa and David Peterson to look into building a high-speed train link between Quebec City and Windsor. Though the project never materialized, Pelletier and others remained convinced that it was something that should be done as long as it was financially viable and could be made to operate on a convenient, punctual schedule. Without giving the idea the green light, I was impressed by his arguments. For me, despite the fact that Canada's development had been based to a large degree on the expansion of our railway system, we had fallen far behind the other members of the G8 in building modern, high-speed trains. In September 2001, after consulting with David Collenette, I appointed Jean Pelletier chair of VIA Rail, with a mandate to reopen the file on a rapid passenger service in the Quebec-Windsor corridor. He was working hard at it and making a great deal of progress when my successor, Paul Martin, in an act of petty political revenge, abruptly and unjustly had him fired for nothing more than making an off-the-cuff remark to the press about a completely trivial matter.

From the Cabinet, too, I watched the retirement of Marcel Massé, Lloyd Axworthy, Sergio Marchi, and other good people. I was sorry to see them go, but I understood that a job in public life is rarely a lifelong career—and I would be following them soon enough. Meanwhile, I had been given an increased majority by the Canadian people to govern for five years, and I still had a job to do for the party and the country.

I made two crucial mistakes, however. First, I rejected the advice of those who were urging me to do what I had done after the 1997 election and call for an immediate leadership review, which I undoubtedly would have won by a significant margin. Knowing I was to leave by the end of 2003, I simply didn't want to go back to ask my hundreds of friends and organizers across the land to get to work once more. They had done enough, in my opinion, and I saw no purpose in rallying them to raise the money, elect the delegates, and organize the convention on my behalf. In effect, I surrendered control of the party. My second mistake was to keep my schedule to myself, simply because I didn't want to look like a lame duck. I was wrong, but that was the kind of theory you can prove only by testing it in practice. By not announcing a date for my departure, I created a false impression in the minds of Paul Martin's supporters, the media, and the public that I might be intending to cling to power forever.

At times I went too far with my teasing. At my third swearing-in, for example, I showed my cravat pin to one of the Martin clique with whom I was on friendly terms and said, "You know, this is the pin that Laurier wore when he was prime minister and he won four consecutive mandates from the people of Canada with it." Or I liked to joke that I was younger than Ronald Reagan had been when he started his presidency, or St. Laurent his nine years in office, or de Gaulle his eleven years, and I would still have more than a decade to go to beat Mackenzie King's record—"though I'm sure," I always threw in when they started to look nervous, "that I won't be able to do that with the same spouse." Still, when I offered to meet with Paul Martin after the election to discuss my retirement plans, he declined. "I'm not interested," he said.

Predictably, the press kept trying to build up a fight between Martin and me. Everyone knew that he had been working hard for a long time to gather support in the riding associations and he was obviously the front-runner by a mile, but I didn't go out of my way to help him or to hurt him. I even felt there would be poetic justice if the son were able to succeed where the father had failed three times. But, with no particular preference as to the ultimate winner, my only concern was to see a fair and wide-open race, because I didn't think that a coronation would revitalize the party or create the momentum we needed to get another majority in the next election. I assumed that everything was being done according to the best traditions of the Liberal Party, and I didn't think it was up to me to look after the interests of the competing candidates. I was naïve.

As Martin's organizers became rougher in their tone and their tactics, the other likely contenders became more discouraged. Things came to a head at the end of 2001 when Brian Tobin, in his capacity as minister of industry, got into a battle with the Department of Finance over his plan to provide rural broadband service across the country. Some around Martin thought it was a bad idea because the technology was changing so quickly; others thought it was a ruse by which Tobin could hire political organizers in every riding from coast to coast. Even so, I gave instructions that the initial development cost of $100 million be put into the next budget, in December. At the end of November, while on a trade mission to Dallas and Los Angeles, I discovered that Tobin's money was to be allocated over several years. I phoned and gave Eddie Goldenberg hell. Some official had made a mistake, I was told, and it was too late to fix it now. After the budget was announced on December 10, I called Tobin and told him not to worry, the remedy was simple—he would get what he wanted through a supplementary spending estimate later in the year. Instead, after thinking about it over the holiday, he came to see me at 24 Sussex on the evening of Sunday, January 13, to tell me he had made up his mind to quit the Cabinet and leave politics altogether.

I was surprised. I knew Tobin had been soliciting the support of some of my friends, raising money, and trying to tie up enough constituencies to launch a serious leadership bid. Perhaps he felt that Martin had an unfair advantage and feared he might use his power as finance minister to undermine the other candidates. Perhaps he didn't want to make the personal sacrifices that the contest required of him and his family. Perhaps he didn't think he had what it takes to be prime minister, lacking especially French. I didn't ask, though I suspected he had come to realize that the race was already over for him. In my experience, while it's very pleasant to dream about being prime minister, there are plenty of hardships and obstacles along the way and very few people willing or able to overcome them. There's no humiliation in that. I was only the twentieth Canadian prime minister since 1867, after all, so it's no wonder there aren't hundreds of people ready to gamble their time, their financial security, and their domestic happiness on a long shot.

Tobin's departure precipitated a major Cabinet shuffle, which brought in ten new ministers, dropped seven, and switched the portfolios of thirteen others. Because I wanted a senior minister to deal with the crucial issues arising out of the terrorist attacks on New York and Washington the previous September, I put John Manley in charge of infrastructure and national security and made him deputy prime minister in place of the long-serving Herb Gray, whom I appointed head of the U.S.-Canada International Joint Commission. To fill the gap left by Manley in Foreign Affairs, I reached into the backbenches and selected Bill Graham, an MP who had done an excellent job as a member of caucus and had found an influential and prestigious niche for himself as chair of the Foreign Affairs Committee for seven years without ever being in the Cabinet. Though Graham was happy to be elevated from the B team to the A team, he had already demonstrated how a good committee chair can sometimes be more powerful than the minister of a minor department. Allan Rock, no doubt with an eye to his own leadership prospects, asked me if he could be given an economic portfolio now that he had tackled the big jobs at Justice and Health, so I appointed him to succeed Tobin in Industry.

As usual, the media found the shuffle interesting from only two angles: scandal and succession. The first involved the resignation of Alfonso Gagliano as minister of public works and government services and his subsequent appointment as Canada's ambassador to Denmark. Both Gagliano and his department had come under intense scrutiny in recent months because of irregularities uncovered in the sponsorship program, leading to the assumption that I was firing him or at least putting him at some distance from the government. On the contrary. I had always found Gagliano to be an honest, popular, and extremely hard-working person. He had immigrated to Canada from Sicily, learned two new languages, worked as an accountant, become active in a school board in Montreal, and been elected to the Commons in 1984. He fought hard for Canada in the 1995 referendum. I gave him a heavy responsibility as minister of labour in 1996, and when Marcel Massé left politics, I made Gagliano my Quebec lieutenant, in charge of relations with the Quebec caucus and the Quebec wing of the federal Liberal Party. In 1997 he became the minister of public works, and he did a good job, as far as I was concerned. Thus, in February 2000, when Jean Pelletier brought my attention, during our regular morning meeting, to rumours in the press about some misspending by Public Works in the sponsorship program, I told him to go see the minister, who immediately ordered an internal audit. When that reported in August, calling attention to a number of administrative errors, Gagliano acted on its recommendations and set the program right.

However, the more the opposition and the media went after him personally, the more discouraged and tired he grew. He sensed, rightly or wrongly, that he was being singled out for attack because of unfair stereotypes of Sicilians, and he had had enough. He certainly didn't intend to remain in politics after I left, he told me, and he wanted another challenge before completing his career. Though I was usually reluctant to give former ministers diplomatic posts ahead of Foreign Service officers, I made an exception in this case, given Gagliano's dedication to his country.

As for the leadership issue, the gossip all had to do with whether or not the shuffle was a deliberate slap in the face for Paul Martin. I never thought about it that way. Manley and Rock might have gained a bit of strength, but they were first-rate, highly regarded ministers whose ability and experience I needed for a couple of important jobs. Certainly, neither of them ever asked me to bring any of their friends into the Cabinet to help them in the leadership race, and I had always made a point of trying to appease Martin's fear that I was out to isolate him. Anne McLellan, who moved from Justice to Health, was a known Martin supporter, as was Maurizio Bevilacqua, the new secretary of state for science. And though I never discussed it with Bill Graham, I was told that he and Martin had been good friends from their law-school days.

The shuffle also helped Martin, at least indirectly, by causing a certain number of MPs who had been passed over for the Cabinet to harden their hearts against me. The ones who didn't make the cut vastly outnumbered the ones who did, of course, and many of them were mad as hell. So they were susceptible to the first candidate who came along and promised each and every one of them a Cabinet position in the next regime in exchange for their support at the convention. There must have been dozens of people around Paul Martin who were sure they were going to be named minister of this or that, and one second-rate backbencher even announced that he was going to be the minister of transport.

One day in 2000, I remember, a group of Italian-Canadian Liberal MPs had come to me to complain about their colleague Carolyn Parrish. They wanted me to scold her for referring to them collectively as "the pasta caucus," which they considered a derogatory slight. But as the meeting got more and more heated, the real problem soon became clear. They were bitter at having been passed over for a Cabinet post and jealous of the person I had selected. As a result, they had lined up behind Paul Martin and seemed anxious to hasten my exit. "You seem to have forgotten who was the leader under whom you, and you, and you, and you managed to get elected," I said, pointing to each of them in turn. "And let me tell you something. You all think you will be in the Cabinet after I'm gone, but my successor will have to choose among you." It turned out I was wrong. He found a job for almost all of them—except for Maurizio Bevilacqua, who had fallen into disfavour for agreeing to serve as a minister under me.

—

In March 2002, Stephen Harper replaced Stockwell Day as leader of the Canadian Alliance; in January 2003, Jack Layton took over the leadership of the NDP from Alexa McDonough; and, in May 2003, the Tories elected Peter MacKay to succeed Joe Clark. I followed the changes, of course, but more as a student of politics than as someone with something at stake, because I knew I wasn't going to be around to take them on in an election. In retrospect, however, I guess that Paul Martin and his team believed I was going to pull a fast one on them at the last minute and fight to retain the leadership at the review scheduled for February 2003. They didn't want to take any chances. At the same time, my decision not to announce a timetable for my departure was causing problems for my own supporters. They were torn between remaining loyal to me, if I was staying, and getting behind one of the contenders, if I was going. As a result, I asked the president of the party, Stephen LeDrew, and the executive director, Terry Mercer, to establish the last date by which I could announce my retirement and cancel the review without having to pay penalties to the hotels and convention centre. Three months ahead, they told me. Okay, I thought to myself, I'll make the announcement in November 2002 that I will retire following a leadership convention in the fall of 2003.

Still, Martin's supporters became increasingly impatient and began making life difficult for me, hoping no doubt that I would give up and go. At first I thought I could hang on to my plan—six months more wasn't a very long time, after all—but the agitation started to infect the harmony of the caucus, the solidarity of the Cabinet, and eventually the operation of the government. At one point, for example, two Liberal MPs began pressuring the government to give a subsidy to the tobacco producers in their ridings in southern Ontario. When they didn't get an enthusiastic reception from the minister of agriculture, they went to see the minister of finance. Since he wanted to secure their votes in the leadership race, he told them, yes, he had the money; yes, they should get it; yes, he wanted to give it to them—but it was being blocked by the prime minister. So they came to complain to me.

I was frank. "It's not a question of money," I said. "The minister of health is currently engaged in a battle against tobacco because it's harmful to the people of Canada, so what mixed message would a subsidy to the producers give? And the minister of agriculture doesn't want to be placed in the awkward position of increasing the level of subsidy to one commodity while refusing to give subsidies to other, less controversial ones. I'm sorry, I know you're going to be unhappy with me, but it's my duty as prime minister to do the right thing and say no." Needless to say, these two MPs became ardent fans of Paul Martin and probably imagined themselves as future Cabinet ministers, though their ultimate reward was to lose their seats in the next election.

On another occasion, in the spring of 2002, the minister of agriculture was asking for an extra billion dollars to help Western farmers cope with a serious drought. Paul Martin, as finance minister, offered less than $500 million. I settled the dispute with a compromise of $700 million—whereupon Martin rushed to the caucus and the farmers to claim that the reduction was my decision, not his, because he had been in favour of the billion dollars all along. It was irresponsible behaviour on his part, and it made the government increasingly difficult to manage.

No prime minister could live with this type of situation for long. All the confusion was extremely disruptive and potentially destructive, as I had witnessed under Prime Minister Pearson. At one point Pearson even lost a vote in the House because so many of his ministers were off campaigning to succeed him. He was furious, and when they returned he told them in very blunt terms to stop what they were doing and get back to work. Now the time had come for me to follow his example. At a Cabinet meeting on Thursday, May 30, I gave the ministers a stern warning that the leadership race was getting out of hand and had to cease immediately. I may have been looking at Martin when I said it, because he sat directly across the table from me, but my message was clearly aimed at every candidate.

The next night Martin gave a speech in Toronto, not far from where I was addressing a Liberal gathering at the same hour. I was told that his organizers were deliberately trying to make sure that I had a low turnout. If so, they didn't succeed. Then I heard that Martin's chief of staff had been seen handing out his business card to friends at the event and telling them to keep it as a souvenir because his boss wasn't going to be the minister of finance on Monday morning. Meanwhile, Martin himself was telling reporters that he had to "reflect" on his options as a member of the government. "The question is," he said, "will my continuation in the Cabinet, given these events, permit me in fact to exercise the kind of responsibility and influence that I believe a minister of finance ought to have?" But in our system, as Martin must have understood, it's the prime minister who appoints a minister to serve in the Cabinet as an adviser to Her Majesty; it's not the adviser who decides whether or not to serve, unless it's to quit. So the minute he said that in public, I assumed he was intending to resign.

All weekend the press was full of speculation that Martin was leaving. Bay Street and the international financial community were wondering what was going on in Ottawa. There were serious concerns that the dollar, the stock market, and interest rates would take a hit as soon as the world markets opened because of the political uncertainty. Fed up and furious, I was determined that this nonsense had to end. When I finally got through to Martin on the phone in the middle of Sunday afternoon after he had failed to return a number of my calls, I told him that I had accepted his resignation. Later he claimed that I had fired him. Aline, for one, was puzzled. "If he disliked being in your government so much," she asked me, "why isn't he proud to have resigned instead of pretending he was fired?" No matter, I phoned John Manley, who was in the middle of a ministers' retreat, and told him to put on a tie: he was Canada's new finance minister.

Despite the apocalyptic predictions in the press, life went on quite smoothly. Martin got a lift in the polls from people who thought I had been too tough on him, but as far as I was concerned, he had left of his own accord. Caucus members were upset and nervous about losing their seats, no doubt about it, but most of them calmed down when they realized the sky hadn't fallen on their heads. A majority of Liberal MPs and senators even signed a letter supporting my leadership, despite the heavy pressure they were under from the Martinites to withdraw their names. One day two ministers came to urge me to change my mind and stay, but they left telling everyone, including my staff, that I definitely wasn't going to run again. And still the tension and intrigue did not subside.

I did not like what was happening within the party, especially as I knew it was all for nothing. So Aline and I decided I should move up the announcement of my retirement from November to September 10, a date we chose to coincide with the celebration of our forty-fifth wedding anniversary. But a couple of events caused me to move it up even earlier. One was the visit to Canada by Pope John Paul II at the end of July. His Holiness, always a person of great warmth and compassion, offered Aline and me his prayers because of the difficult period we were going through. I came away from my audience with the Pope with a clearer understanding that nobody needs to live with the strain and indecency of unfair attacks.

The second event was the Liberal caucus meeting set for August 20 in Chicoutimi. I was warned that it was going to be a stormy one. Why, I asked myself, put my colleagues through a difficult ordeal where they might do things they would later regret or say things that would threaten the unity of the party? That morning, in front of Bill Gates and a business audience in Toronto, I made what I knew immediately to be a terrible speech. I wasn't confident with the text, my old jokes sounded flat, and I handled the questions without any wit or enthusiasm. Oh-oh, I thought to myself, my heart's no longer in the game. When I got in the car with Eddie Goldenberg, I asked him to prepare a resignation speech. Then I called Aline and asked her to drive from Shawinigan to Chicoutimi, because I was going to announce my decision the next day. By coincidence, we were celebrating the fiftieth anniversary of our first meeting that month.

"For forty years the Liberal Party has been like a family to me," I said in my speech. "Its best interests are bred in my bones. I have reflected on the best way to bring back unity, to end the fighting, to resume interrupted friendships. I have thought about how much time it will take to finish the job we were elected to do, to complete the agenda for governing that I set out last night—for children in poverty; for Aboriginals; for health; for the environment; for urban infrastructure; for public-sector ethics. I have taken into account my duty to protect for my successors the integrity of the office I hold from the Canadian people, an office that is non-negotiable. Here is my conclusion: I will not run again. I will fulfill my mandate and focus entirely on governing from now until February 2004, at which time my work will be done and at which time my successor will be chosen. This will be after three of the opposition parties have chosen their new leaders, so Liberals will know what they are facing. And it will be early enough to give a new prime minister all the necessary flexibility to choose the date of the next election."

It took Paul Martin and his advisers three hours, including the time he spent in a washroom hiding from the reporters' questions, to come up with a three-sentence response. And in this response he claimed to hold me in "the highest respect."

—

As soon as I announced my decision to retire, it was as though I had been given a second lease on life. Contrary to what I and my advisers had assumed, I found I had even more political power than before. In the parliamentary system, a prime minister remains prime minister until he is defeated in the House, and I made no secret that I was prepared to use all the prerogatives of a prime minister for as long as I held the office. Wim Kok, the prime minister of the Netherlands, stayed another year after his party had elected a new leader, while Sonia Gandhi remained leader of her party in India without wishing to be prime minister. As a result, whenever Martin's supporters in the Cabinet and the caucus vehemently opposed any of my major decisions, I simply had to hint that I was ready to lose the vote in the House of Commons to make them either rally to my side or absent themselves with a strategic trip out of town. If the government had fallen on a serious matter, they knew, I would have called a quick election and been almost certain to win another five-year mandate. Some of my own supporters even suggested that I should organize my own parliamentary defeat for just that purpose. It would have been easy enough to do, but I really wasn't interested in remaining as leader. However, the mere possibility allowed me to stay another year and three months—not to cling to power for its own sake but to govern for the good of the country. This was the period, it should be noted, during which Canada decided to send our soldiers to Afghanistan, said no to the invasion of Iraq, took the lead in African development, signed a new multi-billion-dollar health agreement with the provinces, added more billions to the National Child Benefit, and achieved a long list of other significant accomplishments.

One of the most important and controversial decisions the government still had to make was whether to ratify the Kyoto

Protocol to the United Nations Framework on Climate Change, an international obligation to significantly reduce greenhouse gases by the year 2012. It had been negotiated in December 1997 but still required, to take effect, the signatures of a minimum of fifty-five nations responsible in 1990 for at least 55 per cent of the developed world's greenhouse gas emissions. The scientific evidence was increasingly clear and increasingly alarming: if human beings don't cut back on the emission into the atmosphere of carbon dioxide and five other noxious gases—and fast—the global warming we're causing will have disastrous consequences for human health and ecological sustainability within the lifetime of our children. In my opinion, the counter-arguments were no stronger than those of the tobacco lobbyists who used to argue that smoking doesn't cause lung cancer.

Protecting the environment had been a personal preoccupation of mine ever since I was put in charge of Canada's national parks in 1968 as minister of Indian affairs and northern development. I created ten new national parks in four years, in comparison with the four that had been created during the previous forty years. "Take care of my parks" had been my words to Sheila Copps when I named her minister of Canadian heritage in 1996, and I was delighted in October 2002 when she announced that her department was going to create ten more national parks and five new marine conservation areas, in effect doubling the area of protected land. The following year, the government passed the *Species at Risk Act,* to preserve and recover endangered wildlife species, thanks to the concerted efforts of Environment Minister David Anderson and Environment Committee chair Charles Caccia.

However, the issues of greenhouse gas emissions are much more complex and the alternatives much more costly. And, because the problems are caused by the habits of millions of individuals, no one can legislate an instant solution. You can decide to force the production of energy-efficient cars, but people will complain that they're too small or too slow, and a huge sector of the national economy will suffer. You can argue that every province ought to convert to nuclear energy, because it's cleaner than oil or coal, but once you try to build a nuclear generator, all hell breaks loose, despite the industry's safety record. You can go out to sell CANDU reactors in Eastern Europe or Asia, but the protesters will yell that you're aiding in the proliferation of nuclear weapons, as though nations that want to build bombs won't find a way to make them without your help or as though they can't be monitored by international agencies. In other words, the debate is often based on emotion rather than reason.

Nor are the statistics always based on fair comparisons. Canada may emit more carbon dioxide per capita than most other industrialized countries, for example, but we're 31 million people stretched in a thin ribbon along the U.S. border from one ocean to the other. If you want to deliver a product by truck from Halifax to Vancouver or haul wood from northern Ontario to the American market, you're necessarily going to emit more carbon dioxide than if you're transporting goods the length and width of the Netherlands. Moreover, our population was increasing, our economy was growing, and the oil sands were coming into production. During the G7 summit in Denver in 1997, I remember, Bill Clinton and I were forced to listen to the Europeans brag about the great strides they had made in greenhouse gas reductions during the previous decade. But I had studied my briefing notes and noticed something very interesting. The British had done well because they had the good fortune of discovering natural gas and therefore stopped burning coal, while Germany had done well because it closed down the old inefficient factories in the east—not because the factories were emitting carbon dioxide, but because they were losing money. If you took those extraordinary factors out of the equation, I said to the other leaders, Europe's record was actually worse than North America's.

Clinton breathed with relief. As chair of the meeting, he had been feeling trapped by Helmut Kohl, in particular, who was heading into an election against the Greens and wanted an environmental commitment in the final communiqué that was obviously too strong for the American administration to be willing or able to fulfill at the time. My intervention opened the way for a consensus that ultimately avoided an embarrassing and ultimately unproductive division among the leaders in the eyes of the world.

Though Canada may not have been pushing as hard as the Europeans wished, we were, nevertheless, pushing hard for what the Denver communiqué called "meaningful, realistic, and equitable targets." I reacted impatiently whenever I was told that the opposition within the business community, the provinces, the Cabinet, and the bureaucracy made an agreement on any targets unlikely. I spoke with Clinton to see if and how we could act in concert. I consulted with dozens of other leaders at the Commonwealth Conference in Edinburgh, La Francophonie in Hanoi, and the APEC summit in Vancouver, as well as in bilateral meetings or by phone. By December 1997, when our delegations arrived in Kyoto, both Canada and the United States were prepared to do better than merely reduce emissions back down to their 1990 levels. In our case, I wanted to reduce them to 6 per cent below our 1990 levels, which was a point lower than the target the United States set itself. However, our signatures on the Kyoto Protocol were just a first step toward ratification by our legislators, and ratification could not happen until we knew what the rules would be to allow us to achieve our goals.

During the next five years, while enacting the *Environmental Protection Act* in 1999 and investing more than $1 billion in our Action Plan 2000 and other measures to promote energy efficiency, clean technologies, and alternative fuels, the Canadian government worked diligently to get what we needed from Kyoto. First, we wanted to have a market-based trading system recognized, both domestically and internationally, so that countries and industries could buy or sell "carbon credits" from each other to help meet their quotas. Second, since trees absorb huge amounts of carbon dioxide, we wanted to be credited if we launched a massive program to plant trees on our underutilized land. Third, we thought we should be credited for promoting and developing the use of clean energy, either by selling natural gas and electricity to the Americans, thereby reducing their dependence on "dirty" oil and coal, or by selling our CANDU reactors, the cleanest source of power and the safest nuclear system on the market, to customers around the world. Though we didn't get everything we wanted, we got enough by the summer of 2001 to keep moving forward.

In the meantime, however, Bill Clinton had failed to get congressional approval and been succeeded by George W. Bush, who was ideologically suspicious of multilateral agreements, governmental regulations, and the science of global warming. Even before September 11 and the war in Iraq, it was apparent that the United States had a stand-alone attitude and other priorities. The worry in Cabinet, in the provinces, and among Canadian business leaders was that if we ratified Kyoto and the Americans did not, our economy would be placed at a serious competitive disadvantage. Of course, most of the hand-wringing came from the anti-government, pro-U.S. ideologues on the right, including the Canadian Alliance, Ralph Klein of Alberta, Mike Harris of Ontario, the Canadian Council of Chief Executives, and the *National Post*. In February 2002 Klein played a stunt on me in front of the international media during the Team Canada mission to Moscow. Out of the blue, at the crowded news conference on our final day, he handed me a letter in which all the premiers and territorial leaders purportedly stated their reservations about the economic impact of Kyoto. I had to be defended by Premier Bernard Landry, of all people, who pointed out that the Quebec National Assembly had voted in favour of Kyoto.

At the heart of Klein's objection was the fear that implementing Kyoto was going to cause the cost per barrel of oil to soar because of carbon taxes and technological regulations, as a result of which the oil sands investors would flee to non-signatories such as Mexico or Venezuela. It was the same type of anti-Ottawa hysteria that had swept through Alberta in the early 1980s when Trudeau's National Energy Program (NEP) had been introduced to deal with the universal consensus that the world was going to run out of oil by the year 2000. Albertans seemed to have forgotten that the NEP had been toasted by their Conservative premier, Peter Lougheed, with a glass of champagne, and that I had been instrumental as president of the Treasury Board in 1975 in brokering the very costly deal between Lougheed and the federal minister of energy, Donald Macdonald, that helped finance the initial development of the oil sands with grants, incentives, and subsidies. At least Lougheed himself never forgot. When I took on some responsibilities with his law firm in Calgary after my retirement, he told the press, "If we have the oil sands today, we owe Jean Chrétien a big thank you."

For much of 2002, therefore, we discussed climate change at the G8, developed our domestic policies, negotiated with the provinces and stakeholders, mobilized public support, and waited to see if the Bush administration would produce a domestic climate-change plan as good as Kyoto. But precious time was passing, and the target deadline was drawing nearer. After dozens of reports dating back to the commitments the Mulroney government had made at the United Nations Conference on Environment and Development in Rio in 1992, after the Kyoto negotiations in which Canada had played an active role, after countless discussions in caucus, in Cabinet, in Parliament, with the provinces and private sector, all that remained was for me to make the final decision, which I did while flying to the World Summit for Sustainable Development in Johannesburg, South Africa.

On September 2, 2002, I announced that Canada would ratify the Kyoto Protocol, with the implementation details to follow later. Not only did I believe it was the right thing to do for the planet and for future generations, but it intensified the pressure on Russia to follow suit, and thus meet the 55 per cent minimum required for the Protocol to go into force. President Putin had already told me he would sign if I did. It took a bit longer than I had assumed, but he made good his promise in November 2004. Even though Canada had failed to get all the concessions we sought, ratifying Kyoto was both a statement of our values and a pledge to reduce greenhouse gas emissions. It was popular at home, especially among the young; it fit our image abroad as an environmentally conscious, socially progressive nation; and, just as with the government's fight against the deficit, I thought it was important first to establish an obtainable target and then to figure out how to meet it step by step, year by year. The fact is, if you have no set destination in mind, you'll never get anywhere.

On September 18, soon after my return from Johannesburg, I flew to Calgary to discuss the challenges of Kyoto with the oil industry and to try to reach some solutions. Canada needs and wants the production of oil in Alberta, I told them, and we weren't going to cripple the development of the oil sands with government fiats or punitive penalties. Rather than increasing the cost of production by $10 or $12 a barrel, we were planning increases in the range of 20¢ or 30¢ at most at 2002 prices. However, like every other sector, the oil producers wanted to protect their maximum profit. In all my forty years in public life, I've never once seen a sector coming to the government and asking us to increase the taxes it's paying so that the country can be better off. Nor was I able, before I left office, to get an agreement on how to establish and operate the carbon-trading system that was necessary to allow us to reach our Kyoto obligations by 2012.

I almost did, however, and I remained optimistic to my last day as prime minister that we were on track with the Climate Change Plan we announced in November 2002 and supported with $3.7 billion in new commitments. Changes in technology were certainly going to help. Using electricity instead of natural gas to extract oil from the oil sands or operating hybrid automobiles would reduce carbon dioxide emissions. So would the use of nuclear generators rather than coal-fired plants, and, as I discussed with Premiers Gary Doer and Dalton McGuinty, the construction of a hydro grid to carry Manitoba electricity to the markets of Ontario. To that end, the government invested in research and development in all kinds of emission-reduction innovations, infrastructure projects, and cutting-edge businesses that had the potential to make a substantial difference. Indeed, I saw this global crisis as a major job-creation, wealth-creation opportunity for Canada if we could develop and export leading environmental technologies around the world through initiatives such as the Sustainable Development Technology Foundation or the Canadian Foundation for Climate and Atmospheric Sciences that John Manley had done so much to foster. Unfortunately, whether for political or ideological reasons, my successors succumbed to the fears and threats of the anti-Kyoto forces and did serious damage to Canada's progress and our reputation in the process—until the Canadian people spoke up once again and demanded action.

—

Suddenly, in June 2003, the federal government was confronted by an unexpected problem that threatened to pit Canadians against each other in a bitter clash of policies and values if it was not handled with sensitivity and experience. The Ontario Court of Appeal ruled that, under the Charter of Rights, same-sex marriage was legal, equal in all respects to the union of a man and a woman. Changing the word probably didn't change the reality a great deal, but it became a symbol for both sides, in the same way that the words "distinct society" had become a symbol for those who held differing views about Quebec's status in the federation.

While the opposition to same-sex marriage crossed all political boundaries and even divided the Liberal caucus, it was generally true that Conservative voters were more progressive on social issues than Alliance voters and didn't want to be seen in league with the religious right. As a result, many Tories either came over to us on this issue or split the anti-Liberal vote to our advantage. Unlike gun control, however, this wasn't an issue I chose to play up. It was complicated, emotional, divisive, and maybe not as important as all the sound and the fury suggested, given how few gay couples actually bothered to tie the knot. For me it was a problem best handled by the slow and steady evolution of society. There had been some controversy, for example, the first time we gave gay people paid leave when a partner had a death in the family, but further social benefits were extended to gay couples with much less fuss. These steps were accomplished the way I liked, with little fanfare and no deliberate provocation.

Once the court had made same-sex marriage a matter of human rights, I decided not to dodge the issue. Even though I am a Roman Catholic, I wasn't elected as a Roman Catholic, and in a multi-racial, multi-religious society, a prime minister has to leave his religion at home. I had also evolved in my own thinking about homosexuality from a very conservative view of what was normal to a tolerance and understanding of human diversity. When I was minister of justice, a government official came to me with a terrible problem. He was a closet gay man, and his former partner, with whom he had built a house, was blackmailing him:

give me the house or I will reveal to the world that you are a homosexual. "Tell this guy to go to hell," was my advice. "If he reveals that you're a homosexual, so what?" Years later, when I was prime minister, a Liberal senator stood up during a very emotional caucus discussion and said he was homosexual. He had had that orientation all his adult life, he told us. At first he fought it. He got married, had kids, and pretended to be like most other men, but his nature never changed. Now he was divorced and had been living with a companion for many years. After so much misery, he was at long last a happy man. It was a very moving story. So, while homosexuality, multiple divorces, and babies born before the honeymoon may be upsetting for many traditional people, they are the modern realities we have to recognize.

That's not to say I didn't have a lot of sympathy and respect for those who sincerely held the opposite view, such as Pat O'Brien, the Liberal member of Parliament from London, Ontario, who eventually resigned from the caucus over the issue to sit as an independent. I liked the guy, I liked his straightforward style, and I understood his discomfort as an Irish Catholic with gay marriage. Perhaps we made a mistake by not getting rid of the word "marriage" for everyone. Perhaps we should have called the union of any two people a legal contract for the sharing and division of assets, and let the churches give it whatever description they wanted in their private arrangements. But I had less sympathy and respect for those self-righteous types who were all talk about family values while working on their second divorce or cheating on their spouse. Nor did I have much sympathy and respect for the right-wingers who chose to exploit this emotional debate by using it as an opportunity to bash the Charter of Rights and insult judges as Liberal hacks. They claimed that the courts, especially the Supreme Court, had usurped the power of the politicians to make social policy and, worse, that the kind of social policies the courts were making was based on liberal biases.

With regard to the first, power still rests with the politicians because, notwithstanding the Charter, a federal or provincial government is allowed to override a certain right or freedom by a simple piece of legislation. During the intense discussion I had with Pierre Trudeau about Mulroney's constitutional reforms over dinner in the Toronto hotel room in 1992, he even accused me of having weakened the Charter of Rights by surrendering to the premiers' demand for the "notwithstanding" clause. "You gave them that," he said.

"Sorry, Pierre," I countered. "I recommended it. *You* gave it."

As objectionable as the idea was, I had gone along with it in 1982 as the minister of justice responsible for the constitutional negotiations for two reasons. One was pragmatic: Canada probably wouldn't have had any charter without it. At first Trudeau had insisted on a perfect charter, but I convinced him after a vigorous argument to compromise; otherwise, he would lose the support of every single premier in his battle to patriate the Constitution. It helped that any application of the notwithstanding clause had to be renewed every five years, which meant that the voters would have a chance to make the ultimate judgment.

My second reason for supporting the notwithstanding clause was that I had become convinced of its validity in principle too. Under the Charter, for example, Canadians have freedom of speech, but society has set limits to that. You cannot shout "fire" in a theatre—that's a clear abuse. But what if the Supreme Court were to rule that freedom of speech took precedence over any laws against hate literature or child pornography? I would have no problem if the government of the day used the notwithstanding clause in order to prevent the spread of discrimination or to protect the innocence of children. And if a future Canadian government should decide to resort to the notwithstanding clause in the matter of same-sex marriage, it would have the power to do so, though it would probably have to pay a very heavy political price. On the whole, I'm pleased that the option has not been used at the federal level in twenty-five years.

As to the notion that the courts were packed with left-leaning Liberal appointees, I always challenged the opposition to give me an example of one bad judge. While the appointments were technically made by the prime minister, they came after a broad consultation with the minister of justice, the bar association, the provinces, and the legal community. Since 1988, as well, every major region of the country had an advisory committee of seven distinguished representatives, of whom only three were federal appointees. These committees screened the applicants in confidence and ranked them according to their qualifications. I never appointed anyone as a judge who had not been recommended by this independent process.

We live these days in an upside-down world when it comes to these so-called conflicts of interest. If you know somebody, no matter how competent, the opposition and the press say that he should be disqualified from any government service for no other reason than that you know him. But if you appoint somebody you don't know and he turns out to be no good, neither the opposition nor the press accepts the excuse that it's not your fault, you didn't know the guy. Of all the judges whose appointments I was involved with, either as minister of justice or as prime minister, there were very few I knew beforehand. Suspicions were raised when I named Michel Bastarache to the Supreme Court, for example, because he and I had been together in the Ottawa offices of Lang Michener for a short while. The reality was that we had never shared a file or developed a social relationship beyond an occasional cup of coffee. The only thing that mattered to me was that he had a first-rate brain, an excellent record as a lawyer, and a superb reputation among his peers as one of the best judges in Atlantic Canada.

Nor did ideology and party affiliation play any role. Of course, as a liberal, I would have hesitated before appointing a person with a record on the extreme right or the extreme left, but I never tried to find out if someone had voted Liberal or had supported a particular piece of legislation. I was looking for people who had demonstrated an understanding of the law, solid reasoning, decent behaviour, and the mental flexibility to let the evidence trump their biases and prejudices. Has this person been a good judge? Can this person write a clear opinion? Is this person too hard or too lenient? Can this person, however brilliant, work collegially?

If people look at the results rather than complain all the time about the process, I think they will conclude that the system works well. Why? Because any responsible prime minister knows that his own honour is attached to making a good appointment. Yes, he has the sole power to appoint a less-qualified friend, but that only means he alone will be blamed. He's completely responsible and can't hide behind anyone else or run away. Therefore, he is extremely prudent in the use of his power. But if the decision is given to a parliamentary committee, for instance, who will take the responsibility if it goes wrong, and what will prevent the selection process from turning into a political circus? When I look at what's happening with Supreme Court appointments in the United States, all I see is a lot of partisan dogfights in Congress. Why would the candidates submit to a process in which the smallest details of their lives are examined under a microscope in public—their family situation, their financial affairs, their associations, every word they wrote as a law student or every judgment they made on the bench? I don't believe that any of us could emerge without flaws if we were put under the same sort of intense, partisan, and unforgiving scrutiny. Nor do I think that anyone of the quality and integrity of, say, Beverley McLachlin would step forward under those conditions.

—

In March 2002, Don Boudria, who had replaced Alfonso Gagliano as minister of public works in the recent Cabinet shuffle, came to me with stories that all was not as it should be with the government's post-referendum sponsorship program. Up until that moment, as far as I knew, except for the administrative problems outlined in the audit report that Gagliano had commissioned and acted upon in 2000, the program had been running smoothly and honestly. No one—not the minister of public works, the president of the Treasury Board, the minister of finance, the clerk of the Privy Council, or my chief of staff—had alerted me to any other concerns, so I had no reason to preoccupy myself with the file. I had enough problems on my desk without having to invent new ones in my imagination. Hadn't I told the ministers at the outset to bring their troubles to me or to the PMO but otherwise to look after their departments by themselves?

I heard nothing more after the audit report until the day Boudria showed up with his news. "I'm tempted to call in the auditor general," he said, "to do a special investigation."

"Go ahead," I told him, "and call in the RCMP while you're at it. If anybody's been stealing money from the federal government, he or she should be caught, tried, convicted, and thrown in jail."

Sadly, there will always be some bad apples in every organization, private or public—people who will try to steal money if they think they can get away with it. That's why we have the RCMP; that's why we have the auditor general. And though neither may be perfect at all times, both are extremely professional, with reputations for integrity and competence known around the world. In fact, the federal government probably has more auditors producing more reports annually than any other organization in Canada, and in 1994 we increased the number of reports by the auditor general from one to four a year. In this case, far from demonstrating that the administrative system didn't work and needed to be overhauled, events proved that it worked quite well. Even the auditor general, Sheila Fraser, concluded in her blunt report in May 2002 that the rules were in place—they just hadn't been followed as they should have been.

As a result of the RCMP investigation I had ordered, two advertising executives, Paul Coffin and Jean Brault, were arrested and subsequently found guilty of fraud, as was Charles Guité, the bureaucrat in charge of administering the sponsorship contracts. Not one of them, I should add, was a Liberal. Indeed, Coffin had been president of a Tory riding association in the Montreal region; Brault had been a well-known péquiste who gave $100,000 to the Parti Québécois illegally; and Guité had been a civil servant appointed by the Mulroney government.

In our system, the prime minister and his Cabinet have a collective responsibility for everything that is right or wrong in the federal government. If they decide to send Canadian troops to war, for example, they have to bear the political consequences. That doesn't mean they're to blame if an armoured vehicle goes off the road and a soldier gets killed in the accident. Similarly, if the prime minister selects a finance minister, and that minister approves a budget for sponsorships, and the president of the Treasury Board distributes the money, and the public works minister delegates the implementation to his officials, Cabinet solidarity makes them equally and jointly responsible for the program, yet none of them can be blamed for stealing money or defrauding the treasury. Therefore, though I repeatedly said how sorry I was that a few rogues had broken the rules, betrayed the very notion of public service, and let me down personally on my watch, I was accepting the responsibility—but the blame lies with Coffin, Brault, Guité, and anyone else the courts might find guilty.

Increasingly, with the passage of time and the cooling of rhetoric, I believe that most fair and dispassionate observers will come to the same conclusion. On June 27, 2006, for instance, Conservative Senator Hugh Segal bravely and forthrightly told his colleagues in the Upper Chamber, "I do not accept for one moment that there was any corrupt intent on the part of the previous government or its leadership, and I am offended by suggestions to the contrary." With hindsight, too, Chantal Hébert, an Ottawa columnist for the *Toronto Star* and a persistent critic of the federal Liberals, viewed the whole sponsorship business as a "mouse of an affair" that would have soon faded into oblivion if Paul Martin hadn't reacted like "an elephant panicking at the sight of a mouse" and "tried to climb any tree in sight, breaking branches at every turn, and generally creating havoc in all directions." And what of the commission of inquiry headed by Justice John Gomery? "At the end of it all," Hébert had to admit, "it did not find fault with a single sitting politician, and it rapped the knuckles of a very limited cast of public actors."

—

Like "Peppergate," like "Shawinigate," the sponsorship scandal had more to do with party politics and the newspaper wars than the public interest. With no ongoing war in Iraq to debate, no unmanageable controversies over Kyoto or same-sex marriage, no third referendum in Quebec, no downward trend in the opinion polls, the opposition and the media had nothing better with which to attack us than muck. It tarred the reputation of many innocent people, destroyed the effectiveness of a national-unity program, and refuelled the cynicism of Canadians about their democratic institutions. It also created a most unfair impression of Quebec as a corrupt province full of corrupt politicians and corrupt party organizers. Quebecers were angered by that insinuation, and rightly so, because it fed upon an old prejudice about French Canadians and a lack of respect for the province, whereas, for example, Quebec had been the first province to introduce serious legislation to tackle one of the toughest and most important issues in modern democracy: the issue of political contributions and election expenses.

I had been watching that issue unfold in Canada and other countries, especially the United States, where campaign costs had soared by hundreds of millions of dollars at every election. Hillary Clinton had needed to raise more money to win her New York seat in the Senate in 2000 than our party had to raise for all 301 Liberal candidates across Canada. As a result, political parties everywhere were under increased pressure to generate greater and greater amounts of cash to pay for mass advertising and new technologies, which in turn generated a widespread suspicion among the media and the public that every elected official had to be in the pocket of big business and the rich. This suspicion, in my experience, had little foundation in reality. Traditionally, for instance, the banks were among the largest contributors to the Liberal Party, as well as to the Tories and the Alliance, but when they came to ask to be allowed to merge, we decided that it wasn't in the public interest and didn't flinch from saying no.

Perception is everything in politics, however, so I decided that it was essential to reform the system in order to clear away the myths and restore the public's trust in their representatives, in the same way that we had established the office of the ethics counsellor and strengthened the regulations involving lobbyists and ministerial conduct. On February 11, 2003, therefore, I personally introduced the second reading of Bill C-24, an amendment to the *Canada Elections Act*, requiring full disclosure of all contributions and expenses over $200 for parties, candidates, riding associations, nominations, and leadership candidates, and setting an annual contribution limit of $5,000 for individuals to a national party, and $1,000 for corporations or trade unions to a candidate or riding association. The bill made up the difference by increasing the maximum tax credit for individual contributions from $200 to $400, more than doubling the national party rebates for election expenses to 50 per cent, and giving each party $1.75 per year for each vote it had received in the previous election. No one was more relieved than the corporations themselves. Not only were they now spared all the bagmen knocking constantly on their doors, but they didn't have to put themselves in the uncomfortable position of supporting the Liberals or the Tories more than the NDP or the Bloc.

The strongest opposition came from within my own party. The fundraisers were furious with me for making their job more difficult; the party president denounced the legislation as dumber than a bag of hammers; and I had to impose it on the Martin supporters in the caucus by threatening to call an election. The Quebec MPs were particularly irritated by the fact that the government of Canada was going to have to give money to the Bloc. "Yes," I said, "I don't like it either, but there is a positive side for us. In normal circumstances, as long as the Bloc exists, it will split the anti-Liberal vote with the Tories and let us take more seats in the province."

———

During the fall of 2002 the Martinites became so anxious to measure the drapes in the PMO and ride in a limousine that they got the party executive to bring the leadership convention forward to November 2003. In my mind, nevertheless, I was still intending to follow the schedule I had announced in Chicoutimi and to remain prime minister until February 2004. If I resigned as soon as my successor was chosen, I reasoned, it would be hard for him to call an election during the depths of winter. If I waited until the new year, he could take office in the fourth year of the Liberal mandate, call back the House or not, make a few Cabinet changes around the ministers who didn't want to run again, slide into an election in the spring, and win another majority against the divided opposition. And that, according to Paul Martin, had suited him just fine. As the convention drew nearer, however, he changed his mind and let me know through Alex Himelfarb, the clerk of the Privy Council, that he was now expecting to take over as quickly as possible.

"Okay by me," I told Himelfarb. "If that's what he wants, that's what he'll get. I'll give him a month following the convention to organize his Cabinet and prepare the transition while I fulfill my commitment to be at the Commonwealth meeting in Nigeria, attend the farewell dinner Jacques Chirac has long been planning in my honour in Paris, and greet the prime minister of China in Ottawa on December 11. I'll be gone the very next day."

Not waiting until February would prove to be a fatal error in judgment on Martin's part. If I was going to be leaving as soon as the convention was over, I felt it would be inappropriate for me to be up on my feet answering questions in the House on behalf of a government of which I would no longer be a member in a matter of days. Besides, there was nothing urgent on the agenda, nor was there any point in asking Liberal MPs and senators, most of whom were heavily involved in the leadership race, to stick around for routine matters such as the tabling of the auditor general's latest report on the sponsorship program. So, on November 12, I prorogued Parliament.

Though I had neither seen Sheila Fraser's report nor been briefed about it, I knew, like everybody else in Ottawa, that it was going to be tough. But I didn't prorogue Parliament because I was afraid to face it or wanted to pass it like a kiss of death to my successor. It had always been my intention to receive Fraser's report, thank her for her good work, and say what I had been saying over and over again for a year: if there is evidence of theft or fraud, let the police catch the crooks and let the courts put them in jail. Of course, I expected to have to take some hits in the press for a couple of weeks, but that hadn't frightened me in the past and it didn't frighten me now. By the time Martin was to take over, the whole issue would have been history and he could have begun his mandate without that albatross around his neck.

At one point in November, Paul Martin must have figured out the logic in my scenario, because he sent Alex Himelfarb to see me with the message that he, Martin, had again changed his mind. He now wanted me to remain in office until the end of January. However, since many of his associates were in the media every day accusing me of clinging to power for dear life, I replied, "Please tell Mr. Martin that I would be happy to stay, but only if he asks me officially." I never even had a phone call from him, with disastrous consequences for him and the Liberal Party.

—

On Thursday, November 13, at the Liberal convention in Toronto, I set aside my feud with Paul Martin and gave him my whole-hearted support. "My friends," I told the delegates in my closing speech, "I am passing on the leadership of the party to a new leader, a new prime minister, a great Liberal, who has been a big part of the record we are so proud of."

As I reminded the Liberals at the convention, Canada had come a long way in ten years. We had taken the largest deficit in Canadian history and turned it into seven balanced budgets in a row. We had paid off more than 10 per cent of our national debt and gone from spending 37 cents in every tax dollar to 17 cents on servicing that debt. Interest rates were at their lowest levels in decades; inflation was steady; the dollar was rising rapidly. We had created three million new jobs. We had made the largest tax cuts ever. We had introduced the National Child Benefit, the most important new social program since medicare.

We had put the Canada Pension Plan on a sustainable financial footing for another generation. We had invested vast new sums in health and health research. The Millennium Scholarships, the Canada Research Chairs, and the Canada Foundation for Innovation had begun to reverse the brain drain and to make us pioneers in the new global economy. We had put a stop to the deceptions of the separatists through the *Clarity Act* and had regained the respect of a majority of Quebecers through good government. We had enacted one of the toughest gun-control laws in the world. We had defended human rights overseas and at home, including same-sex marriage. We had limited the power of special interests and returned power to the people through the election-expenses legislation. We had upheld our values abroad, whether with our peacekeeping missions with the UN and NATO, the Ottawa Treaty on landmines, the International Criminal Court, or our work in Africa with the New Partnership for African Development. We had strengthened the greatest trading relationship in the world through NAFTA and had stood shoulder to shoulder with the United States in Haiti, Afghanistan, and on that terrible day in September 2001, but we had also maintained our independence and commitment to multilateralism by not going to war in Iraq. We had taken measures to protect the global environment with Kyoto, the Fish War, and our new national parks. We had remained a haven of tolerance and diversity in a world racked by extremism and hatred, kept our doors open to immigrants and refugees, and solidified our reputation on the international stage as enthusiastic free traders and a humanitarian people.

Above all, we had restored the spirit of confidence, pride, and unity in Canadians. In 1995, the *Wall Street Journal* had called us an honorary Third World country. In 2003, *The Economist,* sporting a cover illustration of a moose wearing rose-coloured glasses, declared us "cool," while *L'Express* described us as the country that the French could only dream of having. As a result, in the fall of 2003, the Liberal Party was at the top of the polls and poised for a fourth consecutive majority government—not because we had a sense of entitlement or had bought the votes of the people, but because we had earned their trust through hard work, tough decisions, firm leadership, fair values, and good government. In Quebec, too, 57 per cent of the voters said they were intending to vote Liberal, and most of the pundits were predicting that we were sure to win most of the seats in the province, because of Kyoto and Iraq. In personal terms, after all the years of vilification at the hands of the separatists and all the charges that I had been too tough with the *Clarity Act,* my single greatest regret about not running one more time was that I missed the opportunity to prove that I had gained back the confidence of a great majority of Quebecers.

"My friends," I said in my farewell address, "we cannot be complacent, at a time when the opposition is getting together, when in a country of the centre the opposition is moving to the right. Canadians should beware of those on the right who put the interests of Bay Street over the interests of Main Street. Canadians should beware of those on the right who put profit ahead of community, who put the narrow bottom line ahead of everything else. Canadians should beware of those on the right who would reduce taxes at the expense of necessary public services, beware of those on the right who do not care about reducing social and environmental deficits. Canadians should beware of those on the right who would weaken the national government because they do not believe in the role of government. My friends, my fellow Canadians, my fellow Liberals, if you remember only one thing that I say tonight, remember this: we must never ever lose our social conscience."

—

The morning of December 12, 2003, was emotional for my family and me. Some of the staff were in tears when Aline and I left 24 Sussex Drive to be driven across the road to Rideau Hall, where I submitted my resignation to Governor General Clarkson and invited her to ask Paul Martin to form a government. The plan had been for me to say a few words to the media afterwards, then Aline and I were to get into her car—a Liberty, no less—and drive away. But it was a beautiful winter day, so we decided to walk across the grounds and exit by the gate near our new condominium. As we walked down the street, people came out of their homes to say thank you and wish us good luck. Poor Aline, assuming that the ceremony at Rideau Hall was going to be brief and businesslike, had worn her fur coat over a plain sweater and a hat to cover her hair, so she got quite a surprise when we arrived in our new home and found that a small group of family and staff had gathered for a party to welcome us. But she didn't care, because she had finally got her wish: she was out of the public eye, and I was out of politics.

Aline knew, of course, that I could never stop working, even with a decent pension and no extravagant needs. I still had too much pep, too many interests, and lots of curiosity to get out and about, meeting people, talking, learning, and helping. Today, wherever I go on business or for pleasure, whether to Paris or Kazakhstan, London or Senegal, Shanghai or Cyprus, Moscow or Dubai, whenever I'm asked what's going on in Canada, I say, "The economy is booming, separatism has been checked, we're not at war in Iraq, but we do have one terrible problem. We don't know what to do with our surpluses."

That's not to say that we don't have a lot more work to do. There are still too many poor families, too much regional disparity, too little opportunity in our Aboriginal communities, not enough fast answers to global warming, on and on and on. My point is that our problems are relatively minor and easy to solve when compared with the problems of war, disease, starvation, and environmental disaster that hundreds of millions of the Earth's inhabitants face every day. We are the envy of the world. Our passport is the most valuable document we possess. In other places, Catholics battle Protestants, Muslims battle Jews, Hindus battle Buddhists. Here those same communities live side by side in peace, often without knowing or caring about the faith of their neighbours.

When I hear people say, for example, that the system can't be changed or that an individual can't make any difference, I think back to the Canada that existed when I entered Parliament in 1963 and compare it with the Canada that existed when I left office in 2004. It's not the same country at all, and a great deal of its transformation came through political action. Bilingualism, immigration, education, medicare, the aerospace industry, the oil sands, the Charter of Rights, the Canadian music and magazine industries, the ugly turbot, Rwanda, Iraq, everything big and small—there is nothing that hasn't been touched and shaped by politics, sometimes for better, sometimes not.

As I've often said, politics is like skating on thin ice. You never know when you're going to fall into a hole and disappear forever. One minute everything is just fine. It's a beautiful day and you're on top of the world. The next minute you make a stupid statement or show bad judgment, your name is mud, you feel guilty, you feel angry, you hide in shame. If you're lucky, however, you're alive and still have your skates, so you climb out of the hole and carry on—bruised and shaken, perhaps, but you've survived one more day. And the days become weeks, the weeks become months, the months become years, the years become decades, and you're still on your feet. That's how I survived in public life for more than forty years—one day at a time.

It's not the life for everybody, of course. Many of my friends, no matter how smart and accomplished, could not have endured it even a day. You need a thick skin. You need a determination to persevere and to not let yourself be humiliated by the setbacks. You need to be ready to go wherever necessary, left, right, above, below, to reach your goals. You need optimism and confidence. You need a strong and understanding family who are willing to share the terrible struggles and unjust attacks you will encounter. But if you have all that, and if you have the interest, the feeling of achievement and satisfaction is truly wonderful. You feel you have participated in a noble endeavour.

Aline and I have travelled a very long, very hard road together, from our working-class homes in rural Quebec to the palaces of London, Paris, Moscow, and Beijing. Politics was the route, public service the reward. No matter how rough and complicated it was—and at times it was very rough and complicated indeed—when I look back I am pleased that I made public life my occupation. The difficulty was only one element. There was also the challenge, the excitement, and the accomplishment. To be absolutely honest, I didn't do what I did only for the glory of the nation. There was the sheer fun of it, too—the personal thrill of the sport.

More and more these days, however, I'm happy to follow current events from a distance, confident that the sun will come up tomorrow anyway. I'm following the advice given to an old friend of mine who's always sick and grumpy. "Come on, Dad," his kids keep telling him. "You have nothing to worry about, it's a lovely day, the summer's short. Just turn off the TV and get outside. The news is always so bad, it's depressing you." Now, just as my father shook hands with Wilfrid Laurier, so in another generation there may arise a young Canadian whose father shook hands with me. In that way and to that person, I pass on the great mantle that I was privileged enough to wear: the responsibility to preserve and foster the peace, tolerance, generosity, prosperity, and compassion that have made Canada the best nation on earth.

When Aline and I aren't travelling, we spend the winters in our new house in Ottawa, where I have an office in a law firm downtown. Every summer we come home to my old riding in Quebec. I keep an office there, too, though I'm often out on the golf course if it's a nice morning, and I can rarely resist interrupting my work to escort visitors through the National Gallery of Canada's extraordinary museum in the renovated aluminum factory next door. If I go downtown for lunch, people call me Jean as often as they call me Prime Minister, and it makes me feel good to know that they still identify me as one of their own, the son of Wellie and Marie, the little guy from Shawinigan.

Sometimes Aline and I will go to a political event or state occasion if we're invited, but that happens less and less. It's healthier for us to live with the fact that when you're out, you're out. We're in the stage of our lives in which we would rather be with our children and grandchildren, enjoy a home-cooked meal with friends and relatives, savour each moment together as it passes, and prepare for our next journey, hopefully hand in hand to a paradise as beautiful as Lac des Piles.

Vive le Canada!

ACKNOWLEDGMENTS

All memoirs run certain risks, and mine are no exception. If you have been successful, you have to walk the thin line between boastful pride and false modesty. If you have been attacked, you have to defend yourself without sounding defensive. If you have been hurt, you can't allow yourself to become bitter. You have to be honest about others without being harmful or gossipy. And because your recollections have historical value simply by being yours and yours alone, they tend to put you and your point of view at the front and centre of every event you remember. Worse, your memory isn't always a reliable resource. It plays tricks on your mind, not just over the years, but within hours of what actually happened. The times you've been proven right come back with much more facility than the times you've been proven wrong. Your best lines and finest moments remain remarkably vivid, not least because you've kept replaying them in your head or over a glass of wine with friends, while your inappropriate wisecracks and embarrassing faux pas gradually fade—if they haven't immediately been shoved—into oblivion. Loudmouths, troublemakers, and rogues tend to steal the spotlight from those who performed their jobs quietly, competently, and honestly.

In my own case, though my recall of events, conversations, and numbers is reasonably intact, I have never kept a diary, have rarely written letters, and have seldom dictated a memo, and my mind has the habit of deleting most of the minutiae of an issue once it's been solved and I've moved on to the next one. As a communicator I have always been more of a storyteller and a populist than a lecturer, which may explain why I had more success speaking from the heart at a podium than reading a dry text prepared by an official. If I had been more preoccupied with my place in history, I might have kept a better record, but I was focused on doing the best job I could at the moment without worrying too much about how it would look in the future.

Fortunately for me, I have been saved from the worst of these dangers by the collective memory and blunt advice of the many friends and colleagues who volunteered to read the draft versions, in whole or in part, for errors in details or tone: Jean Pelletier, Eddie Goldenberg, Chaviva Hošek, John Rae, Raymond Chrétien, Marcel Massé, Stéphane Dion, Allan Rock, John Manley, David Zussman, Bruce Hartley, James Bartleman, Claude Laverdure, Patrick Parisot, Percy Downe, Peter Donolo, Paul Genest, Paul Heinbecker, Robert Fowler, David Scott, Jean Carle, John English, David Dodge, Dr. Gerald FitzGibbon, and, of course, Aline, France, Olivier, and André Desmarais. I am grateful to each one of them, even while I am solely responsible for any mistakes that may have crept into the text and remained there undetected.

As busy as I have been since my so-called retirement, I felt that, if I were ever to record my thoughts and recollections for posterity, I should do it sooner rather than later, while they were still fresh and relatively clear in my mind. As it happened, the dedicated people at Library and Archives Canada had the same idea. Indeed, having already received miles of documents and hundreds of thousands of photographs from my term in office, they wanted me to literally record my memories as part of their oral-history program. Since I've always been a fast talker and a slow writer, I jumped at the opportunity to kill two birds with one stone.

To help me, I turned again to my old friend Ron Graham, one of our country's most distinguished political journalists, with whom I had worked on my first book with such satisfying results. Over the course of more than a year, Ron challenged me with questions about every episode in my public life, then, with the help of Frances McNeely, turned my dozens of hours of answers into more than twelve hundred pages of transcripts. In draft after draft, he and I worked closely together to cut away the repetitions and digressions, arrange the narrative, clarify the arguments, and polish the wording, without losing my true voice in the process. At the same time, Ron interviewed many of my colleagues; he worked his way through my official papers; he acted as my agent with the publishers; he selected the photographs; and he did it all with professionalism, discipline, and good humour. I honestly couldn't have done this book without him.

Similarly, while I was still at work on the English edition, I turned to another distinguished Canadian author, Daniel Poliquin, to collaborate with me in producing the French edition. Though the texts of the two editions are similar in structure and content, Daniel got me talking and thinking in ways that seemed more suitable to my mother tongue. We had a lot of fun doing it, and our days of work often ended in an enjoyable game of billiards and a beer by the fire. Thank you, Daniel.

My thanks, too, to the staff at Library and Archives Canada in Ottawa and in Shawinigan: Élizabeth Mongrain, Peter de Lottinville, Maureen Hoogenraad, Ann Maurice, and Guy Tessier, who worked closely with Jean-Marc Carisse on the photographs. Their assistance was invaluable and much appreciated. At Knopf Canada, I owe an enormous debt of gratitude to executive publisher Louise Dennys, senior editor Rosemary Shipton, copy editor Stephanie Fysh, proofreader Gena Gorrell, and the entire team in production, marketing, and sales. They believed from the start that I had another good book in me, and their skill and encouragement made a believer out of me. At Éditions du Boréal, I would like to thank Pascal Assathiany for his enthusiastic support and strong editorial judgment.

Finally, my thanks and my love to my children, my son-in-law, my grandchildren, and my Aline. Without you, nothing.

PHOTO CREDITS

———

All photographs by Jean-Marc Carisse / Fonds Jean Chrétien / LAC and Fonds Jean-Marc Carisse / LAC, with the following exceptions:

Reuters / Shaun Best: second insert, page v (bottom); fourth insert, page iii (bottom);

Diana Murphy / Fonds Jean Chrétien / LAC: third insert, page i (bottom), page ii (bottom), page iii (bottom), and page v (bottom); fourth insert, page v (bottom), page vii (top, middle, and bottom);

Serge Fournier / Fonds Jean Chrétien / LAC: third insert, page v (top).

INDEX